DEBT AND ADJUSTMENT IN
THE WORLD ECONOMY

INTERNATIONAL FINANCE AND DEVELOPMENT SERIES
Published in association with the Institute of Social Studies

General Editor: E. V. K. FitzGerald, Professor of Economics, Institute of Social Studies, The Hague, and Director, Finance and Trade Policy Research Centre, University of Oxford

The *International Finance and Development Series* reflects the research carried out at The Hague and associated centres in Europe, Asia, Africa and Latin America on the relationship between international capital flows and the process of structural adjustment in less-developed economies. The studies in this series share a common analytical approach based on the use of advanced social accounting techniques and the explicit modelling of the economic behaviour of institutional sectors, which in turn permit a new approach to macroeconomic policy design.

Debt and Adjustment in the World Economy

Structural Asymmetries in North–South Interactions

Rob Vos
Senior Lecturer in International Finance
and Development Economics
Institute of Social Studies, The Hague

Institute of
Social Studies

St. Martin's Press
in association with the
INSTITUTE OF SOCIAL STUDIES

First published in Great Britain 1994 by
MACMILLAN PRESS LTD
Houndmills, Basingstoke, Hampshire RG21 2XS
and London
Companies and representatives
throughout the world

A catalogue record for this book is available from the British Library.

ISBN 0-333-62506-4

10 9 8 7 6 5 4 3 2 1
03 02 01 00 99 98 97 96 95 94

Printed in Great Britain by
Ipswich Book Co Ltd
Ipswich, Suffolk

First published in the United States of America 1994 by
Scholarly and Reference Division,
ST. MARTIN'S PRESS, INC.,
175 Fifth Avenue,
New York, N.Y. 10010

ISBN 0-312-12437-6

Library of Congress Cataloging-in-Publication Data
Vos, Rob, 1955–
Debt and adjustment in the world economy : structural asymmetries in North–South interactions / Rob Vos.
p. cm.
"In association with the Institute of Social Studies."
Includes bibliographical references and index.
ISBN 0-312-12437-6
1. Debts, External. 2. Structural adjustment (Economic policy)
3. International economic relations. I. Title.
HJ8015.V67 1994
336.3'435—dc20 94-30588
CIP

For my parents, and for Irene, Ricardo and Jessica

Contents

List of Tables and Figures

Tables

Figures

International Finance and Development Series

Editor's Introduction

The dramatic changes in the structure and behaviour of international finance since the collapse of the Bretton Woods system some twenty years ago have transformed the nature of global macroeconomics in general and the processes of growth and adjustment in developing countries in particular. Clearly, the financing of development has become an issue far more complex than a simple 'transfer of resources' from rich to poor countries which has traditionally concerned development economists and policy makers, because national patterns of public and private investment and savings (and thus sustainable growth and income distribution) now form part of international capital markets and the wider economy. The Finance and Development Group at the Institute of Social Studies in association with research teams and individual scholars from a considerable number of developing countries, has since 1985 carried out at The Hague an integrated research programme on international capital flows and their effect on the processes of structural adjustment and economic growth. The volumes in the *International Finance and Development Series* aim to communicate the insights gained from this programme to the community of scholars and policy-makers concerned with the current and potential role of external finance in supporting a process of sustainable development in the poor and middle-income countries which are home to three-quarters of humanity.

The traditional view of development finance was based on two propositions that are now widely regarded as implausible. On the one hand, the assumption that external and domestic finance are closely complementary conditions for high rates of productive investment no longer appears tenable in the light of the sovereign debt crisis, doubts as to aid effectiveness and capital flight. However, there is insufficient understanding as to how developing countries gain access to international capital markets and how macroeconomic shifts within the OECD economy are transmitted through these markets. A number of studies in the *Series*, therefore, address the supply factors underlying aid flows, commercial bank lending and direct foreign investment, and suggest that the form of finance itself plays an important role in both the transmission of shocks and the nature of domestic response to them. On the other hand, the traditional assumption that effective development finance requires extensive government intervention as banker, investor and planner has been replaced by reliance on the private sector and market forces, as a consequence of a wider perception that poor governance is responsible for economic stagnation. However, little is known about private sector behaviour in developing countries, and particularly about the financial decisions of firms which range from peasant families and petty traders to large industrial corporations and multinational enterprises, and which have very distinct aims while facing quite different institutional constraints. Thus much of the research reported in the *Series* is concerned with the nature of the private sector finance and the structure of markets in developing countries, and suggests that economic policy effectiveness is conditioned by the specific nature of private sector response.

Unstable financial markets have characterized the development experience of the last two decades, as the level, composition and destination of capital flows to the developing world have changed dramatically. In the 1960s these flows were relatively small, on average little more than about two per cent of the GDP of the receiving countries, and were mostly bilateral official development assistance (ODA) and, in a few cases, private direct foreign investment. In the second half of the 1970s capital flows to developing countries increased suddenly, reaching over five per cent of the GDP of the capital-importing developing countries, while the composition of the flows changed towards commercial bank loans. This apparently structural shift was abruptly reversed in 1982 when, after the Mexican debt crisis, bank lending to the developing countries stopped; during the 1980s ODA flows declined as well due to budget constraints in the donor countries. In the 1990s, ODA flows have regained significance (with Japan becoming the largest single donor) for the poorer countries, while direct foreign investment flows to some middle-income countries have increased substantially. A few countries have also regained access to commercial market borrowing, although these flows now largely reflect portfolio investments rather than bank credits. Despite this recovery, however, capital flows to the developing world in the 1990s is now at a much lower real level than in the 1970s and likely to remain so for the foreseeable future.

Despite worldwide financial liberalization, international capital markets are still highly segmented as far as developing countries are concerned. Not all countries have access to commercial bank loans, nor do all countries receive direct foreign investment. In the 1970s, the boom in commercial bank lending was largely confined to a limited group of middle-income and resource-rich developing countries, while the resurgence of direct foreign investment flows in the 1990s appears to be equally concentrated. Poorer developing countries appear to have no access to private sources of external finance because they present high risk and little attraction as markets or export platforms; and thus have to rely on official sources of external finance from OECD governments and multilateral institutions. There thus seems to be little empirical support for the traditional theoretical view that private capital will automatically move towards capital-scarce regions once financial markets are liberalized.

The sharp fluctuations in capital flows to the South created both positive and negative shocks to which both public and private sectors had to adjust. A host of country studies assessing the success or failure of adjustment efforts have been published in recent years, but they are mainly either confined to macroeconomic aggregates or concerned with particular sectors. However, as in the case of international capital markets, domestic financial markets in developing countries are highly segmented. The country studies in the *Series* consider these structural characteristics explicitly, giving particular attention to the behaviour of private sector agents as they operate in different institutional and market contexts. For example, poorly-developed capital markets and credit rationing by banks clearly constrain the investment decisions of some agents more than others. Typically, small firms and unincorporated businesses are the first to face such financial constraints, with disproportionate consequences for output and employment of credit squeezes and real interest rate regimes. Modern corporate firms are less constrained by the availability of finance because of interlocking ownership patterns and links to banks, but their investment decisions tend to be negatively affected due to the impact of stabilization policies and structural adjustment programmes on their balance sheets and the portfolio decisions of their shareholders. As a result, private investment has failed to respond to orthodox economic reform in most cases.

The country studies in the *Series* also suggest that in many cases the effective domestic response (i.e. of both public and private sectors) to shifts in external finance have been more shock-accommodating than incentive-generating. The availability of foreign resources in the 1970s, often in excess of the finance needed to compensate for external shocks such as higher oil prices, encouraged the public sector to engage in large-scale investment programmes. Meanwhile, the reduced availability of adjustment finance following the debt crisis led to severe macroeconomic instabilities in cases where public finances were generally difficult to control and the development of export industries had been neglected structurally. In such circumstances, new finance was conditioned by policy reforms prescribed by the multilateral creditor agencies and donor community. In these adjustment schemes the private sector is given a predominant weight via privatization and liberalization programmes, but this was largely to be achieved by eliminating presumed inefficient intervention of the state. While it is certainly true that government intervention in a vast majority of developing countries has been far from optimal, there is no reason to believe that the premise of orthodox adjustment policies as currently propagated – that private agents are socially efficient resource allocators and that markets clear optimally – is generally true either. A proper understanding of the behaviour, structure and performance of all major institutional agents in the economic process is required *before* any attempts to redefine the role of external finance in adjustment and growth can be made. By extension, the potential role for state management of the economy can only be assessed once private sector behaviour is understood.

The studies in this *Series* share a common methodological approach, informed by the following basic propositions:

First, that international capital markets are segmented and imperfect; they do not clear through interest rate variations, but rather through the portfolio choices of financial intermediaries based on assessment of future income flows, asset values and liquidity in an uncertain world; thus developing countries do not have equal access to ODA, commercial bank loans and direct investment;

Second, that the determinants of the level and distribution of capital flows to the developing countries are mainly to be found in the North; both the macroeconomic balances of the rich countries of the world and specific microeconomic factors driving decisions of international financial intermediaries and aid donors determine the total level of capital available to the South as well as its overall distribution over the major forms of capital flows;

Third, because the flows are determined to a large extent on the supply side, the South has to adjust to changes as they occur; the impact of external finance on the receiving economy depends critically on type of international capital - ODA, bank credits or direct investment - to which the country has access, each of these has a distinct effect on public and private sector savings and investments;

Fourth, the impact of external finance depends upon the institutional structure of the economy in general; and the rational but distinct investment and savings behaviour of the main economic agents (governments, parastatals, corporations and households) operating in segmented capital markets in particular;

Fifth, policy making and policy effectiveness are constrained by the international conditions facing the country and the behaviour of the main economic agents within it; any principles of economic policy must therefore be based on implicit assumptions about private sector behaviour which are in fact institutionally contingent.

In order to apply these propositions and to test their validity in a rigorously comparable manner, a common methodological approach has been applied throughout the research programme reported in this *Series.* In order to integrate the analysis of the global context of trade, savings and investment demand, an appropriate accounting framework had to be designed, within which a mass of inconsistent data could be organized. The Finance and Development Group has thus constructed a 'World Accounting Matrix' (WAM) in collaboration with the United Nations, the LINK Project and the Erasmus University Rotterdam, in which the various current-account transactions and the financial flows between the major regions of the world (including several groups of developing countries) are measured by level, origin and destination. The matrix form of the WAM enables consistency to be achieved between various data sources according to their respective reliability, and demonstrates both the interactions among trade and finance flows between regions and the dimensions of financial market segmentation. Although WAM itself is a purely *ex post* descriptive device, it provides the basis for more analytical work on the determinants of capital flows, the interaction between financial and trade flows, and dynamic world modelling of financial markets and the place of the developing regions in the global capital market.

Standardized accounting frameworks were also required at the country level which could be compared with each other, thus integrating financial variables with macroeconomic balances on an institutional basis, and providing the local counterpart for the World Accounting Matrix (WAM). The country studies are hence articulated around a Macroeconomic Social Accounting Framework (MSAF), which is a Social Accounting Matrix (SAM) in which the institutional categories are fully specified and the flow of funds properly integrated with public and private savings and investment balances on the one hand and the capital account of the balance of payments on the other. Only in this way can the link between the real and financial sides of the economy be established, through the accumulation decisions and portfolio behaviour of the main economic agents.

The country studies identify the microeconomic behaviour of institutions in terms of the driving forces underlying savings, investment and portfolio decisions of different economic agents. These may include: international commercial banking firms, donor governments, multilateral institutions, borrowing governments and firms, small and large farmers, corporate and unincorporated enterprises, public and private firms, urban wage earners, self-employed and other household sectors, and so on. All the studies test these behavioural relationships economically using specially constructed time-series; a number of them also contain a computable general equilibrium (CGE) model built around the MSAF in order to simulate the macro- and microeconomic interactions between external shocks, international finance and domestic adjustment processes. These country models allow for counterfactual analysis of the effectiveness of structural adjustment policies, and form the counterpart to those studies in the *Series* focusing on the global macroeconomy which apply a modelling approach built up from the WAM and segmented global markets for aid flows, commercial bank lending and direct foreign investment.

In the *Series,* therefore, the use of a single accounting framework means not only that rigorous comparison can be made between the countries studied, and conclusions can be drawn for larger groups of similar economies, but also that the interactions between countries and regions can be studied and the implications for international policy coordination derived.

In sum, the authors of the studies in the *Series* share a common perception that the currently orthodox paradigm that underpins most contemporary studies of macroeconomic adjustment – and by extension informs dominant policy advice – give inadequate attention to the behaviour of different institutional agents involved in the process of financing economic development. In order to redress this imbalance, we try to apply a consistent methodology to the analysis of the world economy and international capital markets, country studies of external finance and economic adjustment, and cross-country comparisons of response to external shock. The volumes planned for the *Series* thus include analyses of various aspects of the pattern of world capital flows and the relationship of particular developing regions to the core market; a set of case studies of the interaction between international and domestic finance in individual countries including Bolivia, Colombia, Mexico,

Pakistan, Philippines and Thailand; and finally, two volumes bringing together the work of the Group in the fields of data methodology, model building and comparative policy analysis.

Valpy FitzGerald
The Hague, July 1994

Editor's Preface

The present volume by Rob Vos constitutes a particularly suitable start to this *International Finance and Development Series* as it bridges the global and country level analyses discussed above. The primary focus of the book is on the functioning of international financial markets and on the impact of external finance on the economies of the South. The author approaches the workings of international financial markets as they affect developing countries from both historical and theoretical perspectives. The characteristics of the capital flows to the South in successive historical periods are explored and the patterns of segmentation of the financial markets are clearly identified. The microeconomic determinants of the boom in private (bank) lending to developing countries in the 1970s are shown to involve both credit rationing and a vigorous oligopolistic competition of large international bank firms for market shares. These conditions, combined with imperfect risk assessment and uncertainty, were intrinsic causes of a tendency towards over-lending and heavy concentration of bank loans in a limited number of developing countries that were considered to be creditworthy.

Some borrowers, in particular the low-income countries, were effectively rationed out of private international financial markets. The threat of widespread default, originating from Mexico's debt payments problems in 1982, transformed creditors' expectations and led to a collective retreat of the international banks from lending to developing countries, including those without debt-servicing problems. Similar factors had generated the booms and crises in international lending that took place both in the 19th century and in the 1920s and 1930s. Such instability in the supply conditions of external lending naturally hampers the applications of optimal borrowing strategies by developing country governments and public enterprises. Vos suggests that sudden booms in lending (as well as in aid inflows) led to so-called Dutch-disease effects, including real exchange rate appreciation and resource reallocation towards non-tradable goods sectors, thereby reducing the capacity of the indebted economies to respond to external shocks in commodity and financial markets.

These findings are then introduced into a structuralist North-South (STAC) model, built up from the basic global accounting methodology that underlies the World Accounting Matrix. Equations are added to describe the behaviour of international financial markets, and the supply and demand determinants of trade and production, and accumulation behaviour in prototype Northern and Southern economies. The model is then used to simulate the worldwide effects of capital flows to the South, and suggests that debt crises are systemic and are the result of the way in which financial markets operate and borrowing countries are inserted in the world economy. It is also demonstrated that a doubling of development assistance (i.e. to the OECD target of 0.7 per cent of Northern GNP) may have negative effects on growth in the developing region, depending on the way in which such a fiscal expansion is financed in the North. Public borrowing would push up the world interest rate and affect Northern output growth, while the South would suffer from an increased debt burden, lower export earnings and falling terms of trade; tax-financing or expenditure cuts in the North would largely mitigate or offset the negative welfare effects that would emerge under a regime of no fiscal adjustment and bond-financing in the North.

The policy implications of Vos' analysis are considerable, even though his model is highly aggregated. The theoretical notions and stylized facts of the STAC model are more plausible than those of most models of the world economy, which are influential in designing national and international macroeconomic policies. This book thus not only provides a solid analytical basis for a critical reassessment of the role of development finance in an uncertain world economy, but also elements for the overdue revision of international economic policy models.

Valpy FitzGerald
The Hague, July 1994

Author's Preface

This book results from the research project *Money, Finance and Development* carried out at the Institute of Social Studies (ISS), The Hague. Institutional support from the ISS and funding by the Ministry of Education, the Dutch Council for Scientific Research (NWO), and the Directorate-General for International Cooperation of the Ministry of Foreign Affairs, facilitated the realization of this study. Within the context of the broader research project, I received helpful comments and suggestions from many people.

I am especially indebted to Dr. Karel Jansen, who invited me to join the project, causing me to divert my attention temporarily from the down-to-earth problems of poverty and basic needs towards the higher echelons of finance and global interdependence. Our frequent and lengthy discussions provided tremendous support as this part of the research took shape, and his comments on several drafts of the manuscript undoubtedly helped to improve it.

A special tribute should also be given to Professors Hans Linnemann and Valpy FitzGerald for many supportive and challenging discussions. Their encouragement helped me through stressful periods when I felt this study was taking too long and wished to return to 'normal life'. Moreover, Professor FitzGerald's stimulating ideas on structuralist economic theory were a continuous source of inspiration.

Professors Jan Willem Gunning and Wouter Tims provided me with very helpful and detailed comments and corrections on more than one draft of the manuscript and thereby did much more than they were asked to do. I am grateful for their very concise reading and observations.

I also owe a special word of gratitude to Professor David Vines who went through a previous version of the entire manuscript, providing critical, but extremely helpful comments. I should also thank two other, anonymous, referees for their useful comments.

Papers that provided the bricks and mortar for several parts of this book were presented at seminars and conferences, among others at the conference on 'Macroeconomic Interactions Between North and South' organized by the International Economics Study Group and the Centre for Economic Policy Research at the Isle of Thorns (UK) in 1987, at the conference on 'North-South approaches to trade and development' at the University of North Carolina at Chapel Hill in 1988, at the Development Economics Seminar, The Hague, in 1988 and at the IDS/ISS conference on 'Finance' in Brighton in 1991. Participants at these conferences provided helpful comments. I owe special gratitude to Ronald Findlay, Alasdair I. MacBean, Lance Taylor, Adrian Wood and David Evans for their comments and suggestions.

I owe many thanks to Adri S. Louter for his skillful help in the programming of the model applied in Chapter 8. Linda McPhee and Josephine Bosman have made my unruly English readable and Joy Misa has skillfully prepared, designed and typeset the book.

Last, but by no means least, I thank Irene, Ricardo and Jessica for their patience and caring, although I know that this book by no means can compensate for my many hours of absence.

R.V.

1 Introduction

1.1 Debt, Adjustment and Global Interdependence

The debt crisis which affected developing countries in the 1980s has once more revealed the vulnerability of their economies to shocks in world commodity and financial markets, raising questions about the precise nature of their dependence on growth and economic policies in the industrial countries.

Traditionally, debates around dependence and interdependence between the countries of the industrialized 'North' and the developing 'South' have focused on interactions through trade and commodity markets. Trade was long seen as one of the major vehicles for growth in the South, with gains from trade crucially dependent on economic growth in the North and trade elasticities (cf. e.g. Lewis 1977, Riedel 1984). A complementary role was given to capital flows from North to South, as a way of financing investment and, like exports, as a source of foreign exchange. Such a simple view of external finance in development seems unsustainable in the light of the events of the 1970s and 1980s. It has been several decades since questions first were raised with respect to inefficient uses of foreign capital inflows which caused these to substitute for domestic savings (Griffin 1970). In the light of the events over the past two decades, it may well be argued that global economic factors causing instabilities in the supply and lending terms of external finance can be another reason why foreign capital inflows are not necessarily beneficial to development.

This study critically assesses the extent to which capital movements between rich and poor countries contribute to the reduction of the income gap between the two. The main hypothesis is that because developing countries do not have full and free access to international capital markets and because these markets are inherently unstable, the poor nations of the world are unable to reap the full benefits of aid, bank credits and other capital transfers. To make this clear, this study inquires into the institutional features of world capital markets, the factors determining developing-country access to these markets and the mechanisms through which macroeconomic policies in the creditor countries are transmitted to the debtor countries. The analysis suggests that because of systemic market failure in the international financial markets, international aid and debt-management strategies should include a better supervision of global capital markets and a set of rules for international macroeconomic policy coordination which explicitly target the growth and development objectives of the developing countries.

While in the 1960s international development finance related largely to a modest scale of official lending and aid to LDCs, in the 1970s there was a move towards large-scale lending by international banks. This shift coincided with the first oil-price shock and a slowing down of economic growth in the industrialized countries that affected the trade positions of LDCs in the early 1970s. Commercial bank lending seemed a new solution to the foreign-exchange problems of LDCs. The international financial system appeared an efficient mechanism to deal with the successive shocks in the 1970s: savings surpluses of the major oil-exporting countries and decreasing investment finance needs in the industrialized economies allowed the international banking system to increase its role as intermediary for the financial needs of LDCs. Some observers interpreted this process as an indication of both more integrated and efficient financial markets and as indicating the success of development efforts, as it appeared that only middle-income countries gained access to the international bank-loan market (see e.g. McKinnon 1977, Dufey & Giddy 1978, Bruno 1984, Krueger 1987).[1] However, the system proved to be not so robust and efficient in dealing with the shocks that affected the international economy in the 1980s. A second oil-price rise in 1979/80, increasing interest rates and less buoyant export opportunities for LDCs due to a fall in commodity prices and increased protectionism, created debt-servicing problems. Although foreign-exchange constraints were tightening, this time the banks tried to reduce their exposure and showed a clear revulsion to new lending to LDCs.

An emerging debt crisis became manifest in August 1982 when Mexico declared itself unable to service its debt. The highly-indebted countries plunged into a deep crisis, from which they have been unable to recover. Table 1.1 shows a few indicators of the economic crisis in the South. The heavily indebted countries that borrowed heavily from private sources ('private borrowers') and that ran into major debt problems, most of whom are exporters of primary commodities and located in Latin America, felt negative real *per capita* GNP growth through the 1980s, after a respectable 3.5 per cent annual average in the 1970s. The investment rate (as a share of GNP) fell dramatically, from 22 to 14 per cent; the prolonged loss in investment will undoubtedly delay the recovery of economic development for many years to come. Debt-export ratios have continued to rise steeply until the late 1980s, despite substantial (but unstable) expansion of export volumes; a falling trend sets in only after 1989 with the initation of officially-supported debt reduction schemes. For the entire group of private borrowers, these indicators show a better performance, reflecting the relatively good economic performance of particularly the Asian countries in the group with dynamic manufacturing export sectors. Their investment and growth rates could be kept up and debt-export ratios were brought down after increases in the early 1980s. An economic crisis and also an apparent debt crisis can be observed among the generally low-income countries without access to private capital markets who must rely on official sources of external finance ('official borrowers'). On average, 'official borrowers' show low per capita output growth in the 1980s, on top of poor performance in the 1970s. Debt-export ratios have increased for 'official borrowers' at least as dramatically as for 'private borrowers' with debt problems, despite higher export volume growth rates than in the 1970s. Unlike private bank lending, there was no actual fall in official lending in the 1980s; the major factor contributing to the dramatic increase in debt-export ratios has been the collapse of primary commodity markets and a sharp deterioration in the terms of trade of these countries.

Many explanations have been given for these economic-*cum*-debt crises in developing countries. Many observers have blamed debtor country governments for bad economic management, emphasizing a lack of fiscal discipline, overvalued exchange rates and protectionist trade policies. (Representative statements can be found in Sjaastad 1983, Balassa et al. 1986, World Bank 1985 and Harberger 1985.)

Another influential view emphasizes unforeseen exogenous shocks brought on by OPEC price policies, a rather unexpected policy shift in the North leading to high real interest rates and a prolonged world economic recession. As a result of these 'random shocks', the debtor countries have been confronted by a falling demand for their exports, a collapse in commodity prices and a sudden and steep increase in the cost of external borrowing. This position has been put forward by influential authors like Cline (1983) and Dornbusch & Fischer (1987) and is implicit in policy reports of the IMF (*World Economic Outlook*, various years) and World Bank (1985). For some, this explanation led to optimistic perceptions about solving the crisis. An improved macroeconomic environment was expected, with the major economies climbing out of their downward cycles aided by better policy coordination in the North to reduce interest rates. The expected resumption of growth in the North would resolve the liquidity problems of the debtor coun-

Table 1.1 The economic crisis in the Third World in the 1980s

	1970-79	1980-82	1983	1984	1985	1986	1987	1988	1989	1990
All LDCs[a]										
GNP per capita growth	3.7	0.5	-1.0	2.2	2.5	2.9	2.3	2.2	1.6	0.6
Investment rate	22.1	23.1	19.9	18.9	19.4	19.4	20.8	21.8	23.2	22.5
Export volume growth	4.0	3.6	4.9	12.4	2.3	4.6	9.0	10.5	4.1	4.2
Debt-export ratio	146.5	185.5	242.4	232.5	264.5	306.6	295.2	254.1	232.7	222.5
Official borrowers[b]										
GNP per capita growth	1.2	1.8	2.9	0.3	1.8	1.2	1.9	4.6	2.4	2.3
Investment rate	18.9	20.7	19.3	20.0	21.0	20.2	19.8	20.8	20.6	20.2
Export volume growth (%)	3.1	-2.4	2.3	6.6	2.5	5.3	4.5	3.6	13.5	1.4
Debt-export ratio	165.9	225.7	296.9	300.0	360.2	402.9	416.4	380.8	362.1	353.0
Official borrowers in Sub-Saharan Africa										
GNP per capita growth	1.3	-0.6	-1.1	-0.6	-1.0	0.6	1.2	0.4	1.2	-1.0
Investment rate	19.0	18.3	16.9	19.1	19.0	18.1	16.6	18.4	18.8	18.1
Export volume growth (%)	2.1	-3.7	1.0	7.7	3.3	8.1	-4.5	-1.9	6.3	-3.5
Debt-export ratio	136.0	262.8	336.9	345.0	412.2	453.3	483.4	428.6	418.0	392.4

(Continued...)

(Table 1.1 *Continued*)

	1970-79	1980-82	1983	1984	1985	1986	1987	1988	1989	1990
Private borrowers[c]										
GNP per capita growth	3.8	-0.6	-3.1	1.0	1.7	2.4	1.3	0.8	1.2	-0.7
Investment rate	24.1	24.6	20.2	18.9	19.6	19.9	21.7	22.3	23.8	22.5
Export volume growth	3.1	3.4	6.4	12.0	1.6	4.2	8.8	12.4	2.8	4.1
Debt-export ratio	132.5	180.3	237.0	222.9	239.0	285.7	256.8	213.1	190.1	173.7
Private borrowers with debt problems[d]										
GNP per capita growth	3.5	-1.1	-5.6	-0.0	1.5	2.0	0.4	-0.9	0.3	-2.7
Investment rate	22.7	17.2	12.7	10.7	11.3	13.6	15.9	15.9	16.4	14.1
Export volume growth	1.6	1.5	4.4	12.6	1.5	-7.1	4.1	10.3	-0.2	0.7
Debt-export ratio	153.0	230.3	321.2	297.5	314.4	409.9	393.0	329.0	292.1	264.7
Diversified borrowers[e]										
GNP per capita growth	4.8	4.0	5.4	8.0	6.1	5.5	6.3	6.4	2.4	4.5
Investment rate[f]	16.1	18.5	18.7	18.4	17.4	17.2	18.0	20.8	22.0	23.8
Export growth	7.7	7.4	0.8	16.7	4.6	5.8	12.1	6.9	4.1	5.9
Debt-export ratio[f]	153.8	162.9	209.2	195.9	231.5	266.1	263.1	222.0	201.2	199.9

Sources: World Bank, *World Tables* (diskette 1992) and *World Debt Tables* (diskette 1992).

Notes:
a. See Table A.1.1 for country classification and coverage. Major oil exporters, Eastern European countries and former Soviet Union are not included.
b. Countries with two-thirds or more of outstanding external debt owed to official creditors.
c. Countries with two-thirds or more of outstanding external debt owed to private creditors.
d. Includes Argentina, Brazil, Chile, Côte d'Ivoire, Ecuador, Mexico, Nigeria, the Philippines, Uruguay and Venezuela.
e. Countries falling between the criteria indicated under b and c.
f. Country group estimate excluding China.

tries, restore their creditworthiness and avoid a collapse of the financial system (see particularly IMF 1983 and Cline 1983).[2]

Yet other explanations have emphasized the potential instability of the international loan market in which lenders can only imperfectly assess creditworthiness of sovereign borrowers. On the demand side, borrowers in turn may have a different perception than lenders about their future payment capacity and the cost of default. Optimism about the future payment capacity of developing countries in the 1970s is seen to have stimulated bank lending and to have contributed to an overexpansion of developing country debt. A threat of default by one borrower, like Mexico's in 1982, may be sufficient to alter market perceptions and cause banks to retreat from this market segment, but potentially could give rise to a widespread financial crash. This type of explanation has been put forward by scholars from various theoretical perspectives. Kindleberger posits that international private lending follows a boom-bust cycle that has occurred numerous times throughout history (Kindleberger 1978, 1982). Sachs (1984a), among others, has shown that debt crises and bank runs may be logical consequences of lenders' and borrowers' behaviour once factors like risk, uncertainty and imperfect information have been included in the theory of optimal lending and borrowing. Darity & Horn (1988), Ensign (1988) and Devlin (1989) have argued further that the managers of oligopolistic banks had particular incentives, such as substantial bank commisions, which led them to aggressive lending behaviour that contributed to the emergence of the debt crisis.

These different explanations are not necessarily mutually exclusive; on the contrary, they might be complementary. Clearly, however, each emphasizes a particular aspect of a complex set of factors.

This study is an attempt towards a more integrated approach. It will look into the microfoundations of lending and borrowing behaviour in various segments of the international capital market. These, however, will need to be fitted into a global macroeconomic context explaining how financial and commodity markets interact. From this perspective it is hypothesized that the source of the developing country debt crisis is not so much 'random shocks', but more systemic factors underlying the functioning of financial and commodity markets. More particularly, it is hypothesized that supply factors have dominated the pattern of capital flows towards developing countries. In the 1970s and 1980s these related to donor constituency and political factors in the case of official concessional loans and aid flows and oligopolistic banking behaviour in a context of uncertainty and imperfect sovereign risk assessment in the case of commercial bank lending. In the latter case, supply conditions were unstable, both because of shifts in bank behaviour and because of uncoordinated policy decisions in the major economies. These supply conditions have vast implications for adjustment processes in the South.

Firstly, for Southern borrowers the world capital market appears strongly segmented, as creditworthiness assessments by banks have largely excluded low-income developing countries from private lending, separating the South broadly into 'official' and 'private' borrowers.

Secondly, the current account balances of the South appear to be determined less by trade elasticities or activity in the rest of the world than by access to external finance and so more by donor government policies, commercial bank behaviour and the macroeconomic policies of the major economies.

Thirdly, instability in the levels and terms at which external finance was available constituted by itself a source of external shocks to many Southern borrowers. The unexpectedly vast availability at low cost of commercial bank lending in the 1970s found eager public sector borrowers in many middle-income countries. It is argued that these borrowers considered the sudden access to largely free-disposition funds as a 'windfall profit', producing a structural sectoral shift towards non-traded sectors, in turn producing adjustment problems when external financing conditions reversed. Such shifts may vary depending on the initial structural features of the economy, i.e. it is hypothesized that shifts tend to be larger in economies which are net primary exporters and have inward-looking industrial sectors.

1.2 The Concept of International Finance

International finance involves the acquisition by institutions or individuals in one country of assets in another. External assets may be of a purely financial nature, i.e. loans, bonds, bank deposits, foreign currency etc., or may include direct investment involving ownership of physical capital abroad. International finance has a logical counterpart in commodity trade. The capital-exporting country – international finance and international capital movements are synonymous here – requires a current account surplus to allow the acquisition of foreign assets to take place. The capital-importing country in turn can finance a current account deficit after allowance for the capital inflow.

International finance involves both a *flow* and a *stock* concept. The *stock* concept relates to the value of outstanding foreign assets (or external liabilities), while the *flow* involves a change in the stock value. The stock value may be further affected by asset revaluations, e.g. due to changes in market values of assets or exchange-rate movements. However, in this study the focus will be on flow-related changes in foreign asset and liability holdings and their interrelationships with commodity trade.

For an economy as a whole, international financial transactions involve changes in the capital account of its balance of payments. However, since international finance usually involves a reward of some kind (interest, profit remittances) which usually flows back to the country of origin, there will also be a direct relation between the outstanding stock of foreign assets and the economy's current account through interest rates and rates of return on capital. Additionally, debt-creating capital movements (loans, bonds) involve repayment schedules. Commodity trade is affected as a net transfer of financial resources from abroad (net capital inflow less net factor payments) will provide additional foreign exchange, permitting higher imports (or a larger trade deficit). This is a one-period effect. However, an economy that is borrowing from abroad is in fact taking a mortgage on its future income, and, more precisely, on its future foreign-exchange income because of the related factor payments and amortization obligations. Accumulations of foreign liabilities and future asset prices (rates of return) and exchange rates will determine claims of foreign asset holders on the home economy's future commodity flows representing future income streams. Assuming these payments have to be realized in the currency of the lending economy, the financial interactions between the two economies will affect their trade balances and foreign asset holders may be seen to have a claim on future trade surpluses of the borrowing economy.

This direct correspondence between commodity trade and international finance may be further identified in terms of standard national accounting concepts applied to the world economy. For each individual economy it holds that the external balance of the economy will have to match the internal balance. The external balance is defined by the current account balance of the balance of payments, consisting of the trade balance *less* net factor payments and net current transfers to the rest of the world. The internal balance is the balance of savings and investment, reflecting in the aggregate the balance between domestic production and domestic demand for goods and services. For a two-economy world the accounting identities, detailed in Chapter 2, can be summarized as follows. For economy A, say the capital-exporting North:

$$
\begin{aligned}
&\textit{Net increase in foreign assets}\\
&\equiv \textit{exports} - \textit{imports} + \textit{net factor income}\\
&\equiv \textit{savings} - \textit{investment}
\end{aligned}
\qquad (1.1)
$$

where:

$$
\begin{aligned}
&\textit{Net factor income}\\
&\equiv \textit{world interest rate} \times \textit{accumulated net foreign assets position}
\end{aligned}
\qquad (1.2)
$$

In equations (1.1) and (1.2) it has been assumed for simplicity that current transfers are zero, that capital flows consist only of interest-bearing assets and that there is a single, uniform world interest rate. The *net* increase in foreign assets indicates the gross outflow of capital, less (debt) repayments and capital inflows. The current account balance is represented here by the trade and factor income balance. By definition, in a two-economy world the external balance of economy *A* corresponds to its internal balance, i.e. the capital export reflects a savings surplus, as well as to the external and internal balance of the capital-importing economy *B*, in this case the South:

$$
\begin{aligned}
&\textit{Net increase in external liabilities}\\
&\equiv \textit{imports} - \textit{exports} + \textit{net factor payments}\\
&\equiv \textit{investment} - \textit{savings}
\end{aligned}
\qquad (1.3)
$$

Thus the savings surplus of the North simultaneously finances, *ex post*, the current account deficit and investment-savings gap of the South. Northern imports are equal to Southern exports, showing that trade and financial interdependence are sides of the same coin. This becomes even clearer if we define the 'non-interest current account' or 'net financial transfer' for the South as:

$$
\begin{aligned}
&\textit{Net transfer}\\
&\equiv \textit{net increase in external liabilities} -\\
&\quad (\textit{world interest rate} \times \textit{accumulated net external liability position})\\
&\equiv \textit{imports} - \textit{exports}
\end{aligned}
\qquad (1.4)
$$

In other words, a net inward transfer will correspond to a trade deficit; an outward transfer, e.g. caused by an increase in the world interest rate, will have to correspond to a trade surplus. These accounting relations define the link between trade and finance.

1.3 Trade, Finance and Institutions

A traditional way of analysing the role of foreign capital flows in economic development is the celebrated two-gap model (e.g. Chenery & Bruno 1962, Bacha 1984). Economies could be either savings or foreign-exchange constrained. The view that foreign capital inflows would help to lift the major constraint on growth and generate positive welfare effects for the recipient economy was already being challenged during the early stages of development of the analytical framework; empirical analyses suggest that foreign capital tends to substitute for rather than complement domestic savings (Griffin 1970, Weisskopf 1972). The debt crisis of the 1980s has provided ground for a widely held view that growth in output in the South is essentially 'debt constrained' (e.g. UNCTAD 1987a). Inadequate official flows, the high debt-servicing burden and the virtual cessation of private lending constrain import capacity and therefore output growth. More aid, resumption of bank lending and debt reduction are, according to this view, the critical means to reactivate the economies of the indebted South.

Undoubtedly, the unfavourable external environment in the 1980s has contributed to the severe foreign-exchange problems faced by many developing countries. From a global perspective, more capital for the South could be beneficial, but welfare effects need not be unambiguously positive. Welfare effects are highly dependent on the conditions under which capital transfers are supplied and how these affect other key variables in the process of global interdependence, such as commodity prices, growth in the industrialized North, interest rates and so on.

According to the traditional view of the complementary role of foreign capital flows, output growth in the South (g_S) is constrained by its stock of capital (K_S), which has an essential import component. The implied model contains relationships of the following kind:[3]

$$g_S = f(K_S, \ldots) \tag{1.5}$$

and

$$K_S = g(M_S, \ldots) \tag{1.6}$$

where M_S is the volume of imports permitted by the external resource constraint, i.e.:

$$M_S = h(\Delta F_S, \ldots) \tag{1.7}$$

where a reduction in net capital inflows (ΔF_S) leads to a decline in imports and so in output growth, and *vice versa*. This view is incomplete in that it assumes capital flows to be exogenous or dependent upon unspecified supply conditions and does not consider interactions with commodity markets. Taking notice of such elements, the external constraint could be respecified as:

$$M_S = h\,(\Delta A_S,\ \Delta B_S, i_W, p_m, p_e, g_N, \ldots) \tag{1.7a}$$

where the net capital flow has been split into official development assistance (ΔA_S) and private bank lending (ΔB_S), i_W is the interest rate on external debt, p_m and p_e are the prices of Southern imports and exports and g_N is the rate of Northern output growth, assuming this to be the principal indicator for volume growth of Southern exports. A simple world economy divided into North and South thus demonstrates a few important interactions related to four main areas of investigation of this study.

Finance and commodity markets

Firstly, an exogenous capital transfer will raise import capacity and Southern output. However, if Northern demand (g_N) for Southern goods is left unchanged, downward pressure on Southern export prices (and hence on the Southern terms of trade) may emerge, offsetting the initially positive impact of the transfer. Greater import demand in the South following the transfer, on the other hand, will increase Northern exports and aggregate demand. The net effect on welfare in both economies will depend on demand elasticities for both (Northern and Southern) commodities in both regions and the terms of trade effects resulting from the transfer. This has been a traditional theme in international trade theory, where demand effects have been isolated in the study of the well-known 'transfer problem'. (Chapter 3 surveys the relevant literature.)

Financial institutions

Secondly, supply conditions of capital flows may be interdependent with developments in commodity markets. In private financial markets, creditors may assess the risk of a potential default on debt servicing in relation to the borrowers' solvency or ability to pay. The existence of 'sovereign risk' (related to the non-enforceability of loan contracts in international lending) may lead to risk assessment at the country level using (expected) export earnings in relation to the size of outstanding debt as an indicator of the ability to pay. In terms of equation 1.7a, increasing indebtedness (ΔB_S) and/or adverse trends in Southern export markets may thus enhance the probability of default and limit further lending. This suggests a pro-cyclical interaction between private international lending and trade that may form a source of instability in the process of world economic adjustment.

In orthodox portfolio theory it is usually assumed that creditors consider loan placements at the margin and will charge a higher risk premium (i_W increases) as the probability of default increases (see e.g. Williamson 1983, Llewellyn 1980, Friedman 1983 for a discussion of this approach and further Chapter 3). More recent literature has emphasized that the existence of sovereign risk may create problems of moral hazard and averse project selection of borrowers in face of higher borrowing costs. This will lead creditors to apply credit-rationing rules to select 'good' and 'bad' risk borrowers (Eaton & Gersovitz 1980, 1981; Sachs 1984a; Folkerts-Landau 1985; Eaton & Taylor 1986). Economy-wide solvency indicators are seen to underlie country-risk assessments by creditors, such that increased indebtedness and negative shocks in commodity markets are expected to affect private bank lending (ΔB_S) more than the interest rate (i_W), and given relations (1.5) and (1.6) this will have negative welfare consequences for the borrowing economy. This 'neo-orthodox' portfolio approach has provided a theoretical basis for the widely accepted notion that credit rationing rules underlie the supply of commercial bank loans. However, such models try to derive more or less predictable lending patterns from the borrowers' creditworthiness indicators, saying little about major shifts in the supply curve of bank loans such as those observed in the 1970s (outward) and 1980s (inward).

Such shifts should be explained by looking at the global macroeconomic environment and at the institutional structure of the bank loan market. Regarding the latter, it is suggested that banks may not be the 'arm's length' investors commonly assumed in orthodox and neo-orthodox portfolio theory, but rather should be analysed as large corporations; banks in fact operated in the 1970s and 1980s in clearly oligopolistic market structures. Salesmanship in search of increasing market shares forms a central ingredient of the modern management of commercial banks, as one can see in any management textbook on banking.[4] A disruption of initial market conditions may affect lending behaviour. Before 1970, developing countries had little access to private financial markets, but two factors contributed to a radical shift in market conditions. One is related to a number of financial innovations (discussed at length in Chapter 5), including financial deregulation in the major economies and new mechanisms for better risk sharing in sovereign lending, which made lending to the South more attractive and reduced entrance barriers for new creditors. The second is related to shifts in global macroeconomic balances, including the ones related to the first oil price shock, which affected Northern investment-savings balances and generated large savings surpluses in major oil-exporting countries which were deposited in the international banking system. New entrants and a buoyant financial market triggered a process of oligopolistic competition over market shares. Assertive salesmanship was such that some came to speak of 'loan pushing' (Kindleberger 1978, Darity & Horn 1988), a phenomenon not uncommon in the history of international private lending to developing regions (see Chapters 4 and 5). Despite the competition, lending remained highly concentrated in *loan syndicates* (to share risks and to earn high commissions). While the amounts lent concentrated in a rather small group of Southern borrowers, risk evaluation, rather than being assessed at the margin on a loan-to-loan basis, usually took the form of a ranking of broad and easily identifiable risk classes providing market access to the richer developing countries.[5] A new market disruption, i.e. the threat of a major debt crisis and of a potential collapse of financial markets, provoked within this institutional context a massive retreat from lending to the South in the 1980s.

Such a view of financial markets immediately complicates the analysis of the relations hypothesized in equations 1.5 to 1.7a. Firstly, broad categorization of classes of sovereign borrowers has led to the virtual exclusion of the poorer countries from private capital markets and suggests market segmentation from the point of view of the South. The lower-income countries consequently rely on official (bilateral and multilateral) capital flows as a main source of external finance. In line with most of the literature, such flows are considered to be determined essentially by political factors on the supply side. Secondly, access to private sources of borrowing may be highly unstable (taken over larger periods of time) and difficult to predict, which will influence borrowing strategies ('loan pushing') and spending decisions if a prolonged period of capital market access is expected. Official flows may be more stable, but may be tied to particular projects and be less responsive to shifts in the other components of equation 1.7a.

Global macroeconomics

A third major area of North-South interactions relates to international 'spill-over' effects of macroeconomic policies. Again, welfare effects on the South are not one-directional. For example, a contraction in Northern monetary policy, either as a result of coordinated Central Bank action in the major economies or as the net result of uncoordinated policies among, say, the USA, Japan and Germany will increase interest rates in the North while output and prices in the North are likely to fall below the paths they would otherwise have followed.[6] In terms of equation 1.7a, import capacity in the South will be lowered as a result of both the rise in i_W and the associated fall in ΔB_S (higher sovereign risk and tightening of credit markets). A lower g_N will affect demand for Southern exports, so that, if supply effects from lower imports are relatively slow, there will be downward pressure on p_e. The downward effect of the policies on p_m (assuming that the South buys most of its imported goods in the North), is the only element that allows import capacity to expand in equation 1.7a. However, it is likely that this positive effect will not offset the unfavourable effects on the other factors. A second-round effect would be lower Northern exports due to lower Southern imports, affecting g_N. On balance, one would expect under the given assumptions a detrimental impact on Southern welfare.

Outcomes may be less transparent for other macroeconomic policies. Fiscal expansion in the North, e.g. via tax reductions stimulating private investment, will raise aggregate demand in the North and positive spill-over effects may be expected for the South via higher g_N and upward pressure on p_e. On the other hand, expanded demand may create inflationary pressures in the North, raise p_m, and, with unchanged monetary policies, induce pressure on Northern capital markets leading to higher interest rates, and causing ΔB_S to fall. The net effect on Southern growth is an empirical matter, of course, but not independent of the underlying model.

Southern adjustment and demand for borrowing

A fourth area of investigation relates to the hypothesis that the nature of capital movements and instabilities in its supply (especially commercial bank lending) may affect spending behaviour and resource allocation processes in the borrowing country. In terms of the relations (1.5) to (1.7a), this could be reflected, for instance, in structural parameter shifts in (1.5) and (1.6) (e.g. a higher capital- and import-intensity of production). Here, however, such structural shifts are hypothesized to be linked to sectoral shifts between traded and non-traded goods producing sectors. In the case of the countries that had relatively easy access to commercial bank loans in the 1970s, 'loan pushing' and optimistic borrowing prospects led to indebtedness often far beyond the adjustment finance needs arising from the external shocks provoked by, among other events, the first oil-price hike. Even those countries with booming export sectors, including oil producers such as Venezuela, Mexico, Ecuador, and Nigeria, borrowed heavily. Finance was available at low costs, which many borrowers may have seen initially as a 'windfall gain'. Borrowers showed initial signs of absorption problems, upward pressures on real exchange rates (defined as non-traded to traded goods prices) and subsequent resource shifts towards non-traded sectors (mainly through public investment), symptoms also observed in literature analysing so-called 'Dutch-disease' effects in economies with booming export sectors (see e.g. Corden 1984, van Wijnbergen 1984a, Bevan, Collier & Gunning 1987).

Under the hypothesized structural conditions of the world economy, capital flows need not necessarily lead to efficient resource allocations; debt crises, inefficient allocations and negative welfare effects are plausible outcomes.

1.4 North and South

Given structural asymmetries (differences in insertion in commodity markets, a credit-rationed South and control of financial markets from the North), a North-South divide can be seen as analytically meaningful to international linkages and the role of finance in development. Naturally, such a level of aggregation is a great over-simplification. While it helps to isolate key processes, a classification of North and South is not sufficient to give persuasive answers to questions like which international factors contribute most significantly to the occurrance of debt crises. Neither North nor South forms a homogeneous group of economies.

In this study the North generally refers to the group of industrial market economies, essentially the OECD countries. In the analysis the leading role of the major economies (particularly, the USA, Japan and Germany, and for historical reasons Great Britain) is recognized. As a group, the North has overwhelming importance in the world economy, encompassing most world trade and finance. Table 1.2 shows, for instance, that over 80 per cent of world savings and investment is concen-

Table 1.2 Matrix of North-South economy characteristics, 1985

	Percentage share in: World		World finance			Destination of total exports			Export structure (%)			Import structure (%)		
	Popul.[a]	*GDP*[a]	*Exports*	*Savings*[a]	*Investment*[a]	*North*	*South*	*Other*[d]	*Non-oil*	*Oil*	*Manufac.*[b]	*Non-oil*	*Oil*	*Manufac.*[b]
North	17	81	69	85	83	75	20	5	21	7	72	17	19	64
South	83	19	22	15	17	67	26	7	21	43	36	18	16	66
Major oil-exporters	0.5	2	5	4	5	67	27	6	2	94	4	22	5	73
Official borrowers	36	3	2	1	1	75	21	4	72	7	21	28	25	47
Private borrowers[c]	46	14	15	10	11	66	26	8	27	36	37	19	16	65
Other	--	--	9	--	--	47	19	34	16	30	54	20	15	65
Total	100	100	100	100	100	69	22	9	22	20	58	17	18	65

Sources: World Bank, *World Development Indicators* (population data); IMF, *International Financial Statistics* (GDP, savings and investment); UNCTAD *Handbook of International Trade and Payments Statistics, 1987* (trade); GATT *International Trade 1987-88* (trade); and IMF, *Direction of Trade Statistics Yearbook 1981-87* (trade).

Notes:
a. Excluding former socialist economies of Eastern Europe.
b. Includes unspecified merchandise trade.
c. Includes also 'diversified borrowers' and China.
d. Refers to former socialist countries of Eastern Europe.

trated in the North. (The economies of Eastern Europe are excluded basically for reasons of insufficient data.)

The South has been traditionally characterized in international economics as a group of less developed countries relatively specialized in the production of primary commodities. Table 1.2 shows that in the aggregate this characterization remains in accordance with stylized facts. The South principally exports primary commodities (to the North) and its import structure is dominated by manufactures supplied by the North. For the South as a whole, primary exports constituted 64 per cent of total merchandise exports in 1985, with 43 per cent of the total being oil exports. For the non-oil developing countries (the weighted average of groups 2.2 and 2.3 in Table 1.2) oil represented 33 per cent of the total; non-oil primary products had a share of 32 per cent, leaving a fair share for manufactures (35 per cent). Thus, although in the aggregate the South can still be considered a net exporter of primary commodities, such a characterization obscures relevant differentiations. A not insignificant group of countries are now net exporters of manufactures.

To isolate major differences in vulnerability to Northern macroeconomic policies and fluctuations in international financial markets, this study takes structural differences in financial dependence as a first classification criterion for Southern economies. This leads to three main types – *private*, *official* and *diversified* borrowers – a distinction defined by the principal source of external finance. Official borrowers are nations with more than two thirds of their total outstanding external debt originating from official (bilateral, multilateral) sources, private borrowers are those with more than two thirds of their external liabilities owed to private sources (banks, bond markets, international firm credit supplies), and the rest are defined as diversified borrowers. Most LDCs appear to fall in the first two categories on the basis of a stock-taking exercise using average data for 1982-86. The average share of official debt in total debt of official borrowers is 84 per cent, while that for private borrowers is 25 per cent. Of a sample of 76 LDCs, 61 belonged to one of these two categories, while 15 fell between the demarcation lines and could thus be labelled as diversified borrowers. (See Appendix A.1 for the complete country classification.) Table 1.2 identifies official borrowers as closest to the traditional Southern trade typology, being essentially non-oil primary exporters. The trade dependence of private borrowers seems more diversified, with important export shares for oil and manufactured goods.

1.5 Chapter Outline

Chapter 2 identifies the main variables and basic accounting relations for the study of the world economy (along the lines of section 1.2). *Chapter 3* reviews existing theory on the microeconomic determinants of international capital flows and the interactions with trade and growth in North and South.

Chapter 4 gives a historical analysis of international capital movements and world economic adjustment patterns. The chapter seeks parallels with present-day problems of global interactions between finance and commodity trade. It appears that booms and crises in international lending have occurred long before the latest episode. Particular attention is given to the experiences of upward and downward cycles in international lending from rich to poor countries in the late nineteenth century and in the 1920s and 1930s. The behaviour of financial institutions as well as the business cycle in the major creditor countries (Britain and the United States) are shown to have played critical roles in the emergence of financial booms and crises.

The same ingredients feature in the analysis of the recent period (1970-89) of enhanced financial interdependence between the industrialized North and the developing South, discussed in *Chapter 5*. Despite a rapid growth of financial markets in the North, private capital flows to the South did not regain importance until the early 1970s. The chapter describes the general market conditions under which commercial bank lending to LDCs expanded in the 1970s. It also describes the effects of the subsequent boom and crisis on the Southern adjustment process. During the boom period of external finance, investment rates increased significantly and fiscal deficits widened. High growth rates could be sustained, but the use of funds increased capital intensity and expanded non-traded goods sectors. When the crisis set in, pressure on high fiscal deficits was sustained (partly to service external debt), forcing the private savings-investment balance into surplus. Private capital outflows ('capital flight'), exacerbating the adjustment problem, were a logical result. The chapter describes the major differences in the shifts in the macrobalances in different types of Southern economies, i.e. official, private and diversified borrowers.

From the analysis of Chapter 5 the major empirically generalizable assumptions about the functioning of world commodity and financial markets and the main actors are derived. *Chapters 6* and *7* elaborate on a *structuralist* theory of North-South interdependence (some of the key elements of the approach were already mentioned in section 1.3). *Chap-*

ter 6 reassesses the theories discussed in Chapter 3, drawing conclusions about the driving forces underlying official capital flows and reconciling theoretical approaches to oligopolistic banking behaviour and credit rationing of Southern borrowers. These behavioural rules need to fit the global budget constraints related to investment-savings and trade balances in North and South. *Chapter 7* pieces these together in a theoretical North-South model in order to trace the impact of international capital market imperfections on growth, trade and terms of trade in a simple North-South framework. The chapter adopts the structuralist North-South trade model elaborated by Taylor (1981), but introduces a role for different types of capital flows, including aid flows, bank credits and foreign asset demand of private agents in the South. It further introduces the effects over time of asset accumulation. Under the given assumptions, the model reveals asymmetries in the global adjustment process, with control over growth in the South constrained by external factors (controlled in the North), and demonstrates the conditions under which debt crises may occur. The model shows further how the interaction between capital flows and trade and the pattern of world economic growth depends on institutions (in this case financial institutions and official suppliers of capital).

Chapter 8 offers a number of simulations with a numerical version of the model elaborated in Chapter 7. The results emphasize structural tendencies of creating trade-offs between gains from trade and different forms of international finance in North-South transactions, as well as potential sources of system instability. One key finding is that increased aid flows from North to the South tends to impose a secondary burden on the recipient region, i.e. the South. This effect is particularly strong if aid transfers are financed through an increase in Northern government borrowing, which pushes up the world interest rate triggering a recession in the Northern economy with world-wide repercussions. This 'transfer problem' can be mitigated for the South and the world as a whole, if the North undertakes the appropriate fiscal measures offsetting the pressure on the world interest rate. These results are compared with those obtained by a number of existing empirical world models that focus on North-South interactions.

If institutional factors determining supply-led finance and credit rationing towards the South are explicitly taken into account, Southern policy options appear constrained and strongly influenced by spill-over effects of Northern macroeconomic policies. New sources of lending, major debt reduction schemes or structural adjustment policies stimulating export production in the South, are by themselves insufficient ingredients to overcome debt problems, as negative spill-over effects from structural asymmetries in the interactions with Northern goods and financial markets and from uncoordinated Northern macroeconomic policies may fully offset the positive welfare effects resulting from international debt management. On this basis a case could be made for new regulatory measures in international finance and for more cooperative and coordinated policy action involving all major actors, creditor country governments, international banks, debtor country governments and multilateral institutions.

However, as suggested in the concluding *Chapter 9*, not only does the institutional framework to implement such a policy scenario seem to be lacking, parties may also disagree on the appropriate policy model to capture current key interactions. This study does not provide a ready-made model for such policy discussions, but hopefully provides useful building blocks for a proper understanding of the key processes underlying North-South economic interdependence and for more elaborate and realistic frameworks for policy analysis and institutional reform.

2 Accounting for the World Economy

2.1 Introduction

For national economies the accounting rules for 'real' macroeconomic aggregates and financial (flow-of-funds) balances are well established and standardized in the United Nations' SNA system (United Nations 1968) and are part and parcel of textbook macroeconomics. No standardized counterpart system exists to account for the world economy. Early proposals by for instance James Meade (1951) to construct consistent multi-country accounting systems for international trade and finance have never become as elaborate and familiar as the national accounts. This chapter defines a set of very basic global accounting rules which will serve as a key reference in the analysis of the subsequent chapters, but which may also form the basis for a more elaborate system to integrate data on trade, accumulation and international finance (see Vos 1989).

2.2 The World Accumulation Balance

Standard national accounting rules state that, in the closed economy, total investment must equal total saving *ex post*. If this holds at the country level, then also at the level of the world economy (which is, of course, a closed system) the sum of investments of all individual economies must equal total world savings. If one economy receives foreign savings, there must be another with excess national savings, such that in a particular year the sum of all ingoing and outgoing foreign savings or capital flows must add to *zero* on a world scale. National accounting conventions imply that this is the same as saying that, *ex post*, the sum of the current account balances of the balance of payments of all economies must add to zero as well. The following identities hold for the open economy (in current prices):

Gross domestic product:

$$X \equiv C + I + E - M \tag{2.1}$$

Gross national product and disposal of income:

$$Y \equiv X - R \equiv C + S \tag{2.2}$$

From (2.1) and (2.2) we can derive:

Accumulation balance:

$$I \equiv S + (M + R - E) \tag{2.3}$$

Foreign finance:

$$\Delta F \equiv M + R - E \tag{2.4}$$

where:

X ≡ Gross domestic product
C ≡ Total consumption
I ≡ Total gross domestic investment
E ≡ Total exports of goods and non-factor services
M ≡ Total imports of goods and non-factor services
Y ≡ Gross national product (or income)
R ≡ Net factor payments and other current transfers to abroad
S ≡ Total gross national savings
ΔF ≡ Net capital inflow or foreign savings

The world may be subdivided at its highest level of aggregation into two major country groups: the North (N), composed of the industrialized countries of the OECD, and the South (S), comprising the heterogeneous group of developing countries. In each region the *ex post* macro-balance is established by the equality of the internal and external balances. The internal balance is defined by the investment-savings gap ($I - S$). A positive investment-savings gap ($I > S$) expresses an excess of domestic spending ($D \equiv C + I$) over national income (Y). The external balance is the trade gap, imports (M) less exports (E), plus (*less*) net factor payments and other current transfers to the rest of the world (R). Thus we define the external balance as the current account deficit of the balance of payments ($CA \equiv M - E + R$). From the standard national accounting rules the accumulation balances for each region can be derived as:

$$(I_N - S_N) \equiv (D_N - Y_N) \equiv (\theta M_N - E_N + R_N) \tag{2.5}$$

$$\theta(I_S - S_S) \equiv \theta(D_S - Y_S) \equiv (M_S - \theta E_S + R_S) \tag{2.6}$$

where θ is a relative price index ($\theta \equiv P_S/P_N$) and all variables are assumed to be valued in Northern currency. In a two-commodity world with complete specialization between North and South, θ may be interpreted as the terms of trade for the Southern economy. In a two-region world Southern exports must equal Northern imports by definition $(\theta E_S \equiv \theta M_N)$ and vice versa $(E_N \equiv M_S)$. Further, the net external factor payments and other current transfers paid by the South equal by definition those received by the North. As both are valued at the Northern price, it holds that $R \equiv R_S \equiv -R_N$. From these identities it follows that the *ex post* world balances for accumulation, trade and factor payments must be zero:

$$(I_W - S_W) \equiv (I_N - S_N) + \theta(I_S - S_S) \equiv (D_N - Y_N) + \theta(D_S - Y_S) \equiv 0 \qquad (2.7)$$

where the subscript W stands for World, the sum of the Northern and Southern economy. Equation 2.7 defines the *ex post* global macroeconomic identity (or global constraint) in terms of the global investment-savings balance, the world current account balance and the sum of the demand and supply balances of the Northern and Southern commodities. All aggregate balances add to zero.

A more detailed analysis would require a further disaggregation of the principal balance equations into (i) more country groups; (ii) separate commodities, specifying regional excess demand functions by commodity (groups) (indicated by subscript j):

$$\sum_j (D_N - Y_N)_j; \quad \sum_j \theta_j (D_S - Y_S)_j; \quad \sum_j M_{Nj}\ , \text{ etc., } (j \equiv 1 \ldots n);$$

and/or, (iii) institutional sectors (e.g. public and private). Such breakdowns are in keeping with the underlying logic of the accounting rules. The institutional breakdown between public and private sectors and principal agents in the supply of international finance (official creditors, commercial banks and multinational firms) will be important in this study. Regarding the public-private sector distinction, the link between government budget deficits and the current account can be formulated as:

$$\begin{aligned}(I_W - S_W) &\equiv D(I_N - S_N)_p + DEF_N + \theta(I_S - S_S)_p + \theta DEF_S \\ &\equiv CA_N + CA_S \equiv 0 \qquad (2.8)\end{aligned}$$

The internal savings gaps in both regions have been split into a private sector $[(I_i - S_i)_p\ , i = N, S\ ]$ and a public sector deficit (DEF_i), while CA_i represents the current account balance of each region. From equation 2.8 it follows for instance, all other things being equal and starting from an initial *ex post* equilibrium, that expansionary fiscal policies (higher DEF_N) in the North will lead to a corresponding *ex ante* world current account deficit. To bring the world economy back into balance, either the private savings surplus in the North or the Southern economy, or both, will have to adjust. If the increase in Northern government spending is not (fully) compensated by an increase in the private savings surplus, the accounting tells us that internal and external balances in the South will require adjustment.

2.3 International Flow of Funds and Wealth Accounts

Basic world accounting requires that financial variables be added to the basic real economy relations. This is done by applying UN/SNA conventions of flow-of-funds accounting to international financial transactions (United Nations 1968). Very few references exist for the construction of international flow-of-funds accounts. The multilateral institutions collecting external debt statistics agree that the proper framework to conceptualize external debt should be the SNA and, in its footsteps, the IMF Balance of Payments manual (World Bank/BIS/IMF/OECD 1988: 15-18).

A strongly simplified world flow-of-funds system is presented in Table 2.1. On the basis of stylized facts discussed in subsequent chapters it assumes that the international monetary system is fully controlled by the North and that reserve currencies are only created in the North. The major international banks are located in the North and are under control of Northern monetary authorities. The South may borrow and hold deposits in the international banking system and it may hold foreign reserve currency, but it cannot issue international money to finance domestic deficits.

The relevant financial balance equations can be derived from Table 2.1. The financial system comprises the central banks of the North and international commercial banks (omitting multilateral financial institutions). On the liabilities side it has total bank deposits, (J), and international money or currency, (H). Reserves for bank deposits would appear on both sides in this consolidated balance sheet and thus can be omitted. On the asset side appear outstanding commercial bank loans (B) and government debt with the Central Bank (DC_N). In flow terms the balance sheets of the international monetary system are given as follows:

$$\Delta B \equiv \Delta J + (\Delta H - \Delta DC_N) \qquad (2.9)$$

The Northern economy finances its internal and external deficits $[CA_N \equiv (I_N - S_N)_p + DEF_N]$ with bank credits and sales of government securities to the Central Bank. On the asset side, money demand takes the form of bank deposits (J_N) and cash holdings (H_N), while foreign aid (*concessional loans*) by Northern governments (A) and direct investment by international firms (IF) are presented as *direct* capital transfers to the South, i.e. they are not mediated through the international financial system. The financial equilibrium of the Northern economy is given by the balance between the supply of and demand for credit:

$$\Delta B_N \equiv (I_N - S_N)_p + (DEF_N - \Delta DC_N) + \Delta A + \Delta J_N + \Delta H_N + \Delta IF \qquad (2.10)$$

Equation 2.10 shows the accounting relations between real and monetary variables in the North. The *ex post* supply of commercial credits will have to balance with the private savings gap and the budget deficit

Table 2.1 Consolidated world financial and flow-of-funds system

Changes in Assets		**Changes in Liabilities**	
	International Financial System		
Commercial bank lending	ΔB	Bank deposits	ΔJ
Northern government debt	ΔDC_N	International currency	ΔH
	North		
Investment-savings gap equals current account	CA_N	Bank credits	ΔB_N
Bank deposit holdings	ΔJ_N	Government debt	ΔDCN
Cash balances	ΔH_N		
Foreign aid	ΔA		
Net direct investment	ΔIF		
	South		
Investment-savings gap equals current account	CA_S	Bank credits	ΔBS
Capital flight, bank deposit holdings	ΔJ_S	Foreign aid	ΔA
Foreign exchange holdings	ΔH_S	Net direct investment	ΔIF

which is not financed by drawing on Central Bank credits (or money creation). In the Southern economy the financial balance is established as:

$$\theta\,(I_S - S_S) \equiv CA_S \equiv \Delta B_S + \Delta A + \Delta IF - \Delta J_S - \Delta H_S \qquad (2.11)$$

Equation 2.11 can be seen as a presentation of the balance of payments. The items of the capital account are given on the right-hand side and include borrowing on private credit markets (ΔB_S) and foreign aid (ΔA) and investment (ΔIF) as sources of external finance. Acquisition of foreign assets by the South, particularly in the form of bank deposits, has become associated with capital flight in recent years. Estimates of the accumulated value of these assets indicate that they are considerable and of macroeconomic significance in a North-South context (see, for example, Deppler & Williamson 1987, and Chapters 3 and 5 of this

Table 2.2 Assets, liabilities and net wealth in a consolidated world financial system

Assets		Liabilities	
	International Financial System		
Commercial bank lending	B	Bank deposits	J
Northern government debt	DC_N	International currency	H
	North		
Physical capital stock	K_N	Bank credits	B_N
Bank deposit holdings	J_N	Government debt	DC_N
Money (cash) holdings North	H_N	Net wealth	W_N
Foreign aid (official loans)	A		
Net company equity holdings	IF		
	South		
Physical capital	K_S	Bank credits	B_S
Foreign financial assets	J_S	Foreign aid (official loans)	A
Foreign exchange holdings	H_S	Net direct investment	IF
		Net wealth	W_S

study). The final element in equation 2.11 is the use of foreign exchange reserves *(ΔH_S)* (omitting a term for asset revaluation).

The total supply of commercial credits is: $\Delta B \equiv \Delta B_N + \Delta B_S$. Using this identity and equations 2.9 and 2.10 the accounting balance for the supply of credits to the South can be written in terms of the Northern financial balance:

$$\Delta B_S \equiv \Delta J + (\Delta H - DEF_N) - \Delta A - [(I_N - S_N)_p + \Delta J_N + \Delta H_N + \Delta IF] \quad (2.12)$$

Substituting equation 2.12 into equation 2.11 gives:

$$\theta\,(I_S - S_S) \equiv CA_S \equiv (\Delta H - DEF_N - \Delta H_N) - (I_N - S_N)_p - \Delta H_S \quad (2.13)$$

Equations 2.12 and 2.13 make clear by simple accounting rules that the availability of bank finance to the South *(ΔB_S)*, Southern growth *(θI_S)* and adjustment are conceptually linked to the South's own savings decisions *(S_S)*, the Northern fiscal and monetary policy mix *($\Delta H - DEF_N$)*, determinants of the supply of foreign aid *(ΔA)* and portfolio decisions by the Northern private sector $[(S_N - I_N)_p - \Delta J_N - \Delta H_N - \Delta IF]$.

The balance equations give the overall framework for the analysis of international finance and global macroeconomic adjustment. They show how international financial relations are conceptually linked to the real economy, as reflected in commodity trade and domestic spending balances.

The *flow* variables of the accounting system also logically relate to a set of *wealth* and *stock* variables. This may become immediately clear if one transposes the financial variables in Table 2.1 into assets and liabilities, by deleting the delta and, again, omitting terms for asset evaluation. One obtains a system of real and financial wealth balance sheets for the world economy.

Table 2.2 presents such a system. The system is a multi-country adaptation of Tobin's stylized balance sheet accounts constructed for single, closed and open, economies (Tobin 1969, 1980; also van Wijnbergen 1983). New variables in this system are the capital stock (accumulated physical investment valued at historical prices), K_i, for each region and net wealth, W_i $(i = N, S)$. The stock of accumulated material wealth is interpreted here as all tangible assets that store economic value consisting of physical capital and various forms of (domestic and international) financial assets. The net wealth of each region therefore represents the total accumulated value of these assets less that of outstanding liabilities.

2.4 World Accounting and Data Limitations

The previous paragraphs elaborated an accounting system for a two-economy world system with five principal agents (i.e. public and private sector non-banking agents in both economies and international banking institutions). This is of course a very simplified and reduced representation of the world. Ideally, the accounting system should be more flexible, allowing for the introduction of more country groups (or individual countries), agents and different types of commodities. In such a more generalized set-up a double-entry balance sheet such as that presented in Tables 2.1 and 2.2 is less appropriate than a single-entry matrix presentation showing commodity trade and international flow of funds on a source-use basis. Such a framework could subsequently be labelled a *World Accounting Matrix* (WAM). The elaboration and construction of a WAM, will not be pursued here (but see Vos 1989 ; Luttik 1990, 1992; and de Jong, Vos, Jellema & Zebregs 1993).[1] The level of analysis in this study will remain strongly aggregate; very detailed world accounts are not required for the present purpose. Moreover, due to the massive data problems involved, the construction of detailed WAMs would require a study by itself.

Data problems also limit the empirical analysis of international trade, finance and adjustment. A good summary indicator for these data problems is the world current account discrepancy. IMF balance of payments statistics report a growing *ex post* world current account *deficit*, running as high as 107 billion US dollars in 1982. Thus, the accounting rule of a zero *ex post* world current account balance (equation 2.7) is not reflected in the statistics. The relative importance of the discrepancy is also brought out by the data in Table 2.3. The size of the discrepancy has been 1.5 to 7.5 times larger than the accumulated current account deficit of the non-oil developing countries as a group since 1982. Before 1983 it exceeded the size of the US current account deficit, while it fluctuated between 30 and 80 per cent of the huge US deficits between 1984 and 1987. The discrepancy was largest between 1981 and 1984, fluctuating between 0.7 and 1.1 per cent of world GDP, which is about equal to the size of each of the three major shocks that affected the world economy since the early 1970s: the two oil crises of 1973-74 and 1979-80 and the progressive deterioration of the US federal budget position starting in 1981 (see also Marris 1985). Table 2.3 also shows that the discrepancy is much less pronounced when based on national accounts data and defining the world current account deficit as the balance of world investment and savings ($CA_W = I_W - S_W$).

Table 2.3 *World current account balances (billions of US $)*

	Balance of Payments Data						National Accounts Data[a]				
	ICs	Oil exp.	LDCs	CMEA	World		ICs	Oil exp.	LDCs	World	
					Total	*% of Y_W*[b]				*Total*	*% of Y_W*[b]
1975	19.8	35.4	-46.3	n.a.	8.9	0.2	30.8	31.6	-35.6	26.8	0.6
1976	0.5	40.3	-32.6	n.a.	8.2	0.1	13.1	36.5	-24.4	25.2	0.5
1977	-2.4	25.0	-25.1	-6.9	-9.4	-0.1	9.9	34.2	-30.7	13.4	0.2
1978	31.9	-0.7	-35.5	-3.5	-7.8	-0.1	45.3	21.9	-46.4	20.8	0.3
1979	-23.1	51.4	-45.0	-2.7	-19.4	-0.2	4.4	42.1	-39.9	6.6	0.1
1980	-60.5	95.9	-65.5	0.8	-29.3	-0.3	-22.7	56.2	-50.7	-17.2	-0.2
1981	-18.7	34.8	-83.2	-3.0	-70.1	-0.7	22.3	80.0	-87.8	14.5	0.2
1982	-22.3	-18.2	-68.8	2.4	-106.9	-1.1	24.0	59.2	-66.8	16.4	0.2
1983	-19.5	-19.5	-44.7	2.7	-81.0	-0.8	34.0	8.3	-39.2	3.1	0.1
1984	-58.5	-5.4	-28.4	4.8	-87.5	-0.7	6.8	-5.1	-8.8	-7.1	-0.1
1985	-51.4	3.0	-26.9	2.3	-73.0	-0.6	2.3	-6.7	-12.9	-17.3	-0.2
1986	-18.1	-37.9	-9.2	-0.2	-65.4	-0.5	-48.2	-10.2	-2.7	-61.1	-1.0
1987	-38.9	-11.9	-7.7	0.7	-57.8	-0.4	n.a.	n.a.	n.a.	n.a.	n.a.

Sources: IMF, *Balance of Payments Statistics*, various years and IMF, *International Financial Statistics* (National Accounts Data).

Notes:
a. Based on a sample of 102 countries (see Appendix A.1). Current account balance calculated as a residual ($CA \equiv I - S$).
b. World GDP (Y_W) corrected for sample size.

ICs = industrialized countries (OECD);
Oil exp. = major capital-exporting oil exporters;
LDCs = all other developing countries;
CMEA = (former) socialist countries of Eastern Europe.

Possible causes of the large discrepancy in world economic accounts have been discussed by, among others, IMF (1987a, 1992), Vos (1988a) and Luttik (1992). These studies have concluded that the major cause of the discrepancy is to be found in the inadequate recording of externally held financial assets and related income streams. This seems to hold in particular for developing countries. Thus, any study of international financial relations in a North-South context should take account of this discrepancy and, where possible, make adjustments. This study does not attempt to resolve such statistical problems, but the world accounting framework will play a pivotal role in cross-checking the information from different data sources.

2.5 Concluding Remarks

The study of the role of international finance in the process of global adjustment requires an appropriate accounting framework. The framework in this chapter emphasizes the role of *net* capital flows in a logical structure that links financial and 'real economy' variables across countries and institutions. It defines the link between the net external (deficit or surplus) position of any institutional sector, country or country group and (changes in) the level and composition of the *stock* of assets and liabilities held by that sector, country or country group. Stock adjustments in one part of the system must have a counterpart elsewhere.

The accounting system provides the basic balance equations for the modelling of the world economy and North-South financial interdependence, as elaborated in later chapters (7 and 8). The accounting identities of the international flow of funds system and the world trade and accumulation balances do not by themselves indicate, of course, cause and effect of changes over time. But they do form a starting point in the analysis of the behavioural patterns, in theory and practice, described in Chapters 3 to 6.

The large discrepancy in the world current account balance, and thus in the aggregate investment-savings balance, to a large extent relates to problems in the accounting of international capital flows and emphasizes the need for a framework that treats internal and external balances, trade and financial flows and foreign assets and liabilities across countries simultaneously. This seems to be the contribution that a more elaborate WAM framework could make towards a better understanding of the world economy. The empirical analysis in this study could not, unfortunately, benefit from a set of adequately disaggregated WAMs at various points in time. The basic conceptualization of the global accounting framework defined in this chapter, however, forms an important starting point for the analysis in the subsequent chapters.

3 A Review of Theories of International Capital Movements and Adjustment: A North-South Perspective

3.1 Introduction

The purpose of this chapter is to review existing theory about international capital movements and their effects on commodity trade, with particular reference to its applicability to North-South interdependence.

Separating more explicitly trade balances and net financial resource transfers (net capital flows less net factor payments), one may write the global accounting identity as follows, using equations 2.5, 2.6 and 2.11:

$$\begin{aligned} \theta(I_S - S_S) - R_S \equiv M_S - \theta E_S \equiv \\ T_S &\equiv \Delta F_S - R_S \\ &\equiv (\Delta B_S - i_w B_S) + \Delta A + (\Delta IF - rIF) - (\Delta J_S + \Delta H_S) \\ &\equiv E_N - \theta M_N \equiv S_N - I_N + R_S \end{aligned} \qquad (3.1)$$

where *TS* is the net transfer of financial resources to the South and net factor payments and current transfers are assumed to consist of interest payments on external bank debt and profit remittances from direct investment only ($R_S \equiv i_W B_S + rIF$).

There are two predominant approaches in the traditional literature which can be related to the underlying adjustment mechanisms of the balancing of the world accounting identity of equation 3.1. A first approach centres around the 'classic' transfer problem, i.e. the adjustment in trade balances to an exogenous transfer T_S. The transfer may be generated by, for instance, demand deflation in the transferring country (reflected in a change in $S_N - I_N$) and subsequently the analysis focuses on adjustment in the terms of trade, which may rise or fall, to effect the transfer. A second approach, based in the pure theory of trade, looks at endogenous, homogeneous capital transfers (ΔF_S) in response to rate-of-return differentials between the two economies. Capital flows involve a relocation of the capital stock affecting income and the supply of importables and exportables with subsequent effects on the terms of trade. A basic notion in this approach is that capital will move from capital-rich to capital-poor countries.

These basic analytical constructs are of course not readily applicable to reality. In practice, capital flows are heterogeneous, may be direct or indirect forms of finance, and may run in two directions. Equilibrium in commodity and capital markets need not result from a smooth price-adjustment process. Section 3.2 discusses both more elaborate versions of the above approaches and alternative theories explaining the institutional behaviour of demanding and supplying agents underlying four main types of North-South capital movements: direct investment (ΔIF), international bank lending (ΔB_S), official transfers (ΔA) and other asset demand, often associated with 'capital flight' (ΔJ_S). Section 3.3 discusses the traditional literature on the transfer problem and trade adjustment under perfect capital mobility. Although not taking adequate account of the heterogeneous and imperfect nature of the global capital market, this literature adresses a number of relevant questions about growth and commodity market adjustment as a result of (specific types of) transfers. Finally, section 3.4 assesses the role of foreign capital from the angle of (global) macroeconomic theory. For the exposition, a simple two-country version of the traditional open-economy Mundell-Fleming model (*'IS-LM'*) is used.

The theories reviewed in this chapter provide several useful insights. However, the theoretical debates reviewed in sections 3.2–3.4 (microfoundations of capital movements, international trade models and global macroeconomic theory) still appear to be largely separate branches of literature. In later chapters these are brought together in a specific application of a North-South model.

3.2 Microeconomic Foundations of International Capital Movements

This section reviews mainstream approaches to explaining the determinants of international capital movements. Most of the existing theory focuses on private capital flows mediated by an international capital market. In the standard neo-classical model, atomistic profit-maximizing agents are the actors in the interplay of supply and demand. In this approach there are two main lines of analysis. One is a theory of capital movements and factor mobility embedded in the 'pure theory' of international trade; the other follows the theory of finance which emphasizes capital movements as a process of international portfolio diversification.

The first line of analysis tends to treat all capital movements as homogeneous and in essence refers to international investment in terms of productive assets (or direct foreign investment). The main interest of this study is in private and official international lending, as these have been the main types of flows between North and South over the past two decades. Neo-classical portfolio theory provides a basis for understanding commercial bank lending to developing countries, particularly when risk, uncertainty and imperfect information are incorporated. Yet, this approach mainly stresses market conditions under perfect competition. Alternative approaches have stressed the specific institutional setting of the oligopolistically structured international bank loan market. Banks, in this view, should be treated as a firm, rather than as the risk-averse investor of portfolio theory. Both approaches to international lending have in common that, contrary to the basic neo-classical trade theory of factor mobility, capital no longer needs to move in response to rate of return differentials and market clearing is more likely to be geared by *quantity* adjustment (credit rationing) than by *price* adjustment (interest rates).

Official lending has been addressed by a quite different branch of literature: mainly descriptive, political economy models. Private capital flight from developing countries is discussed in terms of a new, specialized branch of portfolio theory.

3.2.1 The pure theory of international capital flows and direct investment

The neo-classical theory of international capital movements begins with simple models of international trade. The roots of this 'pure theory of capital movements' can be found in the basic model set up by MacDougall (1960). The model assumes a perfect capital market and capital moves following rates-of-return differentials between countries. The essence of the model is that under unconstrained capital mobility both capital exporting and capital importing countries will gain positive welfare effects from capital movements. Consider a two-country world economy with the product in each country determined by domestic supplies of labour and capital. Capital is fully mobile and adds to the respective capital stocks in both countries. Countries will import or export capital until their respective marginal products of capital equal the world interest rate. Output will rise for a capital importer and fall for a capital exporter, but after taking account of factor payments national income rises regardless of the direction of the movement.

Figure 3.1 captures the mechanism. Total world capital stock equals

Figure 3.1 Output and investment under neo-classical conditions and perfect capital mobility

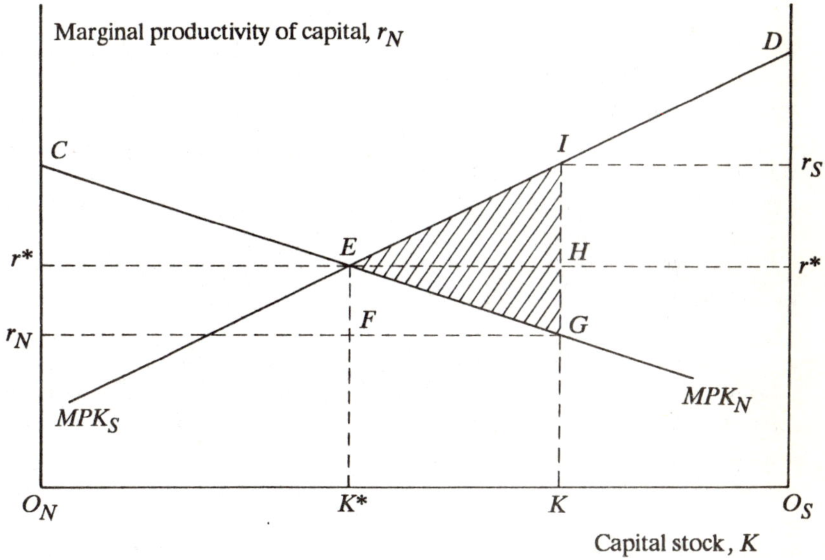

O_NO_S. Initially, under restricted capital mobility, country *N* holds a given capital stock of O_NK and KO_S is held by *S*. The marginal productivity of capital schedules are $CMPK_N$ and $DMPK_S$ respectively, defining world output by the areas under the two curves O_NCGK plus $DIKO_S$. Removal of barriers on international capital flows will induce investors in *N* to buy assets in *S*, since there is a positive real rate of return differential of $r_S - r_N$. Capital movements continue until the rates of return are equalized at Or^*. In equilibrium, output in country *N* has fallen by K^*EGK, while output growth in country *S* equals K^*EIK. World output has increased by *EGI*. Part of country *S*'s output gain, K^*EHK, leaks back to foreign investors resident in country *N* and holding foreign assets to the amount of K^*K yielding a return of Or^*. Country *N* receives a net reward of *EHG* (its increase in national income) as a result of the shift of capital.[1]

MacDougall's model is very basic of course, but it may be seen as the benchmark for much of the neo-classical thinking on international capital mobility. The model presents a kind of 'ideal' case of market efficiency. The crucial assumptions underlying this model are that: (i) markets are perfect and competitive; (ii) capital exporters and capital importers can acquire perfect market information and have perfect foresight, i.e. factors like risk and uncertainty are absent; (iii) foreign investment represents a transfer of factors of production from one country to another, implying international debt-neutrality with (intertemporal) equivalent output effects regardless of the form that the capital movement takes; (iv) capital transfers, whether through equity investment or loan contracts, are specified in real terms and are costless; (v) money is neutral; and (vi) lending and borrowing agents faithfully honour contracts.

As argued further below, relaxing any of these assumptions crucially influences welfare outcomes. However, an advantage of the approach is that it can be readily integrated into trade theory. The model expands the standard Hechscher-Ohlin-Samuelson theory to the case of capital mobility (see also section 3.3 below). The MacDougall model and its extensions in neo-classical trade theory, e.g. through the Kemp-Jones model, form a traditional starting point for theoretical discussions about foreign direct investment. Apart from the limiting assumptions listed above, there are at least two shortcomings to this approach. Firstly, the concept of capital in the context of the model is confined to capital movements that take the form of exports or imports of capital goods, i.e. no role is assigned to the ability of finance to effect such a transfer of commodities and therefore it fails to distinguish between direct and indirect forms of international finance. Portfolio theory picks up this challenge and is discussed further below. Secondly, the model links decisions about moving capital from one country to another to atomistic profit maximizing behaviour which seems to have little to do with the actual institutional channels of direct foreign investment. It has little to say about the firm as an institution taking strategic decisions whether to invest at home or abroad. Empirical studies have suggested that much direct investment takes place through large multinational firms operating in oligopolistic markets and that capital flow appears dependent on strategic firm decisions rather than on immediate cross-country yield differentials at the margin. As indicated, this study is mostly interested in private and public credit flows to developing countries, as these were the main types of finance available to these countries over the past decades. In order to limit the scope of this study, alternative and more widely accepted approaches to direct foreign investment will therefore not be treated here. As a general reference these alternative theories approach direct foreign investment flows from the theory of industrial organization and the Coasian theory of the firm (see e.g. Hymer 1976, Dunning 1981, Casson 1982, Gray 1982 and Helleiner 1989). New developments in trade theory are attempts to incorporate elements (like product diversification, intra-firm trade and product innovation) of theories of the firm and industrial organization (see e.g. Krugman 1979a, 1979b; Dixit & Norman 1980; Stewart 1984; and Ocampo 1986).

The MacDougall model may be seen as the foundation of neo-classical theory of capital mobility. It is a special case under specific market conditions. Market adjustment and welfare outcomes may alter fundamentally once imperfect competition, imperfect knowledge, information asymmetries and risk are taken into account. This has been taken up in portfolio theories.

3.2.2 International bank lending: portfolio theory, optimal borrowing and credit rationing

Recent literature on bank lending to developing countries is discussed in this section in terms of two broadly defined approaches. The first approach is a modern portfolio theory incorporating elements of risk, uncertainty and credit rationing in competitive market structures, with lending and borrowing agents making risk and rate of return calculations at the margin. The second approach emphasizes the specific institutional nature of the behaviour of borrowing and lending agents. Behaviour of creditors, i.e. the lending decisions of large international banks, is not necessarily based on marginal cost calculations and profit maximization. Borrowing agents, often public institutions, also may be imperfect 'portfolio managers'.

Credit rationing and modern portfolio approaches to international lending

Traditional textbook models of competitive lending are similar to MacDougall's pure international capital theory under perfect market conditions: lenders and borrowers are individual rational beings honouring loan contracts and optimizing profits and consumption utility at various points in time. Optimal borrowing theory is one branch of this literature. In the basic argument (Bardhan 1967), borrowers have ready access to loans at a given interest rate and enter the international loan market to finance all investment projects with positive present value at the prevailing interest rate up to the point where the international interest rate equals the marginal productivity of capital. Similarly, lenders use the same information and make the same considerations as borrowers and will lend as long as the borrower is solvent. A borrower is solvent if the present value of its future income exceeds its indebtedness. Lenders and borrowers will thus meet at the same optimal point.

In an international context, countries would, in this view, be able to borrow and finance all investment generating a positive present value. Creditors would leave no economically productive investment unfinanced. Decisions to raise domestic savings in a situation of credit market equilibrium would simply lead to a transferring of funds abroad.

Neo-classical theory of (international) portfolio diversification is closely related to the optimal borrowing literature (cf. for instance, Williamson 1983, Llewellyn 1980 for reviews). Uncertainty about the solvency of the borrower or about the success of the investment project leads creditors to include risk considerations in their lending decisions. Portfolio theory postulates that lenders try to cover and avoid risks by diversifying portfolios and by charging risk premiums and higher spreads over lending rates on riskier loans. Borrowers are assumed to reduce demand for loans in the face of higher risk-adjusted interest rates. In a competitive loan market, supply and demand for investment funds will clear through the cost of borrowing. Critical assumptions in this model are that lenders can distinguish between less risky and more risky lending projects and that more and less solvent borrowers can be selected by charging higher risk premiums.

However, creditors tend to be faced with market uncertainties and informational problems about a borrower's solvency. In the context of international lending, there is an additional dimension of risk, i.e. creditors may be faced with sovereign risk, which is the risk of default or debt repudiation in the absence of legal enforcement – due to sovereign immunity – of loan contracts written between nationals or institutions of one country and those, including government, of another. A growing literature has emerged addressing these issues and the consensus is that such 'market imperfections' tend to lead to credit rationing mechanisms as the predominant form of risk aversion (see e.g. Stiglitz & Weiss 1981, Eaton & Gersovitz 1981, Sachs & Cohen 1982, Sachs 1984a; reviews are in Eaton, Gersovitz & Stiglitz 1986 and Eaton & Taylor 1986).

This literature has provided useful insights into the potential determinants of credit rationing in international lending. The nature of the argument may be illustrated through the model developed by Stiglitz & Weiss (1981). This model, developed for a competitive loan market (domestic or foreign) with imperfect knowledge, has provided the basis for a large literature on international bank lending to developing countries.

For Stiglitz & Weiss (1981: 394-5) the term credit rationing applies to situations in which (i) some applicants receive a loan and others do not, even if they would be prepared to pay a higher interest rate; and/or (ii) there are identifiable groups of potential borrowers that would not receive loans at any interest rate, although they might receive one with a larger total supply of credit.

In a world of uncertainty, creditors attempt to maximize their expected returns on loans subject to the risk of non-payment. Creditors will lend even if there is a positive probability of default if they can be compensated with risk premia. They will expect, generally, that the risk of default will rise with the quantity of outstanding loans. This suggests an *upward sloping* supply curve of loans: creditors will increase lending to a particular borrower only at a rising premium (a higher interest rate) to compensate for the enhanced risk of non-repayment. However, this relationship between the volume of lending and the interest rate is neither linear nor infinite. Credit limits must be imposed at some point. The loan volume may grow to a point where the probability of default will be equal to *one*. At this point, a higher interest rate will not induce new lending.

The literature points to three possible sources of default. One is *insolvency*, the case where the present value of the borrower's future income stream is less than that of the future debt service. In the case of international lending, this includes instances where the present value of the future stream of *trade surpluses* falls short of the present value of scheduled external debt service payments. Creditors will always try to limit lending to below the point of insolvency. A second reason for default is *illiquidity*. A borrower may fall short of resources to meet its immediate debt service obligations, even though it is not insolvent. In the case of a developing country, for instance, the country may be faced with a lack of foreign exchange to meet external debt servicing. Here, the present value of the trade surplus achievable in the short run falls short of of the present value of the short-term scheduled debt service in foreign currency. A third source of default is not so much related to the *ability* to pay, but rather to the *willingness* to pay. Theory allows for the possibility that borrowers are rational, but to some extent dishonest as they violate loan contracts. This has been labelled debt *repudiation*. Sachs (1984a) and Eaton & Gersovitz (1981), among others, make this point explicitly as they allow for the behavioural rule that borrowers repay loans only if the cost of non-payment exceed the benefits. The costs are the loss of income due to sanctions imposed by creditors and possibly their governments, like interruption of access to finance and of trade relations, seizure of assets, etc., while the benefits are defined by the present value of future income derived from not servicing debt.

Creditors will try to limit lending to levels below that which could make it beneficial for the borrower to default.

With perfect foresight and perfect information, creditors would always be able to calculate the points of insolvency, illiquidity and repudiation. In the real world uncertainty prevails, however. Future returns on investment, future export earnings and thus the repayment capacity of borrowers cannot be determined with full certainty; in many cases it's not even close to that. Also the precise cost of sanctions are difficult to know in advance. Finally, creditors cannot be sure whether loan contract terms will be honoured, while their enforcement may be difficult, particularly as said if sovereign immunity is involved.

Stiglitz & Weiss clarify the theoretical implications of including *uncertainty* in the theory of loan markets under the heading of *adverse selection*. They show that in a competitive loan market with imperfect information this is likely to lead to credit rationing. A key element underlying this analysis is that borrowers and lenders may have different perceptions about the riskiness of a loan and the investment project financed by it. The lender will set the interest rate on the loan commensurate with the perceived risk of the investment project. For the borrower, revenues above debt service requirements are retainable and may permit or encourage a more risky project. Stiglitz & Weiss argue that the borrower can have an incentive to alter its behaviour after the loan has been made. Under these conditions, inclusion of a higher risk premium in the interest rate may stimulate the process of 'adverse project selection' as the present value of the borrower's returns on the initially chosen project will fall with the higher interest rate. Suppliers of funds are thus faced with problems of adverse investment project selection and moral hazard; the interest rate may therefore fail to clear the market.

Given the difficulty to control the borrower's behaviour, the lender will try to lump diverse projects of the borrowers together and classify types of projects and borrowers into different risk classes (rather than assessing individual cases) and apply rationing criteria to screen high-risk projects. Beyond a certain point higher interest rates will no longer accompany a larger lending volume, rather a smaller one. This will be the case as the creditor becomes aware that a higher interest rate may raise the average riskiness of the portfolio due, from the point of view of the creditor, to adverse selection of investment projects.

Stiglitz & Weiss therefore add a backward slope to the upward-sloping loan supply curve discussed above. These features lead to Figure 3.2 (adapted from Stiglitz & Weiss, 1981: 394) which relates the lender's ex-

Figure 3.2 Interest rate – expected return loci for borrowing company groups A and B

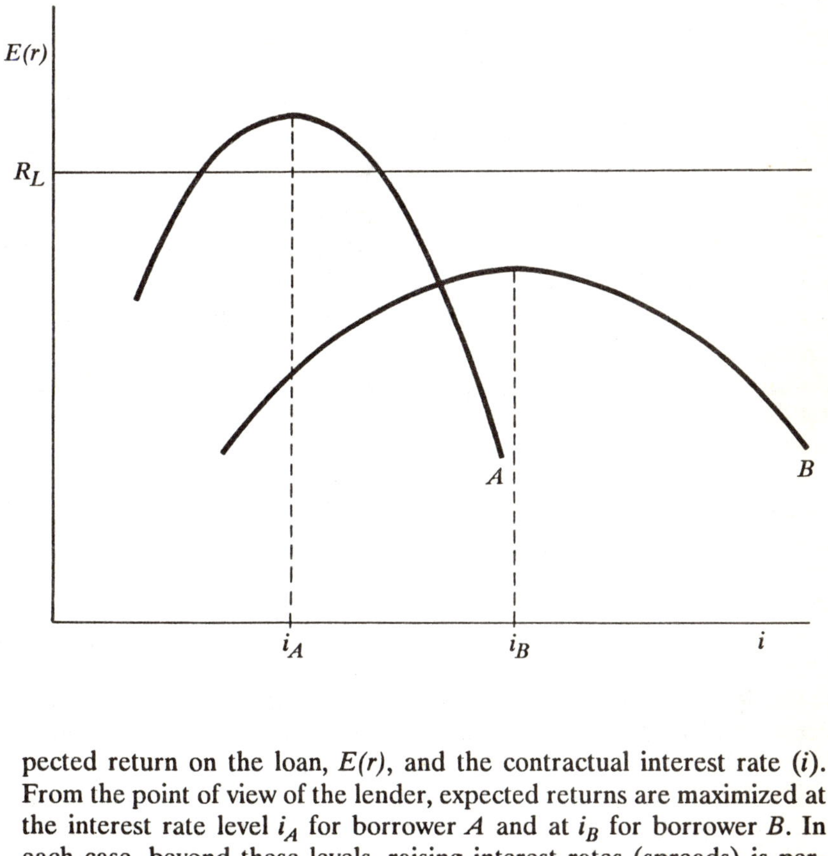

pected return on the loan, *E(r)*, and the contractual interest rate (*i*). From the point of view of the lender, expected returns are maximized at the interest rate level i_A for borrower *A* and at i_B for borrower *B*. In each case, beyond these levels, raising interest rates (spreads) is perceived to become counterproductive as high interest rates may lead to adverse selection and increase the risk of default and thus threaten the lender's expected return. Suppose that the bank's costs of funds (e.g. LIBOR) is at R_L in Figure 3.2. At this level group A of borrowers will have access to loans, but B will not because of higher default risk. Group B will be rationed out of the loan market at any finite interest rate or spread.

A similar result can be obtained allowing for default risk in sovereign lending (e.g. Folkerts-Landau 1985, Eaton, Gersovitz & Stiglitz

Figure 3.3 International bank loan market and credit rationing

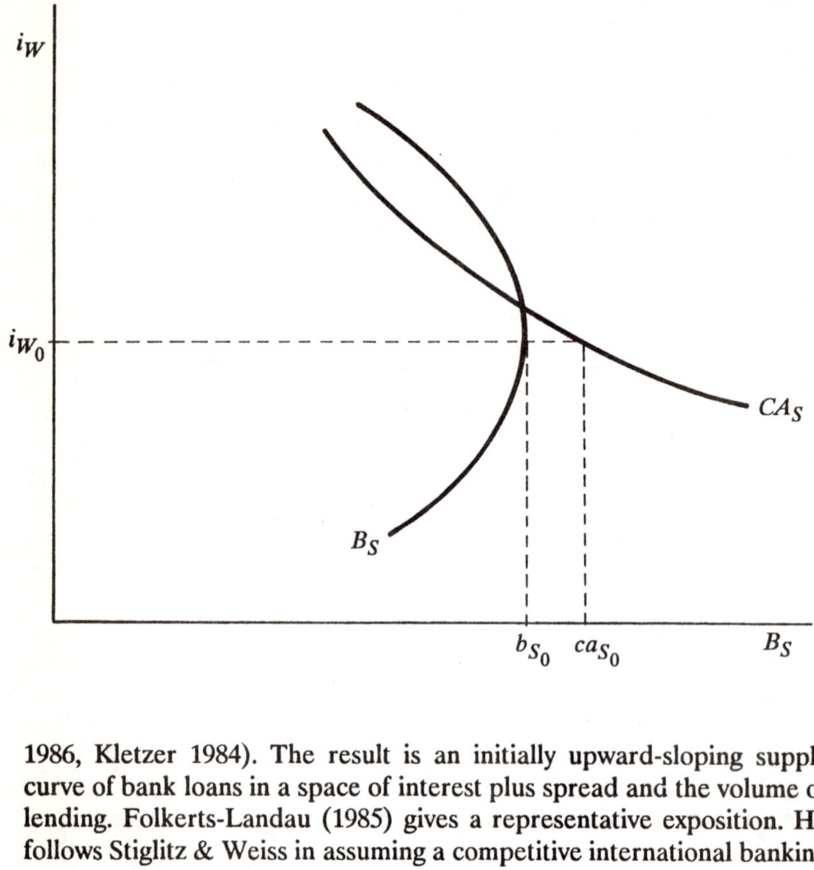

1986, Kletzer 1984). The result is an initially upward-sloping supply curve of bank loans in a space of interest plus spread and the volume of lending. Folkerts-Landau (1985) gives a representative exposition. He follows Stiglitz & Weiss in assuming a competitive international banking market with many (non-collusive) bank lenders and borrowers. Banks are seen as price-takers in deposit markets, but set lending rates (i.e. spreads) to maximize expected returns. Higher lending rates may have an adverse selection effect on borrowers and thus increase default risk along with higher levels of indebtedness. Thus, in interest-loan supply space the supply curve of banks will tend to be backward sloping beyond a certain interest rate. Folkerts-Landau assumes a downward-sloping demand curve for bank loans. Individual borrowers are assumed to maximize expected returns. Net expected returns fall with the level of the interest rate. Borrowers will consider default if gross expected returns fall short of the discounted value of borrowing costs and the possible costs of sanctions.

Figure 3.3 depicts this international bank loan market in a situation where equilibrium in the market is reached through credit rationing. Curve B_S represents the backward bending supply curve and CA_S the downward sloping demand curve for external borrowing of an economy in the South. Banks are willing to lend up to point b_{S_o} at interest rate i_{W_o}, where the bank expects its returns on outstanding loans to be maximized. Beyond this point, a larger loan volume is expected to lead to solvency problems with the borrower, while a higher interest rate induces adverse selection and higher default risk, and banks would tighten credit rationing.

In the figure, the demand schedule of the Southern borrowing country intersects the backward-bending supply curve at an interest rate higher than the banks' expected profit-rate-maximizing i_{W_o}, implying that the demand for external finance of the borrowing country exceeds the amounts supplied by $(ca_{S_o} - b_{S_o})$. The bank could charge different interest rates to borrowers belonging to different risk classes to compensate for any expected shortfall in loan repayment. However, banks tend to have imperfect knowledge about the riskiness of loans and solvency of their clients and fear adverse selection. At best, they can distinguish between broad risk classes of borrowers, but do not have sufficient information to discriminate among borrowers in the same risk class. As a result, as in the model of Stiglitz & Weiss, borrowers will be charged an interest rate reflecting their risk class, while an entire risk class of borrowers may be denied access to the international bank loan market.

Of course, a lower demand schedule would intersect the supply curve at its lower end and creditors would face a demand-constrained market and credit ceilings would not be reached. In this part of the demand and supply schedule for international bank loans, banks would be willing to supply more credit at a higher interest rate, given their creditworthiness assessment of potential borrowers. Theories of the bank firm suggested that this part of the supply curve may in fact not have a constant and upward-sloping shape in a dynamic, oligopolistic market. In a dynamic market situation triggering an oligopolistic competition for market shares, this part of the curve may be horizontal or even downward sloping, as banks start 'pushing' loans and slashing spreads on interest rates in order to maintain market shares. This hypothesis is discussed further below; investigated empirically in Chapters 4 and 5 and incorporated into the credit-rationing literature in Chapter 6.

A critical question not directly answered by the loan market models explained so far is whether the risk-averse and credit-rationing behaviour of banks is sufficient to ensure a *stable* market situation. Referring to the spurt in bank lending to developing countries in the 1970s and the 1980s, Folkerts-Landau (1985) and others have pointed to exogenous market factors to explain shifts in the supply curve. In the 1970s, financial innovations reducing sovereign risk (e.g. cross-default clauses and syndicated lending, see also Chapter 5, section 5.3.1) preceded the boom in bank lending to the South and the loan-supply curve shifted to the right (i.e. a seeming relaxation of credit rationing points to groups of borrowers). The crisis in the 1980s is seen as having been provoked by a policy-induced higher world interest rate and subsequent, increased default risk, leading to a shift in the supply curve to the left and tighter credit rationing.

Sachs (1984a) models a financial panic in the loan market inducing a debt crisis as a form of 'contagion effect' in bankers' expectations. Sachs identifies a loan-supply function which lets risk-averse behaviour of banks also depend on portfolio diversification (i.e. loan supplies of bank i to country j should not exceed a pre-defined share of the bank's capital). It is subsequently shown that liquidity problems of the borrower (i.e. it cannot meet debt obligations out of current income), as distinct from insolvency, can lead to a debt crisis. New loans could solve the liquidity crisis without necessarily risking a solvency or repudiation crisis, but no individual bank is willing to put up the required new loan as it might put the bank at risk (given its ceiling on lending to a single borrower as a share of bank capital). If banks expect all other banks to make the same portfolio consideration, a debt crisis may become a self-fulfilling prophecy. It may thus be safe for a group of banks to help country i out of its liquidity crisis, but it may not be safe for any single bank to do so (Sachs 1984a: 29-32). Collective action by creditors thus becomes a rational device, even among competing banks.

To a large extent one may see this credit-rationing literature as an extension of neo-classical portfolio theory by successfully incorporating uncertainty and informational asymmetries. Given its wide acceptance, it may be viewed as the 'new orthodox' approach to international lending. Creditors remain the rational cautious portfolio managers who evaluate risk at the margin, as in the traditional portfolio models. Although many 'country-risk' models describe the commercial loan market for sovereign borrowers in the South as one characterized by loan syndicates and aggregate lending behaviour, these features do not play a major role in explaining the existence of credit rationing or the dynamics of the market. In most of these studies, amounts of credits supplied are strictly determined as a probabilistic function of creditworthiness indicators. Although the explicit inclusion of uncertainty and credit rationing mechanisms in standard portfolio theory should be seen as a major theoretical advance, there are other approaches that have emphasized the role of the institutional structure of the international banking market and of, apparently, less rational forms of lending behaviour to explain the functioning of this market in recent decades.

The bank as a firm, and 'loan pushing'

A less orthodox approach in international economics, but orthodox in textbook approaches to banking and finance, is to start off with an institutional theory of the bank as a firm (Guttentag & Herring 1985; Darity & Horn 1988; Devlin 1986, 1987). As argued by Weston (1980: 24), portfolio theory treats a bank as an investor, not as a firm. Firm strategies may serve more than one goal, including stability, market share expansion, and so forth. Profit maximization need not be the single rationale determining bank behaviour. Client relationships tend to be important in risk evaluation, more so than the notion of price (interest rates).[2]

This approach provides a different perspective of the dynamics of the international loan market. Referring to the recent history in international lending and the degree of market concentration, the oligopolistic banking behaviour of the larger banking firms is a central feature in explaining the boom and crisis in lending to the South. Syndicated lending, interpreted by among others Folkerts-Landau as a sovereign risk reducing financial innovation, is in this view an attempt by the large banks to maintain market shares in a situation where the market was flooded with excess liquidity and access to the market for new entrants was eased by new risk-reducing forms of guarantees and cross-default clauses. This view of oligopolistic competition over market shares by large bank firms has been put forward by Devlin (1986, 1987). The struggle for market shares, in this view, led to a maximization of loan volumes by the leading banks and, since the cost and risk of market entry were reduced, an oligopolistic price competition in the form of a lowering of spreads. The market in this stage of expansion of international lending is seen as demand constrained.

Other approaches, based on more narrative analyses of banking history, have added a role for specific bank managers' behaviour, de-emphasizing risk-averse behaviour. Kindleberger (1978) and Darity & Horn (1988), among others, emphasize the interests of managers who earn fees and commissions which are a positive function of the size of the loans. This leads to – informally discussed – hypotheses of loan-size maximization and loan pushing, for which they find historical evidence in international lending behaviour in the late nineteenth century, the 1920s and the 1970s.

Less (economically) rational bank managers' behaviour has been described by Guttentag & Herring (1985, 1986), who argue that lending to developing countries was not particularly profitable as spreads were not very high in this market segment, and managers must have banked on their confidence in the market. When emerging debt service difficulties became visible in many countries around 1980, they continued to 'push' loans for some time, thus hastening the crisis. Guttentag & Herring see this apparent 'disaster myopia' as an example of 'cognitive dissonance', a term derived from psychology to explain the behaviour of a decision maker who tries to ignore information that is likely to cast doubt on previous decisions and may put the manager's position into question.

Both the 'new orthodox' portfolio theory and the 'international bank firm' approach suggest that the international loan market, seen from the perspective of the South, is strongly supply-side determined, i.e. by credit rationing or 'loan pushing'. The two views need not be mutually exclusive. Devlin (1986), exponent of the 'bank firm' view, in fact suggests as much. He puts forward the proposition that banks *do* rank customers by creditworthiness. However, informational problems to precisely calculate creditworthiness, particularly in the case of sovereign borrowers, lead to the identification of only broadly defined credit categories (risk classes) with different credit ceilings for borrowers in each category. Loan-size maximization will then take place within the limits of pre-set (adjustable) credit ceilings. This hypothesis is assessed further in Chapters 4–6.

In a similar search for a synthesis, it may also be hypothesized that the bank-loan market is potentially unstable due to asymmetries in the behaviour of lenders and borrowers. In the portfolio approach creditors and borrowers face informational problems leading to diverging assessment of creditworthiness and expected, risk-adjusted rates of return at the margin. In the theory of the bank as a firm, credit rationing is part of a marketing strategy in a context of uncertainty and imperfect creditworthiness. An oligopolistic market structure and market destabilizing factors may provoke a lending boom and loan pushing. In both approaches bank runs and debt crises may result. This critical issue will be looked at in more detail in the subsequent chapters. However, since the loan market does not operate in isolation, this behaviour in the loan market will further have to be assessed in the context of its interactions with commodity trade and capital accumulation (see Chapters 6–8).

3.2.3 Official capital flows

Public capital flows have formed a major source of external financing to developing countries in the post-war period. In the 1960s almost two thirds of net capital flows to the South were from official sources. Although in more recent decades there was a growth in private, commercial bank lending to the South, many (particularly low-income) countries did not have access to this market and have remained mainly reliant on public sources of external finance. Further, stagnation in bank lending in the 1980s has made official capital flows increasingly important, also for the richer developing nations. Official capital flows can be channeled through bilateral or multilateral channels, and a major share of these (65 per cent) are on concessional terms and considered to be development aid (OECD 1985; and Chapter 5).

Both the sheer existence of large public capital flows and the fact that private capital does not seem to move massively to capital-scarce nations like Zambia and other low-income countries in Sub-Saharan Africa and Asia, suggests there is no efficient capital market identical to the neo-classical benchmark. 'What market "distortions" and public-good considerations would justify government involvement?' Eaton (1989: 1308) quotes the World Bank's *World Development Report* for 1985 (p. 99), saying that official capital flows can improve the worldwide allocation of resources. The argument is that, despite the fact that rates of return on investment are often higher in developing countries, there is an underprovision of private funds to these regions for a variety of market limiting factors. These limitations include, among other things, sovereign risk in international private lending (see above), capital market and exchange restrictions in developing countries and investment opportunities with high social returns but little directly capturable private return. As Eaton comments quite rightly, one may doubt whether such limiting factors on private capital movements form adequate explanations for the size, nature and direction of public capital flows. It is therefore unlikely that a strictly economic analysis will give a full explanation for public capital flows from rich to poor countries and most theoretical approaches recognize the strong political motives involved. Since aid flows comprise the largest share, the discussion below is able to touch upon most of the available literature by focusing on this part of total official lending from North to South.

Most of the existing literature focuses on the supply determinants of aid flows. Broadly, one could distinguish two types of studies. One part of the literature follows a largely descriptive and empiricist approach, describing the institutional setting within which official lending from North to South takes place and trying to find correlations between the volume and direction of aid flows and a vector of determinants without specifying a particular theoretical framework. Another part of the literature provides attempts to link official capital flows to theories of public finance.

Starting with the first approach, descriptive theories of the motivations for Northern governments to provide public capital to developing countries can be found in, among others, Mikesell (1968), OECD (1985) and Mosley (1987). These studies identify economic and political self-interest (export benefits, former colonial ties, geo-political motives) or altruism (humanitarian reasons, views of global welfare effects), or a mixture of the two. A number of econometric studies have tried to quantify the relative importance of such supply determinants and their impact on the distribution of aid and official capital flows among developing countries. Beenstock (1980) concludes that donor countries' decisions about aid supplies reflect, as indicators of political decision-making, a range of macroeconomic indicators such as unemployment, the balance of payments position, the central government budget and GNP growth. Others (e.g. VerLoren van Themaat 1982) have given empirical evidence that (smaller) donor countries with highly developed welfare states project their social-democratic tradition in their aid policies. This is reflected in a high positive correlation between the aid effort and the level of public expenditures or tax and social welfare-premium burden in relation to GNP. Other single-equation regression work has identified biases in the distribution of aid across developing countries. Many studies (see also Chapter 5) find that the ratio of aid flows to the GNP of recipient countries tends to be inversely related to *per capita* income, that is low-income countries are more dependent on aid than middle-income countries. However, middle-income countries tend to receive more aid in *per capita* terms (see for such results, among others, Isenman 1976, Edelman & Chenery 1977, Crosswell 1981 and Dowling & Hiemenz 1985; and Chapter 5).

Econometric studies of this kind can be helpful in verifying certain existing patterns and hypotheses about patterns in aid supply and distribution. However, most of the cited studies basically provide a form of econometrics without theory. The estimated regression equations are not reduced forms of an explicit model explaining the observed trends and correlations.[3]

Approaches with a more solid theoretical basis have treated aid as a public good (Pincus 1965, Dudley & Montmarquette 1976, Frey 1984, Mosley 1985). The supply of foreign aid is explained by the demand for it in the donor country (exercised eventually by the taxpayers and voters). In these approaches, taxpayers' demand for aid is defined in terms of their expectations about the impact of aid on both the recipient country (e.g. in the form of development and poverty relief) and the donor country (export increases, political influence). From the point of view of the (citizens of the) recipient country, though, aid is entirely supply-side determined. Thus, in this approach aid is treated as a public good benefiting the donor countries. Pincus (1965) defines aid, like defence, as an international public good. Small countries are seen as 'free riders' spending little themselves, while deriving benefits from larger donor countries. This view has led to policy recommendations towards more equal 'burden sharing' in aid giving among donor countries. At the time of the Pincus study, a 'free-rider problem' seemed to exist. The larger donor countries of the OECD aid community (UK, US, France) supplied more aid in absolute terms and as a share of their GNP than the smaller countries. However, by the 1970s the smallest countries had become the most generous donors (OECD 1985).

Of more substance is the question of whether the aid community considers aid as a homogeneous 'commodity' from which all can reap benefits. If the 'benefits' from aid are tied to particular interests of respective donors in particular recipient countries by ex-colonial ties, geopolitics and trade links, then no 'free-rider problem' will exist. More recent theoretical models explaining aid as a public good have been elaborated by Dudley & Montmarquette (1976), Mosley (1985) and Frey (1984). The political process behind the supply and distribution of aid is simplified in these models to actions of optimizing agents, i.e. the taxpayers in the donor countries maximizing the utility of aid (that is, its impact on the recipient country). This utility maximization determines both the amounts of aid supplied by the donor country *and* its allocation among recipient countries. Such an approach has serious conceptual problems. Foremost, one should seriously doubt whether political processes can be described in these terms. Taxpayers, and even government officials, may know very little about the precise impact of aid on recipient countries, let alone be aware of the 'price' of the commodity they are 'buying'. Unsurprisingly, the econometric evidence supplied is far from convincing. For instance, after a long series of conceptual and measurement problems related to indicators measuring taxpayers' perceptions about the 'quality' of the aid programme of their government,

Mosley (1985) could not produce any unambiguous empirical evidence in support of his theoretical model. Dudley (1979) and Frey (1984) show econometric estimates that could be interpreted as evidence *against* aid being an international public good. They find that there are externalities in aid giving. Governments tend to increase aid budgets if other donors show higher relative aid efforts.[4] Frey's (1984) interpretation is that donor countries resent the aid given by other countries and thus try to increase their own aid budgets to maintain their influence in the international arena.

There is no clearcut theoretical explanation for the observed 'bandwagon' effect. It might be the result of a certain amount of political leverage the donor wants to gain in the recipient country, but it is doubtful whether the quantity of aid is the main determinant. A possible alternative explanation, for instance, could be that foreign aid agencies and government bureaucrats can press more easily for budget increases by pointing to large aid budgets in other countries. Neither model nor evidence is conclusive.

Most of the literature focuses on the supply side and the donor interests determining aid flows to developing countries. There seems to exist a consensus that 'recipients needs' play no direct role in determining aid budgets. Referring to US, British, French and German aid in the 1960s, McKinley & Little (1978a, 1978b and 1979) bluntly concluded that OECD aid disbursements are simply an instrument of power politics masked by 'developmental rhetoric'. Their conclusions have been challenged by Mosley (1981, 1987) on methodological and empirical grounds. Mosley (1987) concludes that even in the 1960s, recipients' needs (i.e. their poverty as measured by their GNP per capita) did affect the allocation of aid across countries, although not so much the size of the aid budget. Furthermore, Mosley also pointed out the existence of much more complex bargaining processes between donors and recipients, again not so much on the size of the budget, but on the allocation of aid to specific projects and programmes. In this context, conflicts of donor and recipient interests may lead to both 'aid pushing' from the donor side (to get budgets spent) and underspending of budgets where recipients, mainly governments and (semi-)government institutions, fail to meet required criteria of project or programme design (see Cassen et al. 1987 and Mosley 1987 for detailed discussions).

In sum, the picture emerging from the literature related to bilateral aid flows is that in the various donor countries decisions regarding the quantity and allocation of aid usually result from a complex set of motives, related to historical ties (colonialism), expected gains from aid-induced trade, and geo-political as well as humanitarian factors. Public finance approaches and econometric studies have been elaborated, but the efforts to find purely welfare economic criteria or other generalizable economic determinants of aid flows have yielded far from fully convincing results. A consensus seems to exist, however, that at the macro-level, i.e. the aggregate size of budgets and their allocation among countries, donor interests predominate, although to some extent the allocation of aid budgets may respond to recipients needs (e.g. poverty in terms of GNP per capita, as well as, more incidentally, food aid and disaster relief) and be subject to bargaining between donors and recipients. In the aggregate, the size of aid flows appears to be supply determined in the North and exogenous to (public sector) recipients in the South, i.e. largely independent of Southern needs for external finance.

This view of the nature of official capital flows has a bearing on the interpretation of processes of external and internal adjustment in countries that are highly dependent on aid. Firstly, exogenous capital flows (in the form of unrequited transfers) have played an important role in the transfer problem debates in the traditional international trade literature. (The relevance of this debate for the present study is discussed in section 3.3.) Secondly, the supply-side determination of official capital flows implies that aid flows are not intrinsically accommodating the *ex-ante* current account deficits of recipient countries. If these are the main source of external finance, changes in the components of the current account balance (for instance, a terms of trade shock) will require adjustment in other parts of the current account and the internal balance for a given amount of foreign assistance.

3.2.4 Two-way capital movements: private capital flows from South to North

Most theoretical studies on international capital movements tend to focus on *net* flows which, at a particular point in time, only move in one direction. In a North-South context such flows would normally move from rich to poor. The simultaneous occurrence in the 1970s of large private capital movements from South to North along with large bank credit flows from North to South has been a source of new theoretical considerations.

There are some conceptual problems in defining the phenomenon. Most of the literature labels it as 'capital flight'. As the term suggests, it is seen as money that 'flees', usually to escape particular risks and taxation (Cuddington 1986). In the literature a distinction has been made between 'normal' capital outflows and capital flight on two different grounds: one based on different motivations and one on a difference in welfare consequences. Dooley (1986), Khan & Ul Haque (1985) and Deppler & Williamson (1987) define capital flight in relation to specific motivations of private agents in developing countries to invest in foreign assets. 'Normal' capital outflows are seen to be part of 'normal' portfolio decisions, that is demand for foreign currency assets is part of the investors' desire to optimize their portfolios based on rate of return and risk considerations. 'Capital flight' is a deliberate attempt to escape the tax base of a source country (including the inflation tax) or to avoid particular risks associated with the political situation (e.g. fears for nationalization) or with the external debt situation. The latter type of risk refers to fears of private agents that the public external debt overhang will lead to an (implicit) expropriation of their assets (e.g. eroded by inflation) as foreign creditors are given a preferential treatment by their governments.

Cumby & Levich (1987) take the other approach and make a distinction between 'capital flight' and other capital exports based on a presumed difference in welfare effects. In contrast to 'normal' capital outflows, capital flight would be a source of national disutility, thus being regarded as disadvantageous by the government.

The measurement and analysis of capital flight may vary considerably depending on whether it is defined by its motivations or by its consequences for national welfare. However, apart from practical measurement problems (see e.g. Deppler & Williamson 1987, Lessard & Williamson 1987 and Vos 1992), some authors have argued that in the case of developing countries it is pointless to distinguish between 'normal' capital outflows and 'capital flight'. Rodriguez (1987), taking Cumby & Levich's position to its logical end, argues that *all* private capital outflows from developing countries should be termed capital flight. This is because in capital-scarce and foreign-exchange constrained economies all leakages of savings and foreign exchange are likely to produce welfare losses. Cardoso & Dornbusch (1989a: 1425-6) comment that a definition based on investor's motives for private foreign asset acquisition requires a good deal of insight and judgement to distinguish capital that is 'fleeing' from capital flows which should be seen as being part of a normal process of portfolio diversification. They doubt whether it is possible to come to an operational definition of such a concept of capital flight. Dooley (1986) and Khan & Ul Haque (1985) claim that while all capital flows are motivated by investors' desire to maximize return on capital, capital flight is motivated by risks of expropriation or market distortions such as capital controls, taxation and financial repression. However, as Cardoso & Dornbusch argue, for a capital outflow to be classified as capital flight it must be a response to risks and losses that are perceived to be large in relation to investable resources. It may be impossible to identify this in practice. Moreover, while different motivations for capital outflows may be separable in principle, they are likely to overlap in practice (Cardoso & Dornbusch 1989a, Vos 1992): if investors choose between domestic and foreign currency portfolios based on a risk adjusted rate of return differential and if investors are risk averse, then all factors implying enhanced risk of capital losses will be part of their diversification into foreign assets.

Differences in concepts used to define the phenomenon are one source of substantial differences in measurement concepts and consequently have led to widely different estimates of capital flight from developing countries. These come on top of important data problems which are discussed at some length in Deppler & Williamson (1987), Vos (1992) and Anthony & Hughes-Hallet (1992). The issue of measurement is discussed further in Chapter 5.

While there is apparently little agreement about the precise concepts and measurement of capital flight from the South, there seems to be greater consensus that a(n) (eclectic) portfolio approach seems to be the most fruitful way to analyse its determinants and consequences. Most authors point to the existence of structural asymmetries between domestic capital markets of developing countries and foreign asset markets, which are seen to determine capital flight. In a perfect world capital market with no asymmetries in asset market structures at home or abroad, an outflow of domestic savings would be offset by a subsequent inflow of foreign savings, equalizing rates of return at home and abroad.

There are at least three, not necessarily mutually exclusive, explanations of why the absence of such a symmetry could lead to two-way capital flows between North and South. Firstly, rate-of-return equalization may be impeded by some form of domestic distortion. Distortions may be associated with macroeconomic policies in both the North and the South. Dornbusch (1985), Cuddington (1986) and Ize & Ortiz (1986), among others, emphasize overvalued exchange rates and anticipation of devaluations as causes of private capital flows from North to South. Real exchange rate appreciation is in turn related to fiscal deficits and related public borrowing and expectations about inflation. Expected yield and risk differentials have been further associated with financial repression and other domestic capital market distortions (Lessard & Williamson 1987), capital controls and tax differentials on financial assets at home and abroad (Dornbusch 1987, Williamson 1987, Lessard & Williamson 1987).

Secondly, domestic and foreign loan contracts may not be equally enforceable. Khan & Ul Haque (1985) model this. If foreign capital inflows are rationed and acquired by the public sector providing public guarantees (see section 3.2.2), private agents may perceive that foreign creditors have a preferential status and that domestic assets are subject to a greater risk of expropriation. This will induce private acquisition of foreign assets which is not matched by a corresponding inflow and will involve welfare costs. This type of analysis has been further dimensioned by Eaton (1987) and Eaton & Gersovitz (1989), who take into account that agents will expect higher future taxation in the face of heavy public external borrowing, which will reduce after-tax returns, affecting private investment and lead to a portfolio shift towards foreign assets.

Thirdly, stock adjustment behaviour may be a complement to the previous explanations. Not only foreign credits, but also foreign exchange markets at home may be rationed and limit the capacity of residents to make international payments. This may lead to the formation of parallel foreign exchange markets, and form a reason for residents to endeavour to acquire a (minimum) target level of foreign assets. Minimum amounts of foreign asset holdings may be targeted by both firms and households for production and consumption purposes. The latter has been related to lifestyles and internationalized consumption patterns of the rich in many parts of the South (Vos 1992).

In principle these determinants could be complementary, although particular determinants may be paramount in some cases and not in others as is suggested by the available econometric evidence (see Chapter 5). This in turn suggests that in applied analysis the specific institutional and economic conditions will have to be taken into account to determine which particular set of portfolio considerations explain private capital outflows in particular developing country contexts.

3.3 Capital Movements, North-South Interactions and the Transfer Problem

The introduction to this chapter noted the so-called transfer problem emerging from capital movements from one country to another and to unclarities in economic theory about the directions of causality between capital movements and adjustments in trade and accumulation. A large literature in international trade theory addresses these issues, but mostly in the context of homogeneous capital flows. In this section this literature is reviewed, without striving for comprehensiveness. Section 3.3.1 discusses the classic transfer problem literature relating to exogenous transfers representing unrequited commodity transfers not directly affecting the capital stocks of the transferring economies; section 3.3.2 discusses the orthodox literature on exogenous and endogenous capital movements involving direct foreign investment; section 3.3.3 looks at a special branch of the trade literature related to North-South interactions; and, finally, in section 3.3.4 the issues are addressed from a different branch of the literature, one derived from standard open-economy macroeconomics.

3.3.1 The transfer problem and exogenous transfers

The economic consequences of the German reparation payments after World War I provoked considerable theoretical debate. The dispute centred around the question of whether the transfer to be made by Germany would involve not merely a 'primary burden' to effect the transfer, but also a 'secondary burden' as the terms of trade of the transferring country might deteriorate. Keynes (1929a,b,c) determined that there would be a secondary burden, while his major opponent in the debate, Ohlin (1929, 1935), argued this was not necessarily the case.[5] For a given level of output, Keynes argued, the primary burden for the transferring country was to mobilize and transfer savings at the expense of domestic investment. The transfer would affect aggregate demand in the transferring and recipient country and thus each country's demand for imports (at unchanged prices). The transfer problem in this context is whether the import demand effects resulting from the transfer will be sufficient to create the trade surplus in the transferring country needed to effect the transfer. Keynes expected the transfer always to be *undereffected* as the recipient country is likely to save part of the transfer, so that net exports of the transferring country would increase by less than the transfer itself. Using the Keynesian income multiplier model it has been shown in subsequent analysis that this is always the case if marginal savings rates are larger than zero (Metzler 1942, Machlup 1943, Dornbusch 1980 and Appendix A3.1). Thus, to effect the transfer (i.e. the required export surplus), the terms of trade would have to turn against the transferring country.

Ohlin argued, however, that this result hinges on the propensities to consume and to import in both countries and thus that the terms of trade could move in either direction. The direction of the terms of trade adjustment depends, in his view, on whether the recipient country's marginal propensity to consume the exports of the transferring country (m_S) differs from the donor's marginal propensity to consume its own commodity ($1-m_N$).

Krugman & Baldwin (1987)[6] give a recent statement of the problem. Assume a simple two-country world economy (countries S and N). The world excess demand equation is given as:

$$(\theta D_S - \theta Y_S) + (D_N - Y_N) = 0 \tag{3.2}$$

where D and Y stand for total expenditures and income, respectively, in countries S and N, and θ is the relative price or terms of trade of country S. Each country is assumed to be fully specialized in the production of a single good. Import demand in S and N is specified as fractions of domestic absorption in each country, m_S and m_N, so that:

$$Y_N = (1 - m_N) D_N + \theta m_S D_S \qquad 0 \leq m_N < 1 \quad 0 \leq m_S < 1 \tag{3.3}$$

and since the trade surplus of country N equals $T_S = Y_N - D_N$ (or, the transfer to S), the equations can be combined to:

$$T_S = \frac{1 - m_N + \theta m_S Y_S}{1 - m_N - m_S} \qquad \text{if } m_S + m_N \neq 1 \tag{3.4}$$

and

$$\theta = \frac{m_N Y_N}{[(1 - m_N) Y_S - (1 - m_N - m_S) D_S]} \tag{3.5}$$

Given Y_S, an increase in the transfer to the South ($T_S = D_S - Y_S$) requires an increase in domestic spending in the recipient country, D_S. Thus, the terms of trade, θ, will improve for the recipient country S and deteriorate for the transferring country, N, if $1 - m_N - m_S > 0$. Thus, in this case the secundary burden falls on the transferring country N. This burden falls on the recipient country if $1 - m_N - m_S < 0$. This is exactly Ohlin's criterion for the presence or absence of a secondary burden for the transferring country.

As other reviews of this literature have concluded (Eaton 1989; Reisen & von Trotsenburg 1988), most of the subsequent debate resolved things in favour of Ohlin. Johnson (1958: 70-77), generalizing the income multiplier model, showed that the transfer need not necessarily be undereffected (as Keynes suggested), once the assumption that the spending (savings) and import demand functions in both countries remain unchanged in face of a transfer is relaxed. If import demand and savings respond directly to the transfer, the transfer may be either under- or over-effected depending on the size of the savings and import propensities in both countries (see also Appendix A3.1).

Two other critical issues have emerged from this literature. Firstly, as initially stressed by Keynes, does a *stable* adjustment path require price flexibility (or else, demand inflation or deflation)? In other words, will a small change in the terms of trade affect the trade balances in the right direction, such as to restore external equilibrium after a transfer? Secondly, the possibility of *negative* welfare effects for the *recipient* country has been raised.

The economic meaning of the question of stability has received remarkably little attention, less than it probably deserves (see also Chapters 6–8). Johnson (1958, reprinted 1971: 63-64) more categorically begs the question by suggesting that the stability problem is 'an empirical one on which theory can render little assistance'.

More discussion has been devoted to the second issue, i.e. the so-called 'transfer paradox', discussed in the context of neo-classical trade theory. Leontief (1936) suggested that there might be a case in which transfers make the recipient country worse off, as the primary income raising effect of the transfer might be outweighed by a secondary effect of a deteriorating terms of trade for the recipient country. Samuelson (1947) argued that such a result in a context of two countries, two commodities and free trade is not consistent with a stable Walrasian general-equilibrium solution and defended subsequently (Samuelson 1952 and 1954) the 'orthodox' case of worsening terms of trade for the donor country in case of transport costs and the 'unorthodox' case (Ohlin) when tariffs form impediments to trade. The defence for 'orthodoxy' in the case of transport costs results from the presumption that transport costs will likely produce a tendency for economies to have a higher marginal propensity to consume their own commodity, and hence $1 - m_N - m_S > 0$, if both countries export different commodities, and the 'orthodox' case of a secondary burden for the transferring country would hold.

In more recent discussions the transfer paradox, also labelled 'immiserizing transfers', has received renewed attention. Lysy (1985) reworks a North-South model initially elaborated by Chichilnisky (1980).[7] Lysy assumes a world with two regions, North and South, each producing two commodities, basic goods and investment goods. The North exports the capital-intensive investment good and the South the labour-intensive basic good. A possible outcome in this framework is that, if the supply elasticity of the investment good is not too high, a shift towards more Northern exports (which is the same as a higher trade surplus, i.e. a transfer to the South), yields a worsening of the distribution between profits and wages in North and South, a deterioration of the Southern terms of trade, and higher Southern export volumes, but lower earnings due to a strong decline in the terms of trade. The deteriorating terms of trade in this case are mainly due to the shift in income distribution which leads to a reduction in demand in the South for its own export commodity, which is larger than the fall in supply. In the adjustment towards a new equilibrium this has the perverse effect of eventually a higher volume of exports of the Southern commodity at a lower relative price. The outcomes of Lysy's version of the Chichilnisky model critically depend on the closure rule, which in this case is the assumption of a rigid supply of investment goods. Lysy acknowledges this may be just a 'special case', but argues this basic assumption would be broadly consistent with 'structuralist' views of the world saying that the South cannot produce itself all the investment goods it needs.

Bhagwati, Brecher & Hatta (1983, 1984) attempt to provide a general framework, but in doing so add the existence of a third country. Donor enrichment may arise if third countries, not directly involved in the transfer process, are net importers or exporters of the commodity exported by the donor and/or have a lower or higher marginal propensity to import the commodity exported by the donor than the country receiving the transfer. Bhagwati, Brecher & Hatta establish the necessary conditions for a transfer paradox to arise. Bridging much of the previous literature, they show that transfers can enrich donors and impoverish recipients in a generalizable three-country, two-commodity case and that this transfer paradox depends critically on the presence of a distortion.[8] Generalizable necessary conditions for donor enrichment following a transfer are that commodity *A* (produced and consumed in all countries) is an inferior good to the country receiving the transfer (i.e. import demand for this commodity falls with a higher welfare level) and/or when the country not involved in the transfer process has an inelastic offer curve (i.e. a higher relative price for commodity *A* reduces the export supply of it by the uninvolved country). A similar condition underlies the possible loss in welfare following a transfer for the recipient country. Bhagwati et al. contend that the perverse welfare effect of a transfer can be avoided if the donor and the recipient country impose an optimal, common tariff against the third country (i.e. the rest of the world).[9]

An important point highlighted by this literature is that international transfers, e.g. in the form of commodity aid but probably also other forms of capital flows (see also next sections), can have important secondary effects affecting the terms of trade between the transferring and receiving countries, as well as the welfare of countries not directly involved in the transfer process. The issue returns, though under different conditions, in subsequent chapters.

3.3.2 Pure trade models and capital mobility

The pure theory of capital movements extends readily to the Heckscher-Ohlin-Samuelson (HOS) framework. Ruffin (1984) points out in his review of static neo-classical theory of (endogenous) capital movements that in the HOS framework factor-price equalization means that trade and factor movements are perfect substitutes: abundant production factors (e.g. capital) are exported indirectly through the goods they produce, whereas scarce factors can be imported indirectly in the form of imported goods that have been produced by making use of those scarce factors. This holds as long as technologies do not differ and both countries have the same constant-returns-to-scale technology.

If trade patterns are more Ricardian, that is reflecting technology differences rather than factor endowments, capital mobility may complement trade rather than substitute for it. As shown through the so-called Kemp-Jones model (Jones 1967, Kemp 1966, Ruffin 1984), trade may increase with capital flows because the technologically more advanced country will tend to have a comparative advantage in the capital intensive good, since with perfect capital mobility rents (marginal productivity of capital) in the more advanced and the less advanced country will be equalized, while the more advanced country will have a higher wage-rent ratio. Following Ruffin (1984: 273-4) this can be made intuitively clear, after adding a few assumptions. Consider a two-commodity, two-factor, two-country world with country *N* technologically more advanced in both industries than country *S*. With equal factor endowments and no capital movements, *N* will have higher wages and rents. Being fully mobile capital will flow to *N* since $r_N > r_S$. Now trade will expand with capital mobility under conditions of the Rybcyznski theorem (Rybcyznski 1955); that is, if *N*'s export sector is capital-intensive relative to the import-competing sector, and otherwise trade would be discouraged by the capital movement.

In these static 'pure trade' models, capital movements are interpreted as increases (decreases) in the capital stock of the capital-importing (exporting) country. This will affect supply conditions in both countries, but the distribution of welfare gains among capital-importing and -exporting countries depends on how trade and capital mobility interact. 'Immiserizing growth' may also result in this context of neo-classical trade models with capital mobility. Bhagwati (1958) demonstrates this in a general setting of the standard 2 × 2 × 2 neo-classical trade model with *exogenous* capital movements. Welfare in the capital-importing country may fall if the foreign investment inflow (i.e. capital stock increase) yields a sufficiently strong output expansion causing a fall in the terms of trade exceeding the positive income effect of output expansion at constant relative prices. Necessary conditions for this result are either that the foreign demand for exportables of the capital-importing country is inelastic to the relative price change, or that the country's export sector is capital-intensive, i.e. the growth in the capital stock will stimulate trade, while growth is biased against the production of the importable (see Bhagwati 1958; and also Findlay 1984: 198-99). A parallel can be drawn with the transfer paradox discussed in the previous section: optimal trade intervention would eliminate the 'foreign distortion' and immiserizing growth effects would no longer occur (see also Bhagwati et al. 1983: 611).

Brecher & Diaz-Alejandro (1977), among others, have analysed 'immiserizing' growth effects in a two factor, two commodity context with a 'production distortion' present in the capital-importing country, specifically the case in which foreign capital is attracted by a tariff (following an earlier argument by Johnson 1967), and in the case of foreign ownership of the growth of the capital stock. In the case of a tariff, Johnson showed that welfare may deteriorate in the capital-importing country if factor endowments change due to the capital movement such that the inefficient, protected production sector expands at the expense of the competitive (efficient) export sector. Any other distortion with a similar effect can lead to immiserization, i.e. lower welfare than in the case without capital mobility. Brecher & Diaz-Alejandro (1977) add that if the additional capital is foreign owned and foreign capitalists appropriate the rents from output expansion, welfare *must* go down (in Johnson's analysis this was a possibility, not a necessary result).[10]

These models could be applicable to capital movements which take the form of direct foreign investment, assuming these respond to yield differentials and involve a change in location of capital stocks. Indirect forms of finance (e.g. public and private forms of international lending as discussed in section 3.2) are not explicitly considered in this context. (Of course, if capital markets were perfect, financial investments would eventually end up in investment in productive assets and rates of return are equalized across countries and alternative types of assets.) The possible welfare losses as a consequence of a fall in the terms of trade which exceeds the gain in domestic factor productivity, also underlie traditional structuralist views on North-South trade and the negative consequences of foreign investment in countries exporting primary exports, as analysed by Prebisch (1959) and Singer (1950) and through the North-South models discussed below.

3.3.3 North-South models and capital mobility

Another tradition of international trade models is that of so-called North-South models. The key notion of these models is that North and South have fundamentally different economies. Usually complete specialization prevails with the industrialized North producing and exporting a manufactured commodity and the less developed South specializes in a primary product. Existing models include income distribution and accumulation behaviour and specify explicit savings functions for both regions and a function determining investment demand in the North only. It is assumed that the South cannot determine its own investment and growth rates as these are determined endogenously by the rest of the system. This relates to familiar, structuralist views on how the world economy works (e.g. Prebisch 1959). Key questions addressed by these models are the effect of a change in the terms of trade on growth in both regions and how a change in autonomous investment demand would affect the terms of trade and Southern growth. The model results depend crucially on the assumptions made with respect to the operation of commodity markets and about macroclosure in the North and South.

To start with the macroeconomic closure rules, the endogenous character of growth and investment in the South has already been mentioned. The best-known theoretical models (Findlay 1980, 1984; Taylor 1981; Vines 1984; see also the survey in Ocampo 1986) assume that the typical Southern economy has 'Lewis-type' labour-surplus characteristics (Lewis 1954): (i) the region's real wage is fixed and its output is determined by available capital; (ii) the capital stock must be imported from the North under modern techniques of production so that growth in the South does not automatically reduce the labour surplus; and (iii) the economy is price-taker for its exports, as world primary commodity markets are assumed to be cleared by a flexible price.[11] While these dual world-economy models agree about the functioning of the Southern economy, they differ with respect to the assumptions about macroclosure in the North. The industrial economies may expand at their natural rate of growth assuming neo-classical, steady-state conditions (as in Findlay 1980, 1984), with excess capacity, mark-up pricing and an accelerator-type investment along Kaleckian lines (as in Taylor 1981), or have savings-constrained Northern investment and a fixed real wage (due to surplus labour in the North) along Kaldorian lines (as in Vines 1984 and Molana & Vines 1988).

In the trade versions of these models (without capital mobility), adjustment centres around the terms of trade. In the Findlay model (see Findlay 1980, 1984 and Appendix A3.2), Northern growth is determined by the natural rate, whereas growth in the South directly depends on its terms of trade in the short run. The terms of trade increase with the relative scarcity of the Southern good and this will lead to an increase in the Southern growth rate. Alternatively, excess supply of the Southern good will deteriorate the Southern terms of trade and Southern growth will decrease. Southern growth thus depends on commodity markets in the short run. In the steady state long run, if income elasticities for both commodities are unitary, growth rates in North and South must be equal, that is the rate of growth of the South will equal the North's natural rate. The terms of trade play a key role in ensuring the growth rate of the South conforms to the exogenously set long run Northern growth rate. In the words of Findlay (1984: 225): 'Trade is the "engine of growth" for the South, but the pace of the engine is set by the growth rate of the North.' The long-term terms of trade are derived as a function of the natural growth rate in the North, the Southern savings rate and Southern productivity (see Appendix A3.2). In the long run, employment in the South is governed by its capacity to import capital goods from the North. Its import capacity, in turn, is determined by the long term terms of trade and the equilibrium per worker capital stock in the North. The South will benefit from Northern technological change (e.g. higher productivity) in the form of higher employment. On the other hand, an autonomous increase in the Southern savings rate or productivity level will lead to an increase in the Southern growth rate (allowing for higher investment), but higher Southern output will lead to a deterioration of its terms of trade (excess supply of the Southern good and excess demand for the Northern good) both in the short and long run. Improved resource mobilization or more efficient production in the South would thus imply that the South would permanently 'export' higher savings to the North with the decline in the terms of trade. The movement in the terms of trade offsets (at least in part) the positive effect of higher savings and productivity on Southern growth and employment. The net effect on Southern growth and employment is not certain and depends on the responses of import demand in both regions to relative price and income changes.

In the Taylor model (Taylor 1981) the South has more opportunities to expand, since Northern output is not on a 'natural, steady-state' growth path, but is characterized by excess capacity. Exogenous factors causing the Southern terms of trade to fall are mitigated by higher Northern real income growth. If income elasticities of the demand for both goods are unitary, then the long-run, steady-state equilibrium of the world economy is given by the same key relationships as in the Findlay model. However, Northern dynamics are completely different. Contrary to the Solow-Lewis model, in the Kalecki-Lewis model the South does not benefit from exogenous productivity increases in the North. As the price of the Northern commodity is fixed, due to the mark-up pricing rule, the productivity increase will not be reflected in an improvement in the terms of trade for the South, but rather lead to a rise in the Northern real wage and a fall in Northern employment. If, however, the autonomous technological change activates the 'animal spirits' of Northern capitalists, the investment demand function will be pushed outward, Northern growth will increase and the South will benefit from better terms of trade, a higher import capacity and so a higher growth rate. Whether the South benefits evenly from the Northern expansion depends, as in the Findlay model, on the import demand functions. Taylor incorporates the traditional structuralist assumption that Northern demand for the Southern commodity is relatively inelastic (Prebisch 1959, Singer 1950). The consequence is a net outcome in which the South cannot fully benefit from the expansion of the world economy and the regions will develop unevenly.

Capital movements between the two regions can be introduced into these kind of models, although relatively little work has been done in this field. Several authors have introduced factor mobility assuming a perfect capital market (see e.g. Burgstaller & Saavedra-Rivano 1984, Quibria 1986 and Dutt 1988). Outcomes are that capital movements are 'immiserizing' for the South (Burgstaller & Saavedra-Rivano 1984 and Quibria 1986) or at least generate uneven development paths widening the income gap between North and South (Dutt 1988). Burgstaller & Saavedra-Rivano (1984) extend the Findlay model with foreign-owned capital moving to the South and rising primary commodity production (see also Findlay 1984 and Appendix A3.2). The result appears as a special case of the Brecher-Diaz Alejandro (1977) finding discussed earlier, with Northern capital 'crowding out' Southern capital. Northern ownership of part of Southern capital stock leads to a transfer of income back to the North, increasing Northern income. Southern output growth is now not only offset by the profit remittance, but also by falling terms of trade as Northern spending and import propensities from foreign-earned profits do not fully compensate for the tendency towards excess supply of primary commodities.

The assumption that the North is on a neo-classical growth path seems critical. Once this assumption is replaced by a production function characterizing Northern excess capacity, as in the Taylor model, the economies may stimulate each other, as higher Northern income from foreign investment may stimulate Northern activity. Taylor (1985) shows this in a case where capital flows from North to South take the form of bank debt, which is, however, as in the previous cases, attracted by a higher profit rate in the South (and a vague, exogenous confidence parameter). A higher rate of profit in the South, for instance resulting from an exogenous productivity increase, would encourage lending to the South. Enhanced capital flows from North to South should be matched by a larger Northern trade surplus, which will be stimulated by increased import demand in the South. Monetary expansion in the North may also increase total loan supply, including lending to the South, and reduce the world interest rate. Increased access to loans will stimulate Southern growth and import demand, while falling interest rates will stimulate Northern investment demand and Southern growth will stimulate demand for Northern exports. The North and South may thus engage in a mutually reinforcing growth process initiated by a capital transfer injection. This could provide support for the global Keynesianism underlying certain international policy analyses such as the report of the Brandt Commission (Brandt 1980).

However, also in this extension of the Taylor model (Taylor 1985) the result crucially depends, on the one hand, on the respective savings and import propensities in both regions determining the effect on the terms of trade and, on the other hand, on the fiscal and monetary policy mix in the North and the specific features of asset markets (whether interest rates are flexible or sticky), factors determining the cost of borrowing and availability of credit. As before, a low income elasticity of demand for the Southern commodity will cause the South to lag behind Northern growth. Also, monetary expansion will produce inflationary pressures. If this leads to a fall in investor confidence (this effect is to be imposed exogenously in this extended Taylor model), there will be an unfavourable effect on Northern growth that will affect the Southern growth rate and terms of trade. If interest rates fall rapidly following the monetary expansion, Northern investment demand and worldwide growth may recover; if they are sticky and adjust slowly, both North and South may for some time find the pace of economic expansion is slowed, again with the South lagging behind.

However, as will be shown in Chapter 7, other outcomes are possible using alternative behavioural rules for international capital movements, differentiating between international bank lending under credit rationing rules, aid flows from North to South and private capital outflows from South to North.

Despite the highly simplifying assumptions, the models discussed here provide useful insights into possible structural conditions that determine asymmetries in the global adjustment process. A central role is given to the terms of trade. World prices are determined by growth equilibrium conditions, rather than by supply and demand. In the Solow-Lewis model, the South may benefit from Northern technological progress in the form of higher employment. In the Kalecki-Lewis model the industrial pricing rule governed by a mark-up over unitary production costs converts Northern productivity changes into higher Northern real wages and unemployment, but the South cannot benefit directly. In both types of models the South is in a seemingly weak position to determine its own growth rate. Higher savings or productivity increases in the South are a mixed blessing, as they have a negative effect on the Southern terms of trade. Also in both models, a difference in income elasticities of demand appears critical to determining whether there is uneven devlopment between the two regions. The inclusion of endogenous capital flows is still quite rudimentary in this type of model, but the analysis suggest these may also be a mixed blessing, given the structural asymmetries between North and South. Chapter 7 builds on this type of models, but allows for a more elaborate specification of financial interactions between North and South.

3.3.4 Global macroeconomics: the Meade-Mundell-Fleming model

The literature discussed in the previous sections is embedded in the tradition of international trade theory. A not entirely dissociated branch of literature provides a macroeconomic perspective. For the last quarter century, the Mundell-Fleming model has been a standard analytical framework to study macroeconomic relations in closed and open economies, as well as global macroeconomic interactions. The foundations of the model were laid by the classic writings of Robert Mundell (1960, 1963, 1968) and J. Marcus Fleming (1962), extending the pioneering work of James Meade on the Keynesian internal-external-balance-adjustment analysis (Meade 1951) and incorporating the modern version of Hume's price-specie flow balance-of-payments adjustment mechanism (Hume 1752|1971), the monetary approach to the balance of payments (Polak 1957, Frenkel & Johnson 1976, IMF 1977). The Mundell-

Fleming model has provided a framework for the systematic analysis of the effectiveness of macroeconomic policies under international capital mobility and alternative exchange rate regimes. It has received the widest application in the specification of small, open economies. In recent years its application in a two-country specification, prominent in the early writings (Meade 1951; Fleming 1962; Johnson 1958; Mundell 1968), has received renewed attention in the face of the policy debates of the 1980s on the international repercussions of US macropolicies and the policy-coordination debate (see e.g. Frenkel & Razin 1987 and Hickman 1988, but also recent issues of IMF *World Economic Outlook* implicitly seem to apply the framework).

The basic characteristics of the model for an interdependent world economy with two countries can be explained in a simplified three-equation system.[12] As before, the two economies are North and South, but in theory they could represent any economy as the standard approach is to model the interactions between two identical economies that function by the same behavioural rules.

$$Y_N = D_N(Y_N, r) + M_S(Y_S, \theta) - M_N(Y_N, \theta^{-1}) \tag{3.6}$$

$$Y_S = D_S(Y_S, r) - M_S(Y_S, \theta) + M_N(Y_N, \theta^{-1}) \tag{3.7}$$

$$B_N + B_S + H = L_N(Y_N, r) + L_S(Y_S, r) \tag{3.8}$$

Domestic demand (D_i) aggregates private consumption, investment and public expenditures and depends positively on income and negatively on the real rate of interest (r). Import demand (M_i), and implicitly exports, depend on income and the terms of trade ($\theta \equiv P_S / P_N$). If capital mobility is perfect, interest rates tend to equalize across countries. The world interest rate depends on the balance of world supply of and demand for money specified in equation 3.8, where B_i is the supply of domestic credit in each economy (exogenous or determined outside the model) and L_i represents the demand for credits. H is the world stock of reserves, which for reasons of convenience is treated here as an outside asset (SDRs or gold). The perfect capital market assumption also includes perfect substitutability between domestic and foreign assets.

The model solution now depends on the exchange rate regime. With fixed exchange rates and prices, the money supply is endogenous, while under a flexible exchange rate regime the money supply will be exogenous. In each case different slopes for the *IS*- and *LM*-schedules will result, as implied by equations 3.6 to 3.8. Figure 3.4 shows downward sloping *IS*- and upward sloping *LM*-schedules for the Northern and

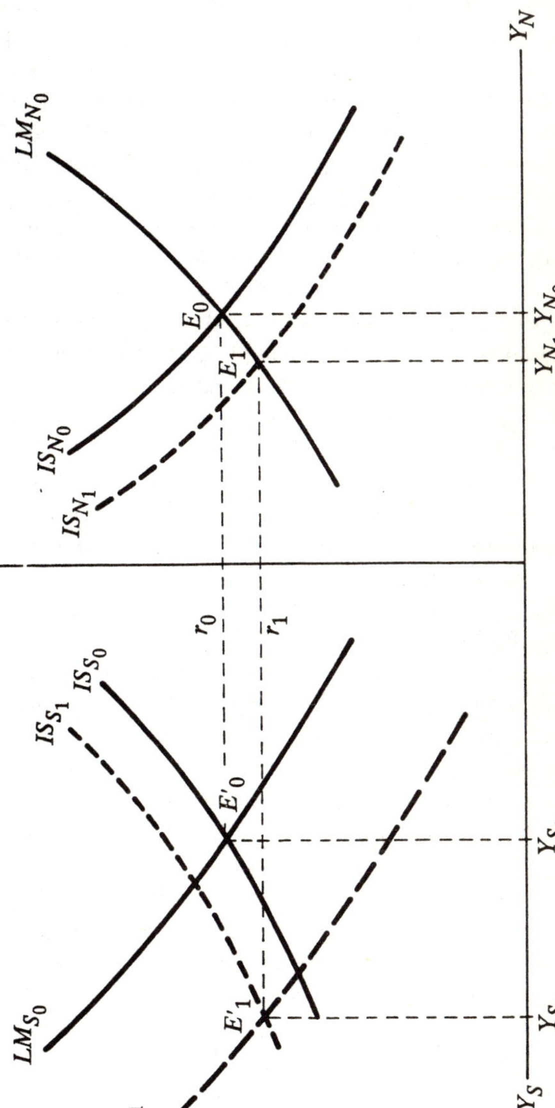

Figure 3.4 Two country IS-LM model: adjustment to a tax-financed transfer

Southern economies under a *fixed* exchange-rate regime (see Appendix A3.3 for the derivation of the respective slopes).

Equilibrium is at point E_0 in Figure 3.4, where the goods and money markets clear for the world economy. A tax-financed autonomous transfer from North to South will reduce disposable income and spending in the North, which is depicted in Figure 3.4 by a shift of the IS_N-schedule to the left. If the credit supply in the North is left untouched, this will create a tendency towards a decline in the world interest rate (to r_1). In the South disposable income increases and puts pressure on the IS_S-schedule to shift to the left. Southern spending is further stimulated by the decline in the interest rate. If the transfer is spent fully on domestic goods in the South (say, non-tradables), a new equilibrium at E_1 will only be established if the Southern central bank allows the Southern money supply to expand sufficiently (to LM_{S1}) so as to equalize interest rates in the two regions. Else, the exchange rate would have to be adjusted to achieve equilibrium. At E_1,Northern output will have fallen, that of the South will have expanded.

The outcome on regional output and *ex post* trade balances will be mitigated if part of the transfer is spent on Northern goods, as Northern income loss is dampened by increased foreign demand. The net outcome depends on the marginal spending and import propensities, the goods demand elasticity with respect to the interest rate and the credit (money) demand elasticities with respect to the interest rate (cf. the multipliers derived in Appendix A3.3). Similarly, one could imagine bond-financed fiscal expansion in the North, which would shift the IS_N-schedule to the right, and with restrictive Northern monetary policies this would push up the interest rate and attract foreign savings (LM_S shifts to the right). Output expansion in the North – assuming the expansionary effect is not offset by lower domestic private sector demand in response to the higher interest rate – would thus be financed by contraction in the rest of the world. Mitigating effects may result from increased demand for foreign goods in the North.

What net outcomes of the international transmission mechanisms are to be expected from a net transfer in the international *IS-LM* model? The short answer is that it depends. In the static Mundell-Fleming model, outcomes depend directly on the spending propensities and elasticities in each economy. The contribution of the model lies in supplying a framework to analyse the interactions, not in supplying unique answers.

The model has been successfully extended to include private and public sector demand (see Frenkel & Razin 1987), imperfect substitution between domestic and foreign assets (Kouri & Porter 1974, Dornbusch 1980) and expectations and exchange rate dynamics (Dornbusch 1976). In the case of imperfect asset substitution, portfolio adjustment analysis is introduced in the essentially 'flow'-specifications of the Mundell-Fleming model. If investors do not consider domestic and foreign assets to be perfect substitutes, determining the 'offset coefficient' of portfolio adjustment becomes a central question. Under perfect substitution a credit expansion in country *N* will lead to a proportional loss in foreign reserves, as the domestic interest rate in *N* will go down, inducing capital exports to *S*. The offset coefficient H_N/B_N will thus be -1. With imperfect substitution the coefficient will tend to fall short of unity, implying that it will take a relatively large change in the interest rate for investors to shift their asset demand to foreign assets. In terms of the Mundell-Fleming model, imperfect asset substitution implies that with capital mobility there is also scope for monetary policy, since interest rate changes and changes in the credit supply are not fully compensated by offsetting capital flows or exchange rate adjustments.

Other limitations of the basic Mundell-Fleming model have been dealt with in modern versions. These include a role for the intertemporal budget constraints of private and public sectors and relative price adjustment (see Frenkel & Razin 1987 for an evaluation). Discussions around the so-called 'debt-neutrality' or Ricardo-Barro Equivalence Theorem, stimulated by Barro's 1974 paper, have led to the inclusion of intertemporal decision-making within this framework with some important international repercussions. The Ricardo-Barro hypothesis asserts that if private sector agents (individuals and firms) expect bond-financing of current fiscal deficits to lead to increased future taxation and if they can properly discount the level of future taxation, then the way in which fiscal deficits are financed will be neutral with regard to its effect on private savings. Further, it would follow that private intergenerational transfers compensate for government-induced intergenerational transfers and so leave the welfare of current and future generations unaffected by increased government deficits, i.e. a rise in the fiscal deficit would be exactly offset by a higher flow of private savings. Under this hypothesis fiscal deficits will have no international repercussions. Most of the subsequent studies, albeit staying within the intertemporal *IS-LM* framework (see e.g. Buiter & Tobin 1979, Masson & Knight 1986, Buiter 1989) have challenged Barro's proposition and argued that private agents may not be able to fully discount future taxation for various reasons, including uncertainties and capital market imperfections. Debt *non*-neutrality implies that fiscal policies will tend to have international repercussions affecting trade and the global capital market. Similar to the type of mechanics of the basic static *IS-LM* model, bond-financed fiscal expansion under debt non-neutrality in the intertemporal framework tends to push up the world interest rate, lead to a deterioration of the Northern current account balance and attract foreign savings.

The *IS-LM* framework nevertheless provides a basic framework to think through the basic global *macroeconomic* interactions and clearly sets out the global budget constraints. From the North-South perspective, the basic *IS-LM* model would require modification in order to allow for, firstly, differences in the behavioural structure of both types of economies (the North-South models discussed in the previous section provide special cases for such global modelling); and secondly, behavioural rules for heterogeneous capital market access and credit rationing mechanisms, as discussed in section 3.2. After the historical and descriptive empirical analyses of Chapters 4 and 5, these two challenges are taken up in Chapters 6–8.

3.4 Foreign Capital and Growth and Adjustment in the South

The review of theories supplying microeconomic determinants of international capital flows suggests that Southern borrowers may be rationed by commercial and official creditors. Alternative theoretical assumptions, including a freely accessible world capital market, suggest that international capital flows may have negative welfare effects. Such assumptions have a bearing on a number of standard notions of the impact of foreign capital on growth in developing countries.

The approach, based on the 'optimal borrowing' literature referred to earlier in this chapter, in its simplest and crudest form links the debt dynamics of borrowing countries to the rate of growth of their economy. Domar (1950) extends the Harrod-Domar model to analyse the link between debt, solvency and development and this type of debt-dynamics analysis has been popularized by Avramovic, et al. (1964) and more recently by Simonsen (1985) and Dornbusch & Fischer (1987). The borrowing rule derived from these models is that the planned growth rate (or export growth) should exceed the interest rate on debt for the borrower to maintain solvency. A severe limitation of this approach is that it precludes the possibility of rationing in the foreign credit market and default on debt payment obligations by borrowers (see above). Other limiting standard assumptions are that all foreign capital is invested and that the savings and capital-output ratios are treated as constants. In a global context, national savings – for instance – may be affected if capital flows have an effect on the terms of trade or on remittance of profit income (cf. above).

The two-gap model has been another influential approach to analysing the role of foreign capital in development (see Chenery & Bruno 1962 for a first presentation). The Harrod-Domar growth model is again a cornerstone. Growth can be limited by either the savings ratio or the availability of foreign exchange. The latter may be the case if investment is strongly dependent on imported capital goods (or intermediates). If the foreign exchange constraint is binding, foreign capital inflows will raise both the growth rate and the domestic savings rate. The model has been intensively used to assess the growth effects of exogenously given availability of foreign capital and to calculate aid and foreign borrowing requirements for a target growth rate.[13] The model has been criticized from various perspectives. Empirical and institutional analyses have challenged the assumption that foreign and national savings are complementary. Griffin (1970, 1987) and Weisskopf (1972) suggest that foreign capital, and in particular aid, is essentially a substitute for national savings. Such a substitution effect can arise for various reasons and may, among other things, be related to the nature of the capital inflow. Aid, for instance, may be directly used (and meant) for consumption purposes (e.g. food aid) or lead to higher current government spending (e.g. local costs to run new investment projects). An alternative hypothesis underlying the possibility of a negative relationship between foreign capital inflows and national savings could be based on the international transmission mechanisms discussed above, namely capital transfers leading to deteriorating terms of trade and/or profit remittances exceeding income growth. This matter will return in the subsequent chapters.

From the neo-classical side the two-gap approach has been criticized, for, among other things, omitting relative price effects and for the model's pessimism regarding the possibility of overcoming the foreign-exchange constraint via a more elastic supply response in tradables (see e.g. Findlay 1973, 1984). Prices (the real exchange rate or terms of trade) and price responsiveness can of course be built in without too much complication. Cardoso (1987), one example of how this can be done, shows that foreign capital will foster growth and domestic savings in the presence of price rigidities or low price elasticities.

Van Wijnbergen (1984a, 1984b, 1986a, 1986b) and Edwards & van Wijnbergen (1989) reinterpret the two-gap approach, merging it with a disequilibrium ('fixed-price') version of the dependent-economy model to assess spending and resource reallocation effects of aid transfers.[14] The savings gap reflects excess domestic demand over income and the trade (or current account) gap reflects excess demand for traded goods. An *ex ante* disequilibrium between the two gaps will thus reflect a disequilibrium in the non-traded goods market. Adapting the accounting relations from Chapter 2, the essence of the problem may be stated as follows. Using subscripts T and NT for traded and non-traded goods sectors respectively, one may write (cf. equation 2.6):

ex ante savings gap

$$\begin{aligned} &= \theta\,(I_S - S_S)_p + \theta\, DEF_S \\ &= \theta\,(D_S - Y_S) \\ &= \theta_T\,(D_S - Y_S)_T + \theta_{NT}\,(D_S - Y_S)_{NT} \end{aligned} \qquad (3.9)$$

and

ex ante current account deficit

$$\begin{aligned} &= M_S - \theta_T E_S + R_S \\ &= \theta\,(D_S - Y_S) - \theta_{NT}\,(D_S - Y_S)_{NT} \end{aligned} \qquad (3.10)$$

In (3.9), the savings gap reflects excess spending over income, the sum of excess demands for traded (T) and non-traded (NT) goods. In (3.10), the external balance reflects excess demand for T-goods, and thus, from (3.9), an excess demand of total spending over income or an excess supply of NT-goods. If the NT-goods market clears, the external gap reflects excess spending over income equal to the savings gap. The relative price between non-traded and traded goods sectors is given by: $\theta_{NT}/\theta_T \equiv (P_{SNT}/P_N)/(P_{ST}/P_N) \equiv P_{SNT}/P_{ST}$ which is usually defined in dependent-economy models as the real exchange rate.[15] The economy is assumed to be small, so the foreign exchange price of traded goods is given. Assume the economy is initially in equilibrium. A disequilibrium situation may result from an aid transfer in a situation of a price rigidity (e.g. indexed wages). Increased aid (reflected in higher Y_S) leading to a higher demand for non-traded goods, may yield a real exchange rate appreciation (higher θ_{NT}/θ_T) and Keynesian unemployment (following Malinvaud's terminology) if wages are indexed and if the share of non-traded products in the wage-goods basket is large enough.[16] This type of disequilibrium during the adjustment period following an aid transfer may also apply, for instance, to the 'Dutch disease' effects following an oil boom in countries with most wage goods produced in import-substituting (effectively non-traded) sectors, like Mexico and Ecuador in the 1970s (see van Wijnbergen 1984b on the various cases). Extending the analysis into an intertemporal framework, van Wijnbergen (1986a) also suggests that an aid increase (even if temporary) may lead to permanently lower export growth. The higher real exchange rate (lower real traded goods price) means foreign exchange is relatively cheap at first, but is likely to become more expensive. If capital markets are imperfect (as is likely in developing countries) higher future costs of foreign exchange are not fully discounted by producers in export sectors and sub-optimal investment in traded goods sectors reduces future productivity. This trade-off between aid and export performance would call for active export promotion policies accompanying aid programmes.

How such sectoral resource reallocation affects the internal or savings gap(s) (cf. equation 3.9) is not immediately clear from the models discussed above. It would seem this would require a further elaboration of the distributional impact. For instance, it could be hypothesized that the (aid) transfer leads to a widening of the fiscal deficit (DEF_S). If the aid transfer is temporary, but the budget increase is structural, adjustment will fall on the private savings balance ($I_{Sp} - S_{Sp}$). However, if export earnings tend to fall with aid inflows, this may also create a downward effect on private savings, assuming that high-saving profit earners are hurt most and that most private sector savings are generated in traded goods sectors. Under these conditions, the internal disequilibrium widens and eventually requires either fiscal adjustment or a cutback of private investment and growth. Internal adjustment may be even more complex, if past and current transfers are debt creating and interest bearing. In a case where most external borrowing is by the government, the fiscal deficit will be partially endogenous to the cost of borrowing and the accumulated debt burden (R_S). This cannot be financed perpetually from further external borrowing and debt repayment will require siphoning off of tradable income, which may further affect both profitability in the export sector and investment confidence. The adjustment problem could be exacerbated, in such a pessimistic scenario, by private capital outflows ('capital flight').

Though subsidiary to this book, such hypotheses – based on the linkage of the two-gap approach with disequilibrium dependent-economy analysis and applied to different conditions of access to external finance – will be used to assess adjustment options open to the South discussed empirically in Chapters 4 and 5.

3.5 Concluding Remarks

Despite the length of this theoretical review, the main points to be retained for the analysis in the subsequent chapters can be summarized rather briefly.

Firstly, capital movements between North and South are heterogeneous in nature. This is recognized by specialized, and as such useful, microeconomic theories elaborated to address the specific features of each type of flow, or market segment. Theoretical approaches relating to direct investment (theory of international firm), international bank lending (credit rationing and theory of bank firm), official flows (political-economy models of aid) and two-way capital flows ('capital flight' theory), have been developed at some distance from traditional micro (pure trade theory) and macro (global *IS-LM*) approaches to global adjustment processes. The challenge to combine these approaches into an integrated North-South framework is taken up in the rest of this book.

Secondly, differentiation by type of capital movement also involves, for reasons of market imperfections, inclusion of aspects of uncertainty and particular institutional settings and recognition of the likelihood of asymmetric behaviour of lenders and borrowers and of donors and recipients in the process of adjustment. For these reasons, market outcomes of the processes of international financial intermediation may be unstable and welfare effects may be distributed unevenly. Existing theory gives partial answers and possible directions. The likely direction of adjustment will have to be based, however, on the specific, historically determined institutional context of lending and borrowing behaviour.

4 Trade, Finance and Institutions: Lessons from the Past

4.1 Introduction

This chapter traces the nature and determinants of capital movements, debt crises and global adjustment processes from 1865 to 1970. The analysis centres around the international lending institutions and the interactions between the investment-savings balances and trade patterns of capital-exporting and capital-importing countries. More specifically, this chapter will stress four facets of capital market performance and global adjustment.

Firstly, the nature and pattern of the process of international finance have varied over time. In the period preceding the World War I, capital moved principally between private sectors in creditor and debtor nations and was invested in export sectors. In the 1920s much more public sector borrowing took place, which was more often than not used for consumption or invested in non-traded activities.

Secondly, the institutional setting of international financial intermediation, and changes therein, are at the heart of the driving forces underlying international lending. Bonds were raised through the mediation of specialized investment banks before 1914 or through US banks in the inter-war period. The historical evidence lends much support to the hypothesis, at odds with many standard theoretical models, that in these periods a predominance of unstable supply factors determined the balancing of loan markets and that, during booms, 'loan pushing' was not uncommon. Where international lending was largely driven by political factors, as in the case of French and German lending to Eastern Europe before 1914 and official development assistance after 1945, finance was supply-led as well.

Thirdly, the nature of the macroeconomic interactions between creditor and debtor nations was important. In these historical periods, the major creditor nations also dominated world trade. Available world savings for international finance depended to a large extent on the *ex ante* savings-investment balance in the major economy. The nature of trade interaction between creditors and debtors was crucial as well, i.e. whether exports were largely complementary or not (manufactures versus raw materials). The combination of savings and investment determinants and trade patterns formed basic ingredients of trade and finance, interacting 'anti-cyclically' (as under British rule before 1914) or 'pro-cyclically' (with the US as the leading economy in the 1920s and 1930s).

Finally, the source of finance and the nature of the politico-economic relations between debtor and creditor country often also shaped the adjustment process of the borrowers once debt-servicing problems emerged. The direction of foreign lending differed with its national origin. Financial markets in London, New York and Paris were not perfect substitutes and there were indirect allocation biases arising from trade interests. The direction of trade and finance was not independent of political interests. The need felt by creditor governments to intervene in times of debt crisis was often decisive for the adjustment process in the debtor country; both debt reschedulings (as before 1914) and defaults (1930s) could result.

4.2 Lending Cycles and Net Transfers

Under normal circumstances a period of external borrowing must be followed by a time in which the borrower makes a net outward transfer to service the debt. Additional loans may delay the switch point, but necessarily there will be periods in which the net transfer is from borrower to creditor. As equation 3.1 in the previous chapter makes clear, to make the outward transfer, the borrower must run a trade surplus. For this it will have to ensure adequate growth of net exports to meet payment obligations. If it fails to do so the lending cycle may be disrupted. Lenders may respond to the debtor's payments problems by tightening credit rationing. If debtors continue to face adverse export markets, they will either have to run into arrears or cut back on imports, which may affect its economic growth. Both will further undermine creditworthiness and payment capacity and a debt crisis is borne.

This can be exemplified further, using the analytical essentials of the debt dynamics as decribed by among others Avramovic et al. (1964), Simonsen (1985) and Dornbusch & Fischer (1987). Adding a time element, t, to the accounting identity (3.1) one may write:

$$M_{S0} - \theta_0 E_{S0} \equiv T_{S0} \tag{4.1}$$

$$M_{S1} - \theta_1 E_{S0} \equiv \Delta B_{S1} - i_1 F_{S0} \equiv (\dot{f}_{S_1} - a - i_1) F_{S0} \tag{4.2}$$

where, as before, M_S and E_S are imports and exports of the borrowing economy (South), are the terms of trade, and T_S is the net inward transfer equal to the trade deficit. Starting from zero debt the initial outstanding debt created in year 0 will be F_{S0}. Equation 4.2 gives the current account deficit in year 1 on the left-hand side. The interest rate on external debt is i. The net increment to debt is F_S, which is equal to the growth of new debt less the amortization rate, $(fs-a)\cdot F_{S0}$. Assuming a constant positive interest rate, applicable to international bond lending in the 1890s and 1920s and further constant export (g_e) and import growth (g_m) and a known change in relative prices (θ), one gets,

$$(1+g_{Sm})^t M_{S0} - [(1+g_{Se})(1+\dot{\theta})]^t \theta_0 E_{S0} = \Delta F_{St-i} \sum_{t=0}^{t-1} \Delta F_{St} \qquad (4.3)$$

and from (4.1) and (4.3):

$$F_{St} = (1+i)^t F_{S0} + T_{St} \qquad (4.4)$$

Expressing both sides as a proportion of export earnings this yields:

$$\frac{F_{St}}{\theta_t E_{St}} = \frac{(1+i)^t}{[(1+g_{Se})(1+\dot{\theta})]^t} \cdot \frac{F_{S0}}{\theta_0 E_{S0}} + \frac{T_{St}}{\theta_t E_{St}} \qquad (4.5)$$

If the debt/export ratio is to be kept constant over time, the borrowing country can maintain a sustainable net resource gap, or inward transfer ($T_S > 0$), as long as the denominator in (4.5) is larger than the numerator. In other words, if the growth of exports and the relative price of the borrower's exports exceeds the interest rate. Otherwise, trade deficits cannot be sustained indefinitely, because the debt/export ratio would grow without limit.

Finally, introduce two financial constraints: a solvency constraint set by the creditor and a liquidity, or payment constraint set by the borrower. The solvency constraint may be proxied by $(F_S/\theta E_S)^* < \Omega$, beyond which point the lender will tighten credit rationing. The borrower's liquidity constraint is $(T_S/\theta E_S) = \rho < 0$, where ρ may be set, for instance, in relation to a minimum reserve requirement to cover imports, but may be adjusted over time by the borrower depending on its willingness to pay. Now if export growth falls short of the interest rate the debt/export ratio may increase beyond Ω and credit will be tightened by the lender. Given export growth, this will force the borrower to cut back on imports ($g_m < g_e$) so that T_S falls and tends towards a trade surplus. Unless the negative T_S falls below ρ, the trade surplus will be sufficient to meet debt servicing obligations, until the debt/export ratio drops again below and a new lending cycle may begin. For a positive interest rate i, it follows from equation 4.4 that the accumulated debt must in the long run exceed the accumulated inward transfer; that is the cumulative T_S is negative.

This would represent the 'normal' debt cycle. However, a lender may react to a borrower's solvency problem by lowering Ω to a point which would push the borrower to run trade surpluses beyond its limit ρ. The subsequent arrears on debt service obligations may lead to a further lowering of Ω, and so on. Eventually all lending may be cut off. The debt cycle is thus disrupted by payment crises and the borrower is denied further access to the loan market.

The pattern of the debt cycle depends, on the one hand, on lender and borrower behaviour and, on the other hand, on the borrower's export opportunities and the terms of trade.

In the next sections the hypothesis is put forward that the expansionary phase of the lending cycle could acquire increasingly speculative overtones. In the late nineteenth century and in the 1920s this had to do with the institutional structure of the market and creditworthiness assessment in a world of uncertainty. Specialized financial institutions managing bond issues had strong incentives to maximize loan sales with the risk falling on individual bondholders. Market uncertainty only allowed for imperfect creditworthiness assessment, but unequal access to market information allowed financial intermediaries to spread often over-optimistic news of great market opportunities that attracted investors to the foreign bond market. A lending boom could be triggered following certain financial market innovations or opening up of new markets, such as the 'countries of recent settlement' in the late nineteenth century. In this market constellation, negative news such as a threat of default, would also spread easily, and provoke a sudden reduction in Ω and a cut-off in new lending.

Market perceptions of agents engaged in international lending were obviously guided by expectations about the export prospects of the borrowing countries. In principle, therefore, access to external loans and export performance would interact pro-cyclically: the better the export performance, the more loans may be obtained, even though they may be less needed, and vice versa. Needless to say, this type of interaction between finance and trade would fuel lending booms and speed up the emergence of payment crises. As emphasized in the preceding chapters, however, trade deficits in one part of the world should be reflected in trade and savings surpluses elsewhere ($T_S = E_N - \theta M_N = S_N - I_N$). In the case of lending to the newly developing regions in the late 1800s and in the 1920s borrowers tended to have very strong trade ties with the creditor country. In the 1890s British lending seemed to show an 'anti-cyclical' interaction with trade: overseas investment increased with falling demand for domestic investment and primary imports in Britain, but when foreign lending declined with the domestic investment boom, British demand for the debtors' exports increased. This provided, in principle, an intrinsically more stable system of trade and finance. However, the incentives for financial intermediaries in a market with incomplete information and uncertainty could still produce lending booms, while the shift from a lending boom to a borrower's export boom was often disruptive. The maturing of investment in export sectors financed by the foreign loans, often did not coincide with British demand for primary imports. Excess export supplies could provoke steep falls in the terms of trade. Emerging liquidity problems affected lenders' market perceptions and new lending would be no longer forthcoming. A debt crisis could thus emerge. In the 1920s there seemed to be a very clear positive interaction between the US business cycle and its lending behaviour to, particularly, Latin America, which made the bond market more prone to crises. With investment demand up, there was a larger demand for primary imports from Latin America which in turn contributed to optimistic expectations about returns on loans to that region. With the US business cycle in a downward trend, both external borrowing and export opportunities for the Latin American countries would dry up and contribute to an enlarged risk of payments crises.

The main factors underlying the structurally different cyclical interaction between the creditor and debtor nations in the 19th century vis-à-vis the 1920s are seen to lie in differences in (i) the trade policies of the major creditor nation (Britain was more liberal during its era and the US more protectionist), (ii) the degree of complementarity of the creditor and debtor economies (the British economy was more complementary, providing manufactures and needing raw materials; the US was also a net primary exporter) and (iii) the response of creditor-country investors to trends in international commodity markets (in the 1920s investors wished to invest more at home and abroad with expanding commodity markets; 19th century events showed an inverse pattern).

The historical evidence supporting these hypotheses is given below.

4.3 1865-1914: Anti-Cyclical Lending under British Rule

4.3.1 International flow of funds

Before World War I, private bond markets were the major source of international finance. Britain was the major capital exporter and London acted as the main financial centre. Europe's industrial revolution produced both a spurt in domestic capital accumulation, which pushed up savings rates, and a strong demand for food and raw materials which made investment in other parts of the world necessary to meet the increased demand. The main stream of international capital flows ran from private European sources of saving to private sectors in borrowing countries via the London capital market. Capital moved primarily to resource-rich, higher-income countries, in particular to the so-called

Table 4.1 Debt-claim matrix of foreign securities holdings (liabilities) by principal creditors and debtors, 1914 (billions of US$)

Assets (claims) \ Liabilities (debt)	Europe	US/ Canada	Latin America	Oceania	Asia	Africa	World
Great Britain	1.0	7.0	3.7	2.2	3.6	2.5	20.0 (44.0%)
France	4.7	0.5	1.6	0.1	1.3	0.9	9.1 (20.0%)
Germany	2.6	1.1	0.9		0.7	0.5	5.8 (12.8%)
United States	0.7	0.9[a]	1.7		0.2		3.5 (7.7%)
Other[b]	3.0	1.6	1.0		1.3	0.2	7.1 (15.5%)
World	12.0 (26.4%)	11.1 (24.4%)	8.9 (19.6%)	2.3 (5.0%)	7.1 (15.6%)	4.1 (9.0%)	45.5 (100%)

Sources: United Nations (1949) and Woodruff (1967: 154)

Notes: a. Refers to US foreign assets outstanding in Canada.

b. Includes Belgium (capital exports to Europe and Belgian Congo), The Netherlands (Europe, Dutch Indies), Switzerland (Europe), Japan and Russia (China), Portugal (Brazil) and Sweden (Russia).

areas of 'recent settlement', such as the United States, Canada, Latin America (particularly Argentina and Brazil) and Australia. Financial and real capital movements went together. Britain supplied the capital goods for peripheral investment. The borrowing nations financed imports through bond issues in the London financial market. At the same time, capital followed the massive population and labour movements towards these countries, involving some 60 million migrants from Europe (Nurkse 1954). The expansion of railroads and other infrastructure was externally financed, inaccessible land was 'opened' for production and foreign investors were repaid from the resulting export earnings. International finance thus facilitated a growing world economic interdependence. Unlike in more ancient times,[1] capital was used less to finance trade, or wars and the defence of political allies, than to support production and productivity growth in capital-poor nations.

There was an estimated US$ 45 billion of outstanding long-term debt by 1914 (see the *debt-claim matrix* presented in Table 4.1), up from less than US$ 4 billion in 1865 (United Nations 1949). The bulk of international capital originated in Britain (about 44 per cent of the world total of external assets). Simon (1967) provides data on the allocation of British foreign investment by type of borrower (See Figure 4.1). Classified by institution it shows that 55 per cent went to private enterprises, while more than two thirds went into infrastructure. The countries of 'recent settlement' received nearly two thirds of British lending during this period: a third went to North America, almost a fifth to Latin America and one-tenth to Australia.

While Britain was principally engaged in 'development finance' for newly developing areas, two other creditor countries, France and Germany, provided finance to cover government expenditures, often of a non-developmental nature (including military spending) in Eastern and Central Europe and in the Middle East. Paris functioned as the principal financial centre for these capital movements.[2] Foreign policy objectives played a significant role in promoting and directing these private capital flows. French and German private capital was mobilized and employed as an instrument to cement political alliances, such as the Franco-Russian alliance. German governments stimulated loans to Russia, Serbia and Bulgaria, as well as to the Ottoman Empire and parts of Africa (see United Nations 1949 and Das 1986). A portion of British capital movements also served official interests. Simon (1967) observes that although British governments did not have a formal regulatory system, they did stimulate investors to purchase British colonial and domi-

Figure 4.1 British foreign lending and investment, by destination, 1865-1914

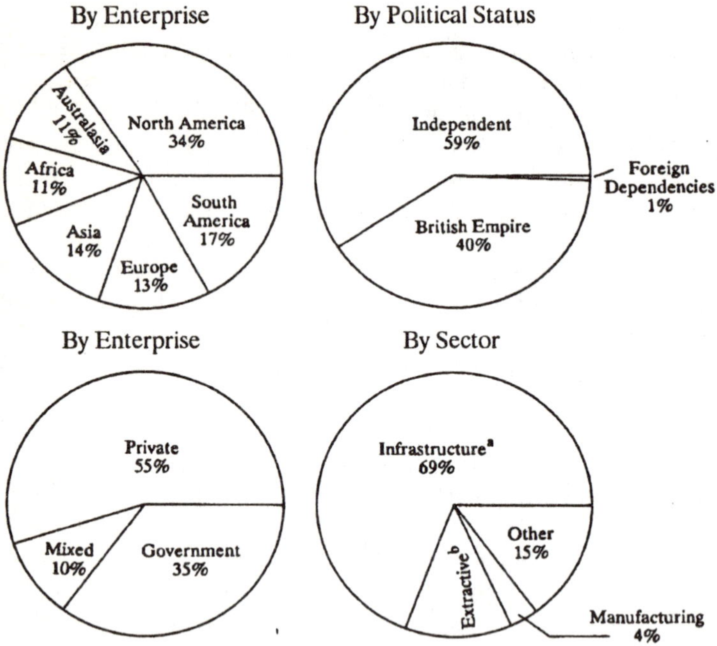

Notes: a. Includes transportation, public utilities and public works.
b. Includes agriculture and mining.

nion securities. Figure 4.1 shows that 40 per cent of British foreign investment was in the different parts of the Empire.

Despite these official interests, the bulk of nineteenth century lending was mediated through the capital market; direct intergovernmental financial dealings were negligible. The terms of lending were predominantly long-term (up to 99 years to maturity and some even perpetual) and took the form of company shares or, most importantly, bonds at fixed interest rates issued by publicly or privately owned railways and utilities.

4.3.2 The magnitude of capital movements

The macroeconomic importance of foreign investment for the British economy was much larger than in the other creditor countries in this

Figure 4.2 UK: net capital exports and domestic investment, 1863-1914 (percentage of GNP)

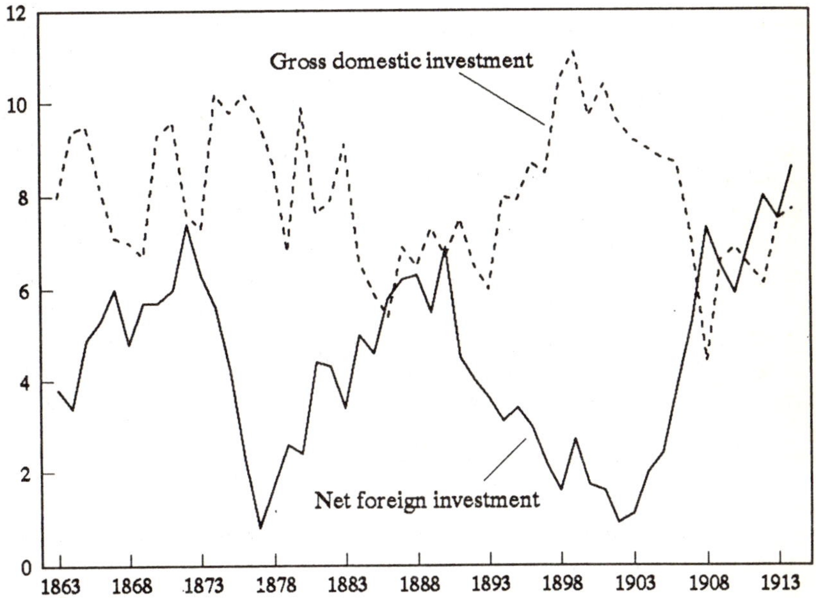

Source: Feinstein (1962)

period and perhaps unique in history. British investment abroad averaged about 5 per cent of its GNP between 1865 and 1914, peaking at around 7 per cent in 1873, 1890 and 1908 and at 9 per cent just before the outbreak of the World War I (see Figure 4.2). During 'trough' periods (1877-1880 and 1898-1903) the rate fell to 1 to 2 per cent of GNP. France and Germany did not invest as much in relative terms: their capital exports averaged 2 to 3 per cent of their respective GNPs in this period.

International investment proved extremely profitable. Net receipts of British investment income from abroad were in the range of 3.0 to 7.5 per cent of GNP. The net transfer of resources (T_S) was even positive for Britain during a large part of the period, as returns exceeded capital exports. The flow of net transfers towards Britain was positive for a prolonged period between 1892 and 1905, averaging nearly 3 per cent of Britain's GNP (see Appendix A.4, Figure A4.1).

The importance of nineteenth century foreign capital inflows for the major borrowing countries varied widely, but on the basis of some fragmentary data sources the following evidence can be supplied. Data provided by Kuznets (1961) and Mitchell (1982) indicate that capital flows to the United States never exceeded 3 per cent of its GNP (Figure A4.2) and, measured over ten-year periods, they financed on average only a minor share of domestic investment (see Table A4.1). Moreover, there were two periods of negative capital inflows: the financial crisis of the late 1870s provoked a reversal of capital movements as debt repayment exceeded new lending, while in the late 1890s to early 1900s there was another financial crisis with reduced capital inflows, followed by the emergence of the United States as a net creditor country. Other major debtors had a much smaller debt in absolute terms, but their capital inflows were much higher in relative terms, financing up to half of domestic investment in countries such as Australia, Canada and Argentina.[3]

4.3.3 Financial institutions and booms and crises in lending

The trend in international lending showed large fluctuations. British capital exports seem to have moved inversely with the domestic investment cycle (see Figure 4.2),[4] which has given rise to the widely held hypothesis that British lending behaved anti-cyclically (see Cairncross 1953, Thomas 1967, Kindleberger 1982, earlier in this chapter and below). Such a pattern could be consistent with lending behaviour based on profit-maximization and responding to yield differentials between domestic and foreign assets, as assumed by MacDougall-type or basic neo-classical portfolio models. Data on yield differentials in this period are hard to come by, but Dunning (1970) reports and analyses some indicators for Britain and the United States. Figure 4.3 plots indices for relative profitability (r_{US}/r_{UK}) and net lending from Britain to the US ($F_{US\text{-}UK}/I_{UK}$). Since no comparable information was available on rates of return on investment in the US and the UK or on domestic UK bonds or on US bonds floating in the London market, indices of share prices in the US and the UK as reported in Dunning (1970) are used as proxies for r_{US} and r_{UK}. The two indices in the figure move in the same direction most of the time, suggesting a positively sloped supply curve of foreign investment in the US in response to relative profitability. This confirms the results obtained by Dunning. Regression analysis on this relationship suggests lending might have responded with a one-year

Figure 4.3 UK investment in the US and relative profitability, 1871-1913 (indices: 1870 = 100)

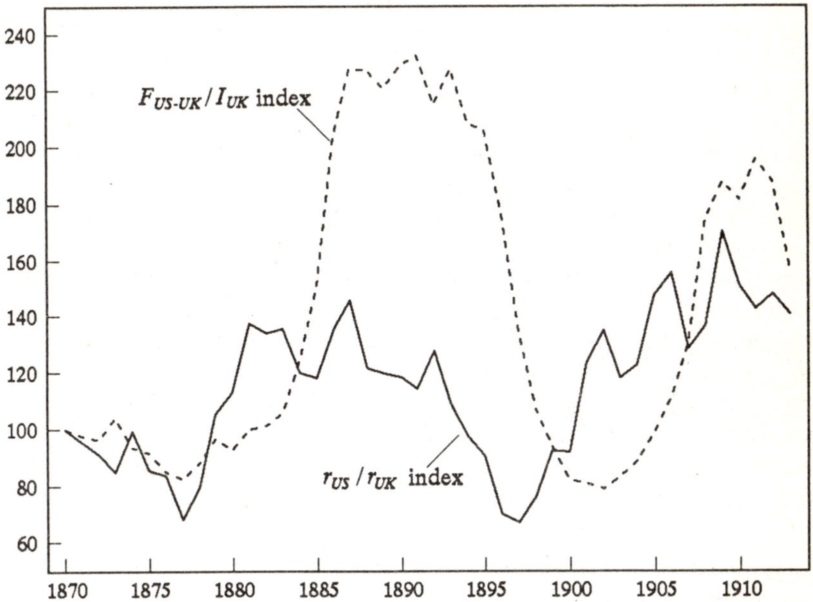

Source: Dunning (1970)

lag.[5] The latter could indicate that *expectations* about profitability played a role.

This is confirmed by accounts of the institutional framework in which international bond lending took place. However, at the same time it appears that lending behaviour was not purely determined by individual investor decisions based on marginal rate-of-return calculations. Specialized financial intermediaries in the London market appeared to have their own interest in raising funds and arranging large bond issues in the countries of 'recent settlement' and were often far from cautious portfolio managers.

Market structure and the role of issuing houses

The nineteenth century saw the establishment of specialized investment banks and acceptance houses specialized in foreign security issues, as well as a rapid growth in the latter half of the century of branches of foreign banks established in London (Kenwood & Lougheed 1971; Kindleberger 1978). This expansion and innovation of financial institutions allowed for the creation of mutual funds, which separated ownership from management of portfolios and spread risks more widely. Individual bondholders required such reputable institutions to assess viability and profitability of projects abroad and to ensure punctual debt servicing. Cairncross (1953: 91-93) emphasizes that foreign borrowers relied on the intermediaries to ensure successful flotation. Feis (1930: 7ff.) documents that the market for foreign bonds was dominated by the large issuing houses owned and headed by powerful private banks, such as Rothschild and Barings. These large issuing houses engaged mainly in raising large government and railway bonds issued in Europe and the countries of 'recent settlement'. Several studies have reported on the substantial risk-free fees and commissions which could be earned by the issuing houses ranging from 2 to 5 per cent of the nominal value of the loan (Davis 1976, Rose & Snowden 1988).

Towards the end of the century, competition in the market increased as new entrants vied for a piece of the cake. Both the market leaders and new entrants engaged in a new practice of *collective* underwriting of bond issues in which the original contracting issuing house invites other financiers and intermediaries to join a syndicate (Morgan & Thomas 1962: 89, Rose & Snowden 1988: 775). Increased competition and collective underwriting put pressure on commissions, which moreover had to be shared with more intermediaries. Collective underwriting was a mechanism to raise the chance of successful flotation of larger loans and thus the absolute value of commission fees.

Such a market structure and competition for market shares shows a striking resemblence to the syndicated lending strategies of international banks in the 1970s (see Chapter 5).

Expectations, 'loan pushing' and concentration of lending

Because of the high fees and commissions to be earned, fundraisers entered the market as active salesmen stimulating representatives of foreign governments and railway companies to issue bonds and spreading information about profitable ventures in newly-developing areas to potential bond holders. With the increasing competition the fee had to be shared among several intermediaries, but Davis (1976: 14-15) documents that the premium would be high enough for the specialized financial institutions to accept initial entrepreneurial risk by buying a large share in a new bond issue as a form of promotion and later selling this to the public. Davis reports further that some promotion campaigns even used part of the premium to attract buyers and allowed banks to buy bonds below the market rate.

The issuing houses had considerable bargaining power *vis-à-vis* borrowers and potential bondholders because of their ability to raise large sums of money and because of the information they possessed on the bond market and, allegedly, on the economies of the countries of 'recent settlement'. Several historical analyses have found clear indications that loan decisions were largely based on the expectations on foreign bond

Table 4.2 Argentina: capital requirements and net borrowing, 1881-91 (millions of gold pesos, current prices)

	Net transfer (net borrow less service charges)	Current account	Net foreign loans	Excess of capital receipts	Paper notes circulation (mln. paper pesos)	Gold premium (1884 =par)
1881	2	-10	14	4	n.a.	n.a.
1882	9	-17	25	8	n.a.	n.a.
1883	27	-40	47	7	n.a.	n.a.
1884	12	-54	40	-14	62	100
1885	16	-31	39	8	75	137
1886	41	-52	68	16	89	139
1887	117	-70	154	84	94	135
1888	198	-78	248	170	130	148
1889	94	-102	154	52	164	191
1890	-25	-101	45	-56	245	251
1891	-24	4	8	12	261	387
1892	n.a.	n.a.	n.a.	n.a.	282	332
1893	n.a.	n.a.	n.a.	n.a.	307	324
1894	n.a.	n.a.	n.a.	n.a.	299	357
1895	-21	-13	17	4	298	344
1896	-3	-35	37	2	295	296
1897	-6	-41	38	-3	293	291
1898	-5	-24	46	22	292	258
1899	-30	13	25	38	291	225

Source: Ford (1962, pp. 135-39); Williams (1920); and *Extracto Estadistico de la República Argentina*, 1915, Buenos Aires, as reproduced in Ford (1962).

profitability created by the issuing houses (Davis 1976, Chapman 1984, Rose & Snowden 1988). Unequal access to information and competition among intermediaries for market shares did lead to lending excesses: demand for foreign bonds would increase particularly during phases when the British investment cycle was low (see also below) and, in the terminology of Kindleberger (1978), speculative mania would emerge. Representatives of investment houses would consequently try to raise more bond issues. There is some evidence showing that this 'loan pushing' in several instances took the form of outright fraud as brokers attempted to sell bonds on non-existing projects (Feis 1930: 106, Chapman 1984: 39-56, Rose & Snowden 1988: 775).[6] At the same time, defaults and threats of debt crises could provoke bondholders to withdraw from lending to a particular country, sometimes for long periods.

Market knowledge and trade relations and economies of scale in the investment projects all played roles in determining the pattern of foreign lending. Firstly, bond issuing was mainly promoted in areas where Britain already had vested interests and where it was expected that raw material supplies could be generated to support the economy. Secondly, investment in infrastructure is characterized by large indivisibilities. Large additions to railroad track were required in the US and Latin America to open up new lands for export production. Fishlow (1985) cites documents from the era evidencing that the issuing houses explicitly used the argument of indivisibilities to raise funds and their promotion campaigns were mutually reinforcing in praising the benefits of raising large bond issues.

These factors led to a concentration of bond lending in the resource-rich, newly developing areas. The bonds were thus mostly tied to investment projects, but due to the loan-volume maximizing behaviour on the supply-side, booms in lending to particular countries were not uncommon, leading to short-term absorption and adjustment problems in the borrowing countries.

A good example is presented by Argentina in the 1880s and 1890s. The Argentinian debt crisis of the 1890s was preceded by considerable balance of payments surpluses (see Table 4.2). Rosy prospects had created higher yields on Argentinian issues and elements of speculative mania began to appear with the encouragement of London issuing houses, particularly between 1885 and 1889. In his authorative study, Ford (1962: 85-88, 140-46) provides data showing that the increase in income opportunities induced new import demand, particularly of consumption goods. The Argentine government, headed by President Celman, stimulated demand further by permitting a lax domestic credit policy and monetary expansion. The expansion of peso paper money was such that the exchange rate did not appreciate sufficiently to correct for the accumulation of gold reserves; instead there was a depreciation as the government let the gold peso-paper peso exchange rate fluctuate freely, thus increasing the gold premium (see Table 4.2 and Ford 1962: 136-40 for a further analysis). By 1889, alarming reports from Buenos Aires of financial excesses and even of issues for investment projects that existed only on paper, led many British investors to withdraw, thereby precipitating the bankruptcy of a major London issuing house, Baring Brothers.[7] Later, Baring was eased into an orderly insolvency through the timely intervention of the British government, the Bank of England and other large banks (Ford 1956). Losses on outstanding Argentinian debt were carried by individual bondholders. This solution, although it averted a financial crisis in London, did nothing to restore the flow of resources to Latin America, and this virtually ceased. Argentina was faced with the need to adjust to its debt servicing difficulties without further voluntary capital inflows. Similarities with the features of the present debt crisis come to mind, although in the present-day context international institutions like the IMF and the World Bank try to compensate for the lack of voluntary lending and avoid a major financial and banking crisis by conducting adjustment lending and arranging debt reschedulings.

In sum, the institutional arrangements of the foreign bond market in London provided strong supply factors that could easily lead to booms in lending provoked by competing issuing houses maximizing the size of bond loans. As the money went largely to investment projects in new and unknown areas, the issuing houses also played an important role in creating expectations among creditors about the profitability of the loans. Emerging repayment problems could disrupt such expectations and lead to a withdrawal lasting several years.

4.3.4 Anti-cyclical adjustment

The booms and crises of international lending were mitigated in the macroeconomic context, which was characterized by the anti-cyclical interaction between British foreign investment and trade. To some observers (see e.g. Cairncross 1953) this pattern made the period a 'golden era' of profitable and developmental international investment with an automatic global adjustment process and an exceptional degree of harmony of interest between lenders and borrowers. The international payments system was governed by the *Gold Standard* and, in theory, its functioning should facilitate the 'automatic' adjustment process. The countries on the gold standard fixed their currencies in terms of gold and balance of payments imbalances were settled by gold transfers. For the system to function well according to David Hume's *'price-specie-flow'* mechanism (Hume 1752), countries should not sterilize the effects of the gold flows on their money supplies. A payments deficit would thus lead to a gold outflow. The subsequent fall in the money supply would lead to a price decline, greater competitiveness and so more exports, fewer imports and a reduction of the payments deficit. However, the price-specie-flow theory assumed capital immobility and Marshall-

Table 4.3 Business cycle indicators, UK and Argentina, 1885-1900 (1885 = 100)

	United Kingdom				**Argentina**			
	GNP	*Import volume*	*Terms of trade*	*Net capital exports to Arg.*[a]	*Export volume*	*Export prices*	*Terms of trade*	*Import volume* +
1885	100	100	100	39	100	100	100	100
1886	101	101	103	68	99	84	90	103
1887	106	101	102	154	97	103	109	127
1888	108	110	101	248	104	115	110	139
1889	110	120	101	154	110	133	120	179
1890	111	120	101	45	121	99	89	154
1891	115	122	106	8	143	85	84	73
1892	114	124	106	n.a.	126	107	113	99
1893	113	122	106	n.a.	142	79	85	104
1894	119	132	108	n.a.	176	69	79	101
1895	123	139	109	17	216	66	77	103
1896	128	146	109	37	194	72	79	122
1897	128	149	107	38	142	84	92	107
1898	136	154	107	46	189	84	88	116
1899	143	158	107	25	239	92	87	127
1900	140	162	109	28	190	97	75	123

Sources: Feinstein (1962), Ford (1962) and Mitchell (1983).

Note: a. Millions of gold pesos.

Lerner conditions to assure this result. The existence of large capital flows implied other mechanisms must have been at work to explain the anti-cyclical pattern.

Keynes (1923) and Taussig (1928) laid the foundations for analysing the functioning of the gold standard with the existence of capital movements. Capital exports could cause a loss in reserves, but central banks could respond by raising discount rates to attract short-term private capital inflows and stem the fall in the domestic money supply. In the Keynesian story of what happens next, higher interest rates would lead to a decline in domestic investment demand, recession and a fall in imports. The balance of payments deficit would thus be reduced, but at the cost of lower output. Such a mechanism could also explain the inverse relation between British domestic investment and *long-term* foreign investment, assuming the long-term flows are less sensitive to the interest rate than short-term capital and domestic investment.

An important study by Bloomfield (1959) has revealed that central banks of the countries that formed part of the gold standard in fact engaged frequently in offsetting policies. Because Britain dominates world trade and finance, such policies proved to be effective and it enjoyed a high interest elasticity of short-term private capital flows. A small change in the discount rate was sufficient to provoke a significant balance of payments adjustment.

This line of reasoning has to be complemented by two further factors in order to explain why international debt crises could emerge. Firstly, the assumption that long-term capital movements did not respond with the same sensitivity as short-term flows to changes in the discount rate seems realistic. As argued in the previous section, indivisibilities, commissions and fees and informational asymmetries between financial intermediaries, lenders and borrowers led to booms and sudden halts in long-term lending. Secondly, trade adjustment was not as smooth as suggested by the price-specie-flow model. Potentially there could be a benign interaction between trade and finance. The liberal trade regime and the complementarity between Britain, as producer of manufactures, and its major debtor countries, as suppliers of food and raw materials, ensured that in the upward business cycle in the UK the decreasing availability of external capital to debtor countries would be compensated by an expansion of their export markets as UK growth would stimulate the demand for their products. However, two disrupting factors seem to have been present. The first is that there was a *time lag* of several years between foreign investment in infrastructure and export growth. This may explain why falling terms of trade coincided with falling capital flows to debtor countries. Spurts in lending led to accelerated growth in export supplies not matched on the demand side. The second factor is a point emphasized by Triffin (1947, 1964). According to Triffin, the cost of credit was an important factor in determining the size of commodity stocks of raw materials held in Britain. As the Bank of England raised the discount rate in response to massive capital exports and possible reserve losses, new purchases of raw materials fell off and the resultant excess supply of products abroad caused a fall in raw material prices, improving Britain's terms of trade and balance of payments. Marshall-Lerner conditions were thus not satisfied and the burden of adjustment fell primarily on the rest of the world rather than on Britain.

Thus, debt crises typically were preceded by falling terms of trade and export earnings, while export volumes tended to increase and, because of emerging debt servicing problems, new lending stagnated. Good examples include the debt crises of the United States in the 1870s and Argentina and Brazil in the 1890s.[8] Table 4.3 supplies figures for the pattern in Argentina. The data indicate that Argentine export volumes increased with income growth in the creditor country. However, Argentine export volumes accelerated disproportionately between 1888 and 1895, provoking (in addition to similar trends in other major capital-importing countries) a fall in its export prices and terms of trade. A debt crisis emerged and British capital exports to Argentina virtually stopped. Debt reschedulings were required in 1891 and 1893 to overcome major liquidity problems (see below). As the British business cycle went upward again after 1894, Argentine export growth continued, its terms of trade were gradually restored and debt repayment could be resumed. Also in the case of Brazil historical accounts have assigned a primordial role to the terms of trade in explaining the timing of the debt crises (see Cardoso & Dornbusch 1989b and Fishlow 1988). Coffee prices collapsed in the second half of the 1890s due to overproduction and British sales out of commodity stocks instead of new purchases overseas. Falling coffee prices eventually led to a threat of default by Brazilian borrowers in 1898 and an interruption of lending to Brazil.

These external factors appeared particularly relevant in the case of capital movements towards the countries of recent settlement relying on private capital sources for export production. Domestic policy responses to falling terms of trade also played a role in these cases, but were more pronounced during debt crises in countries relying on more politically motivated capital inflows. Fishlow (1985) has argued that the debt crises in, for instance, Egypt and Turkey in the 1870s resulted from stagnant domestic revenues and expanding fiscal deficits, while foreign loans had only partly been used to support export production.

4.3.5 Adjustment and conditionality

Typical policy responses in borrowing countries to falling foreign-exchange earnings have been to try to alleviate the liquidity crisis by issuing new foreign (government) bonds. The debt crises in Argentina and Brazil of the 1890s were preceded by steep increases in their budget deficits.[9] Government revenues declined with export earnings, as taxation of foreign trade was the major source of government income. Government spending was stepped up to alleviate liquidity problems in exporting sectors and to finance the accumulation of commodity stocks (see Ford 1962 and Fishlow 1985). These domestic policy responses in Argentina and Brazil hastened their financial crisis as export earnings did not recover quickly enough and foreign investors became more hesitant to continue lending. The liquidity crisis forced Argentina to default on external payments obligations between 1891 and 1894.

Foreign creditors, represented by the issuing houses, got involved in domestic adjustment policies and settlements could be reached with support of politically influential economic power groups.[10] In Argentina in 1891, an international bankers' committee chaired by Lord Rothschild reached an agreement for a new loan. Argentina would meet its obligations in return. The loan that could be raised at the financial centre was far from sufficient, however, and could not prevent heavy import cuts. In 1893 a new agreement, the *Arreglo Romero*, was reached and a more appropriate debt rescheduling was conditioned to stricter budget controls and tighter monetary policies (Fishlow 1985). Argentina was excused from paying 30 per cent of its interest obligations for five years and all amortization for eight years, the costs being borne by the bond holders. As indicated earlier, export growth and terms-of-trade improvement eased the adjustment process after 1895. The Brazilian government and its creditors agreed to a moratorium on new domestic and foreign debt issues and pledged all of Brazil's customs receipts to debt service in exchange for debt settlement (Fishlow 1989).

The creditor country governments played a minor role in these debt renegotiations. They seldom intervened directly, an exception being the bail-out of Baring Brothers to avert financial crisis in the London market (see Ford 1956 on this).

More direct creditor government intervention took place during debt crises in countries where international lending had been more politically determined and where funds were more often used to cover fiscal deficits. In a number of these cases special new foreign loan issues were raised with the help of the British government to solve the 1870s crises, notably in Egypt and Turkey. According to Fishlow (1985), the new loans were conditioned by the acceptance of missions of commissioners, sent to control the spending of the fresh credits. Conditions attached to debt settlements were based in most cases on the debtor's ability to pay. Risks of eventual non-repayment were to be borne by individual bondholders. Nevertheless, there were also many instances, particularly where lending had been determined by political factors, in which bondholders were protected and repayment was forced by a British take-over of custom houses and banks. The British government would thus try to control the debtor's financial and commodity flows, if necessary by making additional use of 'gunboat diplomacy', as Hughes (1979) puts it.

4.3.6 Conclusion

Despite these payments crises, international capital flows between 1865 and 1914 proved profitable to investors. The large capital flows were part of a larger political and economic system with Britain at the centre, providing a financial market for bond issues and a goods market for raw material exports from the borrowing nations. Financial and trade cycles interacted anti-cyclically, but the adjustment was not smooth and could not preclude debt crises. On the supply side, loan-volume maximizing financial intermediaries in the financial centres provided a driving force behind both lending euphoria and withdrawals. The debt servicing capacity of the borrowing nations could not always expand in time to compensate for drops in the financial cycle: the maturing of foreign-financed export production led to rapidly increasing export supplies for which there was not always an adequate market. Particularly, booms in long-term lending led the Bank of England to raise interest rates to stem reserve losses, which in turn stimulated stock liquidation and provoked steep declines in the terms of trade of the capital-importing, raw material-exporting peripheral countries. Emerging debt servicing problems reversed foreign investors' market perceptions (a shift in Ω; see section 4.2) and lending to problem debtors ceased abruptly.

The political and economic pre-eminence of Britain ensured enforceability of the debt contracts. In the case of debt crises, reschedulings usually involved policy conditionality, forcing borrowing nations into domestic adjustment. Borrowers with foreign-financed export sectors had strong incentives to remain inside the rapidly expanding world economy. Foreign investment and imports were crucial to growth, and default would cut off their access to the London capital market. Countries with a larger share of public sector borrowing other than for support of export sectors tended to default unless prevented by direct creditor government intervention, since the incentive to default was great. Particularly countries that had borrowed from France and Germany had much smaller trade ties with their creditors. At the same time, in these cases lending was much more politically determined and public-sector insolvency was less likely to lead to reduced access to new finance. This also provided incentive to default.

The predominant pattern of capital movements in the pre-World War I period depended crucially on the strength and stability of the British economy. The weakening of the major creditor economy would lead to a collapse of this pattern.

4.4 1919-39: Pro-Cyclical Capital Movements and the Decline of British Economic Dominance

4.4.1 Shifting patterns of capital movements

World War I and its aftermath caused a major disruption in the pattern of international capital movements. There were three major shifts: (i) the United States became the major creditor country; (ii) a larger share of borrowing was used for public sector financing and a decreasing share for infrastructure linked to export production; and (iii) British foreign lending now mainly went to the Empire, while US bond lending went largely to Latin America and Europe.

Firstly, Great Britain continued to be an international lender in the 1920s, but the volume of its capital exports declined. Most European countries were forced to relinquish large quantities of their foreign assets during the war.[11] The need to reconstruct their economies required that most savings be invested domestically. This turned Germany into a major debtor country. At the other end of the spectrum, the United States became the major creditor nation in the 1920s: from an initial US$ 6.5 billion of foreign assets in 1919, its external wealth holdings more than doubled by 1929 (US$ 14.8 billion), contributing around two thirds of the world total of new investment in the period (Dunning 1970). New York became the major financial centre during the inter-war period, a shift facilitated by: (i) massive savings in the US during the war; (ii) maturing of the US economy, its strong export position and the weakening of the pound; (iii) financial innovations in the US, particularly the establishment of the Federal Reserve System and expanded capital market facilities; and (iv) the depletion of resources in European countries during the war which forced them to depreciate their currency, leaving the US as the only major country whose currency remained convertible to gold and where foreign bonds could be floated.

Some of the literature (e.g. World Bank 1985, Hughes 1979) suggests that official lending increased in importance as a source of capital flows, but this source should not be overestimated. Official lending by the major creditor country, the US, was important only until 1919, involving

Table 4.4 Central public foreign debt[a] *in some major borrowing countries, 1919-31*

	Foreign debt as % total public debt	**Outstanding public foreign debt (millions of US$)**			**Public foreign debt as % of exports**		
	1929	*1919*	*1929*	*1931*	*1919*	*1929*	*1939*
Germany[b]	10	n..a.	213	787	n.a.	7	34
Austria	92	42	242	283	21	79	157
Australia	52	1578	2862	2852	304	394	658
Canada	20	805	565	532	64	48	99
Argentina	33	321	871	274	32	49	73
Bolivia	88	16	61	69	28	137	333
Brazil	89	440	668	542	70	153	260
Chile	88	222	286	336	79	102	331
Colombia	79	24[c]	69	81	51[c]	58	101
Ecuador	78	17	9	23	83	52	81
Mexico	91	269	486	511	136	171	266
Egypt	97	433	487	482	120	191	369
India	43	1089	1715	1870	82	153	312
Thailand (Siam)	100	32	57	54	50	58	104

Sources: United Nations (1948), Mitchell (1983, 1982, 1978).
Notes: a. Foreign debt of central government and other public administration.
b. Central government debt only; excludes borrowing by municipalities which accounted for most German foreign bond issues in the 1920s. This explains the low German ratios.
c. Refers to 1922.

loans to its allies after entering the war in 1916 and, in particular, to Germany to finance reparations after the war. Practically all US foreign lending in the 1920s came from private sources (See Appendix Table A4.2). Direct foreign investment (about a quarter of total flows) was a fairly new feature.

Secondly, there was an increasing importance of liabilities held by governments and public sectors in borrowing countries. In the 1920s, government borrowings accounted for nearly half of the foreign dollar issues of the United States. Foreign borrowing financed more than three quarters of non-tax budget requirements in Latin American countries (except Argentina) in the 1920s; in Austria, Egypt and Siam (Thailand) almost 100 per cent of budget deficits were externally financed (see Table 4.4).

Thirdly, there was a shift in the geographical and sectoral allocation of international investment. Most US lending was directed to Europe and Canada, but in the course of the 1920s an increasing share went to Latin America. British lending was primarily directed towards the Empire (Table 4.5). Direct investment by US firms was largely in primary producing countries in Latin America and was mainly directed towards raw material production for export markets (United Nations 1949). The

Table 4.5 New foreign security issues raised in New York and London by destination, 1920-31

	US : New York (billions of US $)	UK: London (millions of £)
Governments	7.5	803
British Empire (incl.Canada)	2.1	591
Foreign	5.4	211
Europe	3.0	103
(Germany)	(0.9)	(21)
Latin America	2.0	51
Other	0.4	57
Corporations	1.9	496
Railways	n.a.	96
Other	n.a.	400
Total	9.4	1299

Source: Fishlow (1985: Table 5)

use of security issues was more diversified. In Europe external funds were initially used to finance the reconstruction of industry and infrastructure, the purchase of imported inputs and working capital. In the course of the 1920s European borrowers started issuing central government and municipal securities to finance recurrent expenditure, to avert inflationary finance and for currency stabilization by adding the capital inflows to foreign exchange reserves (Dunning 1970, Fishlow 1985). US bond lending to Latin America was primarily directed towards a further expansion of infrastructure in support of export production (ECLA 1965). However, Latin American borrowers also made substantial use of long-term foreign finance to cover government budgets and in some cases to overcome short-term balance of payments crises.[12]

4.4.2 Macroeconomic role

During the inter-war period the level of international capital movements was not much below that of 1870-1914,[13] but their macroeconomic importance appears to have been much less pronounced. The United States invested on average less than 1.0 per cent of its GNP abroad in the 1920s (Figure 4.4). British foreign investment declined considerably. In the early 1920s it still amounted to around 4 to 5 per cent of GNP, but after 1924 it fell below 2 per cent of GNP, to become negative in the 1930s. Net income from foreign investment could be sustained at around 3 to 4 per cent of GNP, implying that there was a sustained stream of net transfers towards the UK between 1924 and 1939 (See Figures A4.3 and A4.4).

Little comparative evidence is available about changes in the relative importance of foreign capital inflows to debtor countries. In Canada they fell; debt repayments even exceeded new foreign capital inflows between 1923 and 1926, while between 1927 and 1933 net capital inflows averaged less than 3 per cent of GNP, though financing some 20 per cent of domestic investment. In Argentina, however, net capital inflows were around 3 per cent of GDP and 9 per cent of domestic investment between 1922 and 1933, only slightly below nineteenth century levels.[14]

4.4.3 Lending behaviour, credit rationing and 'loan pushing'

As in nineteenth century Britain, financial innovations played an important role in the shift towards actively moving foreign bonds in US financial markets. US investors became acquainted with holding bonds through the Liberty Loan Act of 1917, which authorized the US Treasury to purchase foreign securities issued by governments at war with

Figure 4.4 United States: net capital exports and domestic investment 1918-40

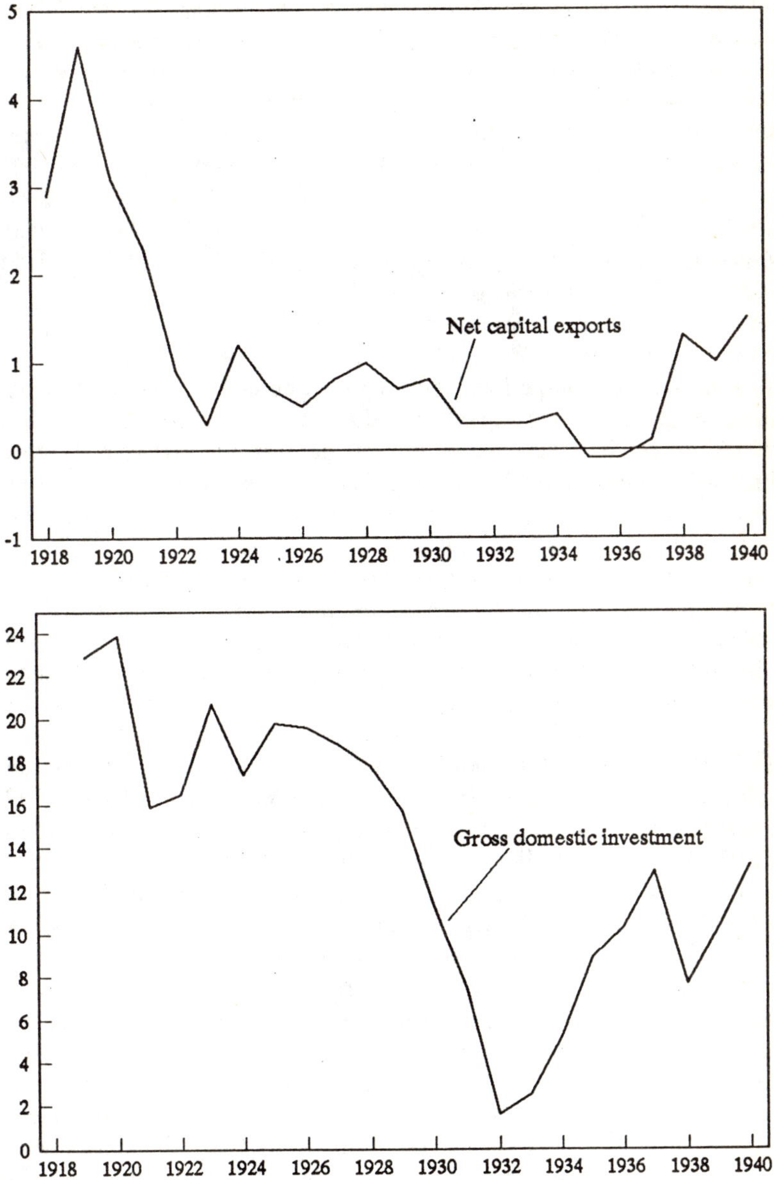

Source: Mitchell (1982)

enemies of the US. Eichengreen (1988) documents that these purchases were financed by selling dollar-denominated securities on the US market. US commercial banks became involved in distributing the Liberty Bonds. At the same time the Federal Reserve Act relaxed the constraint on foreign branching. Banks and their affiliates now could also take an active role in the originating of foreign bond issues.[15] The investment projects financed by these issues helped US producers to create foreign markets for their goods and services (Lewis 1938: 378ff.). The growth of US savings and the low yields on domestic bonds created a potential demand for foreign bonds, while increasing competition among financial institutions provided the supply, often accompanied by aggressive salesmanship. As in the previous period, bankers' commissions on the mediation service were considerable and commissions of a full percentage point were not uncommon (Lewis 1938). The economies of scale associated with marketing large loans and the commissions to be earned may in many cases have outweighed the additional risk to the issuing bankers. This hypothesis emerges in various parts of the literature (Lewis 1938, Darity & Horn 1988) and suggests that the financial institutions tried to maximize the size of the loan, requiring aggressive marketing (loan pushing) towards both the borrowing nation and investors in the US financial market; optimistic forecasts were spread about the economic prospects of the countries where the bonds were to be issued.[16]

US financial institutions and the foreign bond market of course did not operate with full disregard to risk and yield differentials. Booming foreign lending in the mid-1920s coincided with a positive rate-of-return differential between foreign and domestic bonds raised in the New York market. Figure 4.5, taken from Eichengreen (1988), shows the trends in the yields on domestic and foreign dollar bonds between 1922 and 1929. When the yield on domestic bonds declined between 1923 and 1927, foreign bonds became more attractive and US foreign lending increased. The fall in foreign lending after 1927 coincides similarly with a fall in the spread over domestic yields, however without explaining the full variation. Eichengreen (1988: 29-34) further provides econometric evidence which suggests that US lenders used higher spreads to discriminate between broad categories of risk classes of borrowers based on past debt reputation rather than on project evaluation and risk assessment at the margin. Higher spreads were charged to some of the smaller Latin American borrowers with a history of defaults (Peru, Bolivia) as well as to Eastern European borrowers; but risk premia were lower on public than on corporate bonds, German bonds and bonds issued by the larger Latin American borrowers.

Figure 4.5 United States: yield differentials on domestic and foreign bonds and foreign bond issues, 1922-29

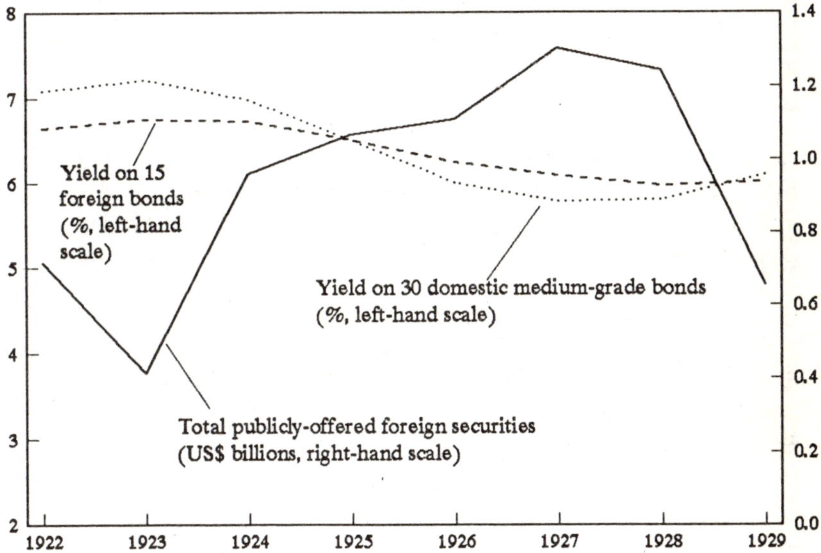

Source: Eichengreen (1988))

Eichengreen (1988: 22-28) finds further that *the size of the loans* raised in the New York market did not bear any significant relationship to *the spread*, meaning that the risk premium apparently was not used as a mechanism to deter borrowers from floating larger bond issues. The evidence does show an *inverse* relationship between the commissions charged by the banks to borrowers and the loan size. This might be associated with economies of scale in the marketing of large loans, as suggested by Eichengreen (1988: 28). However, more in line with the observations made above, this result may well relate to the increasing competition in the bond market with new entrants and collective underwriting driving down commissions and enlarging loan issues. Such an interpretation would also be consistent with the falling commissions after 1925 following the entrance of new banking houses, as documented by Lewis (1938) and Mintz (1951).

Table 4.6 Growth, trade and finance indices for industrialized countries and Latin American and Asian countries, 1929-38 (1929 = 100)

	Industrialized Countries[a]				Latin America[b]				Asia[c]			
	GDP	*Import volume*	*Terms of trade*	*Net capital outflow; 1929 prices (mln. US$)*	*GDP*	*Export volume*	*Terms of trade*	*Import volume*	*GDP*	*Export volume*	*Terms of trade*	*Import volume*
1929	100	100	100	355	100	100	100	100	100	100	100	100
1930	95	95	106	145	96	83	82	77	101	91	90	90
1931	89	90	112	-1422	90	90	67	52	101	87	84	82
1932	83	77	114	-1661	87	75	72	40	104	78	84	79
1933	84	78	115	1006	93	78	74	47	105	80	82	71
1934	89	80	111	-1254	101	79	93	55	99	83	87	77
1935	94	82	108	- 406	106	86	87	57	104	85	92	83
1936	102	86	101	- 176	113	83	96	62	110	94	95	81
1937	107	97	104	-1677	121	92	103	86	110	n.a.	n.a.	n.a.
1938	109	87	108	-1413	121	83	86	72	107	n.a.	n.a.	n.a.

Source: Maddison (1985); ECLA (1950); Thorp (1984); Mitchell (1982).

Notes: a. Weighted averages for US, Canada and major European economies, taken from Maddison (1985).
b. Weighted averages for 12 Latin American countries; GDP is for 6 countries only (Argentina, Brazil, Chile, Colombia, Cuba and Mexico), and is taken from Maddison (1985). Other variables and indicators for other Latin American countries are derived from ECLA (1950), Thorp (1984: statistical appendix) and Mitchell (1982).
c. Weighted averages for China, India, Indonesia, Korea and Taiwan taken from Maddison (1985).

Table 4.7 Dollar denominated debt owed to US and debt in default, 1935 (billions of US$)

	Debt outstanding (owed to US creditors)	**% of debt with delinquent or defaulted interest payments**
Argentina	0.33	24
Brazil	0.31	93
Chile	0.24	100
Colombia	0.14	100
Mexico	0.14	100
Other Latin America	0.36	81
Europe	2.28	51
Canada	1.83	4
China	0.02	100
Other Asia & Africa	0.69	1

Source: Lewis (1938)

Thus, the financial intermediaries showed risk-averse behaviour, but risk assessment was imperfect. Risk assessment mainly served to identify broad risk classes of borrowers leading to a heavy concentration of lending in a limited number of resource-rich countries, particularly in the Western Hemisphere. Risk premia were not used to limit loan size or exposure to high levels of indebtedness. Informational asymmetries and high commissions to be earned could lead to lending euphoria. This bond market dynamic was not dissimilar to that of the pre-war period. The limited number of potential borrowers and the loan-volume maximizing behaviour of the financial intermediaries could thus lead to high exposure of investors to some borrowing nations after a period of euphoria: fundraising for Latin American bonds was accompanied by favourable information about economic prospects in the region, publicized in the New York financial market by competing US bank managers who mediated in the foreign bond market.

4.4.4 Pro-cyclical lending and the financial crash

A crucial difference between pre- and inter-war capital movements is found in the change of conditions under which the interaction between trade and finance took place. Three major elements feature. *Firstly*, the trade policy of the major creditor countries differed: Great Britain by and large had followed free trade policies and trade was a major source of national welfare; the US was more protectionist and its external trade constituted a relatively small proportion of its GDP. *Secondly*, while British lending had been principally to countries with complementary economic structures, borrowers of US funds in the 1920s had exports which were much more competitive to the US economy. *Thirdly*, in the 1920s capital movements tended to be pro-cyclical with the US investment cycle and with trade for primary-exporting countries. Increasing domestic investment rates coincided with increasing capital exports, implying that the upward business cycle was also accompanied by higher savings rates. Available data confirm this pattern, though with deviations at turning points in peak and trough years (see Figure 4.4).[17] On the 'trade side', the lending cycle went up with exports and commodity prices, when investors were more optimistic about lending to these countries; with commodity markets down, international lending also declined, reducing the ability of borrowing countries to service their debt.

The world-wide depression of 1929-32 originated in the major economies and was transmitted to the periphery through falling demand for the latter's exports, falling commodity prices and finally a collapse of the international capital market. The pro-cyclical character of trade and finance forms the background to this process. Lack of finance contributed to the decline of international trade and *vice versa*, eventually provoking the 'Great Crash'.[18]

Table 4.6 shows the major indicators for the interaction between trade and finance in the major creditor countries and some debtor countries in Latin America and Asia. (The export volume of the sample of debtor countries in the table represents about three quarters of world exports of non-industrialized countries in 1929.)

The crisis led to a sharp fall in the import volumes of the industrialized countries, which affected Latin American and Asian export volumes even further. The terms of trade turned against the 'peripheral countries' and worsened by almost 30 per cent for Latin America and 16 per cent for Asian countries between 1929 and 1932.

A debt crisis followed, starting in 1931 with Bolivia defaulting on its dollar obligations, soon followed by most other Latin American countries (except Argentina, see Table 4.7). In 1932 and 1933 default spread to Southern and Eastern Europe, China and Germany. Default did not occur in colonies like Egypt, India, Indonesia, Korea or Taiwan, where adjustment policies were implemented by the colonial powers. The financial crisis particularly affected private capital market confidence in lending to developing countries. In effect, access by LDCs to commer-

Table 4.8 *Capital-importing countries: annual growth rates of real GDP, industrial production and export value, in the inter-war period (growth rate in percentages)*

	1925-29				1929-32				1932-38			
	GDP	*Indus. Prod.*	*Exports (US$)*	*Import value (US$)*	*GDP*	*Indus. Prod.*	*Exports (US$)*	*Import value (US$)*	*GDP*	*Indus. Prod.*	*Exports (US$)*	*Import value (US$)*
Germany	2.5	3.8	9.8	1.8	- 6.9	-15.3	-24.8	-29.6	11.8	14.8	- 1.5	2.7
Austria	2.7	6.2	3.3	3.6	- 7.1	-14.9	-29.6	-24.9	1.5	9.7	9.8	1.0
Australia	-1.1	..	- 2.7	-2.1	- 2.8	..	- 5.1	-29.3	4.5	..	6.6	16.4
Canada	6.1	3.3	- 1.6	9.9	- 9.2	- 3.2	-25.0	-29.7	4.5	8.9	9.3	6.9
Argentina	5.7	5.1	14.4	0.6	- 4.9	- 6.0	-28.5	-36.0	5.3	7.8	4.8	12.8
Bolivia	..	..	2.6	1.1	..	..	-28.0	-32.3	..	..	21.0	29.1
Brazil	7.1	4.4	- 1.8	0.3	- 0.3	- 1.4	-26.5	-36.3	6.9	10.0	7.5	17.2
Chile	9.3	-0.2	5.1	7.2	-12.5	- 8.4	-50.0	-50.9	7.6	8.8	24.6	25.7
Colombia	7.5	4.5	10.3	9.1	1.3	2.9	-18.3	-62.0	4.6	10.4	3.4	19.3
Ecuador	..	..	4.2	11.2	..	..	-17.1	-33.3	..	..	18.1	34.5
Mexico	2.1	3.8	- 4.9	- 2.0	- 5.7	-11.7	-29.4	-31.6	7.6	12.7	11.4	12.2
Egypt	..	..	- 3.6	- 1.4	..	..	-21.2	-16.4	..	..	2.5	6.1
India	1.5	..	- 4.7	1.4	0.0	..	-24.1	-18.2	0.3	..	3.5	2.7
Thailand (Siam)	..	..	- 2.6	4.0	..	..	-16.3	-23.7	..	..	9.7	5.4

Source: Thorp (ed.) (1984: Appendix), Mitchell (1978, 1982 and 1983).

cial loans was cut off until the early 1970s. Several studies (Eichengreen 1988; Lindert & Morton 1989; Eichengreen & Portes 1986, 1989) provide evidence for the conclusion that the closing down of the capital market showed hardly any differentiation between defaulting and non-defaulting countries. This 'contagion effect' mainly affected Southern borrowers and applied less to European borrowers.

4.4.5 Diverging adjustment patterns in debtor countries

In the indebted developing regions, policy responses to the financial crisis of the 1930s were diverse. Firstly, as indicated, some countries defaulted. There appears to have been an intimate relation between the probability of default and the type of trade dependence and the source of external lending. The Latin American countries that defaulted depended for roughly two thirds or more of their export earnings on US markets (Abreu 1984, Maddison 1985) and borrowed mainly from private US sources. The debtor countries relying on US markets were in general more heavily affected by the world economic crisis than those connected to European markets. The recession in the US was stronger and lasted longer than in Europe, where war preparations induced economic recovery. Most Latin American borrowers had close economic (and political) ties with the US, and default was difficult to avoid. Accumulated external debt had increased their vulnerability to external shocks. As most borrowing was undertaken by central governments, the external and internal transfer problems coincided. Central government debt-export ratios in much of Latin America had risen to over 100 per cent by 1929 (Table 4.4). Their debt-servicing capacity was reduced first by the sudden decline in lending by the US, starting in 1928 as the mounting boom on Wall Street diverted funds in the US financial market from foreign to domestic uses. This was followed by the collapse of primary commodity markets, which in most countries simultaneously eroded export earnings and tax income. The ultimate decision to default may still have been political, as argued by Eichengreen & Portes (1989), but it was obvious that with few prospects for new lending most countries were left little room to manoeuvre. With one country announcing default, others soon followed.

In contrast, Argentina, with the UK as principal creditor and export market, did not default on its major debt holdings; only 10 per cent of its exports went to the US. British recovery was more rapid than in the US and as a wheat exporter Argentina suffered milder terms of trade declines than other primary exporters. External and internal political factors reduced the incentive to default further. The UK threatened to cut off imports of major Argentine products (meat and wheat), while the politically influential Argentine *latifundistas* and livestock producers pressed for protection of their private interests. The well-known Roca-Runciman Convention of 1933 formalized an arrangement that reconciled interests of UK bondholders and Argentine export sectors.[19]

Other patterns of trade and finance prevailed in Asia, as evidenced by Maddison (1985: 33-44). The Japanese colonies, Korea and Taiwan, traded mainly with Japan. Japan's effective anti-cyclical policies enabled the colonies to avoid serious payments problems. India and Indonesia, colonies of other foreign powers, tended to have geographically more diversified exports. Their reasons for not defaulting were closely related to the fact that their external borrowing and adjustment policies were conducted under the colonial regime.

Secondly, most countries initially followed adjustment policies according to the rules of the gold standard, i.e. defence of the exchange rate by import reductions, tighter fiscal and monetary policy and loss of reserves. Table 4.8 shows that import reductions in most cases exceeded the fall in export earnings between 1929 and 1932 in order to meet debt-service obligations, while avoiding exchange rate adjustment and reserve losses. As analysed by Maddison (1985), fiscal and monetary policies were similarly strict and deflationary across Asia from 1929 to 1932, but started to diverge thereafter. In India, the British government insisted on a very deflationary fiscal policy, leading to output contraction in 1929-32 and near-zero growth over the entire 1929-38 period. The extreme deflationary policies of the Dutch during the 1930s were transmitted to their colony, Indonesia. The Netherlands adhered to the gold standard until 1936. Ironically, the output contraction in the colony seemed cushioned by deflation in the Netherlands, where prices fell more dramatically than wages and salaries, leaving space for demand increases. The impact of the recession fell primarily on profits in export sectors, but did not induce major changes in the structure of the economy.

In contrast, under the extreme pressure of the depression several Latin American countries switched after 1932 to new, nationalist-developmentalist regimes of protectionism and import-substituting industrialization in an attempt to leave the primary-export growth model. As Tables 4.6 and 4.8 show, their economies quickly recovered and began to show respectable growth rates, particularly in urban and industrial sectors.[20]

4.4.6 The interwar period: conclusions

The strengthening of the US economy provided the basis for a shift from being a debtor country to becoming the major creditor country. This was facilitated by institutional changes in the domestic financial system which made foreign lending attractive. New investment houses and their foreign branches provided market leadership similar to that of the intermediaries in the pre-war London market. Spurts in lending that could occur in the struggle for market shares (and thus for the commissions and fees) were no longer mitigated at the macroeconomic level as the US business cycle and market for debtor-country exports interacted pro-cyclically with the international bond market. These factors made the system prone to crises, more so than in the pre-war period, and a deep financial and economic crisis emerged in the 1930s. Strong interdependence with the US economy appeared to enhance the probability to default. Defaulting debtor countries, outside Europe, had both close economic ties with the US and high central government external debts.

4.5 1946-72: Two Capital Market Segments – Aid and Direct Investment

4.5.1 The end of international financial intermediation

The US continued to be the major creditor country after World War II. The Bretton Woods system established US dominance over the international monetary system with the dollar as the main reserve currency. Most capital movements took place among the industrialized countries. Three types of flows dominated financial interactions in the North. The Marshall Plan dominated in the first years after the war and constituted inter-governmental capital transfers between the US and the European allies. Between 1948 and 1951 about US$ 11 billion was transferred, primarily in the form of aid and commodities for the reconstruction of industry and infrastructure (OECD 1985). The ending of Marshall plan aid produced a slight fall in the US net capital export position in the early 1950s (Table 4.9). Almost immediately, the aid flows were replaced by direct private investment induced by Western European recovery. With economic recovery, capital markets in Europe and the US started to integrate. The late 1950s marked the inception of Eurocurrency markets, when European banks started to deal in dollar deposits using money held by large US companies (see e.g. Dufey & Giddy 1978).

This financial innovation induced the shift away from the dollar reserve adjustment to maintain fixed exchange rates, to a more global dollar as the source of autonomous capital movements. However, the rapidly growing international financial intermediation remained restricted to the economies of the industrialized countries that organized their policy coordination through the creation of the OECD in 1960.

Capital movements towards developing areas remained marginal in terms of volume, but their nature changed dramatically. Whereas previously most of these capital flows were mediated through the international financial (bond) markets, *direct* capital flows became dominant in this period. There were two main segments, one of direct capital transactions (direct investment) between the private sectors of capital-exporting and capital-importing countries and another constituting inter-governmental lending. Bond markets remained shut for Southern borrowers, but direct investment seemed safe and profitable ventures in some resource-rich countries for firms looking for new markets or vertical integration of firms. This applied in particular to Latin America, where in response to the crisis of the 1930s trade regimes had shifted to-

Table 4.9 US net capital exports,[a] 1946–61 (billions of US$)

	Private	Public	Total Net Capital Export (ΔF)	Net Capital Export/GNP (%) (ΔF/GNP=CAB/GNP)
1946-48: Total	0.7	2.8	3.5	1.5
Europe & Canada	0.1	2.4	2.5	
Latin America	0.3	0.1	0.4	
Other[b]	0.3	0.3	0.6	
1949-55: Total	1.0	0.3	1.3	0.4
Europe & Canada	0.5	0.1	0.6	
Latin America	0.2	0.1	0.3	
Other[b]	0.3	0.1	0.4	
1956-61: Total	3.3	0.8	4.1	0.9
Europe & Canada	1.7	-0.1	1.6	
Latin America	0.7	0.3	1.0	
Other[b]	0.9	0.6	1.5	

Sources: US Department of Commerce, Balance of Payments supplement (1961); IMF, International Financial Statistics (computer tapes 1987).

Notes: a. Annual averages
b. Including international institutions.

wards import-substituting industrialization. Industrial investment protected by high tariff barriers and cheap domestic credits provided profitable ventures for private investors. US multinational firms jumped the tariff barriers by setting up or buying Latin American enterprises. According to Griffith-Jones (1984), these private capital flows constituted two thirds or more of total external capital from the US to Latin America in this period.

Although – mainly for political reasons[21] – no Marshall Plan was designed for developing countries, official flows to developing regions became a major source of external finance. This was at least in part a result of the spirit of multilateralism that emerged among the countries of the Western bloc in the 1940s as a response to the experience of the 1930s when a lack of policy coordination had prolonged the crisis (see e.g. Das 1986, OECD 1985). It also led to a new approach to relations between rich and poor countries. In Europe, full employment and high social welfare standards became major objectives of mainstream political parties. The interest in domestic welfare was extended to support for

Table 4.10 External financial resources to developing countries (percentage shares)

	1960-61	1970-72	1975	1980	1985	1987
Aid	56	47	39	41	44	54
Bilateral	54	37	30	31	34	43
Multilateral[a]	2	10	9	10	10	11
Other official	13	9	11	13	17	10
Private	31	44	50	46	39	36
Direct investment	19	17	20	11	8	23[b]
Bank sector	6	16	21	23	16	6
Bonds	n.a.	2	1	1	6	1
Private export credits	6	9	8	11	2	2
Other private					7	4
Total	100	100	100	100	100	100
US$ bn, 1983 prices	34.8	53.6	84.6	93.9	92.3	64.1

Sources: OECD (1985, 1988).

Notes: a. Multilateral aid includes grants by private voluntary agencies.
b. Includes OECD flows to off-shore banking centres.

decolonization and assistance to developing countries in order to enable these to 'catch up' with the industrialized countries. In the evolution of aggregate aid flows two major periods can be distinguished up to the early 1970s (OECD 1985: 92-100): 1950s to early 1960s and early 1960s to 1970. In the first period there was a rapid build-up of economic assistance. Aid flows increased significantly, both in volume and as shares in the donor countries' GNP (Figures A4.5 and A4.6). By 1960 bilateral aid flows had become the major source of external finance to LDCs (Table 4.10). OECD donor countries supplied nearly all development assistance. The United States alone accounted for about half of aid flows until the early 1960s. These were mainly allocated as non-project assistance to countries along the periphery of the Sino-Soviet bloc in the days of the Cold War. Political motives derived from past colonial rela-

Table 4.11 Capital-importing developing countries: net capital inflows, fiscal deficits and private savings-investment balances, 1956-71 (percentage of GDP)

	1956-61	1962-67	1968-72
Aid-reliant countries[a]			
Savings	13.6	12.9	13.8
Investment	17.2	17.8	17.9
Net capital inflows	3.6	4.9	4.1
Fiscal deficit[b]	4.2	4.7	3.7
Private savings gap[c]	-0.6	0.2	0.4
Private borrowers[d]			
Savings	14.9	17.3	19.3
Investment	17.6	18.6	22.8
Net capital inflows	2.7	1.3	3.5
Fiscal deficit[b]	1.4	1.5	1.6
Private savings gap[c]	1.3	-0.2	1.9

Source: IMF, *International Financial Statistics* (computer tapes).

Notes:
a. Sample of 48 developing countries which had more than two thirds of external finance from official sources around 1970 (measured in terms of flows).
b. Central government budget only.
c. Negative sign means private sector savings surplus.
d. Sample of 33 developing countries which had more than 50 per cent of external finance from private sources around 1970 (measured in terms of flows).

tionships tended to shape the aid programmes (including their geographical distribution) of the other major donors (particularly the UK and France) during this period (see also Chapter 3).

In the second period, after 1963, the growth of bilateral aid flows tended to stagnate. American economic aid to LDCs peaked during the Kennedy administration (1961-63), rising from 0.4 to 0.6 per cent of US GNP.[22] However, increasing US budget deficits and increasingly hostile public opinion in the wake of the Vietnam war finally led to a reduction in US foreign aid relative to GNP (OECD 1985: 99). There was also a drop in foreign assistance by the other major donor countries. French aid in particular declined substantially in the first half of the 1960s, with a sharp reduction in aid to Algeria following that country's independence. At the same time, however, the downward drift in aid from the major donor countries was partly compensated by increases in aid from 'new donors', including Germany, Japan, the Scandinavian countries and the Netherlands.

From the early 1960s until 1972 the importance of multilateral aid flows increased substantially: multilateral agencies increased their share in total financial resource flows to developing countries from 2 per cent in 1960-61 to 10 per cent in 1972 (see Table 4.10).

4.5.2 Macroeconomic role

Economic development in the first two decades after World War II took place in a context of rapid trade expansion. Capital flows probably played an initiating role, in particular through Marshall Plan aid, but within the overall pattern capital flows played a limited role. Net capital flows of the major creditor country, the US, fell from an initial 1.5 per cent of GNP in 1946-48 to 0.4 per cent in 1949-55 and remained less than 1.0 per cent thereafter (Table 4.9). Also in the surplus countries in Europe, capital exports fluctuated between 1 and 2 per cent of GNP in the period. On average between 0.3 and 0.5 per cent of surplus countries' GNP was transferred to developing countries.

The relative importance of capital imports in developing countries was more diverse, ranging between zero and 10 per cent of GNP. On average the macroeconomic importance of foreign capital inflows was substantially larger for the low-income, newly independent countries relying on aid flows than for richer countries that received direct private investment. The average for the mid-1960s for the former group was 4.9 per cent of GDP; for 'private borrowers' a low 1.3 per cent of GDP. On average, national savings rates have been substantially higher in the richer developing countries (see Table 4.11).

4.5.3 Cyclical pattern of trade and finance

The interactions of the driving forces of capital flows in world economic adjustment differed from the previous periods. While trade and finance became increasingly integrated between the countries of the Western industrialized world, capital flows to developing regions were largely exogenous to the recipient countries.

Bilateral aid flows primarily served particular political interests and concerns of donor countries (see above and Chapter 3). Direct private investment flowed mainly to resource-rich countries. Investment decisions are taken by large multinational firms, which emerge as a potent force in this period. Theories and empirical analyses of the international firm contend that profits earned on capital invested abroad are probably only one factor underlying such investments. Such decisions are part of a complex of industrial strategy considerations, like diversification, international backward integration by easing the supply of raw materials, overcoming import restrictions, creating new markets, etc. (cf. Hymer 1976, Hufbauer 1975, Dunning 1970 and Chapter 3).

Capital flows by their nature were not prone to debt crises, but appeared, as in the previous periods, largely supply-determined. Perhaps to a much greater extent than in previous periods of long-term private lending, post-war suppliers of funds played a significant role in determining the domestic allocation of the capital inflows. Aid agencies tied lending status to the use of funds and much of the money took the form of project lending subject to project evaluation by the donor. Multinational firms invested according to their market and firm strategy. These mechanisms underlying the supply of foreign savings to developing countries are likely to have had some impact on their macroeconomic adjustment processes.

Aid flows were mainly absorbed by the public sector and financed social and general economic infrastructure. In the 1960s, about a quarter of bilateral aid went to health, education and other social services, while a third was allocated to energy and transport (OECD 1972, 1985). Such uses of aid would support long-term development goals and a mainstream assumption was that, at the macroeconomic level, positive wealth effects would soon be felt. This view was challenged by some in the late 1960s (e.g. Griffin 1970) who argued that foreign aid inflows might have a negative impact on domestic savings and therefore on growth.[23] More recently, the mechanisms underlying macroeconomic adjustment effects in response to aid flows have been analysed with more depth (e.g. Mosley 1987), but without conclusive results. Hypotheses include that recurrent expenditures by recipient governments will increase with the amount of aid and the number of donors because a multiplicity of donors will require more bureaucracy, that maintenance and other local costs will have to be carried by the recipient agent and – perhaps even more importantly – that a fungibility problem may exist, i.e. the resources released by aid money may be used for other, non-investment purposes (Mosley 1987: 85-111). It could thus be hypothesized that aid flows reduce public savings and induce larger budget deficits. Table 4.11 suggests that aid-reliant countries sustained relatively high fiscal deficits in the 1950s and 1960s.

Direct foreign investments were not primarily related to fiscal balances, but generally showed more immediate trade links: (i) demand for imports (raw materials, capital goods) went up; (ii) export production also went up, but in this period a large share of private investment, particularly in Latin America, went into import-substitution industries with little export expansion; and (iii) profit remittances were quite substantial in some cases. Unfortunately, evidence on this subject and on the macroeconomic performance of private direct investment is mostly impressionistic and fragmentary (Dunning 1970; Hufbauer 1975).

In terms of the global adjustment process, these capital movements were probably of marginal importance. It was a period of rapidly expanding trade and aid flows and direct investments to developing countries provided the latter with more foreign exchange to add to this expanding world demand. In this sense one could also speak in this period of a *procyclical* interaction of trade, growth and capital movements. Further, the poor functioning of the gold (exchange) standard in the interwar period had led to its abolishment and it was replaced after World War II by the Bretton Woods system of targeted exchange rate stability at par values expressed in terms of gold or the US dollar. The rules of the game no longer prescribed monetary restriction as the key adjustment mechanism to accommodate reserve losses and to keep exchange rates within the agreed 1%-margin of par values. The gold standard rules were predominantly replaced by discretionary Keynesian demand management. Demand expansion could avoid adjustment costs in the form of output losses as long as there were unemployed resources. The system was viable as long as payments imbalances remained relatively small but proved unsustainable in the longer term. Triffin (1960) was among the first to reveal the system's weaknesses: a growth in dollar reserves generated by the US through a payments deficit was required to maintain world trade expansion as there was no other source of reserve growth. Triffin argued that the US could not expand short-term liabilities infinitely while keeping gold assets constant and sustain the fixed dollar price of gold. The system faced a dilemma, now known as the *Triffin dilemma*: the US should either adjust its payments deficit and world trade would stagnate as a result of a liquidity shortage of world reserve money, or the US would sustain its deficit and a confidence crisis would be inevitable.

As Triffin predicted, the rapid expansion of trade and macroeconomic misadjustment led the world economy into international financial problems towards the end of the 1960s. Rising budget deficits and inflationary financing in the US created tendencies towards persistent current account deficits and the over-supply of dollars. The dollar exchange rate came under pressure and in 1971 the convertibility of the dollar into gold was suspended. The major economic power was not capable of sustaining the existing monetary order of fixed exchange rates under the dollar standard. The shift to flexible exchange rate adjustment between the major currencies coincided with the first oil price rise, which brought about a major shock to the investment-savings balances in the world economy. Its consequences will be discussed in Chapter 5.

The debt problems of developing countries that occurred during this period were not directly related to the major type of capital movements, but to the accumulation of short-term debt and terms of trade losses.[24] Such problems were confined, however, to particular cases and price fluctuations in particular commodity markets important to the countries involved. A major share of these short-term debts were from official sources or officially guaranteed and were rescheduled through consultative groups such as the Paris Club. These small debt crises constituted no threat to the existing world order of trade and finance.

4.6 Some Historical Lessons

Especially preceding World War I and in the inter-war period the role of international capital movements in the world economy was very significant. The historical evidence suggests that – while specifics varied – capital movements towards developing regions were to a large extent driven from the supply-side. Loan pushing, credit rationing, unstable markets and the high concentration of available funds in a few borrowing countries have been intrinsic to the historical pattern of capital flows. The behaviour of financial intermediairies with substantial market power played an important role in this process. Such functioning of markets seems at odds with mainstream theories of international finance discussed in Chapter 3, which assume capital flows are determined by arm's length behaviour of portfolio investors operating in competitive capital markets. Risk assessment of lenders (and their intermediaries) in the bond markets of the late nineteenth century and of the 1920s and 1930s appeared, to put it mildly, to be imperfect, and oligopolistically structured systems of specialized investment houses stimulated spurts in lending which led to a concentration of lending in a limited number of borrowing nations as well as to debt crises in more than incidental cases.

The institutional setting and related microeconomic behaviour are central to the observed peaks and troughs in international lending and its concentration in particular areas. The other crucial element has been the nature of the global macroeconomic context. The essentially anti-cyclical interaction of finance and trade under British rule before 1914 provided a more stable system than the pro-cyclical interaction under US hegemony. Debt crises also occurred in the pre-1914 system, however, since the microeconomic behaviour (of commission-seeking investment bankers) in financial markets could provoke sudden spurts in lending which would not be followed by timely export growth and favourable terms of trade to finance the increased debt burden. Under these circumstances, there were periods during which the debtor countries were required to make a net financial transfer towards their creditors, while facing a 'secondary burden' in the form of falling terms of trade. This resulted in various instances in debt crises. The pro-cyclical interaction of finance and trade that dominated global adjustment in the 1920s and 1930s posed this 'transfer problem' more structurally and bond market failure was part of systemic risks embedded in the world trading and financial system.

These conclusions about the functioning of international bond markets in the 1890s and 1920s may be a relevant historical lesson to those (see e.g. Arndt & Drake 1985 and Lessard & Williamson 1985) who have recently proposed long-term bond lending to LDCs as a less risky and potentially more stable alternative source of external finance to replace the commercial bank loans that dominated the 1970s.

The analysis also indicates that capital movements generally did contribute to economic growth and development in the borrowing nations. The unpredictable volatility in the availability of foreign capital inflows provided adjustment problems. This aspect has not yet been incorporated into standard theories of foreign borrowing, such as optimal borrowing approaches and the two-gap model. The transfer process could be disruptive depending on the particular market conditions for various sources of finance. Growth costs could be severe in the wake of an emerging debt crisis.

Adjustment processes in borrowing countries in periods of debt crisis were mostly country-specific, but some patterns could be detected. In many cases, adjustment efforts were led by the major creditor country. Before 1914 borrowers investing foreign savings in export sectors had little incentive to default. The cost of defaulting was increased by close trade links with the creditor country. Investment bankers would organize debt renegotiations which usually tied export revenues to debt servicing. Politically strong social classes with export interests in the debtor countries would support such solutions. Investment bankers allowed such deals to decrease the value of foreign securities; they were only intermediaries, not final holders of the external assets. Politically motivated international lending before 1914 and most of the lending in the 1920s served export interests to a much lesser extent and played much more of a role in problems of public sector insolvency. The incentive to default appeared much greater in these cases, enhanced in the 1920s by the collapse of commodity markets, the pro-cyclical interaction of trade and finance and the lack of an international lender of last resort. Creditor government intervention to prevent defaults occurred where there was a direct political interest. Again, the intermediaries had no immediate interest in preventing defaults. The penalty was nevertheless severe for both defaulting and non-defaulting countries: denial of access to international financial markets.

In the 1970s, commercial banks would be not merely intermediaries, but also final holders of loans. As we shall see in the next chapter, a debt crisis would thus give reason for fears of financial collapse, and demand a more concerted effort to avoid massive defaults and to enforce debt contracts. The outcomes for the borrowing nations most resemble the settlements of crises in the nineteenth century: developing countries accepted the sacrifices of adjustment and large transfers of resources to abroad. The global context seems different though: pre-1914 adjustment was eased by the anti-cyclical interaction between trade and finance; post-1980 trade and finance tend to interact pro-cyclically, requiring multilateral assistance to soften the blows of adjustment.

5 Global Financial Shocks, Asymmetric Adjustment and the LDC Debt Crisis, 1970-88

5.1 Introduction

North-South financial interactions in the 1970s and 1980s rehashed episodes in the history of international finance. The new ingredient in the 1970s was large scale lending by commercial banks to developing countries. As in the nineteenth century and in the 1920s, this surge was preceded by a number of institutional innovations in private international financial markets which made sovereign lending to the South attractive business. In the most recent period access to these markets was restricted to the richer, middle-income developing countries. Shifts in global macroeconomic balances aided and abetted this new form of large scale international lending. The first oil price shock produced large savings surpluses among a small group of Middle Eastern oil-exporting economies with low domestic absorptive capacity. These surpluses were largely deposited in the international banking system. The industrialized countries of the North adjusted their emerging external imbalances fairly quickly, using deflationary policies to cut back on import demand. This reduced credit demand in the North and allowed the savings surplus heaped in the banks to be funneled to developing countries. In what turned out to be a far from efficient system of international financial intermediation, (i) trade and finance interacted pro-cyclically, as it had in the 1920s; (ii) countries with access to private capital markets benefited from the ample availability of low-cost external finance in the 1970s and adjusted spending patterns without being able to adequately calculate the future cost of borrowing; and (iii) the loans, contracted at variable interest rates, turned out to be highly unstable because the North lacked institutions to adequately coordinate international policy. The outcome was a volatile world economic situation propelling many developing countries into a severe external debt crisis in the 1980s.

This chapter tries to explain these patterns by focusing on the behaviour of the principal agents and the institutional and economic environment in which their decisions were taken, as well as by identifying a number of structural features that could explain diverging North-South adjustment patterns.

The analysis seems to find support for the hypotheses set out in Chapter 3 on oligopolistic banking behaviour, with banks actively selling loans within the credit rationing points determined by the bank managers, and political criteria dominating supply determinants in the allocation of official loans. The role of Northern governments in influencing world economic conditions and financial markets through their macroeconomic policy show that policy asymmetries between the major economies of the North have contributed to world economic instability and a damaging external environment for the indebted South in the 1980s. Policy regimes, initial structural conditions and the use of foreign finance to expand non-traded goods sectors are seen as crucial factors explaining, with hindsight, the likeliness of the occurrence of debt problems within the context of the actual global macroeconomic events. Foreign asset accumulation, a private sector response to the internal transfer problem, is part of that explanation. Northern actors appear to have more bargaining power within the system and this is reflected in the way in which international debt was managed in the 1980s.

5.2 The Pattern of North-South Financial Interactions in the 1970s and 1980s

5.2.1 Sources and uses of North-South capital movements

After having been practically excluded from such markets for thirty years, developing countries of the South regained access to private lending from the financial centres in the industrialized North in the 1970s. As the upper panel of Figure 5.1 shows, Southern borrowing from private financial markets boomed. The accumulation of reserves during most of the boom period (negative values in the lower panel of Figure 5.1) suggests that availability of external resources exceeded immediate adjustment finance requirements following the first oil-price increase. The boom in private lending ended almost as quickly as it began: after 1982 there was a steep decline and by 1985 finance from private financial markets had virtually disappeared. This decline in private lending coincided with increasing debt problems in a large number of developing countries, as indicated by the recorded arrears on debt payment obligations in the bottom panel of Figure 5.1.

Private lending took the form of medium- to long-term loans from commercial banks, largely at variable interest rates, unlike the fixed-rate

Figure 5.1 *Net financial resources to the South and use of reserves and arrears (billions of US$; upper panel shows cumulative values)*

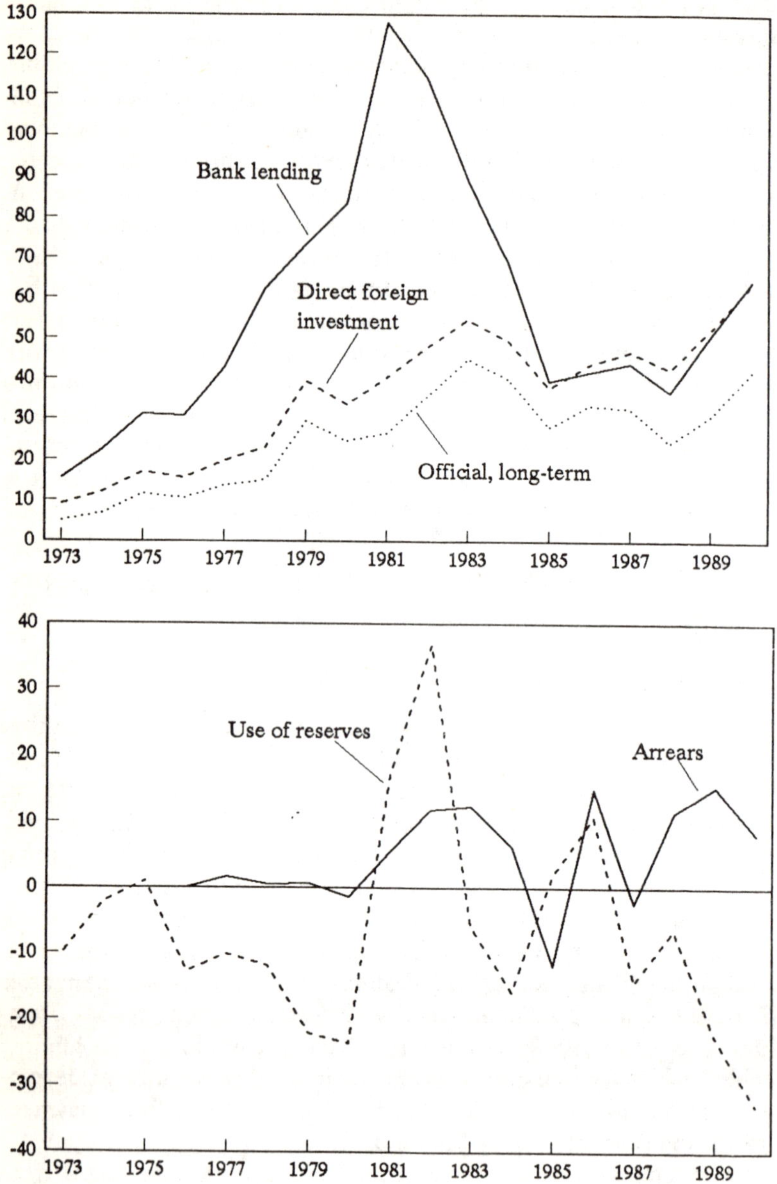

Source: IMF, *Balance of Payments Statistics* (computer tape, December 1991)

bond-financing in the 1920s. This made borrowing countries vulnerable to international financial market conditions and to macroeconomic policies in the North, which exercised considerable influence on international interest rates.

Official lending from bilateral and multilateral sources, the predominant form of development finance in the 1950s and 1960s, remains significant; although its share in the total fell in the 1970s, it became the principal source again in the 1980s with the collapse in private lending. Bilateral sources are much more important than multilateral ones, although there has been a noticeable decline. They constituted 86 per cent of total net official lending in 1970, 80 per cent in 1980 and 72 per cent in 1987 (OECD 1985, 1988 and Table 4.10).

Private direct investment remains fairly constant in absolute terms (and at current prices) at less than one quarter of total external finance over the past two decades.

As in the latter part of the nineteenth century and in the 1920s, funds from private financial markets have been concentrated in a limited number of richer (middle-income) developing countries, apparently considered more creditworthy by bankers (see below). Official flows have been supplied to both low- and middle-income countries, but to the former these constitute the principal source of external funding. Most financial resources flow to public borrowers in the South. This holds for nearly all official lending and development assistance.

Most external finance to developing countries is absorbed by the public sector. Table 5.1 shows (for a sample of 65 countries) that in 1980 80 per cent of long-term external debt was incurred by the government and public enterprise sector, up from 70 per cent at much lower debt levels in 1970. The 1980s show increasing shares of external debt owed by central governments and the central banks of these countries, a shift partly due to the 'nationalization' of much of public enterprise and private sector debts after 1982 (see also section 5.3). Aggregate data also show that around 1980 about half of long-term debt had been allocated to capital-intensive investment in infrastructure and energy. Much of this investment is essentially in non-traded activity. Some of the uses for investment in energy production are likely to have led to substitution of oil imports, although, given the nature of most projects (e.g. huge hydro-electric dams in Brazil, Ecuador and elsewhere), after long gestation lags and after the debt crisis emerged. The observed trends in sectoral uses of external borrowing are most pronounced in countries which mainly relied on finance from commercial banks (private borrowers), as shown by the more disaggregated figures in Table A5.1. Offi-

Table 5.1 *Capital-importing LDCs: outstanding long-term debt by type of borrowing institutions and sectoral allocation*[a]

	1970	1975	1980	1985	1988
Total debt country sample (n=65)[b]					
Total debt	58.0	145.9	487.9	797.1	946.5
Total long-term debt	58.0	143.4	373.6	688.8	842.5
By Institutional Borrower[c]					
Total long-term debt	100.0	100.0	100.0	100.0	100.0
Central Bank, incl. IMF credit	5.0	11.6	11.2	17.1	21.8
Central Government	43.9	38.7	39.4	46.7	54.3
Rest of General Government	1.0	1.0	1.1	1.7	0.8
Non-financial Public Enterprises	19.4	21.0	25.6	18.3	12.8
Priv. sector, incl. non-guaranteed	30.6	27.7	22.7	16.3	10.3
By Borrowing Economic Sector[c]					
Total long-term debt	100.0	100.0	100.0	100.0	100.0
Traded goods sectors[d]	14.7	16.4	17.7	16.4	15.3
Non-traded goods sectors *of which:*	59.2	61.8	63.3	55.0	52.9
– Physical infrastructure	34.3	32.7	29.3	26.5	25.3
– Energy	15.1	14.4	17.2	13.2	13.6
– Publ. adm., defence	6.3	7.0	7.8	6.8	5.2
Other allocations *of which:*	26.1	21.8	19.0	28.6	31.8
– Debt reorganization	6.1	6.5	6.2	11.5	16.5
– Balance of paym. support	11.9	8.9	7.2	7.9	8.4

Source: World Bank, *Debtor Reporting System*.

Notes: a. Sample includes 65 LDCs, of which 36 are Official Borrowers, 16 are Private Borrowers and 13 are Diversified Borrowers. See appendix table A5.1 for data by country groups.
b. In billions of US$.
c. Percentage shares.
d. Includes agriculture, forestry and fishing, mining and manufacturing industry.

cial development assistance by its nature tends to be allocated to the public sector, and OECD data (OECD 1985, 1988) indicate that, though a declining share in the 1980s, project aid is still the major form of official capital transfers (65 per cent of bilateral and 87 per cent of multilateral flows), of which on average about 60 per cent goes to investment in social and physical infrastructure.

In the second half of the 1970s and during the 1980s, a substantial amount of capital flowed *to the North* from the private sector in the South, particularly from countries with access to private financial markets. This acquisition of foreign assets by residents in the South largely took the form of bank deposits and is referred to in the literature as 'capital flight' (see also Chapter 3). Determinants of private capital outflows are discussed later in this chapter.

5.2.2 The world capital market and global macroeconomic balances

The growth in the 1970s of international private lending to developing areas is peripheral within the context of the total international flow of funds. Alongside expanding trade and internationalized production, international financial intermediation has expanded rapidly among the industrialized countries in the North since the 1950s (see e.g. Bryant 1987 for an analysis) and in the 1970s most of the world's finance was generated and absorbed in the North.

No standard quantitative measures of the world capital market exist. One possible measure would be to estimate a world aggregate of savings and investment, which could be *broadly* defined (in flow terms) as the theoretical world supply of and demand for finance. This aggregates domestic and international finance, different forms (bank loans, bonds, aid or direct investment) and different channels (self-finance or intermediation) of finance, definitionally corrected for possible double counting of sources and uses of finance.

Table 5.2 clearly shows the heavy concentration of world finance by source and use in the North. The high savers of the oil-exporting Middle East supply about 4 per cent of world savings (1 per cent of world GDP). Following the first oil-price shock of 1973/74, the savings *surplus* of these oil exporters averaged about 0.5 per cent of world GDP in the 1970s, of which more than half was deposited in banks located in the North.[1] The Southern, non-oil developing countries generate about 10 per cent of total world savings. Their average savings rate as a share in world GDP fluctuates between 2 and 3 per cent.

Table 5.3 shows the pattern along which world savings have been transacted internationally. It shows stocks and flows of *international* finance by institutional origin and aggregate country group of destination. By showing only *cross-border* sources and uses of finance, the data supply a *narrow* measure of the size and structure of the world capital market. It appears that in 1980 over two thirds of the stock of international

Table 5.2 World accumulation balances, 1965-86 (percentage of world GDP)[a]

		1965-72	1973-77	1978-82	1983-86
World					
Savings	*(S)*	22.7	23.8	22.8	20.9
Investment	*(I)*	22.5	23.3	22.8	21.0
Current Account /Net capital export[b]	*(S–I)*	0.2	0.5	0.0	-0.1
'North' (OECD)					
Savings	*(S)*	20.4	19.6	18.2	17.7
Investment	*(I)*	19.8	19.4	18.1	17.6
Current Account	*(S–I)*	0.6	0.2	0.1	0.1
of which:					
United States					
Savings	*(S)*	8.5	6.7	6.2	7.1
Investment	*(I)*	8.2	6.4	6.0	7.7
Current Account	*(S–I)*	0.3	0.3	0.2	-0.6
Germany and Japan					
Savings	*(S)*	4.9	5.8	5.7	6.0
Investment	*(I)*	4.6	5.6	5.6	5.4
Current Account	*(S–I)*	0.3	0.2	0.1	0.6
Rest OECD					
Savings	*(S)*	7.0	7.1	6.3	4.6
Investment	*(I)*	7.0	7.4	6.5	4.5
Current Account	*(S–I)*	0.0	-0.3	-0.2	0.1

(continued...)

liabilities from *private* sources and slightly less than two thirds of that from *total* sources were concentrated in the industrialized North. From Table 5.3[2] it follows that 90 per cent of outstanding international capital stems from private financial markets. Distributional parameters derived on a flow basis are similar to those derived from stock data.

The data on international private financial markets in Table 5.3 refer to commercial bank lending, international bond issues (with governments as principal users) and private export credits. The first two financial instruments predominate. The structure of these capital market segments and the growth in international bank lending to non-banking

(Table 5.2 continued)

		1965-72	1973-77	1978-82	1983-86
'South' (LDCs)					
Savings	*(S)*	2.4	4.1	4.6	3.2
Investment	*(I)*	2.7	3.9	4.7	3.4
Current Account	*(S–I)*	-0.3	0.2	-0.1	-0.2
of which:					
Major capital & oil-exporters					
Savings	*(S)*	0.2	1.0	1.2	0.9
Investment	*(I)*	0.2	0.4	0.7	1.0
Current Account	*(S–I)*	0.0	-0.6	0.5	-0.1
Capital-importing 'South'					
Savings	*(S)*	2.2	3.1	3.4	2.3
Investment	*(I)*	2.5	3.5	4.0	2.4
Current Account	*(S–I)*	-0.3	-0.4	-0.6	-0.1

Source: IMF, International Financial Statistics, computer tapes.

Notes: a. Data are derived from national accounts figures from a sample of 21 OECD countries ('North'), 5 major oil-exporters (Middle East) and 76 developing countries ('South'). See Appendix A.1 for the country listing. The world GDP is the the aggregate US dollar GDP for country sample.

b. In theory, the world accumulation or current account balance should add up to zero. The apparent discrepancy is partly due to inadequate coverage of countries, but mainly due to measurement inadequacies. Notice that this discrepancy is obtained from national accounts data. Sources of the world current account discrepancy apparent in balance-of-payments data have been analysed in IMF (1987a) and Vos (1988a) and are referred to in Chapter 2.

institutions in the 1970s can be inferred from Table 5.4.[3] From these data it appears that Southern borrowers formed an important market of new lending for the commercial banks up to 1982. In the aggregate, private capital markets almost quadrupled (in constant prices) between 1973 and 1987: from US$ 69 to 242 billion. Defined in these terms, international finance kept pace with the growth of international trade: net flows on international financial markets as a share of world merchandise imports remained fairly stable around 6 to 8 per cent. Most of the growth is due to increasing net international bank lending, largely associated with the Eurocurrency market. The ratio of new international

Table 5.3 World distribution of international assets and liabilities, 1980 (stock) and 1978-83 (flow) (in billions of US$; percentages in parentheses)

	Uses / Liabilities						
Sources / Assets	*Industrial North*	*Developing South*[a]	*Soc'ist Eastern Europe & others*	*Intern'l financ'l inst.*[b]	*Total stock (bn $)*	*Total stock (%)*	*Annual flow, (avg.) 1978-83*
Private sources	1332	533	70	[1502]	1935	(90)	257
	(69)	(27)	(4)		(100)		
Financial markets[c]	1018	416	60		1494	(69)	208
Intern'l bank dep. holdings	..	..	..	[1502]	[1502]		
Private direct investment	314	117	10		441	(21)	49
Official sources	..	220	..		220	(10)	54
		(100)			(100)		
Bilateral[d]	..	168	..		192	(8)	42
Multilateral	..	52	..		52	(2)	12
Total (non-bank liab.)	1332	753	70		2155	(100)	311
	(62)	(35)	(2)		(100)		
Source by region							
Total	1332	753	70	1502	3657	(100)	
'North' (direct)	286[e]	299	10	1041	1636	(45)	
Intern'l fin. system (indirect)	993	394	60	26	1473	(40)	
'South'	53	45	..	419	517	(14)	
Other	..	15	..	16	31	(1)	

Sources: World Accounting Matrix (WAM): Debt-Claim Matrix, 1980 (Vos 1989) and the sources mentioned there. For data on the stock of direct foreign investment: IMF (1985); OECD (1987); and Dunning and Cantwell (1987).

Notes:
a. Including major oil exporters of Middle East.
b. Refers to commercial banking system, multilateral financial institutions and IMF.
c. Includes cross-border bank lending, international bonds, private export and supplier credits.
d. Includes outstanding official and officially supported export credits.
e. Refers to stock of foreign direct investment only. No data available on stock value of other intra-industrialized country capital transfers.

Table 5.4 Size of private international financial markets, 1973-87 (billions of US$)

	1973	1974	1975	1976	1977	1978	1979	1980	1981	1982	1983	1984	1985	1986	1987
Total int. lending through banks and bond markets	*40*	59	*58*	*96*	*95*	*114*	*148*	*179*	*194*	*144*	*131*	*152*	*182*	*252*	*329*
of which:															
Industrial countries	19	27	24	50	59	52	85	109	121	94	85	113	119	191	320
Developing countries	14	19	24	32	28	44	48	57	55	37	28	15	18	-1	-6
Int. bonds (net)	*7*	*9*	*18*	*26*	*27*	*24*	*23*	*19*	*29*	*49*	*46*	*62*	*77*	*87*	*59*
Industrial countries	3	5	14	19	20	14	15	13	22	39	36	51	63	77	50
Developing countries	1	1	1	2	3	4	3	2	2	3	2	3	4	2	-1
Int. bank lending (net)	*33*	*50*	*40*	*70*	*68*	*90*	*125*	*160*	*165*	*95*	*85*	*90*	*105*	*165*	*270*
Industrial countries	16	22	10	31	39	38	70	96	99	55	49	62	56	121	194
Developing countries	13	18	23	30	25	40	45	55	53	34	26	12	14	-3	-5
Total lending (constant prices)	*69*	*94*	*84*	*130*	*121*	*135*	*161*	*179*	*177*	*123*	*108*	*121*	*140*	*189*	*242*
Int. bond issues (% world imports)	1.3	1.1	2.1	2.7	2.5	1.9	1.5	1.0	1.5	2.7	2.7	3.5	4.3	4.4	2.5
Int. bank lending (% world imports)	6.0	6.2	4.8	7.4	6.3	7.1	7.9	8.2	8.6	5.3	5.1	5.1	5.8	8.3	11.4
Int. bond issues (% int. bank lending)	21.2	18.0	45.0	37.1	39.7	26.7	18.4	11.9	17.6	51.6	54.1	68.9	73.3	52.7	21.9

Sources: Watson et al. (1986, 1988); OECD, *International Financial Market Trends* (various issues); BIS/OECD, *Statistics on External Indebtedness* (various issues).

bond issues to bank lending fell to 0.12 in 1980, down from 0.45 in 1975. In the course of the 1980s, however, international bond issuing increased rapidly, constituting mainly transactions among industrialized countries. This shift towards bonds is closely linked with fiscal policies in the major economies, particularly public borrowing by the US government (Watson et al. 1988; see also below).

Besides changes in the relative importance of capital market instruments there were noticeable shifts in market shares of Northern and Southern borrowers. Developing countries' participation in international financial markets was virtually negligible in the 1960s, but between 1973 and 1981 they took a share of 35 per cent of total lending from these markets and even 38 per cent of net international bank lending. These shares fell to below 10 per cent, however, after 1982.

Thus, in terms of the *narrow* international financial market concept, the South took a substantial share of private (bank) lending in the 1970s. However, if the *broad* world capital market concept (which reflects more properly the actual *command* over financial resources) is applied to this market segment, the share is much smaller.

Finally, the changes in the structure of the international capital market are closely related to shifts in the global pattern of savings, investment and current account balances. As Table 5.2 indicated, the shift from the North towards the major oil-exporters as the country group with the major savings surplus followed the first oil price increase. After relatively quick adjustment in the North, widening external and internal imbalances in the 1970s mainly show up in the major oil exporters (surplus) and the rest of the South (deficit), both in the order of 0.5 to 0.6 per cent of world GDP. In the 1980s, after the debt crisis, global macroeconomic imbalances mainly show up in the North, with the United States showing a large deficit and Germany and Japan a savings surplus of about equal size (0.6 per cent of world GDP), leaving a minor share of global savings to finance deficits in the South.

5.2.3 Principal actors

The international flow-of-funds system in the 1970s and 1980s included six major actors: public and private sectors in both North and South, international banks and multilateral financial institutions. Focusing on North-South financial interdependence, the remainder of this chapter will concentrate on the behaviour of four of them: (i) international commercial banks, the major suppliers of funds to the South in the 1970s; (ii) creditor country governments in the North, as principal suppliers of official funds to the South and as managers of the international financial system through their financial policies; (iii) governments in the South as principal borrowers; and (iv) private agents in the South, particularly with regard to their role in moving large sums of foreign exchange back to the North (capital flight). Private agents in the North will be examined in terms of their role in the macroeconomic adjustment process in the North and its impact on the world capital market. Multilateral financial institutions have not played a major role as suppliers of funds, but more crucially in the management of the debt crisis of the 1980s. The analysis of this process is not a major objective of this chapter (but see e.g. Griffith-Jones 1988). The major oil exporters could be seen as a seventh actor (as principal OPEC members). Their behaviour will not be analysed in depth either, but – strongly simplified – it will be assumed they exercise considerable influence on international oil prices and have preferred to invest the major share of their surpluses in international financial markets.[4]

5.3 The Supply-side: Institutional Determinants of Capital Flows to the South

Expanding international financial intermediation and the recycling of oil surpluses by the international banking system in the 1970s have been seen by some observers as signs of a growing integration and enhanced efficiency of the world capital market, i.e. corresponding more closely to textbook descriptions of a fully integrated capital market (see e.g. McKinnon 1977, Harberger 1980, Obstfeld 1986, Bruno 1984). The hypothesis of increased global capital market integration has been examined through numerous empirical tests, but there is still an ongoing debate whether these provide conclusive evidence (see the discussion in Bryant 1987: 76-86; IMF 1991 and Frankel 1991). Quite some ink has been spilled over one particular type of test, namely the hypothesis that zero cross-country correlations between domestic investment and national savings rates might reflect perfect capital mobility. This hypothesis was first put forward by Feldstein & Horioka (1980). The argument runs as follows. There is no presumption that each national economy will run balanced external accounts with others. Some run a current account surplus (and thus savings surpluses), others deficits. Capital moves between the countries to finance the imbalances. As suggested in Chapter 4, this process cannot go on forever, because the countries that run deficits accumulate liability positions, and the creditworthiness of the deficit countries will decline over time. However, within efficient national capital markets imbalances can be readily and smoothly financed and market adjustment will be painless. A single, efficient world capital market would emerge if current account imbalances around the world could be smoothly financed. In such a world national savings decisions would be detached from investment decisions, since domestic investors could rely on external finance. Countries with high savings levels need not necessarily have high investment levels, as their surpluses can flow elsewhere. Countries with low savings may have high investment levels as finance is readily available from outside. The test is thus: are saving rates correlated with investment rates? If so, one would conclude, the capital market cannot be fully integrated.

Feldstein & Horioka (1980) found a significant and close correlation, which was interpreted as evidence of low capital mobility. Subsequent papers have mainly reproduced this result,[5] although some recent applications point out that savings-investment correlations have declined across industrialized countries over the past quarter of a century and particularly during the 1980s (Vos 1988b, Dean et al. 1990). The correlations for developing countries have remained consistently high, despite the apparent increased access to financial markets in the 1970s (Vos 1988b, Aghevli et al. 1990). These results may be interpreted as showing both increased Northern financial integration and a strengthening of a North-South dichotomy in access to the global capital market.

Frankel (1991) indicates that the Feldstein-Horioka test rests on the crucial assumption that real interest rates must equalize with perfect capital mobility. If not, low savings can crowd out investment by raising the real cost of borrowing. This also implies that no other factors link savings and investment such that they are correlated across countries. This is questionable, of course, as income growth, demographic factors, government policies and so on are generally seen as factors affecting savings and investment decisions (e.g. Aghevli et al. 1990). Frankel suggests one should take the *covered* real interest parity as the real test of the existence of capital mobility. Covered-interest parity is defined as the case when capital flows equalize interest rates across countries if contracted in a common currency, i.e. if exchange rate risks would have been eliminated. A recent IMF study (IMF 1991: 7-10), gives evidence that this parity has been achieved across the major industrialized countries. Capital markets thus seem fully integrated. Actual real interest rate differentials merely reflect an exchange-rate risk premium. If this is true, then apparently exchange rate volatility make capital markets behave as if they were segmented, even though they are integrated. It may also be, as argued in a review of these issues in *The Economist* (Crook

1992: 24), that the capital markets in the industrialized world are well enough integrated to be the source of exchange-rate and, thus, of interest-rate and economic instability, so as to limit macroeconomic policy control.

Capital markets thus may have become more integrated in the industrialized world, while the developing countries have remained largely at the margin of this process. The correlation of savings and investment has remained high in the developing world, as indicated. A test for covered real interest rate parity is almost impossible and seemingly irrelevant, due to a general lack of currency convertibility and strongly segmented domestic capital markets and financial control measures, which imply that real interest rates do not reflect market conditions.

Moreover, the tests of capital mobility mentioned above say little about the institutional structure of capital markets and the reasons why developing countries do not have ready access to international finance in order to accommodate current account imbalances. The focus in this section will be on these latter aspects and more particularly on the two major market segments in lending to the South during the 1970s and 1980s identified in the previous section: commercial bank lending and official capital flows.

5.3.1 Oligopolistic banking

International bank lending to the South cannot be simply linked to the first oil price shock and a recycling of oil surpluses. Institutional changes in commercial banking in the major economies of the North, initiated in the 1950s, provided incentives to international lending. The shifts in global current account balances provided the macroeconomic context to this process, with lower credit demand in the North and new liquidity arising from savings surpluses deposited by oil exporters. The ground for the growth in international bank lending in the 1970s was prepared by a gradual deregulation of capital markets in the industrialized countries.

After World War II domestic capital markets were subject to a wave of control measures. Bryant (1987) argues that policy makers tended to blame capital flows for the recession and imbalances of the 1930s. The first steps towards gradual financial deregulation were taken at the end of the 1950s and led to the creation of the Eurocurrency market (see e.g. Dufey & Giddy 1978 and Williamson 1983 for a description).[6]

In the 1970s two new impulses led to the further expansion of Eurobank activity. The first relates to the fall of the Bretton Woods system of fixed exchange rates and the delinking of the dollar from the gold price.

The Smithsonian Agreement of December 1971 introduced the floating of the major currencies. In general, flexible exchange rates made fixed-interest bearing bonds riskier than Eurocurrency bank loans and deposits at floating interest rates. The second impulse came from the 'real' side, i.e. the surpluses of the major oil exporters after 1974, who stored most of their new wealth in the Eurocurrency market.

How did developing countries gain access to international bank finance? As described in Chapter 4, prior to the 1970s most capital flows to the South consisted of official flows. Developing countries were not regarded as creditworthy in private capital markets, except for low risk flows like trade-related suppliers' credits and transnational company-controlled direct investment. A particular risk factor considered by creditors in this market is that of sovereign risk, i.e. the non-enforceability of loan contracts in international lending.[7] The recent growth in the share of private financial flows to developing countries is related to two types of institutional changes. Firstly, a number of sovereign risk-reducing financial innovations raised the expected profitability of international lending. This set of determinants is stressed by the 'neo-orthodox' credit-rationing literature (see Chapter 3). Secondly, new entrants in the bank-loan market triggered oligopolistic competition struggling for market shares. These two types of institutional changes are linked processes and both are important for assessing the behaviour of the banks in the 1970s and 1980s.

Three risk-reducing financial innovations stand out. Firstly, central banks and deposit insurance agencies in the industrialized countries have gradually assumed a larger portion of the default risk of the deposit and debt liabilities of the main banks (see Watson et al. 1984 and Folkerts-Landau 1985 for details).[8]

Secondly, developing country governments were asked to provide public guarantees as a condition in bank-loan contracts. This has strengthened the effectiveness of cross-default clauses as these would apply if an individual borrower (the government, its agencies or any private agent that managed to get a public guarantee) defaulted on one of its loans. The system of public guarantees implies the aggregation of risks of individual borrowers in a country. Creditors no longer needed be concerned with the ability of the individual borrower to pay its debt service, but rather with the ability to pay of the borrowing country as a whole, and, since public sectors assume responsibility, with the taxing capacity of the government. During the 1970s bankers actually believed that this was the best insurance against sovereign risk. Citicorp chairperson Walter Wriston justified the heavy lending to developing countries by declaring that 'countries never go bankrupt' (cited in Sachs 1989: 8). Private sector external debt is thus implicitly socialized. After 1982, governments of most developing debtor countries actually took over most of the debt incurred by the resident private sector.

Thirdly, international banks formed loan syndicates which allowed for risk-sharing and for the effective introduction of cross-default clauses, thus raising the cost of default: developing country debt would be collectively monitored and borrowers in default could be denied access to the international banking markets and be threatened with having their external economic relations interrupted (banks could agree to stop trade credits). Loan syndication would thus prevent a borrower from selectively defaulting on loans owed to a subset of lenders. The bulk of commercial borrowing by developing countries in the 1970s came from such bank syndicates acting together in the world financial centres and mostly using Eurocurrency market funds (Folkerts-Landau 1985, Watson et al. 1984, Makin 1984, Ensign 1988; see also below).

Apart from reducing sovereign risk, a number of studies have stressed another important incentive for putting together loan syndicates: *bank commissions* (see Makin 1984: 139, Lewis & Davis 1987, Darity & Horn 1988: 87-88). This was nothing new (see Chapter 4). Loan syndicates proved immediately rewarding because substantial loan fees could be received upon formation of the consortium. These fees or bank commissions were attractive: they were paid in advance, were as a rule collected separately from the borrower, were risk-free and could represent up to *1 per cent* of the total value of a loan.[9] This attracted new entrants to the market and it was, of course, also a motive for economies of scale in banking: the larger the loan, the greater the immediate gains (see also below).

The risk-reducing and rewarding factors not only made international lending to developing countries more attractive, they also seem to have destabilized the international bank loan market by reducing the threshold for new entrants. This, together with the massive liquidity heaped in the international banking system in the early 1970s, may provide support for the hypotheses, put foward in another branch of the literature, that banks engaged in an oligopolistic price competition (Devlin 1986) and 'pushed' loans onto borrowers (Darity & Horn 1988).

The financial innovations took place in what was initially a highly concentrated banking market. Devlin (1986: 150-52) cites evidence showing that since the late 1950s there has been a high and stable concentration worldwide of the banking sector. The top 100 banks owned three quarters of total assets and there was an overwhelmingly dominant position for US banks. Seventy per cent of the total assets of the top ten banks in the early 1970s were held by six US banks (*The Banker*, June 1971: 663-84). International lending in the 1970s was also heavily concentrated in the large banks. Estimates indicate that the top 20 banks (worldwide) accounted for half of the value of international lending and by the end of 1982 the nine largest US banks controlled 60 per cent of international lending and the top 25 controlled 80 per cent (Devlin 1986: Table 22). These banks also directed most of the lending towards the South. Table 5.5 indicates that the largest banks also organized the major share of syndicated loans in the 1970s. In the initial, post-oil crisis period of 1975-77 the top ten mobilized 80-90 per cent of total syndicated loans. This share decreased to roughly one half in the peak years of bank lending to the South, 1978-81, perhaps reflecting oligopolistic competition over market shares. There are two types of complementary evidence to support this hypothesis:

(1) The falling share of the lead banks in total loan syndication suggests an increasing number of *new entrants* to the market. The financial innovations mentioned earlier had reduced the barriers to entry into this market. An estimated 66 banks annually entered the syndicated lending market over 1973-80 (Page & Rodgers 1982: 64, cited in Devlin 1986: Table 20). The challenge to the leading banks came particularly from European banks and regional US banks.

(2) Oligopoly theory (see Clarke 1985 and Chapters 3 and 6) suggests that lowering the barriers to entry and a large number of new entrants may lead to *oligopolistic price competition* over market shares. If this was the case, one would expect a strong fall in spreads, a leng-

Table 5.5 Cumulative distribution of the value of loan syndication among the major banks, 1975-81 (percentage)

	1975	1976	1977	1978	1979	1980	1981
Banks by size							
Top 5	65	67	60	25	33	28	49
Top 10	86	90	79	44	50	47	64
Total	100	100	100	100	100	100	100
Number of listed banks	15	20	20	50	50	50	40

Source: Devlin (1986: Table 23).
Note: Size is defined by value of total assets. The top ten banks are as reported in *The Banker*, 'The Top 300', June 1976: 653-97.

thening of maturities and a high volume of lending. Available evidence seems to confirm this. Figure 5.1 shows that bank lending peaked in 1978-82, despite the fact that world economic conditions worsened and the principal borrowing countries already showed high debt-to-export ratios and signs of emerging payments problems (see below). Average maturities on new bank loans increased from 8.4 years in 1976 to 9.5 in 1981 for all developing countries and from 6.6 to 8.5 for Latin American borrowers.[10] The decline in spreads on international bank loans in the second half of the 1970s is pictured in Figure 5.2: the average bank loans to developing countries fell from 1.8 percentage point over the London Interbank Offered Rate in 1976 to below 1 per cent in 1978-81. However, given the low real interest rates in the second half of the 1970s (see Figure 5.6) and the front-end fees on syndicated loans to be paid by borrowers, price

Figure 5.2 Interest rate spreads on publicly guaranteed loans above LIBOR, 1974-87 (percentages, annual averages)

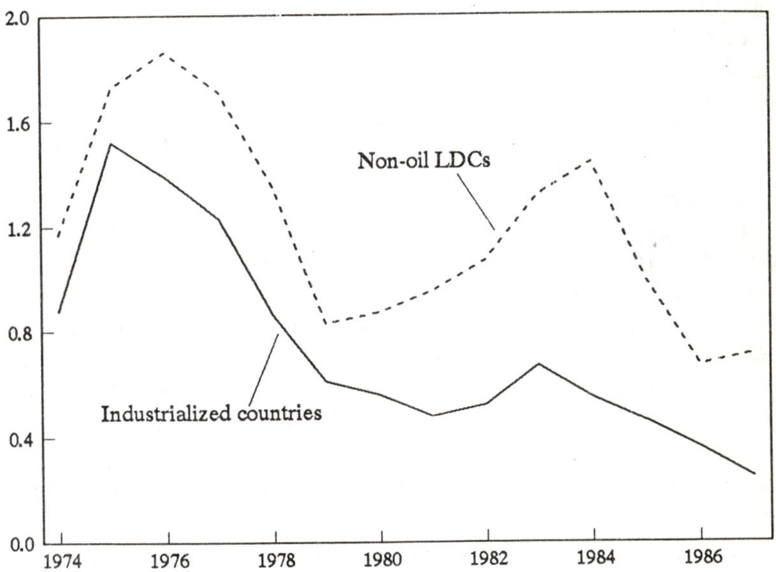

Sources: OECD, *International Financial Market Trends* (various issues); World Bank, *Debtor Reporting System*

> competition may have been much less vigorous than suggested by authors like Devlin (1986). Lewis & Davis (1976) give supporting evidence for downgrading the importance of price competition and observe that the determination of spreads in the 1970s was linked to front-end fees assessed as closing costs on syndicated loans. For borrowers it was sometimes felt politically convenient to have a low publicized spread, which was then traded against payment of a higher, non-publicized commission.

Further supporting evidence has been provided by Ensign (1988). Ensign provides data on modal spreads and loan amounts received from US commercial banks for 48 developing countries during the mid 1970s to the mid 1980s. After ranking the countries by the amounts received (rank 1 for largest sums) and the terms of lending (rank 1 for lowest spread), a high and positive Spearman rank correlation coefficient (r_s) of 0.60 was derived (calculated from Ensign 1988: Table 4.19, pp. 65-66). Data covering the period preceding the lending boom (1972-74) indicated an inverse relationship (r_s = -0.25). Thus, the relationship between the U.S. commercial banks and LDC borrowers changed considerably. Before the lending boom, lending behaviour seemed more conservative: the higher the amounts supplied the higher the spread. During the lending boom an aggressive image comes to the fore: the larger the loan amounts, the lower the spreads. This finding can be explained by both the increased competition in the loan market *and* the commissions earned by the loan syndicate managers and discounted in the publicized spread.

Falling spreads and rising loan volumes do not seem to fit the shape of the backward bending supply curve hypothesized by 'neo-orthodox' credit-rationing approaches, in which initially, at low levels of debt, the curve slopes upward. It does fit the oligopolistic banking behaviour hypothesis, as put forward by Devlin (1986) and Darity & Horn (1988): spreads were cut under a wave of competition for market shares driven by optimistic expectations of future earnings, while bank profits (and managers' fees) were maximized by maximizing the volume of lending. This hypothesis suggests a flattening of the bank-loan supply curve (or even a downward slope).

The above evidence further suggests international lending in the 1970s took place in a borrowers' market. This position has been defended by, among others, Friedman (1983: 45). However, additional evidence shows that not just any potential borrower had access to the market. Banks did not blindly maximize loan volumes. Some red lines were never crossed, particularly those encircling the low-income countries considered uncreditworthy by private creditors. Banks did try assess default risk, mainly by looking at aggregate solvency indicators (e.g. debt-export ratios). The empirical evidence indicates that risk evaluation by banks in lending to developing countries translates into credit limits varying by *country* or *risk class of countries*, not into a differentiation of spreads (as assumed in orthodox portfolio theory) or rationing points per *individual borrower*. A bank sought to place loans within the pre-determined credit ceiling per country (group). Risk assessment was thus rather crude. Market perceptions further shaped bankers' expectations and are part of the institutional setting: risk-reducing financial innovations and a concentrated market structure could trigger a generalized market optimism in the 1970s; one threat of default of a major borrower (Mexico in 1982) contaminated most of the market for other developing country borrowers.

The increased competition among banks in the 1970s could have broadened the market to include many new potential borrowers. In practice, lending was heavily concentrated among a limited number of middle-income developing countries. New entrants in the market did not appear to invest a lot in information gathering and relied instead on information available from the leading banks in the loan syndicates, which invested in information on the economic performance of potential borrowers, but with a certain bias towards countries where they had established contacts or foreign branches.[11] Credit rationing rules and oligopolistic competition for market shares thus appear as jointly operating features of the international bank loan market in the 1970s.

The following data seem to support the hypothesis that the banks used price competition within the boundaries of broadly defined credit rationing rules:

(1) Spreads on international bank loans to developing countries have been relatively small and decreasing during the lending boom. Figure 5.2 showed that public and publicly guaranteed loans from private financial markets to non-oil developing countries have been offered at less than one half of one percentage point higher than to borrowers in industrial countries.[12] Table 5.6 shows more disaggregated data on differentials in spreads among selected borrowers. Remarkably, average spreads on new loans to non-oil developing countries have been systematically below those on loans to large private US firms and those of the latter have been highly variable. Variations in spreads charged to different developing country borrowers

in turn have been very narrow and fairly stable. The spreads for the individual countries are very close to the arithmetic average for the group of non-oil developing countries as a whole. Folkerts-Landau (1985; see also Table 5.6) has shown that the difference in spreads increased slightly after the outbreak of the debt crisis in 1982 largely because most countries that rescheduled their external debt were charged the cost of rescheduling (e.g. Ecuador, Mexico, Argentina and Brazil, but not the Philippines). The change in spreads has been less, or even negative, in countries with fewer debt problems (e.g. Colombia and Korea) or where debt rescheduling raised fewer pol-

Table 5.6 Average interest rate spreads over LIBOR on publicly guaranteed loans from financial markets, 1979Q1 – 1984Q4 (spreads in percentage points; financial flows in billions of US$)

	1979(Q1) – 1982(Q1)			1982(Q2) – 1984(Q2)		
	spread		*net flow*	*spread*		*net flow*
	mean (μ)	*std deviation (σ)*		*mean (μ)*	*std deviation (σ)*	
Industrial countries	0.551	0.069		0.597	0.096	
US corporations	2.754	1.827		2.429	0.914	
Non-oil LDCs	0.878	0.109	38.5	1.244	0.460	15.3
Colombia	0.724	0.053	0.5	0.901	0.374	0.5
Chile	0.816	0.108	2.3	0.954	0.600	0.9
Ecuador	0.682	0.219	0.6	1.449	1.000	0.3
Mexico	0.642	0.149	6.0	1.423	0.843	1.7
Argentina	0.723	0.137	3.4	1.270	0.449	1.3
Indonesia	0.660	0.020	0.5	0.363	0.016	0.8
Philippines	0.951	0.316	0.6	0.790	0.342	0.6
Brazil	1.404	0.507	6.0	2.130	0.000	2.9
Korea	0.829	0.123	2.2	0.629	0.106	2.5

Sources: OECD, *International Financial Market Trends* (various issues); World Bank, *World Debtor Reporting System*; Folkerts-Landau (1985); Board of Governors of the Federal Reserve System, *Federal Reserve Bulletin* (1984).

Note: US corporations refers to large, long-term domestic bank loans with floating interest rates to US corporate firms. Spreads are measured as average bank-loan interest rate less US money centre CD (certificate of deposit) rates of return. Net flow is mean for period.

itical or renegotiation problems, (e.g. Chile and Indonesia). However, for all heavily indebted countries (except Colombia) net flows of financial resources from international financial markets fell sharply after 1982. On the whole, these observations suggest that the pricing of international commercial loans does not reflect creditors' attempts to offset the risk of default.

(2) Banks consider Southern borrowers as *a separate risk class*. This follows from, for instance, the 'Country League Tables of Creditworthiness' which multinational banks tend to use to fix credit ceilings for sovereign borrowers. Most banks keep their own records, but the ratings published in *Euromoney* may be seen as indicative: the twenty most creditworthy countries are industrialized countries plus 'offshore' financial centres like Hong Kong and Singapore.[13]

(3) *Middle-income* developing countries have greater access to the commercial bank loan market. Development level and the structural features of LDCs, like economic size and natural resource endowment, appear to be *a priori* creditworthiness criteria separating Southern borrowers into different risk classes. Low-income and resource-

Table 5.7 Capital-importing LDCs: cross-section analysis of access to private capital markets and level of development

Regression equation: $\ln F_p/F_{tot}$ =	a +	$b\ln(GNP/POP)$	$+ c\ln POP$	R^2	DW	n
1970	-5.11	0.67	0.02	0.29	2.08	66
	(-6.72)*	(5.02)*	(0.23)			
1975	-6.85	0.83	0.17	0.30	1.78	66
	(-6.66)*	(5.16)*	(1.97)*			
1980	-6.19	0.72	0.08	0.39	1.87	66
	(-7.84)*	(6.41)*	(1.23)			
1986	-6.92	0.81	0.17	0.65	1.85	66
	(-13.30)*	(10.60)*	(3.84)*			

Sources: World Bank, *World Debt Tables*, computer tapes (1987/88).

Notes: F_p/F_{tot} = share of debt from private sources in total outstanding debt.

POP = population.

GNP / POP = GNP per capita.

t-statistics are in parentheses.

* significant at 5% level.

poor developing countries have been cut off almost entirely from access to international financial markets. Figure 5.3 indicates the positive relation between a country's share of external debt from private sources and GNP per capita. The figure provides cross-sectional data only for 1986, but as Table 5.7 shows, this relation has been stable over time, with an elasticity parameter in the range of 0.5 to 0.8 since 1970. The regressions in Table 5.7 use population as a proxy of the size of the economy and suggest that, at least during the 1980s, the larger the economy the greater its access to private sources of finance. The upshot is that both lenders and borrowers were concentrated. By 1981, 70 per cent of outstanding bank debt was concentrated in ten countries (Argentina, Brazil, Chile, Colombia, Mexico, Venezuela, South Korea, the Philippines, Malaysia, and Nigeria). Loan syndication created a fiction: what may have seemed

Figure 5.3 Southern borrowers: share of external debt from private sources to total external debt and GNP per capita, 1986

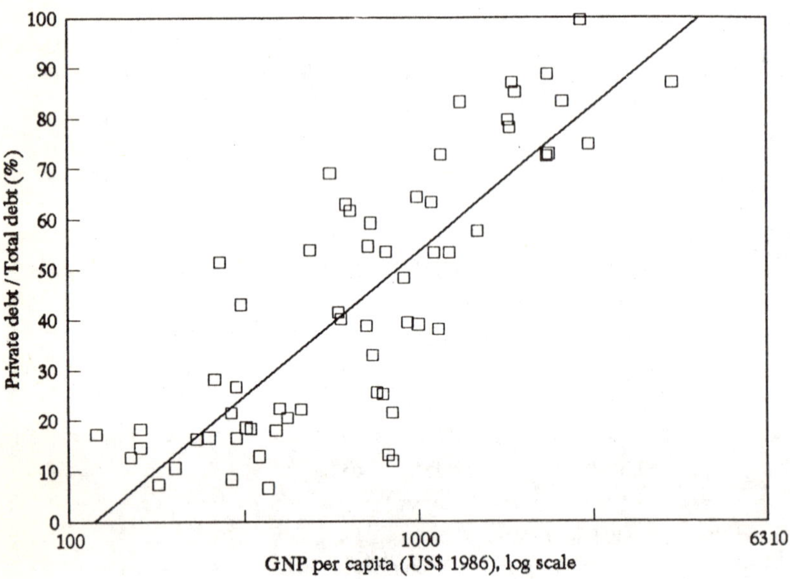

Source: World Bank, *World Debt Tables, 1987-88*

a more diversified portfolio to individual participants sharing usually in more than one package of concerted lending, proved in the aggregate a highly concentrated portfolio for the banking sector as a whole.

(4) The concentration of lending to specific groups of developing countries also seems a result of so-called 'contagion' effects in bank behaviour. Some authors have labelled this the 'follow-the-herd' credo:[14] when financial markets were liquid and developing countries were still considered good risks, all *a priori* selected middle-income countries appear to have had more or less equal access; after the global debt crisis had become manifest, banks retreated *en masse*. The concentration of creditors and loan syndication may explain such behaviour. Evidence suggests, however, that the 'contagion' was to some extent selective. If creditors are able to distinguish properly between 'good' and 'bad' loans and debtors they will set credit ceilings as functions of perceived risk; if not, debt problems in one or more countries may affect lending to other borrowers who may have no apparent debt problems. A rough method is to look at correlations in trends of flows across countries. It is hypothesized that if '*contagion*' effects are present there should be a strong positive correlation (contagion) in the flow of loans to borrowing countries over time, whereas a low degree of contagion (correlation) would imply that lenders apply different credit rationing rules to different borrowers.

Table 5.8 supplies empirical evidence in partial support of the 'contagion-effect' hypothesis. The findings confirm those found by Saunders (1987) using the same methodology applied to a different sample of countries and country groups. The table presents a correlation matrix of net bank lending to a group of 11 major private borrowers for the periods before and after the 1982 crisis. The upper panel gives correlation coefficients from annual data for 1974-81. In this boom period, high and significant correlations are found between most countries in the sample, despite substantial variations in trends in solvency (debt-to-GNP ratio) and liquidity indicators (debt-service ratio). This is particularly the case among the Latin American countries, with Brazil the major exception. But in Africa, Zimbabwe, and in Asia, Korea and Malaysia have high positive correlations with lending to Latin American debtors. Thailand and the Philippines, and two other African private borrowers (Côte d'Ivoire and Nigeria) generally show lower correlations with other

Table 5.8 Contagion effects in commercial bank lending to selected LDCs, private borrowers, 1974-81 and 1983-86

	Correlation Matrix 1974-81[a]												
	Côte d'Ivoire	*Nigeria*	*Zim-babwe*	*Korea*	*Malaysia*	*Thai-land*	*Philip-pines*	*Brazil*	*Argenti-na*	*Chile*	*Colom-bia*	*Ecua-dor*	*Mexico*
Côte d'Ivoire	1.000												
Nigeria	0.838	1.000											
Zimbabwe	0.291	0.467	1.000										
Korea	0.688	0.816	0.680	1.000									
Malaysia	0.391	0.534	0.534	0.705	1.000								
Thailand	0.707	0.789	0.310	0.784	0.537	1.000							
Philippines	0.711	0.522	0.300	0.620	0.524	0.797	1.000						
Brazil	0.249	0.516	0.700	0.418	0.437	-0.005	-0.182	1.000					
Argentina	0.558	0.692	0.729	0.952	0.770	0.784	0.704	0.330	1.000				
Chile	0.770	0.879	0.737	0.924	0.820	0.840	0.706	0.457	0.902	1.000			
Colombia	0.510	0.608	0.803	0.891	0.910	0.730	0.680	0.275	0.938	0.891	1.000		
Ecuador	0.870	0.758	0.641	0.865	0.652	0.633	0.666	0.419	0.772	0.869	0.773	1.000	
Mexico	0.511	0.640	0.900	0.760	0.971	0.617	0.629	0.488	0.832	0.889	0.900	0.716	1.000

(Continued...)

(Table 5.8 Continued...)

	Correlation Matrix 1982: Q1 – 1985: Q4[b]												
	Côte d'Ivoire	*Nigeria*	*Zim-babwe*	*Korea*	*Malaysia*	*Thai-land*	*Philip-pines*	*Brazil*	*Argenti-na*	*Chile*	*Colom-bia*	*Ecua-dor*	*Mexico*
Côte d'Ivoire*	1.000												
Nigeria*	0.419	1.000											
Zimbabwe	0.578	0.974	1.000										
Korea	-0.225	-0.138	-0.186	1.000									
Malaysia	0.715	0.845	0.856	-0.272	1.000								
Thailand	0.273	-0.689	-0.533	0.279	-0.439	1.000							
Philippines	0.760	0.544	0.705	-0.552	0.563	-0.026	1.000						
Brazil*	0.765	0.466	0.495	0.034	0.827	0.006	0.266	1.000					
Argentina*	0.633	0.147	0.300	0.496	0.180	0.574	0.388	0.372	1.000				
Chile*	0.696	0.282	0.350	0.498	0.522	0.349	0.153	0.826	0.777	1.000			
Colombia	0.864	0.505	0.588	0.194	0.765	0.166	0.424	0.922	0.690	0.937	1.000		
Ecuador*	0.661	0.004	0.123	0.476	0.374	0.531	0.051	0.788	0.733	0.966	0.866	1.000	
Mexico*	0.810	0.671	0.666	0.296	0.743	0.105	0.436	0.844	0.756	0.930	0.978	0.820	1.000

(Continued...)

(Table 5.8 Continued...)

Debt indicators for countries in sample

	Debt/GNP Ratio			Debt-Service Ratio		
	1975	*1981*	*1986*	*1975*	*1981*	*1986*
Côte d'Ivoire*	26.3	83.5	128.7	8.7	31.6	21.4
Nigeria*	2.6	13.0	122.6	2.7	4.6	30.7
Zimbabwe	5.5	19.9	45.8	0.8	4.2	22.1
Korea	27.2	19.9	45.8	11.6	12.9	16.9
Malaysia	14.2	23.6	67.0	3.4	3.5	13.4
Thailand	4.1	31.5	45.3	2.4	6.8	16.2
Philippines*	9.2	54.0	95.0	7.4	9.7	22.4
Brazil*	11.6	31.8	42.0	17.9	33.7	34.1
Argentina*	8.2	63.8	66.8	22.0	17.3	51.8
Chile*	53.8	50.2	135.5	27.2	29.6	28.6
Colombia	18.5	24.1	45.6	10.8	13.1	26.4
Ecuador*	10.3	59.2	91.0	4.4	30.9	32.7
Mexico*	12.5	32.5	82.5	24.9	28.1	37.2,

Source: World Bank, *World Debt Tables*, computer tapes (1987/88); BIS/OECD, *Statistics on External Indebtedness* (various issues).

Notes: * = Countries with recent debt problems.
a. Correlation analysis based on annual data.
b. Correlation analysis based on quarterly data.

borrowers and higher ones among themselves. The lower panel of Table 5.8 shows correlations for the debt-crisis period after 1982, applying quarterly data. High correlations are sustained between the Latin American debtors. The fact that this also holds for Colombia, which has no apparent debt problems and for Brazil, the special case in the boom period, clearly indicates Latin American *contagion* effects. Of the non-Latin countries, Côte d'Ivoire (with debt problems) also falls in this category and Malaysia (without debt problems) does so partially. Bank lending to Nigeria and the Philippines (both with debt problems) and Zimbabwe, Korea and Thailand (all without debt problems) appeared fairly correlated in the 1970s, but the correlation coefficients fell drastically after the crisis.

These data suggest that there was contagion in lending behaviour when the bank loan market for sovereign borrowers in the South was buoyant; when credit rationing tightened the revulsion against 'bad' debtors spilled over to *some* countries without debt problems, but this was neither widespread nor systematic.

The change in market confidence, before and after the 1982 debt crisis, is also reflected in a structural shift in the aggregate response parameter of new bank lending to the South and solvency of Southern borrowers, as tested by numerous 'creditworthiness' models.[15] Many such models attempt to quantify the point at which borrowers may (re-)gain access to commercial borrowing. However, on the basis of the observed behavioural shifts and the institutional characteristics of the market analysed above, the predictable capacity of such models should be considered low. Oligopolistic lending behaviour and the apparent contagion effects mean that the probability of regaining creditworthiness cannot be simply extrapolated from economic performance indicators of individual borrowers, such as the solvency indicator.

(5) Southern borrowers with access to bank loans seem to have adjusted demand schedules in face of the sudden availability of private long-term finance in the 1970s. As noted earlier, they are not the careful 'optimal borrowers' suggested in orthodox textbook approaches, and the marketing strategies of banks do not seem to have encountered significant demand constraints.

In sum, the oligopolistic nature of the market for international bank credits and the concentration at the borrowers' end provides a market structure very different from the atomistic auction market assumed in many textbook analyses of portfolio behaviour. There is little reason to believe that unregulated activity will promote an efficient allocation of resources. On the contrary, banks can be expected to use their market power to gain market shares and monopoly rents. If the market structure is destabilized by a lowering of entrance barriers (financial innovations, global macroeconomic conditions), new entrants may provoke price (spread) competition and a struggle for market shares (loan pushing), which is stopped only by a crisis.

5.3.2 Official creditors

By nature, official flows are largely supply-side determined. It is widely accepted that both the amounts supplied and their allocation among developing countries are essentially determined by political processes (e.g. Mosley 1987). As indicated above, about two thirds of official capital flows to the South consists of official development assistance, with the major share supplied through bilateral channels from donor governments in the North (OECD) to recipient governments in the South. Official development assistance (aid), the main type of official capital, is usually said to result from a mixture of motives of which can be summarized as the 'profit' (export interests), 'power' (colonial ties and geopolitical interests) and 'humanitarian' (poverty eradication) principles (see the review of studies in Chapter 3). The stylized facts of the main economic supply determinants are:

Figure 5.4 Net ODA from DAC to LCDs, 1950-87 (percentage share of GNP of DAC members)

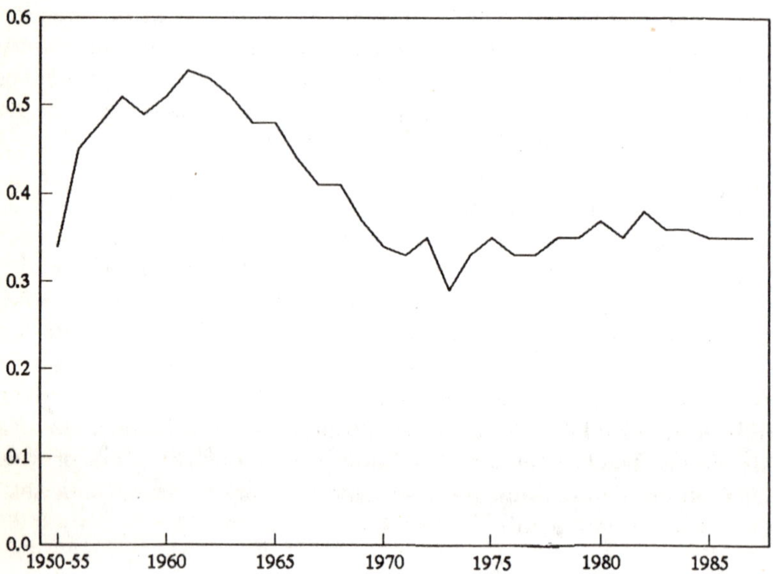

Source: OECD (1985, 1988)

(1) Official flows have remained fairly stable (See Figure 5.4) at around 0.35 per cent of aggregate Northern GNP or around 1.5 per cent of government spending in the North.

(2) Official flows increased by 3.3 per cent per year between 1970 and 1985 (OECD 1985). Since 1980 total official development finance has been virtually stagnant, however, and growth has even been negative if one includes the strong decline in (official and officially guaranteed) export credits. In this sense, official lending showed no noticeable response to increasing current account problems in most developing countries: to the second oil-price increase in 1979/80, to falling real commodity prices (see below) which heavily affected primary exporters and low-income countries, nor to the emerging debt problems of the countries that had access to the private capital market in the 1970s. In fact, development assistance is mostly unconcerned with immediate balance of payments problems, but until recently has focused mainly on long-term development projects. Consequently it has little to no counter-cyclical effect on macroeconomic adjustment. On the contrary, the stagnation in the size of flows in the 1980s suggests this works pro-cyclically, at least at the aggregate level. The disaggregated pattern is more varied. Some donors (e.g. Scandinavia, the Netherlands, multilateral institutions) show more concern with recipients' needs (including balance of payments support) than do others (e.g. the United States).

(3) Low-income countries rely heavily on official flows. The share of official debt in total debt is a decreasing function of GNP per capita (that is, the inverse of Figure 5.3), but the total 'pool' of available official finance tends to be endogenous with Northern growth.

(4) Numerous studies have indicated that the allocation of official flows shows a small-country and middle-income country bias (see e.g. Edelman & Chenery 1977; Dowling & Hiemenz 1985). Expressed in per capita terms, official aid flows tend to decrease with population size and GNP per capita. A re-assessment of this hypothesis using recent data confirms that the relation between aid flows and GNP per capita is non-linear: aid per capita increases first up to a $ 400 per capita income level (1986 US dollars), which is around the World Bank's cut-off line between low- and middle-income countries, and thereafter decreases (see Figure 5.5).[16]

As discussed in Chapter 3, public-goods models of aid have tried to give additional explanations of the allocation of aid, including colonial ties, taxpayers' opinions about the quality of aid, and 'bandwagon' effects among different donors (e.g. Dudley & Montmarquette 1976; Frey 1984; Mosley 1985, 1987). Empirical evidence provided by these studies shows no systematic and generalizable pattern. However, in these cases interpretation of the empirical results is also difficult, due to conceptual and data problems related to the lack of knowledge about the precise impact of aid and the apparent existence of externalities in aid-giving, including possible bandwagon effects.

Despite difficulties in modelling the behaviour of aid donors, the generally accepted notion is that the availability of official capital flows for developing countries is strongly influenced by supply factors, as in the case of bank lending. Where the major private source of external

Figure 5.5 Relation of bilateral aid to GNP per capita from cross-sectional data, 1983-86

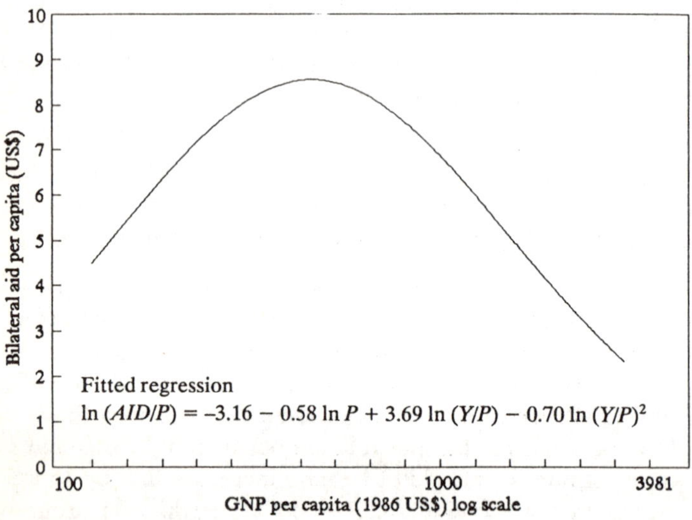

Source: See note 16 to this chapter.

finance for the South is characterized by oligopolistic banking and credit rationing mechanisms, official lending is conditioned by political processes, some degree of competition between donors and, perhaps, public opinion about aid in the major creditor countries. Low-income countries are relatively more dependent on aid as a source of foreign savings, but a country's average income level is in itself a poor predictor of its access to development assistance. Low per capita income is, however, a relevant predictor of limited access to the private capital market, so that – in theory – low average welfare levels would reflect a higher recipient need for aid flows. Aid donors have in the past failed to assign priority to recipient needs defined in this developmental manner, nor to more immediate foreign-exchange needs. More recently, however, concerns about macroeconomic policies in LDCs have become part of conditionality to multilateral structural adjustment lending and in Paris Club reschedulings, but this still reflects the stronger bargaining power of suppliers (see Mosley 1987 for a further analysis of donor-recipient bargaining processes).

5.4 Global Macroeconomic Environment and Northern Financial Policies

The debt problems of a large number of developing countries have highlighted global macroeconomic interdependence. Frameworks for analysing the macroeconomic interactions between North and South have been set out in various recent theoretical and empirical studies. The theoretical literature was reviewed in Chapter 3 and will be elaborated upon in the subsequent chapters. Some applied frameworks can be found in Bruno & Sachs (1985), Van Wijnbergen (1985), Marquez & Pauly (1987), Dornbusch & Fischer (1987), Muscatelli & Vines (1991) and McKibbin & Sachs (1991). Apart from important differences all these studies emphasize, in line with some of the theoretical North-South models discussed in Chapter 3, three stylized features which dominate North-South interactions. Firstly, the Northern economy is viewed as essentially demand-constrained, with (manufacturing) output prices and wages adjusting gradually, while the Southern economy is typically supply constrained with prices of their (primary) export commodities flexible and market clearing. These conditions would make commodity prices more volatile than manufacturing prices, making developing countries vulnerable to Northern demand conditions and macropolicies influencing aggregate demand and inflation. Muscatelli & Vines (1991) add that the presence of speculative commodity stockholdings implies that commodity prices will also directly react to Northern interest-rate changes through stockholding effects. Secondly, there is still relatively little South-South trade, making Southern export growth highly dependent on Northern demand. Well developed capital markets in the North make aggregate demand, particularly private investment demand, highly sensitive to real interest rates which in turn are a function of private portfolio decisions and Northern fiscal and monetary policies. Thirdly, a large part of the external debt of the South was acquired at variable interest rates, which has made adjustment in the South more vulnerable to Northern macroeconomic policies. Since further most of the borrowing was by governments, higher interest rates in the North lead, all other things being equal, to larger fiscal deficits in the South.

The three key variables determining the impact of the Northern economy on the South are interest rates, Northern growth and commodity prices. A lack of policy coordination among the major Northern economies has contributed to a highly uncertain world economic environment with widely fluctuating interest rates, and cyclical fluctuations in world economic activity and real non-fuel commodity prices, all heavily affecting the Southern economies.

Naturally, the impact on different parts in the South depends on their economic structure, trade dependence and debt structure. These aspects will be treated in subsequent sections of this chapter, along with the impact of Southern adjustment on the North, through commodity markets (import adjustment) and financial markets (debt servicing and default risk).

5.4.1 Northern accumulation behaviour, financial policies and interest-rate instability

Figure 5.6 shows the strong fluctuations in LIBOR rates in the 1970s and 1980s. The real rate for developing countries has been even more volatile than for industrial countries: rates were low in the 1970s; and there was a steep increase in the early 1980s. The apparent instability of financial markets is closely linked to the external imbalances of the major economies and to uncoordinated monetary and fiscal policies.

In the early 1970s interest rates tended to fall in nearly all financial markets due to the recycling of the savings surpluses of the oil exporters. Monetary policies among the major economies diverged. The European countries and Japan mainly focused on monetary targets to counteract inflation and to stabilize exchange rates. The United States focused on interest rates, thus allowing for more passive monetary adjustment. Accelerating inflation made interest rate control increasingly difficult and US real long-term (bond) rates became negative by the end of the 1970s. The dollar exchange rate started to fall, making US fiscal deficits unsustainable as government bonds became unattractive and the dollar an uninteresting asset to foreign investors.

In October 1979, US authorities shifted towards monetary targeting through control of the quantity of non-borrowed reserves in the banking system. The shift induced a period of high interest rate variability and appreciation of the dollar. Although the policy shift was announced in advance, the outcome came as a shock to the world economy. There was a sudden, steep rise in real interest rates in 1980/81 as the result of the widening real internal and external gaps in the US economy, led by the

Figure 5.6 Nominal and real world interest rates (LIBOR) in percentages

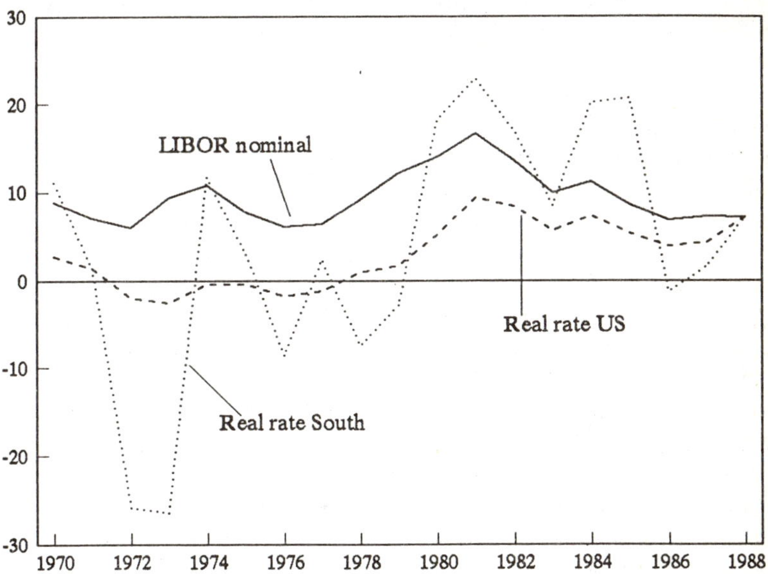

Source: IMF, *International Financial Statistics* (various years)

Notes: US real rate = LIBOR less US inflation rate (GNP deflator)
LDC real rate = LIBOR less change in LDC export prices.

fiscal impulse generated by the Reagan administration, and restrictive monetary policies. The rising fiscal deficit did not 'crowd out', but rather 'crowded in' private investment through an accompanying reduction of corporate taxes. Private savings did not increase correspondingly. US corporate firm savings did not increase significantly despite a major increase in after-tax revenues in 1981-87 (to 11.3 per cent of GNP, up from 9.1 on average in 1971-80), mainly due to a large increase in the interest burden of companies (Dean et al. 1990: Table 5). US household savings declined in the 1980s, suggesting there is no support for the 'debt-neutrality' hypothesis, i.e. that individuals anticipating future tax burdens associated with debt-financed fiscal deficits would increase their savings (see Chapter 3).[17] These factors pushed up private credit demand and real interest rates.

The change in US policy led governments of other major industrial countries to accept more variable interest rates in an attempt to resist even wider exchange rate fluctuations. Since the 1985 Plaza agreement, when it was agreed that an appreciation of the major non-dollar currencies could help to reduce the US current account deficit, interest rates became further subsidiary to exchange rate objectives, thus sustaining high interest rate variability.

'Real' economic balances in the other major economies close to matched the US savings-investment inequality (see Table 5.2). Falling public savings (except Japan) and sustained fiscal deficits characterized most other OECD economies in the 1980s (IMF 1988, Aghevli et al. 1990), implying Northern macro adjustment was achieved via private sector savings surpluses, particularly in Japan and Germany. These surpluses were mainly achieved by private investment rates falling more steeply than private savings rates. As in the US, household savings rates fell in the surplus countries, a phenomenon generally assigned to demographic factors and increases in *net worth* (rising housing and equity values) (Heller 1988, Dean et al. 1990, Aghevli et al. 1990). This was partially offset by higher business savings as a share of GNP, reflecting improved corporate profits, of which an important share would end up in foreign investment.

Although these developments apparently managed to close the Northern savings-investment balance in flow terms, external asset and liability shifts have placed a burden on future adjustment. In effect, trade and financial interdependence among the major economies has become increasingly related to the problem of public and private portfolio adjustment. Recent estimates indicate that the US international asset position had shifted from net assets of US$ 140 billion in 1981 to net liabilities of US$ 533 billion by the end of 1988, with the public sector as main debtor. Inversely the net asset positions of Germany and Japan increased by some US$ 214 and US$ 281 billion respectively over the same period; private sectors being the net creditors.[18]

Obviously, asset shifts of this magnitude have an enormous impact on investment incomes and thus on current account balances, raising the surpluses of Japan and Germany and adding to US deficits. This has two important implications for adjustment in the major economies. Firstly, to reduce external liabilities and current account deficits the US will have to run very large trade surpluses. This can happen only if foreign demand for US output increases, requiring demand expansion helped by exchange rate adjustment in the rest of the world and/or import contraction in the US, affecting exports in the rest of the world. Secondly, a US external deficit can only be sustained if world savings continue to flow to the US. For this effect, US interest rates will have to be kept high in order to attract foreign savings. Tighter monetary policies may help, as these will push up interest rates, but at the same time this will put upward pressure on the dollar, precluding the lower dollar exchange rate needed for the required trade adjustment. Consequently, financial instability and uncertainty are likely to persist, simply because the underlying sources of instability are not cured.

This process of Northern adjustment has affected the South, not only through the impact on the world interest rate, but also through the impact on world economic activity, demand for Southern commodities and commodity prices.

5.4.2 Fluctuations in world economic activity

The world economy experienced a fairly stable expansion in the 1960s, with real world GDP fluctuating rather narrowly between 3 to 6 per cent. The oil shocks of 1973/74 and 1979/80 were among the factors that contributed to a break in this pattern; Northern policy shifts and private sector responses formed another set of factors. The oil shocks contributed to widening current account imbalances in North and South. As evidenced by Pereira, Ulph & Tims (1987), both oil shocks had recessive effects on the North, but the speed of adjustment and recovery differed. Adjustment and recovery were much quicker after 1973/74. The severe recession in 1975, when import volumes in the North fell sharply, contributed to the swing back into surplus of the Northern current account balances, but affected the Southern economies by contracting their export market. The subsequent Northern policy mix was permissive to inflation and real interest rates fell, which contributed to demand expansion and economic recovery (OECD GNP growth averaged 3.6 per cent in 1976-79, up from 1.9 in 1972-75). After 1979, as noted, Northern policies and private sector adjustment were much more deflationary and plunged the world economy into recession (growth down to 1.2 per cent in 1980-83 and 2.4 per cent for 1980-87), leaving less space for developing countries to adjust their external imbalances through higher export earnings.

5.4.3 Commodity prices, pro-cyclical trade and finance and the transfer problem

Real non-oil commodity prices, a key indicator for export-earning capacity of large parts of the South, showed heavy fluctuations in the 1970s (Figure 5.7). When placed in historical context, however, the degree of volatility does not appear atypical (e.g. Grilli & Yang 1988). On

Figure 5.7 LDCs: real commodity and real oil prices, 1970-88 (index 1980 = 100)

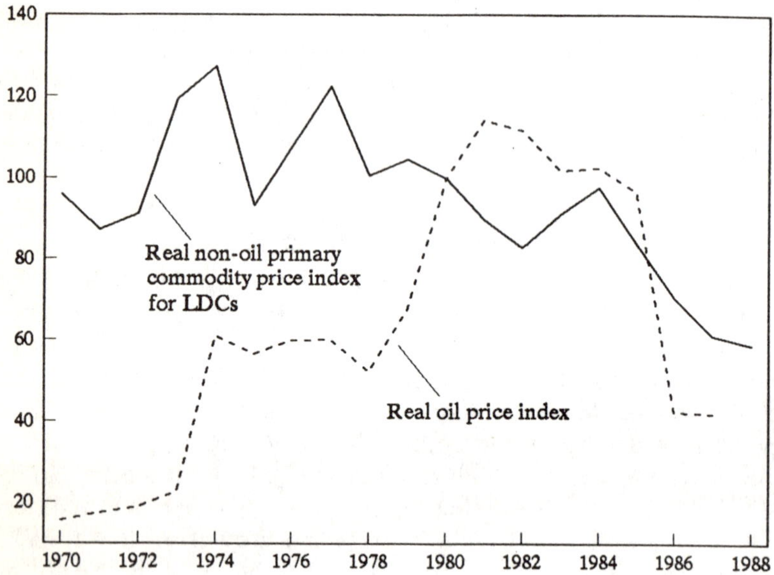

Sources: IMF, *International Financial Statistics* (various years) and IMF, *Primary Commodities, Market Development and Outlook* (various years)

balance, there was a slight upward trend. These gains were lost in the 1980s, when primary commodity prices fell sharply. In real terms (deflated for Northern manufacturing unit value) at the end of 1988 they were 30 per cent below the 1980 level, which was already below the 1970 level. Many explanations of this decline have been offered, ranging from changing technology and increased protectionism to changing world growth patterns (see e.g. Helleiner 1988 and Goldsbrough & Zaidi 1986). However, the pro-cyclical nature of the interaction between North-South trade and finance seems to have contributed to this effect as well.

In the 1970s new lending to the South provided some adjustment finance to cope with negative trade shocks, but many countries continued to borrow even during commodity booms. The clearest examples are of course Nigeria, Mexico, and Ecuador, which became both highly-indebted and major oil-exporters during a decade of skyrocketing oil prices. To the banks, favourable prospects in export markets enhanced perceived creditworthiness. In the 1980s the Northern recession seemed at least in part a consequence of tensions in the capital market and higher interest rates. This hit the South with a double-edged sword: a higher debt burden and lower export possibilities. The incipient debt crisis led to a drying up of new (commercial) lending. Southern attempts to effectuate the required net transfer of resources to the North through increased export volumes (see also below) have contributed to falling commodity prices, as evidenced by Singer (1989) and Thirlwall & Bergevin (1985).[19] This is explained by the low Northern demand elasticity for Southern primary commodities. Dornbusch & Fischer (1987) estimate the aggregate long-term elasticity of Southern (average) export growth to Northern production at slightly above unity (1.15), but complementary estimates show it is below unity for primary exports (Saunders & Dean 1986, Goldsbrough & Zaidi 1986, Marquez & Pauly 1987, Helleiner 1988, Singer 1989). The underlying presumption that commodity prices will fall is, of course, that primary commodity markets are essentially price-clearing. This seems generally the case, as argued by e.g. Williamson (1983), as opposed to pricing of manufactures which in many cases is determined by the mark-up pricing behaviour of international firms (Williamson 1983 and Chapter 7). Higher Northern real interest rates may have contributed to the decline of commodity prices as the higher cost of stockholdings speeded up sales (see e.g. Muscatelli & Vines 1991 and Gilbert 1990 on this).

The combination of a net resource transfer *from* South *to* North and falling terms of trade for the South seems to make the case for an 'orthodox' transfer problem of a secondary burden falling on the transferring country (cf. Chapter 3). This would hold in particular for the indebted countries which heavily depend on primary exports.

5.5 The Demand-side: Southern Borrowers and Macroeconomic Adjustment

Creditors' incentives to transfer capital to the South and global macroeconomic 'shocks', in part provoked by Northern policies, provided a stormy external environment for developing countries in the 1970s and 1980s. Low-income countries were excluded from private capital markets, oil producers could benefit from oil price increases (and were harmed by the decline in oil prices after 1985), and non-oil primary exporters faced unstable and unfavourable commodity market conditions. Many countries faced severe balance of payments and debt-servicing problems in the 1980s. While governments in these countries may be tempted to blame the worsened external environment for these problems, many other observers, including institutions like the IMF and the World Bank, have emphasized – without denying the external factors – the role of domestic policies in developing countries. Countries may have borrowed too much, used funds inefficiently and provided incentive structures which shifted resources away from tradable (export) sectors.

This section assesses the behaviour of actors in the South. It will not be attempted to define 'good' or 'bad' policies, nor to judge whether governments (who are important actors here) behaved properly nor whether such behaviour can explain good or bad performance. Rather, the environment in which such policy decisions took place will be emphasized, namely the domestic structural economic and social features and the external factors. Accumulation behaviour and portfolio decisions of private agents are critical in determining the domestic environment. Choosing between holding domestic and foreign assets ('capital flight') seems particularly interdependent with public external debt problems.

To organize the discussion and to distinguish different country experiences, differential access to the world capital market is taken as the initial criterion to group countries into 'official borrowers' (LDC-OBs), 'private borrowers' (LDC-PBs) and 'diversified borrowers' (LDC-DBs). This distinction exposes structural differences in financial arrangements with the North and in different degrees of sensitivity to shocks in international financial markets. The distinction is not by itself sufficient to separate problem and non-problem debtor countries.

5.5.1 Did countries borrow too much?

In section 5.3 it was argued that supply factors dominate the availability of external funds. In the 1970s commercial banks pushed loans to Southern borrowers in an oligopolistic competition over market shares. Aid donors have their own political-economic motives to supply funds, according to some analysts also involving 'aid pushing'. The need to spend aid budgets and donor conditionality are then more determinant than the specified demand from developing countries. Does this mean Southern borrowers had perfectly elastic demand curves for foreign borrowing?

According to the optimal borrowing literature (see the discussion in Chapter 3), agents will borrow up to a level of indebtedness not exceeding a private, or in the case of government borrowing, socially optimal level. But can governments *implement* such a borrowing strategy?

An optimal borrowing strategy requires free entry into the capital market, but this free access does not and did not exist for developing countries. As analysed in the previous sections, LDCs are rationed in private capital markets and official sources of finance appear subject to donor conditionality. On the demand side, in the 1970s very few countries seem to have adopted explicit borrowing strategies of any kind. In most countries, external borrowing tended to be embedded in simple policy rules for short-term reserve management. Such rules were often based on IMF balance of payments and financial programming 'models' and were not designed for medium- and long-term debt management. In practice, this form of external resource management could induce an upward spiral of borrowing demands. A case in point is the Philippines, where the borrowing rule, installed by the IMF, was such that a larger availability of external finance in the present year would relax the constraint on borrowing in the next (see Dohner & Intal 1989: 512 and Lamberte et al. 1992).[20] In the 1970s the incentive to borrow abroad was great, suggesting a rather flat demand curve for external borrowing. At least with regard to commercial bank loans it seems that:

(i) Long-term bank lending was a new, but attractive phenomenon for most borrowing governments as it attached few conditions to spending (in contrast to aid flows).

(ii) Countries faced increasing current account deficits, in part due to increased (oil) import bills. Structurally, their economies showed substantial import dependence on investment and intermediate goods. Increased foreign-exchange availability eased external adjustment and could support economic growth. Substantial increases in domestic investment rates confirm this (see below).

(iii) There is also evidence that countries took on more external debt than necessary to cover current account needs in the 1970s. In the aggregate, net borrowing was more than sufficient to cover current account deficits in the 1970s. There was a substantial buildup of foreign-exchange reserves by developing countries (cf. also Figure 5.1), particularly by private borrowers (LDC-PBs). Between 1977 and 1981 additions to reserve positions totalled US$ 70 billion against total net borrowings of about US$ 360 billion for all non-oil LDCs and US$ 50 billion (against borrowings of US$ 255) for LDC-PBs (calculated from IMF balance of payments statistics).

Figure 5.8a Net transfers: all sources, by country group, 1978-86 (billions of US$)

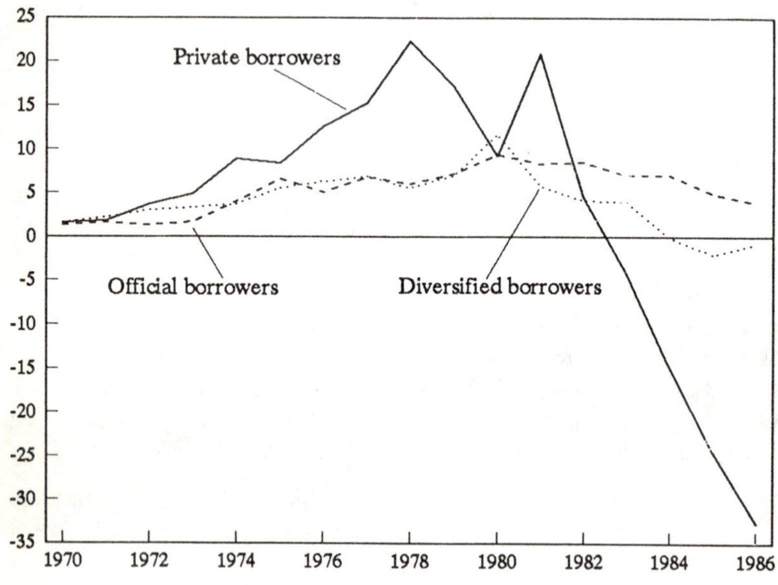

Figure 5.8b Net transfers: official sources, by country group, 1978-86 (billions of US$)

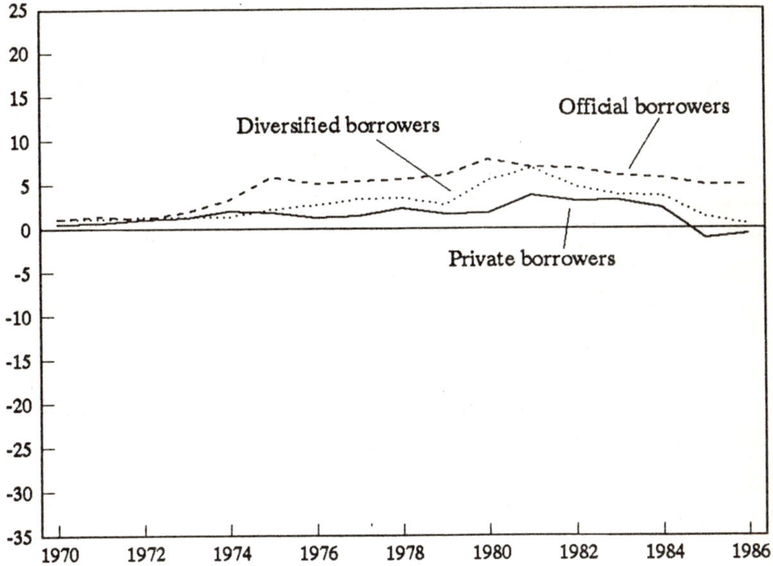

Figure 5.8c Net transfers: private sources, by country group, 1978-86 (billions of US$)

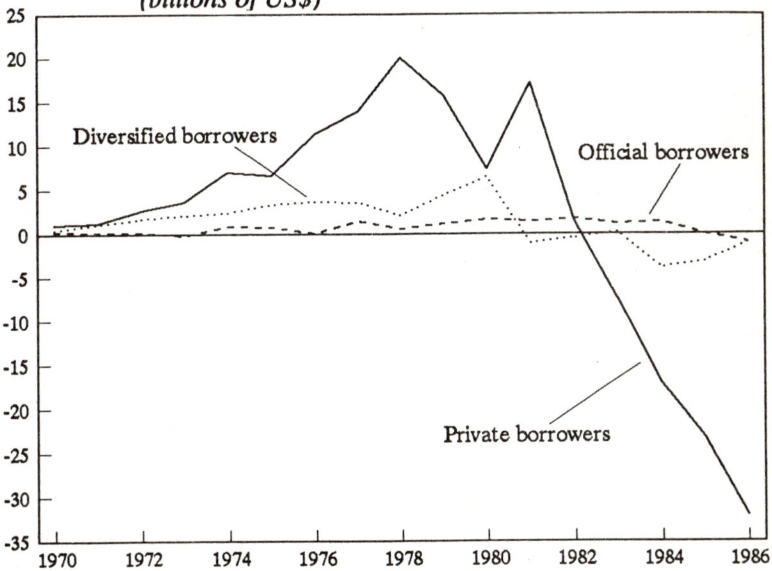

Source: World Bank, *World Debt Tables* (computer tapes, 1987-88)

(iv) Sachs (1989: 12-13), among others, provides a political-economy explanation. Referring mainly to Latin American borrowers, he argues that great inequalities in income may prompt political conflicts which are reflected in chronic fiscal crises: the capacity to tax is constrained by the resistence of the political elite, while government spending is continuously under (upward) pressure from the same political elites, and from inflexible bureaucracies and organized social groups. It may be that foreign borrowing provided the short-term solution to these political dilemmas, by allowing governments to sustain large budget deficits without incurring high inflationary costs in the short run.

(v) Finally, conditions under which funds were offered seemed extremely favourable. Real interest rates were low and it is likely that managers of loan syndicates were generous to responsible politicians in arranging quick deals (Sampson 1981 and Darity & Horn 1988 suggest as much). Low and even negative real interest rates did not provide an incentive to give high priority to maximizing financial returns on investment projects and probably further stimulated the use of foreign borrowing to finance fiscal deficits and government consumption. Some have even argued that the low real interest rates made externally financed government consumption socially optimal (Cline 1983: 28, World Bank 1985: 46-54, Lal & van Wijnbergen 1985: 173, and Sachs 1981: 201-68).

Figures 5.8a-c show the evolution of the net transfers of financial resources by private and official creditors to the South in the 1970s and 1980s. The net transfer is defined as net borrowing less interest payments. While net transfers to official borrowers (LDC-OBs) and diversified borrowers (LDC-DBs) have been fairly stable in absolute terms, and even stagnant in real terms, they shifted strongly upwards for private borrowers (LDC-PBs) between 1974 and 1979 and turned negative after 1982 (Figure 5.8a). Remarkably, just before the outbreak of the debt crisis there was a strong upward shift in the net transfer towards LDC-PBs originating from the commercial banks (Figure 5.8b). This was at a time when real interest rates were already up and banks must have been aware of the threat of major payments problems among LDC-PBs. Observers have seen this as an initial attempt to avoid liquidity problems (Brau & Williams et al. 1983; Eaton & Taylor 1986), but Guttentag & Herring (1985) see this as a type of 'disaster myopia' with multinational bank managers aware of the danger but unwilling to admit their bad lending policies in the past (see also Chapter 3).

Figure 5.8c shows that in the aggregate, net transfers from official sources have been less important than private flows and have been fairly stable and positive throughout the 1970-86 period. For LDC-OBs net official financial transfers have been positive throughout, but for LDC-PBs they were positive up to 1984 and negative thereafter. Official lending to LDC-PBs, particularly from multilateral sources, increased in the early 1980s, thus partly financing the outward transfer towards the commercial banks. Since 1984 net transfers from World Bank and IMF have been negative, however, forcing stronger internal adjustment in these economies.

5.5.2 External Adjustment

A simple debt-growth rule states that if a country wants to borrow up to a given critical solvency level (debt-export ratio), growth of export earnings should exceed the cost of borrowing once that point has been reached (see Avramovic et al. 1964, Thirlwall 1972, Simonsen 1985). However, if external finance is not freely accessible, debt accumulation may be constrained and the trade balance will have to accommodate. This can be shown by expressing the debt-growth accounting rule set out in Chapter 4 (equation 4.5) in terms of exports (θE_S). Assuming that all net factor payments consist of interest payments on external debt $(R_S \equiv i_W F_S)$ and writing the price variables term of equation 4.5 in differential form, one can derive:[21]

$$t_S \equiv \Delta f_S - [i_W - (\dot{p}_S - \dot{p}_N) - g_{Se}]f_S \qquad (5.1)$$

where t_S is the net external transfer or trade deficit as a ratio of exports; f_S is the debt-export ratio; Δf_S is the growth rate of external debt in terms of exports; g_{Se} is the Southern export volume growth rate; and p_S and p_N are rates of change of the dollar prices of Southern exports and imports respectively, the difference being the change in the terms of trade. It also holds (from equation 3.1) that:

$$t_S \equiv (1 - P_N M_S)/P_S E_S \qquad (5.2)$$

so that with external finance, the interest rate and international prices all being exogenous, export and import volumes will have to be the adjusting variables.

The previous sections indicated international trends in access to external finance, world trade and interest rates. Table 5.9 shows how these

Table 5.9 Capital-importing LDCs: external indicators (average growth rates, percentages)

	Export volume	Import volume	Export prices	Import prices	Terms of trade	Interest rate	GDP growth
Total Sample: All LDCs (n = 77)							
1968-72	4.4	4.4	7.0	7.1	-0.1	5.6	5.6
1973-77	-1.1	7.3	22.5	15.3	6.2	6.7	5.2
1978-82	3.1	4.0	10.2	8.0	2.0	9.6	3.4
1983-86	6.2	-0.1	-5.0	-1.8	-3.2	8.2	3.1
1986-88	7.3	5.6	3.2	5.9	-2.5	6.5	5.4
Official Borrowers, all (n = 44)							
1968-72	3.9	0.4	4.4	6.3	-1.8	4.3	3.3
1973-77	3.5	7.2	12.6	15.8	-2.8	5.0	4.4
1978-82	2.0	3.1	6.5	7.8	-1.2	5.9	3.3
1983-86	4.3	1.1	-3.0	-1.8	-1.2	6.7	3.3
1986-88	5.1	0.0	3.5	3.9	-0.4	5.3	3.6
Official Borrowers, Sub-Saharan Africa (n=25)							
1968-72	5.9	2.3	1.6	7.5	-5.4	3.6	3.9
1973-77	-2.0	0.2	12.2	15.6	-2.9	4.7	2.5
1978-82	1.8	-2.1	0.9	7.4	-6.0	5.0	1.5
1983-86	2.6	1.9	-0.1	0.7	-0.8	5.2	1.2
1986-88	2.3	0.5	-1.4	2.4	-3.8	3.2	1.6
Private Borrowers, all (n=18)							
1968-72	3.2	6.0	9.1	8.0	1.0	7.2	7.2
1973-77	-2.6	6.8	25.6	15.7	8.5	8.1	5.6
1978-82	3.2	3.5	11.4	8.0	3.2	11.9	3.4
1983-86	6.6	-0.5	-5.3	-1.5	-3.8	9.4	2.0
1986-88	7.8	7.3	3.2	6.9	-3.4	7.7	5.5

(Continued...)

have impacted on the different groups of Southern borrowers. The figures indicate that in the 1970s the boom in commercial lending coincided with increasing export prices (exceeding the nominal cost of borrowing) and positive terms of trade changes for the private borrowers. These conditions were more pronounced for the countries which would end up with major debt-servicing difficulties in the 1980s. The interest-rate shock and worsening of the terms-of-trade which characterized the 1980s were also more severe for the problem debtors. One important

(Table 5.9 Continued)

	Export volume	Import volume	Export prices	Import prices	Terms of trade	Interest rate	GDP growth
Private Borrowers, primary exporters (n=14)							
1968-72	2.5	5.4	8.0	8.5	-0.5	7.4	7.2
1973-77	-5.7	7.2	29.6	16.5	11.2	8.4	5.3
1978-82	1.0	1.3	13.1	7.7	5.0	12.9	2.9
1983-86	4.4	-6.5	-8.8	-0.9	-8.0	10.7	0.9
1986-88	2.7	-1.1	-3.0	6.3	-8.7	8.5	1.7
Private Borrowers, manufactured exporters (n=4)							
1968-72	7.6	7.1	9.7	7.1	2.4	7.0	7.5
1973-77	9.2	5.9	12.3	14.4	-1.8	7.5	8.3
1978-82	7.8	6.8	7.8	8.5	-0.6	10.0	5.5
1983-86	10.4	5.9	-1.1	-2.0	0.9	8.5	6.1
1986-88	15.0	13.8	8.3	7.3	1.0	7.3	11.5
Private borrowers, with debt problems (n=11)							
1968-72	2.7	5.2	7.5	7.0	0.5	7.4	7.1
1973-77	-5.7	7.4	27.3	15.4	10.2	8.4	5.2
1978-82	1.7	0.7	10.6	7.9	2.5	12.6	2.9
1983-86	3.4	-6.3	-6.7	-1.4	-5.4	8.6	0.6
1986-88	2.3	2.7	-0.6	5.7	-5.9	7.5	1.7
Diversified Borrowers (n=15)							
1968-72	11.4	4.8	1.9	6.0	-3.8	6.0	6.7
1973-77	1.7	9.4	20.2	13.5	6.0	6.7	5.9
1978-82	3.8	7.0	9.1	8.4	0.6	9.2	3.9
1983-86	5.9	-0.4	-5.4	-2.7	-2.8	8.6	3.5
1986-88	7.0	6.8	2.9	4.7	-1.7	7.1	4.6

Source: World Bank, *World Tables 1989-90*; *World Debt Tables 1989-90.*

underlying factor seems that most of the countries that ran into serious debt problems are primary exporters (including oil exporters) and were thus doubly hit by rising interest rates and falling commodity prices. Table 5.9 also seems to confirm the earlier hypothesized inverse relationship between export volume growth and export prices, and also that the implicit elasticity is much higher for the primary exporters (i.e. both the problem debtors and the low-income official borrowers). The export growth of the problem debtors was, however, less than half the increase in real interest costs on external debt. LDC-PBs able to avoid major debt problems were mainly exporters of manufactures who were more than able to compensate rising real interest costs with sufficiently high export growth.

Official borrowers suffered less from the interest rate shock. The increase in the real cost of borrowing for this group of countries was mainly due to the deterioration in export prices.

Import volumes have been the major accommodating variable. Table 5.9 shows that the boom in lending permitted a significant import growth in LDC-PBs in the 1970s. Primary exporters (and LDC-PBs with debt problems) cut back import demand at an annual rate of 6.5 per cent between 1983 and 1986 (a decline of nearly 40 per cent from 1982 levels). The fall in import demand affected GDP growth, although from the table it appears that the elasticity is less than unity.[22]

Falling or stagnant import ratios and rising export-to-GDP ratios in the 1980s, have generated the necessary trade surpluses to finance the net resource transfers of (in particular) private borrowers towards the creditor countries in the North. The adjustment has been of enormous macroeconomic magnitude in the South. Trade surpluses reached an average of 4.4 per cent of GDP for LDC-PBs between 1983 and 1986; a shift from structural trade deficits of 1 to 1.5 per cent in the preceding two decades (see below Table 5.10a). As indicated, no such outward transfer has been required for official borrowers. Nevertheless, net capital inflows in the 1980s have neither compensated for the falling import capacity nor prevented economic stagnation as a consequence of reduced export earnings. This holds particularly for Sub-Saharan Africa.

5.5.3 Internal adjustment: fiscal rigidities and private foreign asset accumulation

The accounting identity linking external transfers to the national savings and investment balance may be formulated as (using equations 2.13 and 3.1):

$$T_S \equiv \theta(I_S - S_S) - i_W F_S \equiv (\theta DEF_S - i_W F_S) - \theta(S_S - I_S)_p$$
$$\equiv \Delta F_S - \Delta J_S - i_W F_S \qquad (5.3)$$

where the net transfer or non-interest current account deficit has to match *ex post* the difference of the non-interest fiscal deficit and the private sector savings surplus. Equation 5.3 includes as simplifying assump-

Table 5.10a All capital–importing LDCs: internal and external balances, 1965-86 (percentage of GDP)

		1965-72	1973-77	1978-82	1983-86
Net Transfer	(TS)	2.7	1.6	2.3	-1.2
Net ext. financing	$(\Delta F - \Delta J)$	2.9	2.5	4.0	1.9
Private cap. exports[a]	(ΔJ)	0.8[b]	1.5	2.2	1.6
'Gross' borrowing[c]	(ΔF)	3.7	4.0	6.2	3.5
External Balance	$(CA = E - M - R)$	-2.9	-2.5	-4.0	-1.9
Trade balance	$(E - M)$	-2.7	-1.6	-2.3	1.2
Exports	(E)	12.2	15.6	16.6	20.5
Imports	(M)	14.8	17.2	19.0	19.3
Factor payments	(R)	0.2	0.9	1.6	3.1
Interest[d]	(iF)	0.4	0.6	1.4	2.2
Internal Balance	$(S - I)$	-2.9	-2.5	-4.0	-1.9
Savings	(S)	16.5	20.7	20.4	19.6
Investment	(I)	19.3	23.2	24.3	21.5
Fiscal Balance	$(T - G)$	-2.6	-3.1	-3.8	-4.4
Govt. expenditures	(G)	14.4	17.0	18.0	19.0
Taxation	(T)	11.8	13.9	14.2	14.6
Private Savings Surplus	$(S_P - I_P)$	-0.3	0.6	-0.2	2.5

Sources: IMF, *International Financial Statistics,* computer tapes (July 1987 update), for national accounts data and government finance statistics. Data on capital flight are author's estimates derived from Williamson (1987) and IMF, *Balance of Payments Statistics;* see also Table 5.13. Data on interest payments on external debt (*iF*) are derived from World Bank, *World Debt Tables* (computer tapes, 1987/88 update).

Notes:
a. Defined as net change in foreign assets held by private resident (bank and non-bank) sector of countries included in country sample. For definitions and methods of estimation see text and Table 5.13.
b. Residual of net external financing and net acquisition of foreign assets by private sector (ΔJ).
c. Estimate based on data for 1970-72 only.
d. Actual interest payments on reported short- and long-term external debt from all sources.

Table 5.10b Official borrowers: internal and external balances, 1965-86 (percentage of GDP)

		1965-72	1973-77	1978-82	1983-86
Net Transfer	(T_S)	1.7	3.5	6.1	5.5
Net ext. financing	$(\Delta F - \Delta J)$	2.5	4.7	5.8	5.9
Private cap. exports[a]	(ΔJ)	1.1[b]	1.7	2.4	0.6
'Gross' borrowing[c]	(ΔF)	3.6	6.4	8.2	6.5
External Balance	$(CA=E-M-R)$	-2.5	-4.7	-5.8	-5.9
Trade balance	$(E-M)$	-1.7	-3.5	-6.1	-5.5
Exports	(E)	10.9	13.8	14.4	13.1
Imports	(M)	12.6	17.3	20.6	18.6
Factor payments	(R)	0.8	1.2	-0.3	0.4
Interest[d]	(iF)	0.5	0.5	0.7	1.0
Internal Balance	$(S-I)$	-2.5	-4.7	-5.8	-5.9
Savings	(S)	15.4	16.6	18.3	14.9
Investment	(I)	17.9	21.3	24.1	20.8
Fiscal Balance	$(T-G)$	-4.1	-5.5	-6.9	-7.9
Govt. expenditures	(G)	15.6	20.0	22.3	24.7
Taxation	(T)	11.5	14.5	15.4	16.8
Private Savings Surplus	$(S_P - I_P)$	1.6	0.8	1.0	2.0

Sources and *Notes*: See Table 5.10a.

tions that net factor payments to abroad consist entirely of interest payments on public external debt, so that the debt-servicing burden $(i_W F_S)$ is jointly presented with the fiscal balance. The stylized fact is that most (about 80 per cent) private and official external finance has been channeled through the public sector. The net transfer (T_S) will fall with private capital outflows (ΔJ_S) and put more pressure on fiscal adjustment.

Tables 5.10a-d show macroeconomic adjustment patterns for LDC-OBs, LDC-PBs and LDC-DBs (diversified borrowers) and Appendix Tables A5.3-A5.4 give results for sub-samples of these country groups. Note that these tables supply (GDP) weighted averages for each country group.

Table 5.10c Private borrowers: internal and external balances, 1965-86 (percentage of GDP)

		1965-72	1973-77	1978-82	1983-86
Net Transfer	(T_S)	1.5	0.5	1.3	-4.4
Net ext. financing	$(\Delta F - \Delta J)$	1.3	1.2	3.8	0.2
Private cap. exports[a]	(ΔJ)	1.0[b]	1.9	3.1	2.9
'Gross' borrowing[c]	(ΔF)	2.3	3.1	6.9	3.1
External Balance	$(CA = E - M - R)$	-1.3	-1.2	-3.8	-0.2
Trade balance	$(E - M)$	-1.5	-0.5	-1.3	4.4
Exports	(E)	12.4	15.8	16.4	21.2
Imports	(M)	13.9	16.2	17.7	16.7
Factor payments	(R)	-0.2	0.7	2.5	4.7
Interest[d]	(iF)	0.5	0.7	2.1	3.2
Internal Balance	$(S - I)$	-1.3	-1.2	-3.8	-0.2
Savings	(S)	19.5	23.6	20.8	20.5
Investment	(I)	20.9	24.8	24.6	20.7
Fiscal Balance	$(T - G)$	-1.5	-2.1	-2.9	-3.0
Govt. expenditures	(G)	11.3	13.8	15.3	15.4
Taxation	(T)	9.8	11.7	12.4	12.4
Private Savings Surplus	$(S_P - I_P)$	0.1	0.9	-0.9	2.8

Sources and *Notes*: See Table 5.10a.

The top halves of Tables 5.10a-d show the shifts in external balances for four main sub-periods. For the South as a whole (Table 5.10a) the boom in external borrowing was concentrated in 1978-82 with 'gross' external financing (ΔF) increasing to 6.2 per cent of GDP, up from 4.0 per cent in 1973-77. The upward shift in the net transfer (T_S) from 1.6 to 2.3 per cent) is much less pronounced due to increases in interest obligations on external debt ($i_W F_S$) and private foreign asset acquisition (ΔJ_S). The corresponding shift towards a larger trade deficit ($\theta E - M$) is due to a major increase in the import coefficient, despite an average increase in the export-GDP ratio. Adjustment in the 1980s reflect a fall in available external finance and a negative resource transfer, despite a fall in 'capital flight' as a percentage of Southern GDP. Confirming the

Table 5.10d Diversified Borrowers: internal and external balances, 1965-86 (percentage of GDP)

		1965-72	1973-77	1978-82	1983-86
Net Transfer	(Ts)	2.3	2.7	1.6	1.1
Net ext. financing	(ΔF)	2.8	3.4	2.5	3.0
External Balance	$(CA=E-M-R)$	-2.8	-3.4	-2.5	-3.0
Trade balance	$(E-M)$	-2.3	-2.7	-1.6	-1.1
Exports	(E)	13.9	17.4	19.8	22.5
Imports	(M)	16.2	20.2	21.4	23.6
Factor payments	(R)	0.5	0.8	0.9	1.9
Interest[d]	(iF)	0.2	0.3	0.9	1.9
Internal Balance	$(S-I)$	-2.8	-3.4	-2.5	-3.0
Savings	(S)	15.0	17.9	21.2	20.7
Investment	(I)	17.8	21.3	23.6	23.7
Fiscal Balance	$(T-G)$	-2.6	-2.5	-2.8	-3.5
Govt. expenditures	(G)	20.3	20.5	20.1	21.2
Taxation	(T)	17.7	18.0	17.3	17.7
Private Savings Surplus	(S_P-I_P)	-0.2	-1.0	0.3	0.4

Sources and *Notes*: See Table 5.10a.

earlier analysis, these shifts are more pronounced in the LDC-PBs (Table 5.10c), than in LDC-OBs (Table 5.10b) or diversified borrowers (Table 5.10d). In the LDC-PB external adjustment reflects both a major increase in export shares and a fall in the import ratio.

The bottom halves of Tables 5.10a-d give the aggregates that indicate internal adjustment. Two salient features come to the fore: fiscal rigidities and private savings surpluses and capital outflows.

(1) *Fiscal rigidities* are a characteristic of adjustment in all groups. A widening of fiscal deficits took place in the 1970s and 1980s,[23] except – within the group of LDC-PBs – manufactured exporters (Table A5.6). The fact that both official and private capital inflows

Table 5.11 Capital-importing LDCs: public investment rates, 1970-88 (percentage of GDP)

		1970	1975	1980	1985	1988
All LDCs	(n= 23)	7.3	8.8	10.5	9.4	9.1
- LDC-OBs	(n= 6)	7.4	8.6	13.0	10.7	11.1
- LDC-PBs	(n= 10)	7.1	8.7	10.2	7.4	8.0
- LDC-DBs	(n= 7)	7.4	9.1	9.1	10.1	8.3

Sources: Pfefferman & Madarassy (1989) and FitzGerald & Sarmad (1990).

Note: Public investment rates refer to investment by general government and public enterprises. Sample includes the following countries:
Official Borrowers (LDC-OBs): Guatemala, India, Kenya, Pakistan, Sri Lanka, Tunisia;
Private Borrowers (LDC-PBs): Argentina, Brazil, Chile, Ecuador, Korea, Mexico, the Philippines, Singapore, Uruguay and Venezuela;
Diversified Borrowers (LDC-DBs): Bolivia, Colombia, Costa Rica, Peru, Thailand, Turkey and Zimbabwe.

have been principally channeled through the public sectors seems an obvious determinant of the observed fiscal expansion. Comparative data on public *investment* in developing countries are scarce, but averaged figures for a sample of countries indicate a substantial increase in public investment ratios during the 1970s and falling ratios in the 1980s but levels remaining higher than in the beginning of the period (Table 5.11).

The fiscal expansion and enhanced public investment can be interpreted as a sectoral shift towards non-traded goods sectors and may create 'Dutch-disease' effects of the type discussed in Chapter 3. Under the managed exchange-rate regimes of most developing countries the demand shift towards non-tradables caused a relative price shift in favour of non-traded goods (also interpreted as a real appreciation).[24] As indicated in Section 5.2.1, much of the external borrowing for new public investment went into capital-intensive projects in infrastructure and energy, characterized by long gestation lags. Data in Table 5.12 suggest this shift in investment pattern has led to increased ICORs in LDC-PBs.[25] Also official capital flows were analysed as being strongly tied to public sector and non-traded goods expansion, particularly in physical and social infrastructure. Additional evidence (Mosley 1987, van Wijnbergen 1986a) suggests further that in many cases ODA flows put upward pressure on cur-

Table 5.12 ICORs[a] for groups of LDCs, 1973-86.

	1973-77	1978-82	1983-86
LDCs	4.5	6.2	8.3
Official Borrowers	6.1	7.8	7.7
– Sub-Saharan Africa	8.0	7.4	7.8
Private Borrowers	4.0	5.7	9.9
– with recent debt problems	4.7	6.6	11.1
Diversified Borrowers	4.6	5.9	3.8

Source: IMF, *International Financial Statistics*, computer tapes.
Note: a. ICOR is calculated as the ratio of the gross fixed investment rate (I_f/GDP) over the average annual GDP growth rate.

rent government expenditures (wage and maintenance costs of aid-financed investment projects), as well as on the real exchange rate.[26] The latter effect is not only due to the sectoral shift towards non-traded goods, but also to the fact that the import component of aid projects is often smaller than the inflow of foreign exchange, leading to initial reserve accumulation.

The external-finance induced expenditure shift towards non-tradables, in many countries aided by trade and exchange-rate regimes supportive of import substitution, created an incentive structure which has been detrimental to export sectors. As long as countries could borrow enough abroad this did not necessarily create growth constraints. However, problems arose when in the 1980s the cost of external finance was pushed up, new lending became scarce, and terms of trade shifted against the indebted countries. Export volumes were increased in most countries, as indicated, but export earnings did not increase enough to allow primary-exporting countries to grow out of debt problems. In these countries real exchange rate overvaluation was considerable, also due to highly protectionist trade regimes. During the adjustment process required in the 1980s, exchange rate adjustment was hampered and resisted by the trade-off between fiscal and external adjustment. A devaluation would raise the domestic-currency cost of external debt-service. Interest payments on public external debt alone constituted *on average* about 30 per cent of total government expenditures of private borrowers in 1983-86 (World Bank 1988: 105ff.). Many debtor countries have achieved substantial increases in tax ratios and cuts in non-interest government spending since 1983, but despite these efforts fiscal deficits have tended to remain high. For the group of LDC-PBs as a whole, non-interest government spending *(G – iF)* fell from 13.2 per cent of GDP in 1978-82 to 12.2 per cent in 1983-86 (Table 5.10c); primary-commodity exporters in this group cut back on these expenditures by 1.5 per cent of GDP to show a budget surplus in 1983-86 with zero interest payments on external debt (Table A.5.2).

Apparently, the probability of emerging debt problems has been closely associated with fiscal policies and the trade and exchange rate regime. This 'domestic policy failure' has been emphasized often in studies of the debt problem. However, the evidence also suggests, confirming findings of other studies (Berg & Sachs 1989, Almansi 1988), that weak fiscal structures and protectionist trade regimes, large non-traded sectors and reliance on primary exports were all important *initial* conditions. These were distinguishing structural features of the economies of problem debtors; the unexpected boom in international lending in the 1970s merely reinforced these as the availability of foreign finance provided little incentive to change policy regimes.

(2) *Private accumulation behaviour*. Negative financial resource transfers combined with sustained fiscal deficits imply there must have been a major shift towards enhanced private savings surpluses. Table 5.10a shows this: the private savings gap shifted from -0.2 per cent of Southern GDP in 1978-82 to 2.5 per cent (private savings surplus) in 1983-86. The shift is largest for the private borrowers (Table 5.10c) and mainly among the primary exporters within this group (Tables A5.3-4). The 1970s showed upward trends in savings and investment rates for the South as a whole. Stagnating or falling rates can already be observed in LDC-OBs in Sub-Saharan Africa (Table A5.3) and LDC-PB primary exporters (Table A5.5), due to falling public savings associated with increased current spending and debt-service burdens and terms of trade deterioration.

After 1982, public and private investment rates fell most dramatically among LDC-PBs while savings rates were sustained in order to match the reduction in the current account deficit and the outward net external transfer (Table 5.10c). 'Official borrowers' in Sub-Saharan Africa (Table A5.3) also felt a substantial decrease in the supply of net official lending as a share of GDP in 1983-86, but adverse external shocks in commodity markets around 1980 had already affected investment and savings rates in 1978-82, a trend which became much stronger as the decade progressed.

A macroeconomically important part of private savings has been used to acquire financial assets abroad. This phenomenon is commonly referred to as capital flight. In terms of the macroeconomic adjustment process, foreign asset acquisition means that part of the private savings surplus leaks abroad. In times of external restraint this enhances the domestic adjustment problem. For this reason it is logical that capital flight now plays an important part in the policy discussions related to the debt problem in developing countries. The estimates reported in Tables 5.10a-d suggest, however, that the acquisition of foreign assets by private sector agents in developing countries is by no means a new phenomenon, nor is it a feature restricted to major private borrowers in Latin America, as suggested in much of the literature.

As pointed out in Chapter 3 there is no standard definition of capital flight. Most applied measurement concepts broadly derive a residual measure of private capital exports (see Deppler & Williamson 1987,

Table 5.13 Capital-importing LDCs: private foreign asset accumulation, 1970-86 (billions of US$; period averages of annual flows)

	1970-72	1973-77	1978-82	1983-86
Capital-importing LDCs	4.3	14.1	33.5	25.3
LDC-OBs: Official Borrowers	1.1	3.7	7.8	2.4
Sub-Saharan Africa	0.1	1.9	2.4	1.0
LDC-PBs: Private Borrowers	3.2	10.4	25.7	22.9
Oil exporters	1.2	5.0	13.5	8.8
Export. of manufact.	-	0.9	1.4	1.5
Primary exporters	2.1	4.5	10.8	12.6
LDC-PBs with debt problems	2.4	9.5	20.7	13.7

Source: Own estimates based on Williamson (1987), *Statistical Appendix* and IMF *Balance of Payments Statistics*.

Notes: Private foreign asset acquisition is defined here as the net change in private (bank and non-bank) external claims and measured on the basis of balance-of-payments statistics as the net change in external liabilities plus net direct investment less the current account deficit and less the change in official reserves and foreign assets acquired by the public (official) banking sector. 'Offshore' banking centres (Hong Kong, Caribbean islands, etc.) are excluded.

Lessard & Williamson 1987 and Vos 1992, for comparisons). Table 5.13 gives aggregate estimates for external asset accumulation by the Southern private sector derived from a residual balance of payments measure and an IMF study (Williamson 1987). The same data were also used to estimate $\Delta J_S/GDP$ in Tables 5.10a-d. Although in absolute terms most private capital outflows stem from LDC-PBs, especially those in Latin America, they have also been significant (around 2 per cent of GDP) in low-income countries (LDC-OBs) in the 1970s. Sudan, for example, ranks among those with large amounts of private capital outflows indirectly financed through remittances from Sudanese workers in the Middle East which are channeled through the black market for foreign exchange and capital exports by the upper class (Harris 1986, Brown 1992). The phenomenon appears to have been negligible in countries with no external debt problems, proxied in Table 5.13 by the exporters of manufactures.

Econometric studies on the determinants of capital flight have found five variables to be most significant, though not equally important in all cases:[27]

(i) The *real exchange rate* (or expected overvaluation) is significant in all studies referring to LDC-PBs. Cuddington (1986) obtains this result in a group of mainly Latin American borrowers; Pastor (1990) for a pooled regression of the seven major Latin American countries; and Vos (1992) for various alternative measures of private capital outflows from the Philippines. Hermes & Lensink (1990) do not find a significant relationship between foreign asset demand and the real exchange rate in the case of six countries in Sub-Saharan Africa.

(ii) The *rate-of-return differential* between foreign short-term assets and domestic financial assets was significant in the case of the major Latin American economies and the Philippines (Pastor 1990, Vos 1992), but not for private capital outflows from Sub-Saharan Africa.

(iii) The *availability of external finance* (ΔF_S) appears to be a significant determinant in all cases, for LDC-PB in Latin America, for the Philippines and for Sub-Saharan Africa (Pastor 1990, Vos 1992 and Hermes & Lensink 1990). Flow related debt indicators, rather than stock indicators of debt overhang (e.g. $F_S/\theta E_S$ or F_S/Y_S) appear significant, which could suggest that there is not so much a response to perceived 'expropriation risk' of domestic assets (cf. e.g. Khan & Ul Haque 1985, Eaton 1987, Cardoso and Dornbusch 1989 and Chapter 3), as foreign exchange availability through new borrowing which is 're-exported' through private channels.

(iv) Agents seem to target a certain stock of foreign assets *(J_{S-1})*. Stock adjustment behaviour has not been tested in all cases, but seems significant in some Latin American countries (Cuddington 1986 shows this for Mexico), the Philippines (Vos 1992) and a re-estimation of the Hermes-Lensink data for Sub-Saharan Africa shows this as well.[28] Stock adjustment behaviour is well founded in orthodox portfolio theory (see e.g. Purvis 1978; Cuddington 1986), but as argued elsewhere (Vos 1992), this may include consumption motives as well, i.e. international lifestyles of the rich in developing countries requiring substantial foreign exchange holdings.[29]

(v) Rather than being a reason for capital flight, as assumed in some orthodox models (see Khan & Ul Haque 1985, Cuddington 1986), *capital controls* have been found significant in *reducing* capital outflows. Available evidence exists for Latin America (Pastor 1990, Dornbusch 1987), but the hypothesis could not be tested in the other cases.

These results must be considered with some caution, because of their sensitivity to the statistical measure (Vos 1992; Anthony & Hughes-Hallet 1992). Nevertheless it seems that in LDC-PBs private capital outflows have been determined by normal portfolio considerations, like exchange risk and rate-of-return differentials, in addition to factors which apply elsewhere: debt accumulation, stock adjustment (possibly related to consumption patterns of the elites) and capital controls. Risk-adjusted rate-of-return considerations do not seem to apply in the case of private capital outflows from low-income countries in Sub-Saharan Africa.

5.6 Borrowing Strategies, Adjustment and Debt Crisis Management

The previous section emphasized the structural conditions (supply of external funds, nature of the economy) under which policy decisions were taken in the debtor countries. The point is not that policy behaviour is entirely endogenous to these conditions, but that structural conditions provide at least a strong limiting factor to available policy options. Supply conditions in private financial markets (oligopolistic banking, loan pushing and excess savings) lifted many financial restraints in LDC-PBs and low costs of foreign borrowing encouraged shifting spending patterns in the 1970s. The shift was largely towards government spending and public investment in capital-intensive projects with long gestation lags. Where chronic fiscal deficits were permitted for political reasons, foreign borrowing was an important source of deficit financing and financing of government consumption. In the sectoral allocation of foreign borrowing there was a strong bias towards the non-traded goods sector. For countries dependent on capital inflows from official sources (LDC-OB) the availability of external finance was more stable. Nevertheless since these flows typically serve to finance public spending and because of donor conditionality such flows also have a bias towards non-traded goods sectors.

These 'borrowing strategies' did not and could not compensate for the interest rate and commodity price shocks in the early 1980s induced by shifting global savings-investment patterns and a policy shift in the North. Following these shocks the commercial banks retreated from new lending to the South, while official creditors did not respond to the pressure on rising current account deficits by stepping up development assistance flows. External and internal adjustment problems had to be faced by all Southern economies, but severe debt problems were largely concentrated among the group of primary exporters. The shift towards non-traded goods sectors created a severe institutional internal transfer problem for these economies: the public sector held the external liabilities, while the private sector (in most cases) generated the foreign exchange. The scope and incentive for adjustment through export expansion was limited by the crisis in commodity markets and a bias towards protecting domestic (import substitution) industries which are not easily transformed into competitive export industries. Adjustment, particularly among LDC-PBs in Latin America and LDC-OBs in Sub-Saharan Africa, thus went through import contraction with negative effects on investment and growth. Fiscal adjustment often remained insufficient, due to political pressures and to endogenous pressures from higher debt-servicing burdens and exchange-rate devaluations intended to improve the trade balance. Sustained fiscal deficits financed by monetary expansion led in many cases to an upward inflationary spiral, domestic financial distress and attempts to avoid exchange rate overvaluation. These factors sustained incentives for private foreign asset accumulation, thus exacerbating the adjustment and internal transfer problems.

Countries, particularly in Southeast Asia, which had already shifted towards a trade orientation based in manufactured exports and with apparently more prudent fiscal policies in the 1960s and 1970s, experienced less stringent medium-term adjustment problems as their incentive structures were already strongly biased towards export expansion.

Differences in bargaining power of creditors, creditor country governments and governments of debtor countries determined the debt renegotiation process in the 1980s. In history (see Chapter 4) debt crises were mostly solved by substantial debt reduction, either through renegotiation (1890s) or default (1920s), for a sustained period. There are recent cases where such financial 'time outs' have been seen to provide successful resolutions of debt problems. For example, Indonesia (1966-71) negotiated reduced payments, Turkey (1979-81), was helped by a substantial increase in official lending, and in Bolivia (1986-87) debt relief was effected via a concerted debt buy-back scheme (cf. Sachs 1989: 23). However, international debt strategy in the 1980s has differed from the historical experience in that debt reduction has played little part. Instead it has reflected differences in power between debtors and creditors and the existence of institutional third parties, such as the IMF and the World Bank. The international financial community feared a collapse of the international financial system and thus pursued a strategy of avoiding debt relief and default by insisting on the fulfilment of debt obligations.[30] Debtor countries feared retaliation by commercial banks in response to a default, particularly the cutting off of trade credits, diplomatic retaliation by creditor governments and lost access to IMF, World Bank and Paris Club support.

This imbalance in bargaining power between debtors and creditors underlies the approaches to the debts of 'private borrowers', specifically: (i) the rescheduling of commercial bank loans, stretching out amortization (in some cases also interest payments) without reducing outstanding debt; (ii) high-conditionality loans supplied by the IMF and World Bank tied to stabilization policy programmes agreed between the IMF and the debtor country governments and providing a 'seal of approval' helpful in commercial-bank and Paris Club debt rescheduling negotiations; and (iii) the agreement of debtors to maintain full and timely servicing of debt obligations.

As shown in section 5.5 this strategy did little to reduce the debt burden of LDC-PBs with debt problems. After six years of this type of debt-crisis management an increasing number of borrowers started to revert to the default option to resolve their internal and external transfer problems. This was more time-consuming and less widespread than in the 1930s, but by the end of 1987 the Latin American borrowers that had unilaterally suspended at least part of interest payments on commercial bank loans (and on parts of the official debt), included Bolivia, Brazil, Costa Rica, the Dominican Republic and Peru, followed by Argentina and Ecuador. The precise point at which countries decide to default is difficult to establish, but again some element of 'contagion' seems to be present. The international financial community in turn optimistically pointed to domestic adjustment and hoped that debtors could 'grow out from under' their debt problems, but as the 1990s begin the US government has launched a new debt proposal (the 'Brady plan') which explicitly recognizes that debt relief is a precondition to resolve the debt crisis.

The 'official creditors' rescheduled their claims through the Paris Club but equally made such reschedulings contingent on an IMF agreement. Most LDC-OBs, particularly in Sub-Saharan Africa, have hesitantly adhered to such conditionality (see for instance, the contributions in Van Arkadie, ed., 1986) to maintain access to IMF and World Bank loans, aid and export credit. While IMF agreements are taken seriously by LDC-OB governments, adherence to debt obligations has been taken less seriously. Accumulated arrears have almost equalled new official financing of LDC-OBs between 1983 and 1988.[31]

5.7 Concluding Remarks

Six major conclusions can be derived from this assessment of North-South financial interactions in the 1970s and 1980s.

Firstly, the most salient feature of the period was the renewed access of developing countries to private financial markets in the North, which was the combined product of, at the microeconomic level, institutional changes in the Northern international banking market (wider sharing of sovereign risk and oligopolistic bank behaviour) and, at the macroeconomic level, shifts in global savings-investment balances following the first oil price increase creating a savings surplus placed in the Northern banking system.

Secondly, the allocation of bank credits among Southern borrowers was determined by creditworthiness assessment by the banks, applying broad risk categories of borrowers. By and large, the richer, middle-income countries had access; the low-income countries did not. The latter had to resort to official sources (Northern donor governments). Flows from these sources were mainly driven by political-economic factors operating on the supply side. From the point of view of the South, the world capital market thus appeared highly segmented. Supply factors were thus strong in determining adjustment in the loan market. The struggle for market shares of commercial banks within the boundaries of apparently fairly uniform credit-rationing rules for broad classes of borrowers led to a strong concentration of bank lending in a small group of countries. Nevertheless, oligopolistic competition during the 1970s did lead *within certain segments of the loan market*, particularly that for middle-income countries, to situations where lending was constrained by demand rather than supply, but always with the boundaries of the credit-rationing points defined by the banks and loan syndicates. Although perhaps with less clear (economic) rationales, donors and their agencies also seem to ensure that their exogenously fixed budgets are spent, at first sight independently of recipient needs.

Thirdly, the supply conditions of bank lending proved unstable. Uncoordinated policies in the North allowed for expansive financial markets in the 1970s and low interest rates. A policy shift in the major economy, the US, inadequately matched by counter-cyclical policies in the other OECD countries, particularly Germany and Japan, and the 'debt non-neutrality' characterizing private sector savings adjustment led to a tightening of financial markets and a strong increase in international interest rates. Other outcomes were recessive tendencies in the North and steeply falling commodity prices (further explained by structural change in the North and protectionist trade policies). Commercial banks responded to the subsequently emerging debt problems by a revulsion to lending to the South (with 'selective contagion' among countries with and without debt problems). Official capital flows provided no alternative to the emerging liquidity problems.

Fourthly, trade and financial interactions between North and South behaved largely pro-cyclically in the 1970s and 1980s. In the 1970s most borrowing countries had to adjust to emerging current account deficits brought on by increased oil import bills; but (with a time lag of a few years) most of the adjustment could take place through external financing instead of domestic adjustment. Export markets and commodity prices showed upward trends in the second half of the 1970s and this provided a further incentive to private lending. In the 1980s, both export markets for most Southern economies (particularly primary exporters) and loan markets were less favourable. Equally, official lending could not ease adjustment for the LDC-OBs by increasing foreign exchange availability when commodity markets collapsed.

Fifthly, the unstable and uncertain external environment did not allow debtor countries to follow 'optimal borrowing strategies'. Different fiscal policy and trade orientations seem to explain, with hindsight, why some countries ran into debt problems and others did not. These factors are initial conditions built up over longer periods of economic development, not – as in many orthodox views of the debt crisis – reflections of 'good' or 'bad' adjustment policies used to cope with external shocks. External borrowing by primary-export economies enlarged their already sizeable non-traded sector and weakened their fiscal structures. When adjustment was required to cope with debt problems and falling export prices, the incentive and capacity to adjust via export expansion (and diversification) was weak and fiscal adjustment difficult. Most manufacturing exporters coped by building on their long-term experience of export expansion and increasing market shares in world trade. Their export markets did not collapse and their industrial structures provided an inherent export drive.

Finally, it could be hypothesized, in line with the argument set out in Chapter 4, that the different behaviour of the principal agents in North-South-North capital movements in the 1970s and 1980s – commercial banks, Northern (creditor) governments, Southern (debtor) governments and Southern private agents – made up an inherently unstable system of trade, accumulation and finance if left to market forces alone. The need for official intervention became effective in the international debt management strategy after 1982. Bargaining strength appeared, unsurprisingly, biased to the creditor side. Management of bank debt reschedulings, coordinated by the IMF and the major creditor country governments, gave priority to safeguarding creditor interests and to limiting the threat LDC debt could pose to the international financial system. Debt could be rescheduled, but this was conditioned to strong policy involvement by, in particular, the IMF. Banks managed to reduce exposure to risky developing-country loans, but the debtors were still deep in debt at the start of the 1990s.

When the Southern debt crisis emerged, no ready-made framework for policy analysis of the specific characteristics of North-South macroeconomic interactions existed. Recent academic research has made some progress, but no consolidated framework has yet been established to integrate the relevant institutional features and behaviour of the principal agents. Moreover, the financial dimensions of North-South interdependence and trade and commodity market interactions seem to be little integrated in analysis. In the next chapters, existing theory is reassessed and the theoretical implications of the empirical findings of this chapter are elaborated.

6 Theories of North-South Capital Movements and Global Adjustment Revisited

6.1 Introduction

This chapter reassesses some of the main theoretical propositions on North-South trade and financial interdependence discussed in Chapter 3, using the empirical evidence supplied in Chapter 5. In particular, the purpose of this chapter is to incorporate the notions of the stylized facts of politically-determined aid supplies and oligopolistic bank-firm behaviour in the international capital market described in Chapter 5 into a model of credit rationing. This alters specifically the loan demand and supply schedules illustrated in Figure 3.3 in Chapter 3. This revisited microeconomic theory of international lending is subsequently embedded into the global macroeconomic accounting framework as elaborated in Chapter 2, setting the basic analytical framework for the subsequent chapters. The focus is on two levels of analysis. Firstly, it discusses the microeconomic determinants of official capital flows and the functioning of the international bank-loan market where the focus is on theoretical foundations of oligopolistic banking behaviour and its consequences for loan market adjustment. Secondly, it reassesses North-South economic interdependence within the framework of the global macroeconomic budget constraints, defined in Chapter 2, and the microeconomic determinants of capital movements as analysed in this chapter.

The resulting propositions form elements for a North-South model of trade, finance and capital accumulation, which will be elaborated in Chapter 7.

6.2 Institutional Determinants of North-South Capital Movements

6.2.1 Official capital

The evidence provided in Chapter 5 on the determinants of official capital flows from North to South supports the following conclusions:

(i) official capital movements from North to South have been a rather stable proportion of Northern GNP over the past two decades; (ii) in line with most theoretical approaches discussed in Chapter 3, supply factors seem to predominate in the determination of the availability and allocation of official capital flows to developing countries; (iii) official flows are the main source of external finance for low-income countries, but a low per capita income does not guarantee greater access to official flows; (iv) the stability of the aid-to-Northern GNP coefficient disguises differences in motives underlying official flows from the various donor countries in the North; these motives relate to specific political motives (colonial history, geopolitics, humanitarian criteria) and are subject to budget constraints set by macroeconomic policy considerations in the North.

One conclusion from Chapter 3 was that microeconomic theories of official capital movements (e.g. the public goods approach) thus far have not yielded convincing and properly testable propositions on the determinants of public capital flows from North to South. In economic models it thus seems safest to treat the supply of aid as determined by exogenous political processes. In macroeconomic terms aid flows (and in the same vein, other non-concessional official capital flows) appear to be supply-side determined. Donors have pre-defined budget constraints on the supply of aid. Within this constraint, aid tends to be allocated among developing countries according to donor-country specific motives and biases. The budget constraints on the total supply of aid might be set by individual donors as a fixed proportion of GNP, but the coefficient may vary with the size of the public sector in the donor country (welfare-state argument) and the political and economic interests in developing countries. There is, however, *a priori* no particular reason for the aggregate supply of official flows to be a stable share of Northern GNP, despite the observed trend over the past two decades. In the subsequent analysis the supply of official capital flows to the South will be seen to be exogenously determined by policy decisions in the North.

Further, it seems justified to assume that developing countries have little means to ensure greater access to aid flows, although in specific cases these may be subject to complex negotiation processes (see Chapter 3 and Mosley 1987). To the extent to which developing countries may be considered foreign-exchange constrained, and given the fact that most official funds are supplied on concessional terms, there will be a likely tendency towards excess demand for such funds. Some rationing mechanism is then required to choke off the excess demand. In the case of bilateral flows the rationing criteria will be linked to the political considerations of the donor governments. In the case of multilateral aid, the basis for rationing decisions may be less obvious. Lending by the World Bank and the International Development Association (IDA) has traditionally been limited to the foreign-exchange component of *approved* projects, while more recently, with the introduction of structural adjustment lending, more general balance-of-payments support is provided under the conditionality that recipient countries are willing to negotiate a package of (often far-reaching) policy reforms.

The international macroeconomic repercussions are closely linked to the classic transfer problem discussed in Chapter 3. In addition to demand and terms of trade effects, the way in which aid flows are financed in the donor countries may also have international repercussions. A tax-financed transfer is likely to produce the deflationary impact on the transferring economy. Fiscal expansion and deficit financing could be an alternative and even provide a demand impulse to the world economy, unless – as discussed below in section 6.3 and in Chapters 7 and 8 – this global effective demand effect is not offset by a 'crowding out' of private spending in the North induced by repercussions from global capital market adjustment.

6.2.2 International bank lending

The empirical analysis in Chapter 5 showed that the particular institutional features of international banking played a crucial role in determining the boom and crisis in private lending to the South in the 1970s and 1980s. The setting was different, but such institutional features also appear to have been central in earlier episodes of major North-South capital movements and debt crises, as concluded in Chapter 4. Oligopolistic banking behaviour and loan syndicates featured in the institutional setting of the most recent cycles in private lending to developing countries. Elaborating propositions suggested by Devlin (1989) and Darity & Horn (1988), the boom in international bank lending to the South in the 1970s was analysed as a process of oligopolistic bank firm competition for market shares. These aspects relating to firm behaviour and market structures are inadequately captured, if at all, in the widely accepted portfolio approach to the functioning of loan markets. 'Neo-orthodox' portfolio theory of international lending, as discussed in Chapter 3, proposes that creditors rationed borrowers in the 1970s and 1980s as a result of sovereign risk and imperfect market information. At first sight, the struggle for market shares (also labelled as 'loan pushing') and credit rationing seem paradoxical, as the former suggests the existence of a demand-constrained market. Chapter 5 suggests that the propositions need not be incompatible, and provides empirical support for this. There it was argued that due to uncertainty and imperfect creditworthiness assessment, banks define broadly defined risk classes of borrowers and credit ceilings for each of them, rather than having market adjustment determined by (risk-adjusted) interest rate adjustment. Depending on particular market circumstances, within different market segments (given by the risk classes) banks may enter into a competition for market shares; i.e. they may operate on a part of the loan supply curve where this part of the market is demand constrained.

The paragraphs that follow give, apart from a graphical exposition, a fairly informal theoretical statement of these central features of the international bank-loan market. They are a starting point for a more rigorous and detailed formalized theory of oligopolistic bank behaviour and the dynamics of the bank–loan market for developing-country borrowers. The model elaborated in Chapter 7 and the model simulations of Chapter 8 try to capture the functioning of the bank-loan market on the basis of some strongly simplified formal rules. For a lack of a fully elaborated theory, some market dynamics, such as the changing expectations and perceptions underlying lending behaviour of banks as observed in Chapter 5, will be imposed on the model as exogenous shocks rather than being endogenized. Nevertheless, despite these limitations the basic ideas can be made clear, at least intuitively.

Before listing the stylized features of the international bank loan market, it is useful to detail the theoretical notions of oligopolistic firm behaviour. Figures 6.1a and 6.1b (derived from Modigliani 1958 and Clark 1985) illustrate the basic notions of oligopolistic firm behaviour as derived from the Bain's theory of oligopoly. Figure 6.1a shows a special case of oligopolistic behaviour of firms that adjust quantity (output) and agree on a market price which effectively bars entrance of new firms. The figure rests on the Sylos postulate (Sylos-Labini 1962) which says that new entrants assume that established firms will maintain their current output level after entrance. Given this assumption, new entrants can calculate how much the market price is likely to adjust after entrance and whether entrance is worthwhile. What is even more important, established firms can determine which price they should set to deter new firms from entering the market. Figure 6.1a assumes there is a minimum efficient scale of production (x^*) or minimum loan value (given informational costs involved in entering new markets). Entrants consider entry only at this scale or above. *LAC* is the long-run average cost curve for established firms and new entrants and *D* is the market demand curve. Under the Sylos postulate, new entrants expect to meet

Figure 6.1a *Oligopolistic behaviour of firms that set quantity (output) and market price to bar entrance of new firms*

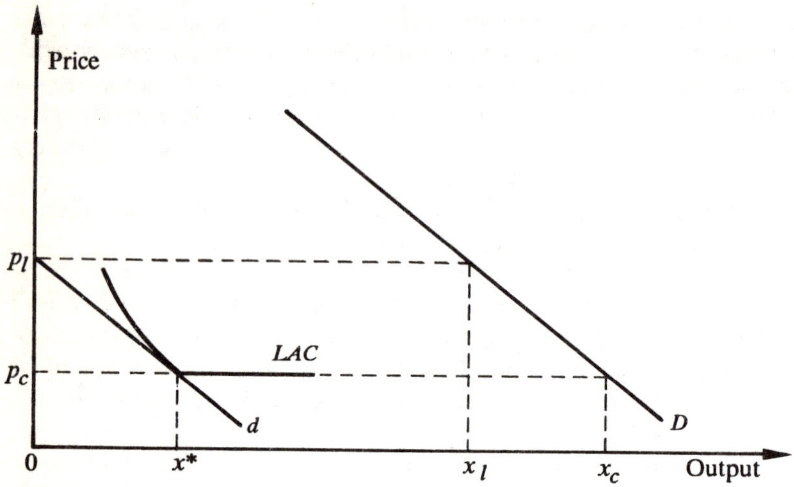

Figure 6.1b *Oligopolistic behaviour of firms that set the limit price to bar entrance at any output level*

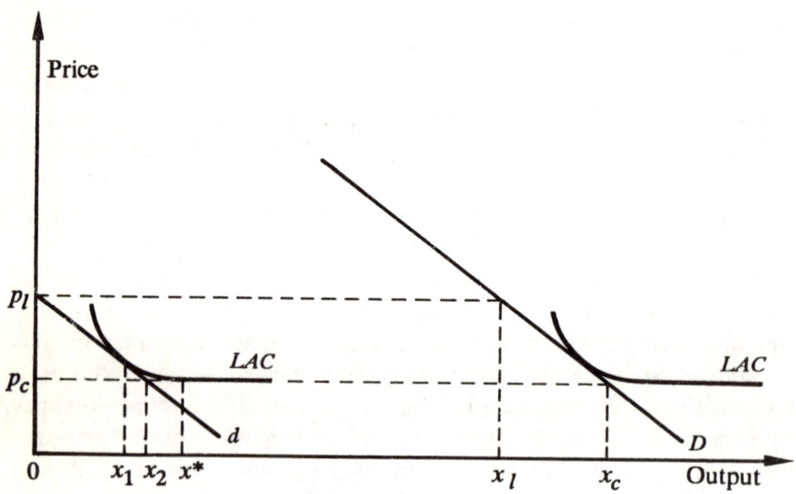

Sources: Modigliani (1958) and Clark (1985)

demand only to the output established by existing firms. To deter entrance, established firms will restrict output such that if new entrants try to enter the market at minimum scale Ox^*, the price would fall below the competitive price, p_c. From the figure it is clear established firms limit output at x_l, such that the minimum scale of entrance equals the difference between the competitive output, x_c, and limit output: $Ox^* = x_l x_c$. In similar fashion the limit price, p_l, is found by drawing the potential demand function for new entrants, d, which lies everywhere below the long-run unit cost curve. The mark-up over the competitive price oligopolistic firms will charge can be derived in its simplest case from a linear market demand function:

$$x = \alpha - \beta p \qquad (6.1)$$

where x is market demand, p is market price and α and β are positive constants. Given that limit output is defined as the difference between competitive output and the minimum efficient scale, $x_l = x_c - x^*$, one may write:

$$\frac{p_l - p_c}{p_c} = \frac{x^*/x_c}{\beta p_c/x_c} = \frac{x^*/x_c}{\eta_c} \qquad (6.2)$$

where η_c $(= p_c/x_c)$ is the market demand elasticity at the competitive price.

The resulting equation shows that the oligopoly mark-up over the competitive price will fall with the minimum efficient scale of production (e.g. because of reduced information costs), with increases in market demand at the competitive price, x_c (e.g. following increased borrowers' demand following external shocks) and with a rising demand elasticity at the competitive price, η_c, implying a flatter demand curve.

Prevention of entry at the minimum efficient scale is only a special case. That this is so, is illustrated by the more general case shown in Figure 6.1b. In this case entry below the minimum scale is also possible while established firms must set the limit price such that entrance at *any* output level is not profitable given the Sylos postulate. The market demand curve for new entrants, d, is drawn tangential to the long-run unit cost curve, *LAC*, such that at no point does d exceed LAC. With the limit price set at p_l threat of new entry starts with the firm of size Ox_l. Clearly, the case in which $Ox^* = Ox_l$ is merely a special one. Generally output is limited at a lower bound, i.e. to $x_l x_c Ox^*$. If established firms fear entry at suboptimal size (i.e. less than Ox^*), limit output will be higher and limit price lower. In this more general case the precise mark-up is less easy to determine, but intuitively the smaller the disadvantage costs of suboptimal production, the lower the limit price should be to deter entrance.

This model of limit pricing and quantity restriction to bar entrance to an oligopolistic market has some obvious limitations and which have been recognized in the literature (Clark 1985: 85-87 provides a summary), but nevertheless it provides a useful benchmark also for analysis of the international credit market. From the description of the international credit market it seems that the stability of market conditions as presumed in Figures 6.1a and 6.1b was interrupted during the 1970s by (i) the expansion of the potential market due to reduced sovereign risk and increased bank liquidity (curve *D* shifts to the right) and (ii) increased risk-sharing and thereby a reduction in the long-run unit cost curve (*LAC* shifts to the left and downwards). As indicated, the banks responded in two ways. Firstly, spreads (mark-ups) were reduced by the established bank firms (the lead banks) as a typical oligopolistic response to the threat of new entrants in order to preserve market shares. Demand curves *D* and *d* flattened as a result, but simultaneously the supply curve of banks also flattened as the banks accept a lower spread while supplying larger quantities. The consequences for the loan market demand- and supply-schedules, starting from the basic framework set out in Chapter 3 (Figure 3.3), are shown below. Secondly, the lead banks organized loan syndicates as a strategic move to maintain market shares. This form of explicit collusion, often introducing new entrants, obviously mitigated the emerging oligopolistic price competition. New entrants tended to be interested to participate as they had less or no experience in international lending, particularly in lending to LDCs; the loan syndicates reduced creditworthiness assessment costs and provided a mechanism of risk-sharing. At the same time, the mechanism attracted even more new entrants as the informational barrier to entry fell for many smaller banks. Loan syndication thus seems to have reinforced the flattening of the demand and loan supply schedules by attracting new entrants, but at the same time mitigated this effect by reducing oligopolistic price competition. Competition between various loan syndicates organized by the lead banks suggest reduction of spreads and a flattening of the supply curve were the predominant changes in the international loan market during the 1970s.

The supply-side conditions of the international bank loan market of the 1970s and 1980s were described in Chapter 5 as follows:

(a) Financial deregulation in the Northern economies led to the creation of the Eurocurrency market and the increasing importance of international banking, particularly by US banks since the late 1950s.

(b) Financial innovations, including cross-default clauses, deposit insurance and loan syndication, made sovereign lending more attractive and enlarged possibilities of risk-sharing.

(c) These innovations took place in a market structure dominated by a highly concentrated banking sector, and lowered the threshold for new entrants. The subsequent tendency towards larger competition in the international credit market was aided by global macroeconomic developments (including the oil price shock) in the early 1970s which enhanced circulating liquidity in Eurocurrency markets.

The large banks responded in two ways to maintain market shares. Firstly, some price cutting (lowering of spreads) took place as a result of the increased competition. Price cutting as a likely response to the threat of new entrants is a well-established hypothesis in theories of industrial organization and oligopoly (see e.g. Clarke 1985 for a survey and below). In the case of the concentrated international banking market 'barriers to new competition' in the sense of Bain's theory (Bain 1956) were broken down as financial innovations reduced some of the absolute-cost and economies-of-scale advantages of the lead banks. Spreads were cut as a consequence. Evidence supplied in Chapter 5 showed that spreads on lending to developing countries were falling in the 1970s and slightly increasing in the 1980s. However, since spreads fluctuated within fairly limited boundaries, quantities (loans) expanded dramatically and real basic interest rates (LIBOR) were already low in the 1970s and high in the 1980s, it seems likely that price competition was not of the 'cut-throat' nature that some theories of oligopolistic competition would predict.[1]

Secondly, the last observation could be explained by the fact that lead banks heavily engaged in loan syndication to extend their loan portfolios, entering new markets (sovereign borrowers in the South) and attracting new entrants (the smaller banks) into the syndicates. Loan syndicates provided a mechanism for risk-sharing and reducing informational costs (including creditworthiness assessment) for new entrants. In terms of the theory of (industrial) oligopoly, the lead banks engaged in a form of 'collusion' and used economies of scale to collect information about the new markets and to keep market shares. As shown by Table 5.5, the lead banks lost some ground, but retained a good share of the market.

To these, one should add two additional supply characteristics:

(d) Despite the drive to expand markets, banks were risk averse and applied credit rationing rules, rather than spreads, to discriminate among different risk classes of borrowers. Banks appear to distinguish only fairly *broad* risk classes of borrowers. In the case of sovereign lending to the South, the average welfare level seems an important criterion to classify *a priori* more and less creditworthy countries. By assessing *country* risk, rather than that of individual borrowers and projects, banks aggregate borrowers within risk classes. Thus, risk assessment is much more related to broad indicators of (expected) economic performance of borrowing countries, than to rates of return on investment projects. The use of broad risk indicators and the selection of broad risk categories forms an important factor in explaining the concentration of lending among a relatively small number of borrowers. The oligopolistic market structure and the aggregation of creditors in loan syndicates, and the related concentration of information, may explain the apparently fairly uniform pattern of creditworthiness assessment and observed 'contagion' effects in lending behaviour.

(e) Substantial fees to be earned by lead banks in the organization of syndicated loans in the 1970s formed an additional incentive to maximize loan volumes within the boundaries of given credit ceilings per country and risk class. Such a driving force may imply that credit ceilings are not merely a function of creditworthiness (default risk) indicators, but are likely to be endogenous to the potential supply of bank credit. This factor should be seen as an additional determinant of the tendency towards a flattening of bank loan supply curves in the 1970s. In addition, these managerial incentives may lead to sub-optimal choices from the perspective of the firm. As suggested by principal-agent theories of the firm (Guttentag & Herring 1985, Holmstrom & Tirole 1989), the principal agents (credit managers) maximize incomes (fees and loan size) but may disregard some potentially costly hazards for the firm. Rational expectations theory assumes market discipline leads decision-makers to form the correct expectations: those making systematic errors will go out of business. If risks are considered low, this hypothesis may have little meaning, since hazards occur so infrequently they may be disregarded. Lending to LDCs was considered low risk in the 1970s, as argued in Chapter 5. Competition drove prudent decision-makers from the market and the managerial incentive systems within the banks (front-end fees) further promoted 'disaster myopia', in the terminology of Guttentag & Herring (1985), in international lending.[2] Heavy concentration of country risk could thus result because of the strategic oligopolistic behaviour to maintain market shares, the managerial incentives to maximize loan size and the lending rules which discriminate between borrowers by broad risk classes, but not so much *within* classes if creditworthy borrowers.

These elements add to a picture of banks as active sellers in broadly defined segments of the loan market during the expansive cycle of lending. Instead of an upward-sloping supply curve, as suggested in the mainstream credit-rationing theory (see Figure 3.3), one would expect the oligopolistic competition to lead to a flattening of the supply curve and possibly become downward sloping (see below). Informational problems and related uncertainties are likely to be the source of the apparently uniform application of credit-rationing mechanisms. These aspects of risk-aversion provide a link with the 'neo-orthodox' credit-rationing literature. However, the rationing of international bank credit in this context is not so much that of the cautious portfolio manager assessing risk at the margin, but that of a bank firm with market shares in mind. Disruption of an initially oligopolistic market situation could trigger a competition for market shares, as in the early 1970s with openings to new entrants and a major expansion in the size of the market. The threat of a debt crisis and a tightening of the market, as in the 1980s, could thus provoke massive retreat from the (broadly defined) market segment of Southern borrowers.

The above suggest a strongly supply-led credit market: not all countries/borrowers have equal market access, which depends on the creditors' perception of the market and creditworthiness. Nevertheless, for those that have access: '*it takes two to tango*', i.e. the supply should be related to factors determining demand. If borrowers follow optimal borrowing strategies and evaluate the costs and benefits of externally financed investment projects, one would expect a downward-sloping demand curve in relation to the interest rate and the level of indebtedness. The higher the interest rate, the lower the incentive to borrow abroad, and the higher the level of indebtedness, the higher the risk of financial distress. However, as demonstrated in Chapter 5, the driving forces on the demand side, aided by supply factors, suggest less 'prudent' borrowing behaviour. In short:

(a) Most commercial bank loans were incurred by public sector borrowers in the South. In the 1970s, most government agencies in these countries were considered 'virgin borrowers' having previously been excluded from private international financial markets. Devlin (1986: 126) emphasizes a possible additional supply factor: as long as new borrowers meet minimum creditworthiness levels, lending may appear to be sound portfolio diversification given the insignificant level of exposure with the bank. Chapter 5 interpreted the same feature as a demand factor: to inexperienced borrowers, commercial bank loans, even though supplied at variable interest rates, were an attractive alternative to official loans tied to donor stringency and direct private foreign investment involving foreign ownership and control of domestic production.[3] Moreover, during the lending boom real interest rates (and spreads) were low.

(b) To most countries, higher import bills following the first oil crisis had increased the demand for foreign exchange, while the new source of finance provided a welcome alternative to inflationary finance in countries with chronic fiscal deficits.

(c) Besides providing finance to postpone or ease adjustment, the rather unexpected availability of low cost loans produced shifts in the spending plans of borrowing agents. The new source of external finance was largely used for large-scale, long-term public investment programmes, probably because borrowers expected a lasting lending boom. With the ending of the boom in the 1980s, public investment programmes in the indebted countries were heavily cut, but pressure on government budgets remained – now caused by the heavy debt-servicing burden. Inadequate export expansion and insufficient capacity of the state to mobilize foreign exchange resources from traded goods sectors to finance expenditures in foreign currencies enhanced, rather than decreased, demand for new external borrowing and debt re-financing in a large part of the South.

On these grounds, one may expect the demand curve to shift, following the availability of external finance. However, for creditors the eagerness to lend will fall after reaching certain levels of indebtedness due to increased default risk, while for debtors the eagerness to borrow may increase in line with debt-servicing needs and if adjusted spending behaviour becomes structural.

The dynamics of the bank-loan market for Southern borrowers as hypothesized above is captured in Figures 6.2a and 6.2b. The first graph shows market behaviour during the expansive phase of lending to the South. In the initial situation the supply curve, schedule B_{S_0}, is derived from Figure 3.3. The curve expressing the relationship between outstanding debt (B_S) and she interest rate (i_W) is initially upward sloping. It is assumed that the lending rate and the level of the spread move in the same direction. For the borrowing country with market access, an almost flat, but declining demand curve – represented by its *ex ante* current account deficit (CA_{S_0}) is assumed. Initially, banks are willing to lend up to point b_{S_0} at interest rate i_{W_0}, where they expect returns on outstanding loans to be maximized. (After this point a larger loan volume is expected to lead to solvency problems with the borrower, while a higher interest rate induces adverse selection and higher default risk; hence, banks supply less financing.) In the figure the demand schedule intersects at an interest rate higher than the expected bank loan-return maximizing i_{W_0}, implying that the demand for external finance exceeds the amounts supplied ($ca_{S_1} - b_{S_0}$). If market conditions change, e.g. the introduction of new risk-sharing loan techniques, new entrants challenging established market interests or a supply shock due to an explosive expansion of loanable funds (cf. the first oil shock), the banks enter a phase of oligopolistic competition, selling loans aggressively and cutting back spreads over the risk-free interest rate (LIBOR). Supply schedules move outward to B_{S_1} and B_{S_2} (reflecting adjusted creditworthiness assessment), but also the schedule flattens during the expansive phase of lending. The demand schedule shifts outward (to CA_{S_1} and CA_{S_2}) following increased supply, but the market may be demand constrained for some time if the supply shock is large. Loan pushing may continue, possibly even beyond critical levels of indebtedness established by the banks themselves. Referring to the 1979-81 period, Guttentag & Herring (1985: 133) see this as a typical case of bank managers experiencing 'cognitive dissonance', i.e. the psychological response of decision-makers to protect self-esteem when new information casts doubt on the wisdom of past decisions (see also Chapter 3).

Figure 6.2b shows the market adjustment to an unfavourable supply shock, e.g. a steep increase in the interest rate at high levels of indebted-

Figure 6.2a International bank lending to South: oligopolistic competition and 'loan pushing' competition

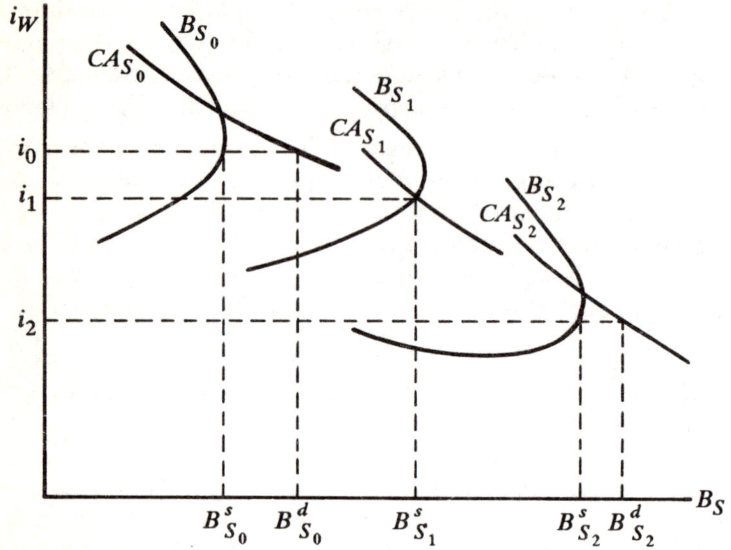

Figure 6.2b International bank lending to South: credit rationing and 'loan revulsion'

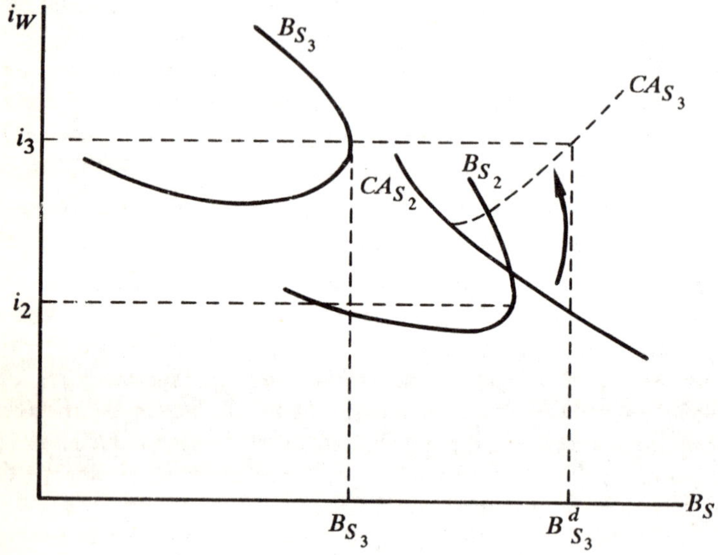

ness followed by a loss of bank confidence in the South in the face of an emerging debt crisis. The cost of funds acquired by banks increases. Borrowers may start facing debt-servicing problems, but find it difficult to adjust domestic spending or to believe they are facing a temporary liquidity crisis, in which case they will demand more external finance at the higher interest rate. The demand schedule will rotate to CA_{S_3}.

Suppliers adjust creditworthiness criteria as they perceive a strong increase in default risk (and risk of bankruptcy if exposure to developing country debt is large *vis-à-vis* bank capital) and lose market confidence. The supply curve shifts back to the left (to B_{S_3}). At the interest rate i_{W_3}, banks are willing to supply the amount b_{S_2} which is less than at rate i_{W_2}, since they expect their loans to become more risky than before as (some) borrowers have run into liquidity problems. With contagion effects from debt-servicing problems of some borrowers, B_S will shift in the same direction for the entire risk class of borrowers (Chapter 5 evidenced the existence of a 'selective' contagion effect). The contagion effects are explained by the aggregation of lenders in syndicates and via cross-default clauses and by informational externalities. Contracting new loans or withdrawal of credit by one lead bank or syndicate will induce a revision in the creditworthiness assessment and perceived likelihood of default of a particular (group of) borrower(s). The loans the banks wish to supply may fall to less than the stock of loans already outstanding, in which case there will be no new voluntary lending.

Excess demand at interest rate i_{W_3} is then given by $(ca_{S_3} - b_{S_3})$. If banks are unwilling to supply the funds to manage the borrowing country's liquidity crisis, default may become a serious option. Otherwise, the country will be forced to domestic adjustment leading to a change in its *ex ante* trade balance to meet debt service obligations (a backward shift of CA_{S_3}).

During contraction of the private lending to the South, tight credit rationing enhances the bargaining power of creditors. However, without a legal mechanism for loan contract enforcement, debt rescheduling seems the second-best option for creditors to avoid major losses and reduce (or at least, postpone) immediate threats of default. As indicated in Chapter 5, this was the predominant debt management strategy during the 1980s. This outcome may be seen as a logical result of the specific institutional context. Firstly, a widely held and plausible assumption (see e.g. Folkerts-Landau 1985; Sachs 1984b, 1989; Krugman 1989) is that debtors perceived default costs to be high given the cross-default clauses (i.e. the risk of losing all access to commercial lending, including trade credits) and possible repercussions by creditor governments. Secondly, the intervention of 'third parties' such as the IMF supplied a mechanism of debt-contract enforcement via high-conditionality loans and rescheduling agreements in an attempt to overcome short-term liquidity. For these two reasons and because of the lack of a debtor cartel, banks found themselves in a strong bargaining position to enter into rescheduling agreements and extract full interest from countries without supplying themselves with new money or accepting some debt relief. Increasing payments problems and instances of defaulting countries have not motivated banks to enter schemes of defensive lending or debt relief, even though it has been argued that this might be in their own interest (Sachs 1988b, Krugman 1989).[4] 'Third party' intervention and the strong bargaining position of the banks reduced incentives to enter such a schemes and in fact made them unnecessary. The banks did not fail to act in their own interest.

The microeconomic determinants of the international loan market for Southern borrowers need to be inserted in the macroeconomic context that sets the budget constraints within which lending is to take place. This issue is taken up in the next section.

6.3 Debt Non-Neutrality, Global Adjustment and the Transfer Problem

A general conclusion from the previous sections is that capital flows to the South are largely supply determined. The microeconomic analysis focused on political determinants underlying the supply of official flows and credit-rationing rules set by oligopolistic bank behaviour underlying private credit flows to Southern borrowers. To assess the implications for the process of global adjustment, these behavioural rules need to be fitted into the global macroeconomic budget constraints of the world accounting framework as defined in Chapter 2. This section broadly identifies the possible implications and how these relate to three other theoretical notions discussed in the previous chapters: the transfer problem, the issue of debt-neutrality and Northern fiscal policies, and the Southern internal transfer problem. In Chapters 7 and 8 these themes will be integrated into a more specified North-South model to analyse the mechanisms of global adjustment.

The global accounting rules stated that, *ex post*, the world current account (deficit) and accumulation balance should equal zero (see also equation 2.8):

$$CA_N + CA_S \equiv [(I_N - S_N)_p + [\theta (I_S - S_S) + \theta DEF_S] \equiv 0 \qquad (6.3)$$

while the financial constraints in each region are given by (using 2.10 and 2.11):

$$CA_N - [\Delta B_N + \Delta DC_N - \Delta A - \Delta J_N - \Delta H_N - \Delta IF] \equiv 0 \qquad (6.4)$$

$$CA_S - [\Delta B_S + \Delta A - \Delta J_S - \Delta H_S + \Delta IF] \equiv 0 \qquad (6.5)$$

The flow equilibrium in the world financial market was defined by (equation 2.9):

$$\Delta B^s \equiv \Delta B_N + \Delta B_S \equiv \Delta J_S + \Delta J_N + \Delta H - \Delta DC_N \qquad (6.6)$$

where ΔB^s is the net change in the total supply of bank loans.

In theory there may be many alternative adjustment mechanisms for this global system, but the analysis to this point suggests that the degrees of freedom, particularly for the Southern economy, may be quite limited. To a large extent the limitations stem from financial constraints. The role for direct foreign investment *(ΔIF)* is likely to be determined by strategic decisions of Northern firms (see Chapter 3, section 3.2.1), but as before the role of this type of capital flow will be de-emphasized. Official capital flows *(ΔA)* are, in the aggregate, exogenous for the South and determined by political factors in the North. The supply of bank credits *(ΔB_S)* is set by the credit-rationing rules of international banks. From the analysis in the previous section one could suggest the following generally specified aggregate supply function:

$$\Delta B_S = \sum \Delta B_{Si} = \sum b_{Si} [(Y_S/N_S)_i ; N_i ; (B_S/\theta E_{Si}) ; \sigma_{xi} B^s] \qquad (6.7)$$

$$\text{if } (Y_S/N_S)_i < (Y_S/N_S)_i^{min}, \text{ then } \Delta B_{Si} = 0$$

where it is assumed, following the analysis of Chapter 5, that (i) banks consider the South as a whole a separate risk class of borrowers to which banks are willing to supply only a certain share in their total portfolio, determined by a confidence parameter x; (ii) banks discriminate between broad risk classes: at the bottom are the countries considered not creditworthy ***a priori***, e.g. because they have a per capita income level (Y_S/N_{S_i}) and economic size (N_i) below a certain minimum set by the banks, while creditworthy countries tend to receive loans in function of a general solvency parameter $(B_S/\theta E_S)_{-1}$; and (iii) credit limits may shift because of economic performance in countries eligible for a loan (changes in solvency parameter), because of changes in overall credit availability (B^s) and/or because of a change in market conditions and confidence (risk-reducing innovations, new entrants, threat of widespread default) leading to a shift in the confidence parameter σ_x. The confidence parameter is equal for all Southern borrowers if there is general contagion ($\sigma_{xi} = \sigma_x$), but may vary for broad risk classes if contagion is selective. If there is vigorous competition for market shares, banks will try to push loans up to permissible credit ceilings.

Starting from these conditions of international finance, the major themes of earlier chapters may be reassessed:

(i) the transfer problem (i.e. trade adjustment after financial transfers);

(ii) global repercussions of Northern real and financial adjustment; and

(iii) the scope for alternative adjustment options in the South.

These three issues will now be briefly assessed in reverse order.

Southern adjustment

Traditional theoretical frameworks to assess the role of international capital flows (e.g. the two-gap model) are mostly confined to one-way movements or net capital inflows. Segmented capital markets and heterogeneous responses of public and private agents to changing conditions of external finance demand a more disaggregated approach. External borrowing by the South has been closely related to public sector deficits and private capital outflows are likely to have restrained domestic private investment. High demand elasticity for external finance by the public sector and the given supply conditions of ΔA, ΔB_S and ΔIF, imply that for a given reserve position (ΔH_S) the Southern current account balance is mainly conditioned by supply conditions of various types of external finance. The remaining component, private foreign asset acquisition (ΔJ_S), is largely a function of financial criteria, implying that Southern external adjustment is conditioned by portfolio decisions of foreign creditors and domestic private agents. The analysis in Chapter 5 suggested private capital outflows are determined by both external factors (availability of external finance, rates of return on foreign assets) and internal factors (real exchange rate, domestic rate of return, and lifestyles of the rich). It was also suggested that these determinants may reinforce each other. External commercial borrowing and aid receipts mainly flowed into the public sector and, almost simultaneously, to non-traded activities. In cases of managed exchange rate regimes this led to upward pressure on real exchange rates, which reduced profitability in traded goods sectors and exchange rate-adjusted interest rates on domestic financial assets.

The fact that a portion of private savings surpluses tends to be invested in the North has hampered Southern adjustment in the 1980s. Fiscal balances in countries with large debts at variable interest rates have become increasingly sensitive to Northern adjustment (and the effects on the global interest rate). The capacity to generate the required trade surpluses to effectuate net financial transfers from the public sector to Northern creditors has varied. The existence of private capital outflows increases pressure on domestic foreign exchange markets. Import cuts tend to dominate adjustment where the growth of export earnings is hampered by a lack of buoyant world commodity markets (particularly in the case of primary exporters) and export diversification cannot easily be achieved due to structural supply bottlenecks and slow policy adjustment (governments resisting major exchange rate adjustments because of their impact on the fiscal balance). The size of the required adjustment appears for the most part endogenous to the behaviour of the principal agents in the North and the resulting levels of available finance, world interest rate and income growth (i.e. demand for Southern exports).

Northern public-private sector interactions and global capital market adjustment

The counterpart accounting balance of the Northern current account balance is given by the Northern private savings and fiscal balances [$CA_N \equiv (I_N - S_N)_p + DEF_N$]. The size of the world capital market defined in the broad sense is largely determined by Northern savings and investment (see Chapter 5). Increasing fiscal deficits in the North may lead to *ex ante* current account deficits (or lower surpluses) as private sector savings balances do not tend to automatically accommodate changes in the fiscal balance. The latter effect has been explained by the empirical literature (i) in terms of debt non-neutrality or the non-existence of the Ricardo-Barro equivalence theorem, i.e. intertemporal savings decisions do not (fully) discount future taxes from bond- or monetary-financed fiscal deficits; and/or (ii) from the standard IS/LM approach, a less than fully compensatory 'crowding-out' effect of private spending as a consequence of government deficit financing. However, the same outcome may also result from alternative specifications as long as private savings and investment decisions are not fully interdependent with fiscal policies and capital markets are imperfect. In other words, the effect of fiscal policies on credit availability and the interest rate is not fully compensated by accommodation of private savings and investment as it is likely that these only partially depend on financial variables.

Chapter 5 provided empirical evidence for this incongruity of private sector accumulation behaviour and financing of fiscal deficits, both within and among the major economies of the North. The observed instability of world interest rates was seen to be a result of this macro-adjustment behaviour. From the global framework set out here, it would appear that a bond-financed increase in the Northern fiscal and inadequate private savings adjustment $(\partial(DEF_N)/\partial(S_N - I_N)_p > 1)$, is likely to lead to an increase in the world interest rate. The underlying assumption is that the global interest rate is a function of the global excess demand for loanable funds, i.e.:

$$i_W = ED_B\,[\Delta B_N^d + \Delta B_S - \Delta B^s\,]$$

where Northern *ex ante* demand for bank credits is given by ΔB_N^d.

The function for the interest rate may also be written as, using equations 6.3, 6.4, 6.6 and 6.7:[5]

$$i_W = ED_B\,[(I_N - S_N)_p + \Delta J_N + \Delta H_N + \Delta IF + \Delta B_S + \Delta DC_N - (\Delta J + \Delta H)] \quad (6.8)$$

All other factors being equal, an increase in Northern government bond financing (DC_N) will tend to lead to a rise in the rate of interest, i_W. Increased aid flows funded by the same type of deficit financing will thus have the same effect. The precise macroeconomic implications will have to be derived, however, from a more complete global model specification as there will be repercussions of the financial market adjustment (and interest rate changes) on demand for other financial assets, incomes, savings and investment and thereby on trade.

Trade balances and the transfer problem

Equation 6.5 assumed that Southern access to private finance is partly dependent on export performance, i.e. finance and trade interact procyclically. Part of export performance depends on the terms of trade (θ), which brings the classic transfer problem back to the fore: how will the terms of trade adjust to effectuate the financial transfer? Chapter 5 suggested that, at least in the 1980s, there may have been a case for the 'orthodox position' of a secondary burden falling on the transferring country: increasing interest rates and a collapse in the availability of new lending turned the indebted parts of the South into net suppliers of financial resources to the North and at the same time they witnessed a terms-of-trade deterioration. However, evidence also supports the opposite case of 'official borrowers' who remained net recipients of transfers while witnessing falling terms of trade in the 1980s. Export structures, differences in the determination of official and private capital movements, adjustment of global financial markets and Northern macroeconomic adjustment seem to provide the complex background to these diverging trends. Firstly, terms-of-trade effects have been strongest in countries heavily reliant on primary exports and may be related to the price-clearing nature of most primary commodity markets and the low income elasticity in the North of this type of goods. Secondly, higher interest rates helped to influence lower investment demand in the North thereby slowing growth and demand for Southern commodities. Primary exporters with a large commercial external debt at variable interest rates were thus doubly affected by higher interest rates and lower real export prices leading to the 'orthodox' transfer problem. Official borrowers were hit less hard by the higher interest rates and the crisis in international lending, but did carry the terms-of-trade burden. The nature of Northern adjustment may be one important factor underlying this apparent trade-off between aid and trade: increased aid flows will increase fiscal deficits in the North and, if financed from the capital market, put upward pressure on interest rates which spills over to commodity markets via decreased effective demand.

6.4 Concluding remarks

This chapter reviewed key elements of theories of public and private capital flows from North to South in the light of the empirical analysis of Chapter 5. Further, it redefined the global budget constraints to North-South financial intermediation and official capital movements, and discussed some implications of the microeconomic determinants of these international financial transactions for the global adjustment process. A more complete model specification would also need to take account of general equilibrium effects. In the next chapter a simple North-South model is elaborated which incorporates the theoretical propositions put forward in this chapter about institutional behaviour in capital markets and the global macroeconomic budget constraints.

7 Global Interactions: Aid Flows and Commercial Bank Lending in a Structuralist North–South Model

7.1 Introduction

This chapter describes the *STAC* model: a Structuralist North–South Trade model with endogenous Aid flows and bank Credits. The focus is on the functioning of global capital markets, as defined in Chapter 6, and their impact on trade and growth in the two regions. That is, the model attempts to capture the workings of a segmented capital market with Southern borrowers having more restricted access to international credit supplies than borrowers in the North and their supply of credit being rationed by Northern banks and donor agencies on the basis of creditworthiness assessment and political factors. The model further brings out interactions between fiscal and private savings-investment balances within and between both regions and, because a role is assigned to foreign asset acquisition by Southern agents, shows that capital may flow in both directions. These capital market characteristics are included in a simple model determining output and trade of North and South (and a third region of oil exporters).

The model fits into a recent tradition of North–South modelling. Some fundamentals were already discussed in Chapter 3. The initial models focused on the essentials of trade interactions between North and South (Findlay 1980, 1984; Taylor 1981; and Vines 1984). More recent models also include a role for capital flows (Taylor 1985, Burgstaller & Saavedra-Rivano 1984, van Wijnbergen 1985, Darity 1987, Beenstock 1988, Dutt 1988, Currie & Vines et al. 1988, Muscatelli & Vines 1989). In this chapter the distinctive features of the STAC model are spelled out. In Chapter 8 the outcomes of the STAC model are further compared with some of the existing applied models.

The modelling of commodity markets is very much along the lines of the North–South models of the type discussed in Chapter 3 (see particularly Findlay 1980, 1984 and Taylor 1981). The model developed here follows in its basic setup that of Taylor (1981), assuming complete specialization in trade with the South producing a flex-price composite primary commodity, the North a fix-price manufactured product, and a region of oil producers selling oil at a fixed price for use as an intermediate good for production in the North. In other words, commodity market adjustment is structurally different between the regions. Following existing North–South models, the economies are also structurally different. The South is assumed to be characterized by labour-surplus conditions à la Lewis (1954) with the real wage fixed at an institutionally determined subsistence level, while output is constrained and determined by available capital and foreign exchange (since investment goods must be imported from the North).[1] The Northern commodity market is demand-constrained and price formation is a function of oligopolistic firm behaviour (as in Taylor 1981)[2], which is also assumed to be crucial – in line with the Kaleckian approach – in determining the real wage and in determining private savings and investment behaviour.

The key addendum to the model elaborated in this chapter is the inclusion of a segmented world capital market. Other models have assumed no capital mobility, as in the basic Findlay model (Findlay 1980), passively adjusting capital movements to match the trade balances of the regions (Taylor 1981), or a homogeneous and perfect capital market with capital moving in response to rate of return differentials (Burgstaller & Saavedra-Rivano 1984, Quibria 1986, Dutt 1988). Beenstock (1988) elaborates an econometric North–South model with mainly neoclassical and monetarist features. The global capital market is interest-rate clearing with sovereign risk taken care of in the spread over the base rate. Neither bank behaviour nor credit rationing play a role. Darity (1987) provides a North–South model with mark-up pricing characterizing the behaviour of commodity markets in *both* regions, but unequal access to bank credits determining the structural difference. In this model commercial banks are the single financial intermediary, Southern agents are residual borrowers and the spread over LIBOR clears the world credit market (Darity 1987: 218). With excess supply of loanable funds, spreads will fall and banks will 'push' loans to the South. Consistent with the analysis of commercial bank behaviour in the previous chapters, the model developed in this chapter emphasizes credit rationing procedures of banks rather than the use of spreads to determine loan supplies to the South.

The STAC model thus allows for an analysis of North–South interdependence under a number of specific assumptions about the nature of world commodity and capital markets and the related behaviour of the agents distinguished in the system. The modelling of commodity markets is obviously strongly restricted by the assumption of complete specialization, but provides a link with a part of the literature in the field and may still have some relevance for the large group of mainly primary commodity exporting developing countries.[3] The modelling of capital flows is, of course, also highly stylized, but is consistent with the analysis of markets and institutional behaviour of the previous chapters.

Another major simplification of the model is that the world economy is treated as a single-currency area, omitting exchange rate movements, the inclusion of which would substantially complicate the model. What is more, money as such plays no explicit role; instead, the Northern commodity serves as a means of exchange. Thus both inflationary processes and exchange-rate effects are omitted. These assumptions allow a focus on the impact of the process of international credit allocation (credit rationing) in global adjustment. In fact under these assumptions, financial assets and liabilities represent future claims or 'options' on Northern *commodities*. Their price (interest rate) should also be interpreted in these terms. A further important implication of the omission of an explicit role for money in the model is that policy-driven demand impulses from the North (deficit financing) are immediately dampened through the impact on the global capital market, since Northern government demands restrain credit availability of the other agents in the system.

Recognizing these limitations, the structuralist North–South model with aid and credit rationing (STAC) elaborated here is conducive to analysing the impact of supply-side driven capital movements operating in different market segments on growth, macroeconomic and commodity-market adjustment in both regions. The existence of public sector fiscal activity in both the North and the South and capital flight from the South introduces the possibility of both crowding-in and crowding-out effects on investment and growth within and between the two regions. The global and regional impacts of Northern and Southern fiscal deficits tend to be strongly asymmetric. This chapter outlines the model and explains its operations analytically.

The key features of the model are described and theoretically justified. The nature of the model closure is discussed and the model for growth interactions between the Northern and Southern economy is solved. Interactions between North and South for different capital market conditions are compared, treating respectively cases with no capital flows, with foreign aid flows only, and with predominantly commercial bank activity. In the final chapters of the book a number of numerical policy simulations with the STAC model are discussed and compared with outcomes and policy conclusions of alternative theoretical and empirical North–South models.

7.2 The STAC Model: Structural Features

Table 7.1 summarizes the basic equations of the STAC model and Table 7.2 describes the variables and parameters. The model takes the Northern price (P_N) as *numéraire*, so that all variables are expressed in terms of the Northern commodity.

The model specifications are set up around three specific commodity markets (primary commodities, manufactures and oil) and a particular institutional structure characterizing the functioning of the global credit market. As indicated, the commodity market specifications of the model define structurally different economies and are largely derived from Taylor's theoretical North–South model. The specification of North–South capital movements follows the analysis of the previous chapters.

The North is assumed to produce manufactures in a market structure dominated by oligopolistic firms producing under conditions of excess capacity. These market conditions are reflected in mark-up pricing rules determining the Northern price and income distribution between wages and profits. Macro-adjustment in the North is demand constrained. In contrast, the production of primary commodities in the South is assumed to be supply and foreign-exchange constrained, i.e. output is determined for a given capital stock and all capital goods are imported. As a stylized fact, primary commodities are assumed to be auctioned at the world market. This commodity market clears for price adjustment and, given Northern price setting, determines the Southern terms of trade. Surplus labour conditions in the South are assumed to set the Southern real wage at an institutionally fixed minimum and determines terms of trade, income distribution and private savings. A third region of oil exporters produces oil at an institutionally set price (e.g. OPEC negotiations, but see also Chapter 5).

The credit market is assumed to be concentrated and dominated by oligopolistic banking behaviour. Banks distinguish between broad risk classes of borrowers and Northern borrowers apparently have unrestrained access, while Southern borrowers are rationed on the basis of their imperfect creditworthiness assessment by the banks. It is assumed that there is enough competition in the market (e.g. triggered by risk-reducing financial innovations) to drive banks to place loans up to the credit ceiling set for Southern borrowers. While the Southern credit market segment is assumed to adjust for quantities, the global credit market as a whole is assumed to adjust, jointly with the market for Northern government bonds, for the world interest rate.

These market structures condition the behaviour of eight agents, namely the six agents discussed in Chapter 5, plus, following other models, the Northern and Southern private sectors split into wage- and profit-earners:

(1) Northern workers are assumed to be passive actors in the present specifications, receiving a wage income which is entirely spent;[4]

(2) Northern profit earners (owners/managers of firms) control their profit shares through mark-up pricing as they are assumed to operate in an oligopolistically structured market; their savings and borrowing behaviour are subject to portfolio considerations;

(3) the Northern government sector acts according to predefined fiscal policy objectives (in the basic model specification, these are a given level of public expenditures and development aid to the South) and affects both the Northern and the global economy through its spending policy, supply of aid flows to the South and deficit financing strategy;

(4) international banks maximize the volume of lending constrained by credit-rationing rules applied to Southern borrowers;

(5) Southern workers are also passive, with no real bargaining power due to the labour surplus;

(6) profit earners (owners of firms in primary production) maximize current income through portfolio behaviour, i.e. by seeking the highest rate of return on domestic investment in physical capital and foreign financial assets;

(7) the Southern government tries to achieve the highest possible public investment rate to enhance welfare, within the constraints of available budgetary finance and limited by its political power to tax private incomes, its access to external finance and debt management criteria.

(8) oil exporters set the price of oil and deposit their savings surplus in the international banking sector.

In the sections below these behavioural assumptions are detailed following the sequence of equations of Table 7.1.

Table 7.1 STAC model: structural equations

	South	
(7.1)	$Q_S=\omega_S(L_S+L_{Sg})+M_{NS}$	Supply-demand balance for Southern commodity.
(7.2)	$Q_S=\sigma_{Sp}K_S+\sigma_{Sg}K_{Sg}$ where: $k=K_S/K_{Sg}$; $\sigma_{Sp}=\delta Q_S/K_S$; $\sigma_{Sg}=(1-\delta)kQ_S/K_S$	Production function.
(7.3)	$L_S=Q_S/q_S$	Southern employment in export sector.
(7.4)	$R_S=(1-\omega_S/q_S)\,\theta Q_S$	Southern profits.
(7.5)	$DEF_S=\Delta F_S^a+\Delta B_{Sg}= =\theta\omega_S L_{Sg}+(1+x_S)\,i_W B_{Sg}+I_{Sg}-t_S R_S$	Southern fiscal deficit and financing
(7.6)	$M_{SN}=\theta M_{NS}+\Delta F_S^a+\Delta B_S-\Delta J_S$ $-(1+x_S)i_W B_{Sg}-(1+x_S)i_w B_{Sp}+i_W J_S$	Southern imports & net transfer from abroad.
(7.7)	$S_S=s_S\,(1-t_S)\,R_S+i_W J_S-(1+x_S)\,i_W B_{Sp}$	Southern savings.
(7.8)	$I_S=S_S-\Delta J_S+(\Delta B_S-\Delta B_{Sg})$	Southern investment (finance constrained).
	Major Oil Exporters	
(7.9)	$Q_O=m_{NO}Q_N$	Actual oil production.
(7.10)	$M_{ON}=m_{ON}\nu Q_O$	Import demand.
(7.11)	$\Delta J_O=s_O\,\nu Q_O+i_W J_O$	Real savings & cur. acct. balance; $s_O=(1-m_{ON})$.
	North	
(7.12)	$1=(1+\tau)\,[\omega_N/q_N+\nu m_{NO}]$ where: $q_N=Q_N/L_N$ and $P_N=1$	Northern mark-up rule & real wage determination.
(7.13)	$Q_N=C_N+I_N+G_N$ $+M_{SN}+M_{ON}-\theta M_{NS}$	Northern supply-demand balance.
(7.14)	$C_N=(1-t_N)\,\gamma\,Q_N$ where: $\gamma=[\omega_N/q_N+(1-s_N)\,\tau\,(\omega_N/q_N+\nu m_{NO})]$	Northern consumption demand.

(Continued...)

(Table 7.1 Continued)

(7.15a)	$\theta M_{NS}=\alpha(1-t_N)\gamma Q_N+A\theta$	Northern demand for Southern good.
(7.15b)	$C_{NN}=C_N-\theta M_{NS}=(1-\alpha)(1-t_N)\gamma Q_N-A\theta$	Northern consumption home good.
(7.16)	$I_N=[g_{0N}+g_{1N}(r_N+u)-g_{2N}(1+x_N)i_W]K_N$	Northern invest. demand.
(7.17)	$r_N=[1-(\omega_N/q_N+vm_{NO})]Q_N/K_N$	Northern profit rate.
(7.18)	$u=Q_N/K_N$	Northern capacity utilization parameter.
(7.19)	$S_N=s_N(1-t_N)[\tau(\omega_N/q_N+vm_{NO})]Q_N+$ $(1+x_S)i_W(B_{Sg}+B_{Sp})+i_WDC_N-i_W(J_0+J_S)$	Northern savings.
(7.20)	$DEF_N=\Delta DC_N=G_N+i_WDC_N$ $-t_N(1-vm_{N0})Q_N+\Delta F_S^a$	Fiscal deficit and financing.
	World Financial System	
(7.21)	$\Delta B^s=\Delta J_N+\Delta J_O+\Delta J_S-\Delta DC_N$	World commercial credit supply
(7.22)	$\Delta J_N=j_{0N}J_N+j_{1N}(i_W-r_N)_{-1}S_N$	Northern demand for deposits.
(7.23)	$\Delta J_S=j_{0S}J_S+j_{1S}(i_W-r_S)_{-1}S_S$ where: $r_S=R_S/K_S$	Southern demand for deposits.
(7.24)	$\Delta B_N^d=b_{1N}I_N$	Northern private sector demand for bank credits.
(7.25)	$\Delta B_{Sg}^d=\Omega^{-1}[(1+x_S)i_WB_{Sg}]-(\theta M_{NS})-\Delta F_S^a$ where: $\Omega=[(1+x_S)i_WB_{Sg}/(\theta M_{NS}+\Delta B_{Sg}+\Delta F_S^a)]^{max}$	Southern public sector demand for international bank loans.
	if: $\Delta B_S\leq\Delta B_{Sg}^d$, then $\Delta B_{Sg}=\Delta B_S$	Limit to debt-servicing cap. set by Southern gov't.
	if: $\Delta B_S\geq\Delta B_{Sg}^d$, then $\Delta B_{Sg}=\Delta B_{Sg}^d$	Credit rationing to Southern govt.
	and further, if: $(1+x_S)i_WB_{Sg}/(\theta M_{NS}+\Delta B_{Sg}+\Delta F_S^a)>\Omega$ then, if $\Delta B_{Sg}<0$, set $\Delta B_{Sg}=0$ then, if $(1+x_S)i_WB_{Sg}/(\theta M_{NS}+\Delta F_S^a)>\Omega$ set $(1+x_S)i_WB_{Sg}=\Omega(\theta M_{NS}+\Delta F_S^a)$	Default option, Southern govt.

(Continued...)

(Table 7.1 Continued)

(7.26)	$\Delta B_S = b_{1S}\,[(B_S/\theta M_{NS})^{emax} - (B_S/\theta M_{NS})_{-1}]\Delta B_S$	Supply-determined bank credit flows to the South.
(7.27)	$\Delta B_N^d + \Delta B_S = \Delta B^s$	Global credit market equilibrium

End-of-year stock variables

$K_{N+1} = K_N + I_N$	Physical capital stock, *N*.
$K_{S+1} = K_S + I_S$	Private physical capital stock, *S*.
$K_{Sg+1} = K_S + I_{Sg}$	Public physical capital stock, *S*.
$B_{N+1} = B_N + \Delta B_N^d$	Outstanding bank debt, *N*.
$B_{Sg+1} = B_S + \Delta B_{Sg}$	Outstanding public sector bank debt, *S*.
$B_{Sp+1} = B_{Sp} + (\Delta B_S - \Delta B_{Sg})$	Outstanding private sector bank debt, *S*.
$B_{S+1} = B_{Sg+1} + B_{Sp+1}$	Outstanding bank debt, *S*.
$DC_{N+1} = DC_N + \Delta DC_N$	Domestic government debt, *N*.
$J_{i+1} = J_i + \Delta J_i \quad (i = N, S, O)$	Total bank deposits by region.

Table 7.2 List of variables

Endogenous variables		
ΔB^s	=	Net total commercial bank credit flow.
ΔB_N	=	Net commercial bank credit demand of Northern borrowers.
ΔB_S	=	Net commercial bank credit flow to Southern borrowers.
ΔB^d_{Sg}, ΔB_{Sg}	=	Net commercial bank credit demand (and realized demand) of Southern government.
C_N	=	Consumption demand, North.
ΔDC_N	=	Northern government debt (net flow).
I_N	=	Private investment in North.
I_S	=	Private investment in South.
I_{Sg}	=	Public investment in South.
i_W	=	World interest rate.
ΔJ_N	=	Bank deposits, North (flow).
ΔJ_S	=	Bank deposits, South (flow).
ΔJ_O	=	Bank deposits, oil-exporters (flow) (equals savings, oil exporters).
L_S	=	Employment in commodity production, South.
M_{NS}	=	Imports of North from South.
M_{ON}	=	Imports of oil exporters from North.
M_{SN}	=	Imports of South from North.
Q_N	=	Output Northern commodity.
Q_O	=	Output, oil.
Q_S	=	Output, Southern commodity.
R_N, r_N	=	Northern profits and profit rate.
R_S, r_S	=	Southern profits and profit rate.
S_N	=	Northern savings.
S_S	=	Southern savings.
u	=	Northern capacity utilization parameter.
θ	=	Relative price (terms of trade) Southern commodity (in units of Northern commodity).
ω_N	=	Real wage, North (in terms of Northern commodity).

(Continued...)

(*Table 7.2 Continued*)

Other endogenous variable labels (not used in model solution)		
C_{NN}	=	Northern consumption demand for Northern commodity.
DEF_N	=	Fiscal deficit, North.
DEF_S	=	Fiscal deficit, South.
L_N	=	Employment, North.
Exogenous variables		
A	=	Constant term in Northern consumption function.
B_N	=	Beginning-of-period outstanding commercial bank debt, North.
B_S	=	Beginning-of-period outstanding commercial bank debt, South.
B_{Sg}	=	Beginning-of-period outstanding commercial bank debt, public sector, South.
B_{Sp}	=	Beginning-of-period outstanding commercial bank debt, private sector, South.
DC_N	=	Beginning-of-period Northern government debt (outstanding).
ΔF_S^a	=	Official aid flows from North to South.
G_N	=	Government expenditures, North.
$(B_S/\theta M_{NS})^{emax}$	=	Creditworthiness indicator, South.
J_N	=	Beginning-of-period bank deposits, North (stock).
J_S	=	Beginning-of-period bank deposits, South (stock).
J_O	=	Beginning-of-period bank deposits, oil exporters (stock).
K_N	=	Beginning-of-period capital stock, North.
K_S	=	Beginning-of-period private capital stock, South.
K_{Sg}	=	Beginning-of-period public capital stock, South.
L_{Sg}	=	Public sector employment, South.
x_N	=	Mark-up determining interest-rate spread on bank loans to North.
x_S	=	Mark-up determining interest-rate spread on bank loans to South.

(*Continued...*)

(Table 7.2 Continued)

	Exogenous parameters and coefficients	
b_{1N}	=	Northern credit demand parameter.
b_{1S}	=	Response (confidence) parameter to South's creditworthiness.
g_{0N}	=	Constant in investment demand function North.
g_{1N}	=	Profit response parameter investment demand function North.
g_{2N}	=	Interest-rate response parameter inv. demand function North.
j_{0i}	=	Constant in deposit demand function $(i = N, S)$.
j_{1i}	=	Response parameter deposit demand function $(i = N, S)$.
k	=	Ratio of Southern private to public capital stock.
m_{NO}	=	Import propensity of oil consumption North.
m_{ON}	=	Import propensity of oil exporters' dem. for Northern commodity.
q_N	=	Labour productivity North.
q_S	=	Labour productivity South.
s_N	=	Savings rate North.
s_O	=	Savings rate oil exporters.
s_S	=	Savings rate South.
t_N	=	Tax rate North.
t_S	=	Tax rate South.
α	=	Income propensity to consume Southern good in North.
σ_S	=	Output-capital ratio South.
δ	=	Distributional parameter Southern production function.
τ	=	Mark-up rate Northern price formation.
ω_S	=	Real wage South.
ν	=	Relative price of oil (in terms of Northern commodity).
Ω	=	Policy determined cap on debt servicing to foreign exchange availability in South, determining upper bound of Southern demand for bank loans.

7.2.1 The Southern economy

The supply-demand balance of the Southern, primary commodity is specified in equation 7.1, with real demand consisting of the real wage bill (the exogenously set uniform real wage, ω_S times employment in primary production, L_S, and public sector employment, L_{Sg}) plus export demand. Thus, Southern wage income is assumed to be fully spent on the primary commodity. The Southern commodity is only imported by the North and the corresponding demand function is specified below (eq. 7.15a). Employment in the primary sector increases, for a given productivity level (q_S), proportionally to output (7.3): [$L_S = (1/q_S)\, Q_S$], while public sector employment is assumed to be a policy variable. Output, Q_S, is constrained by capital, so that there is full capacity utilization (as opposed to demand-determined output in the North, see below). Equation 7.2 reflects a linear production function with two complementary types of capital: public (infrastructure) and private (land and machines).[5] Output will increase with public investment on the assumption that inadequate infrastructure forms a bottleneck in production. The output-capital ratio for Southern commodity production, σ_S , is decomposed into ratios for public and private capital weighted by a distributional parameter (δ). Average capital productivity may decrease, however, if the capital-output ratio of public investment is relatively high (as described in Chapter 5).

Equation 7.4 defines the level of Southern profits in terms of the Northern commodity as primary commodity output less wage costs, where θ is the terms of trade between primary commodities and manufactures. The determination of the terms of trade for the South is described below in the context of the interactions between the Southern and Northern economies.

Total Southern government revenue is determined as a linear function of profits (in eq. 7.5). Current government expenditures in the South consist of the public sector wage bill and interest payments on external government debt [$(1+x_S)\, i_W\, B_{Sg}$], where x_S is a mark-up rate determining the spread over the world interest rate (i_W) for Southern borrowers, set exogenously by the banks. The level of public investment, I_{Sg} , is assumed to depend on the available public finance. In the absence of a domestic capital market and of money printing, as assumed here, public sector non-tax financing must come from abroad and takes the form of pure aid transfers ΔF_S^a and credits from the international banking system (ΔB_{Sg}). Determinants of external finance and borrowing decisions of the Southern government are specified below.

Equations 7.6-7.8, complete the model system for the South. The Southern trade balance in equation 7.6 determines Southern imports from the North (M_{SN}) residually from export earnings and the net transfer of resources, i.e. net new finance ($\Delta F_S^a + \Delta B_S$) less private sector accumulation of financial assets in the North (ΔJ_S) and less net interest payments to the financial system [$(i_W + x_S)\, B_S - i_W\, J_S$]. Equation 7.7 defines Southern private savings as a function of profit income and interest earnings on private foreign assets. Finally, equation 7.8 determines the Southern private investment level as a function of available finance (self-financing and foreign financing) *less* private accumulation of foreign assets, ΔJ_S, where decisions to invest at home (I_S) or abroad (ΔJ_S) are based on portfolio decisions of profit earners in the South (see equation 7.23 below). Implicit in equations 7.4, 7.6 and 7.8 is the assumption that profits are fully spent on the Northern good (either in the form of investment or consumption goods) or are diverted into financial asset holdings abroad.

7.2.2 Major oil exporters

Oil price shocks have played an important role in the generation of external imbalances in North and South over the past two decades. To capture the global effects, a region of oil exporters is introduced. In the model the economy of this region has a rudimentary structure, producing only oil and importing manufactures from the North to satisfy domestic demand. The region sells oil at a given price ($v = P_O/P_N$), negotiated at OPEC meetings. All oil production is assumed (for simplicity) to be exported to the North only. Oil is an intermediate to Northern production and oil production (Q_O) adjusts to output-related demand in the North ($m_{NO}Q_N$), thus assuming slack capacity in the oil-exporting region (eq. 7.9). Alternatively, without affecting the present model results, oil production could have been assumed to be negotiated at OPEC meetings, letting the oil price clear supply and demand. Oil-exporters consume (import) a fixed proportion (m_{ON}) of the oil revenues (eq. 7.10), while the residual is saved ($s_O = 1 - m_{ON}$) and deposited in the international banking system (ΔJ_O; eq. 7.11). Interest income from deposit holdings ($i_W J_O$) is also assumed to be saved and redeposited.

An oil price increase will thus affect the cost of production of the Northern commodity and expand the credit-creating capacity of the multinational banking system.

7.2.3 The Northern economy

Northern manufacturing is seen as dominated by oligopolistic firms that can set prices as a mark-up over variable costs (here consisting of wage costs and intermediate input costs), a premise in Kaleckian macro-economic theory (Kalecki 1971). There is excess capacity. As in the Taylor model, the mark-up rate (τ) is given exogenously.[6] Equation 7.12 specifies the mark-up rule and, in effect, determines – for a given labour productivity (q_N) – the Northern wage rate in terms of the Northern commodity, ω_N,[7] since the model uses the Northern price level as its numeraire, the mark-up (τ) is given and the costs of the intermediate commodity (vm_{NO}) are assumed fixed, so that:

$$\omega_N = [(1 + \tau)^{-1} - vm_{NO}]\, q_N \qquad (7.12a)$$

where: $q_N = Q_N / L_N$

In Kaleckian and Post-Keynesian tradition, the consumption function for the North assumes that wages are fully consumed and that a proportion s_N of profits is saved (eq. 7.14).[8] Of this expenditure a proportion (α) goes to commodity imports from the South (eq. 7.15a) and the rest to domestic production (eq. 7.15b). A traditional structuralist assumption in the debate on North-South trade interdependence is the lower income elasticity of the Southern commodity. In Chapter 5 it was suggested this presumption still fits the reality of primary exporters. Following Taylor (1981), this could be captured through the strongly simplified linear expenditure equation system represented by equations 7.14-15a, b. In equations 7.15a and 7.15b, θ is the price of the Southern commodity relative to that of the North. So long as the constant A is positive the income elasticity for the Southern commodity is less than one (eq. 7.15a).

Equation 7.16 specifies private investment demand as a positive function of profitability (as in Taylor, 1981) and of capacity utilization, and as a negative function of the cost of investment finance $[(1+x_N)\, i_W]$. This function, in conjunction with the real wage/mark-up pricing function and the demand-determined actual output function, may be interpreted as a recognition that firms, even in oligopolistic market structures, operate in an uncertain and changing environment and are unable to calculate exactly optimal price and output.

The private savings function (S_N) in the North reflects decisions of firms and a class of rentiers to retain a share of profit income for self-finance at the firm level and/or as investment in financial assets. Net interest income from financial assets is assumed to be fully saved (eq. 7.19). The equation assumes implicitly that Northern profit earners are the nominal owners of the international banks, receiving the interest income on the assets they own, but also paying interest on the liabilities of the banking system.

Thus, the private savings-investment balance has been made interdependent only indirectly with the Northern fiscal balance, i.e. through the interest rate effect on private investment of bond financing. 'Debt neutrality' is thus not ensured and Northern fiscal policies are likely to have global repercussions, as hypothesized in Chapters 5 and 6.

Northern import demand is given by equation 7.15a (Southern commodity) and equation 7.9 (intermediate input), while exports are determined by equation 7.6 (to the South) and equation 7.10 (to oil exporters). This leaves the Northern fiscal balance as the final function to be specified for the Northern economy. This is done in equation 7.20.

Government expenditures consist of an exogenous component of government services and investment (G_N), interest payments on domestic debt ($i_W DC_N$) and an exogenously set amount of official development assistance to the South (ΔF_S^a). For a given tax rate, t_N, the fiscal deficit is determined through equation 7.20. It is assumed that the Northern government can fully finance its deficits by issuing bonds (ΔDC_N).

7.2.4 The international credit market

The model distinguishes three types of financial assets: bank deposits (J), bank credits (B) and Northern government securities (DC) (eq. 7.21). To simplify and to focus on the functioning of the international bank loan market, the Northern securities market has a rudimentary form. It is assumed that Northern government demand for bond financing to finance fiscal deficits (ΔDC_N) takes the form of open-market operations that act directly on the (implicit) deposit rate of the international banking system (eq. 7.21); or, seen from another perspective, it could be said that the Northern government is a preferential borrower from the banking system.

Following the analysis of Chapters 5 and 6, the allocation of bank credits to the other agents, Northern firms and Southern borrowers is determined by credit-rationing rules set by the banks, which operate in an oligopolistic market structure. Structural asymmetries exist between lending behaviour and Southern borrowing behaviour and debt crises may occur as a systemic problem.

The model specifications for deposit demand and the demand and supply of bank credits are detailed below.

Deposit demand

Bank deposits are demanded by three agents: the principal agent of the oil-exporting economy and profit earners in North and South. Given the low-absorptive capacity of the oil-exporting economy, it has been assumed that in this economy all savings are deposited (eq. 7.11). The demand for bank deposits from North and South is modelled to be mainly driven by expected yield differentials on physical and financial assets.

Deposit demand by Southern profit earners is a function of the Southern terms of trade (eq. 7.4). Equation 7.23 further assumes stock-adjustment behaviour ($j_{0S} J_S$), which was interpreted in Chapter 5 as asset adjustment for transactions demand (for doing business abroad) and demand for a permanent foreign (interest) income demand (reflecting the lifestyles of Southern elites).

Though not investigated empirically, a similar deposit demand function is assumed for Northern agents. In equation 7.22, Northern firms and rentiers are also assumed to have some fixed demand for deposits (e.g. for financing of working capital, captured in the constant (j_{0N}) and to respond to the expected rate-of-return differential between financial assets and fixed investment [$j_{1N} (i_W - r_N)_{-1}$], where it is assumed that expectations are based on past (previous period) experience. This behavioural relationship bears an implicit correspondence to decisions of firms with regard to their corporate finance structure, i.e. portfolio decisions shifting towards holding more financial assets will reflect a lower degree of self-financing and share capital.

Demand for bank loans

The model distinguishes four types of borrowers in a segmented market structure. World demand for credits is exercised by the governments and firms in North and South. Firstly, as indicated, the Northern government has been assumed to have the status of preferential borrower. Its credit demand (DC_N) is determined through equation 7.20, i.e. by the fiscal deficit. Secondly, Northern firms are assumed to demand credit, (ΔB^d_N), for investment finance purposes (eq. 7.24). Thirdly, in the absence of a domestic capital market, Southern non-tax budget finance is assumed to consist fully of external borrowing and foreign aid flows. The objective function of the Southern government was explained above as trying to achieve the highest possible public investment rate. For a given level of foreign aid flows, this would imply a perfectly elastic demand curve for external borrowing in the absence of a debt management strategy. As suggested in Chapters 5 and 6, there may be arguments for this simple presumption. However, the model allows for some form of debt management by Southern governments. It is assumed that the government sets an (adjustable) limit to permitted external public sector borrowing (see also the reserves/debt management practice of developing countries in the 1970s discussed in section 5.5). The model assumes that due to uncertainties and unknown future foreign-exchange earnings a simple 'rule of thumb' is applied to manage external debt accumulation, rather than a sophisticated intertemporal optimization procedure. In equation 7.25 a ceiling on external borrowing is defined as a function of a preconceived maximum debt repayment capacity, (Ω). This ceiling is defined as the point where the debt overhang becomes so large that expected payment obligations exceed a critical level *vis-à-vis* available foreign exchange receipts. The presence of capital inflows in the denominator of Ω implies that debt repayment capacity is conceived in terms of a liquidity constraint (or an external transfer problem), rather than in terms of a solvency constraint. In the model, Ω is assumed to be a fixed ratio, although in practice the critical ratio might be adjusted over time, depending on credit market conditions.

The critical borrowing ratio both determines the upper bound to government borrowing and the limit to debt repayment, i.e. the level at which there will be a high probability to default. The government will limit borrowing, where actual debt servicing tends to exceed the critical ratio:

$$\text{upper bound: } [(1 + x_S)\, i_W B_{Sg} / \theta(M_{NS} + \Delta B_{Sg} + \Delta F_S^a)] \leq \Omega$$

so that the government demand for bank loans is determined by:

$$(\Delta B_{Sg})^d = \Omega^{-1}[(i_w + x_S)B_{Sg}] - \theta M_{NS} - \Delta F_S^a \qquad (7.25a)$$

The upper bound may become binding, that is supply exceeds demand, when bank lending is in an expansive credit cycle (cf. Chapter 6 and below). When it is in the contractionary phase (which may have set in in response to an immediate threat of a debt crisis due to an interest rate shock, or as a 'normal' stage of the debt cycle), the critical ratio also defines the point at which the government will consider default:

$$\text{lower bound: if } \Omega\, [\Delta B_{Sg}^a - \theta M_{NS} - \Delta F_S^a] < (1 + x_S) i_W B_{Sg}$$

then, debt repayment will be limited to:

$$[\overline{\Delta B_{Sg}} - \overline{(1 + x_S)\, i_W B_{Sg} / \Omega}] = \theta M_{NS} + \Delta F_S^a \qquad (7.25b)$$

Payments arrears are capitalized and added to outstanding debt.

These conditions also determine the domestic adjustment process in face of an external debt crisis. Higher debt servicing obligations and reduced availability of external finance will affect public investment, an assumption following the line of analysis in Chapter 5. Given a non-negativity constraint *($I_{Sg} \geq 0$)*, there is an initial limit to domestic adjustment, such that additional policy instruments will have to be imposed on the model once the adjustment limit is reached. These include cuts on public sector wages and employment ($\omega_S L_{Sg}$), a tax reform (t_S)and default on external debt. The various fiscal adjustment options affect Southern growth and private savings and investment through different channels. Higher taxes affect net profits and private savings and so investment (eqs. 7.7 and 7.8). Cuts in current spending reduce domestic demand for the Southern commodity and put downward pressure on the terms of trade (see also below) and thus affect Southern profits. Debt repudiation will postpone private sector adjustment. In the basic specification of the model, the latter option becomes effective first (cf. 7.25b).

Fourthly, and finally, Southern private investment demand is assumed to be finance (and foreign-exchange) constrained. Southern credit demand is perfectly elastic to available supply, so that, for a given total supply of bank loans to the South, Southern firms are residual borrowers (eq. 7.8).

From the demand side, no market clearing through price (interest rate) adjustment is ensured. Only Northern firms show sensitivity to interest rates and will adjust demand for new credit *flows*, for interest rate changes or changes in the spread. Of the Southern borrowers, only the government may adjust credit demand due to interest rate changes, but the sensitivity does not relate to directly to flows; instead, credit demand may adjust as a result of high accumulated debt *stock* and interest obligations exceeding perceived payment capacity.

Supply and allocation of bank loans

Potential bank loan supply depends on total bank deposits less Northern government demand for securities (eq. 7.20). Bank behaviour determines how this supply is allocated. Lending behaviour of the commercial banks is seen as driven by oligopolistic competition and imperfect creditworthiness assessment. The four types of borrowers constitute four broad risk classes of borrowers. Chapters 5 and 6 pointed out that to avert default risk and to discriminate between 'good' and 'bad-risk' borrowers, banks ration credits among different types of borrowers, rather than using the price of the loans, i.e. including a risk-premium in the spread. In the model, Northern borrowers are assumed to be good risks. Northern government, as indicated, is a preferential borrower. Banks consider lending to Northern firms a good risk and do not place a particular ceiling on their credit availability.

Lending to the South, on the other hand, is perceived as more risky, but also as more profitable, because the dominant form of lending to the South, i.e. via loan syndicates, allows high commissions to be earned, and also because the non-market clearing spread x_S for the South is higher than that for North, x_N. Banks put a ceiling on lending to the South. It is assumed that competition among the banks over market shares is sufficient to cause them to actively sell loans to the South and try to place loans up to the credit ceiling. The determination of the credit ceiling by banks differs from Southern perceptions of borrowing. Banks will determine a credit ceiling for lending to the South depending on perceived default risk. Following the analysis of Chapters 5 and 6, this is captured in the aggregate credit supply function (eq. 7.26)[9] through an exogenously set solvency parameter, i.e. a critical debt-to-exports ratio $[(B_S/\theta M_{NS})^{emax}]$. The parameter suggests forward looking behaviour of banks, but given unknown future export earnings in the South, this is only an imperfect creditworthiness indicator and is no insurance against future debt problems. The limit on the bank loan supply to the South depends further on the total size of the market; growth of liquidity in banks will increase competition for lending to South (ΔB_S).

Further, it is assumed that banks prefer to lend to Southern governments (public guarantees). If the Southern government demand for external borrowing exceeds the total credit ceiling for the South then banks will provide the Southern government with loans up to the credit ceiling:

$$\Delta B^d_{Sg} \geq \Delta B^s_S = \Delta B_{Sg}$$

If Southern governments see their country's debt repayment capacity as more limited than the banks do, then government demand will be satisfied. But, given oligopolistic competition for market shares, banks will try to push loans onto the Southern private sector up to the credit ceiling:

$$\Delta B^d_{Sg} = \Delta B_{Sg} < \Delta B^s_S \quad \text{and} \quad \Delta B_{Sp} = \Delta B^s_S - \Delta B_{Sg}$$

These supply conditions ensure the closure of the Southern credit market segment. The assumed structural asymmetries in borrowing and lending behaviour imply, however, that market outcomes need not be fully satisfactory for all actors on the demand and supply side. Particularly, Southern borrowers may not be able to satisfy credit demand. On the other hand, a high debt burden and limited access to external finance may lead Southern government to opt for default, which may disturb the banks' market confidence. Such a disturbance in market confidence is not endogenized in the model, but can be imposed by adjusting the solvency constraint parameter, $(B_S/\theta M_{NS})^{emax}$, or the confidence parameter (b_{1S}) (see further Chapter 8).

Equilibrium in the global credit market segment requires that:

$$\Delta B^d_N = \Delta B^s - \Delta B_S \tag{7.27a}$$

which in effect determines the world interest rate (i_W); as specified below. Competition between the banks ensures that excess demand for bank credits in the North will drive up the interest rate (and spreads in North and South) through equation 7.27, while excess supply will drive down the world interest rate. A higher interest rate will cure excess demand for bank credits in the North assuming that its negative effect on investment demand (eq. 7.16) and its positive effect on deposit demand (eqs. 7.22 and 7.23) are sufficiently large to clear the market. If this condition holds, the global credit market will find an equilibrium in flow terms, even though a debt crisis may exist in one segment of the market.

7.2.5 Stock adjustment

Beginning-of-period stock variables (K_N, K_S, B_N, B_{Sg}, B_{Sp}, DC_N, J_N, J_S and J_O) are assumed to be known and end-of-period values are obtained by adding the equilibrium (or *ex post*) values to the corresponding flow variables. (See bottom of Table 7.1.) The dynamics of the model are determined by the shifts in the asset and liability positions represented by the values of the listed stock variables. As indicated, accumulation of a large external debt may provoke a debt crisis and thoughts of default in the South. However, as also discussed below and in Chapter 8, certain asset and liability shifts also appear to be a source of system instability.

7.3 Model Solution and Global Interactions

7.3.1 Stability

The system of structural equations has 27 endogenous variables (see Table 7.2) in 27 equations. However, this can be reduced to 21 variables which are solved simultaneously in 21 equations, since Q_S is predetermined by (7.2), L_S by (7.2) and (7.3), ω_N by (7.12), while S_S can be eliminated by substituting (7.7) in (7.8), Q_O by substituting (7.9) in (7.10) and in (7.11) and C_N by substituting (7.12) and (7.14) into (7.13). A solution algorithm and some numerical exercises and policy simulations are discussed in Chapter 8.

The model has three commodity markets and a world credit market. The oil market is assumed to have supply adjusting automatically to demand at a fixed price. The primary commodity market is price clearing, while the asset market eventually clears for the interest rate. With three of the four markets clearing, the Northern commodity market must in principle also reach an equilibrium. However, the Walrasian equilibrium condition is slightly more complex. In fact the oil market is automatically adjusting by model assumptions, independent of the rest of the system and therefore can be left aside in determining the stability conditions of the model. Walras' law requires that n prices (or market adjusting variables) are determined in $n+1$ excess demand functions (or markets). Having dropped the oil market, we have only three markets (Southern commodity, Northern commodity and bank credits) to solve three market clearing variables (θ, i_W and Q_N). The fourth market in the background is the bond market.[10] The situation compares to that of Keynes' *General Theory* in which the goods and money markets determine two independent variables; a third market, the bond market, lurks in the background and clears when the other two clear. In the STAC model an exogenous increase in the Northern fiscal deficit leads to an increase in demand for credits (bonds) by the Northern government, but even though the Northern government is assumed to be a preferential borrower in the system the bond market clears only when the other markets clear, since the fiscal balance depends directly on both Northern output and the world interest rate in equation 7.20.

The model solution will thus depend on the interactions between the Southern and Northern commodity markets, the global bank credit market and the Northern bond market. Market clearing functions may be expressed in their general form as:

Southern commodity market: $\frac{d\theta}{dt} = f\ [ED_S(Q_N, i_W, \theta)]$

Northern commodity market: $\frac{dQ_N}{dt} = f\ [ED_N(Q_N, i_W, \theta)]$

Global credit market: $\frac{di_W}{dt} = f\ [ED_B(Q_N, i_w, \theta)]$

Bond market: $DEF_N\,(Q_N, i_w, \theta) - \Delta DC_N = 0$

An analytical version of the Jacobian matrix of this system of excess demand functions is given in Appendix A7.1. Stability of the system is not unambiguously ensured after all non-negativity constraints of most of the variables and parameters have been taken into account. From the specifications in Appendix A7.1, it seems to follow that model stability depends on three critical factors. Firstly, Keynesian stability conditions should rule adjustment of Northern excess demand, i.e. the response of Northern savings to changes in output (and the Northern profit rate) should be stronger than that of Northern investment demand. Secondly, instability may result if the Northern income propensity to consume the Southern commodity is larger than the savings responsiveness to output changes in the North. Thirdly, the composition of private and public net asset positions in both regions may be a source of instability, i.e. – for certain credit- and deposit-demand parameter values – if the sum of the net financial asset positions of oil exporters and *private* agents in North and South exceeds the Northern physical capital stock and government debt service. The last condition is important as it involves stock variables, which adjust from period to period, meaning that the stability conditions also change over time. Initial stability may be disturbed as net asset positions shift. (The issue returns in Chapter 8.)

For the time being, the analysis of the interactions between North and South in the next paragraphs assumes that stability conditions are ensured and that the system converges at equilibrium.

7.3.2 The Southern commodity market and the terms of trade

The price of the Southern good in terms of the Northern price (i.e. the terms of trade, θ) can be derived from the excess demand function for the Southern commodity. Using 7.1 and 7.15a, demand and supply for the Southern commodity balance if:

$$\theta\omega_S (L_S + L_{Sg}) + [(\alpha (1 - t_N) \gamma Q_N + A\theta] - \theta Q_S = 0 \qquad (7.1a)$$

From which θ can be expressed in terms of the Southern real wage and Northern input costs and mark-up, knowing that $\gamma = [w_N/q_N + (1-s_N)\,\tau\,(\omega_N/q_N + vm_{NO})]$ and $\varphi = vm_{NO}/(\omega_N/q_N + vm_{NO})$ as defined before and that $(\omega_N/q_N + vm_{NO}) = 1/(1+\tau)$ from 7.12, so that:

$$\theta = \frac{\alpha (1 - t_N)[(1-\varphi) + (1-s_N)\tau](1+\tau)^{-1} Q_N}{Q_S - \omega_S(L_S + L_{Sg}) - A} \qquad (7.1b)$$

It follows that the terms of trade will adjust endogenously with the rest of the system, improving with Northern output growth and deteriorating with the growth of the Southern exportable surplus. Without (yet) taking general equilibrium effects into account, exogenous shocks in the form of a higher oil price (increase in φ), Northern mark-up (τ), tax (t_N) or savings rate (s_N) will lead to a terms-of-trade deterioration, while a higher Northern demand propensity for the Southern commodity (α) will put upward pressure on θ.

7.3.3 The Northern commodity market

Equilibrium in the Northern commodity market and the equilibrium growth rate for the North can be determined from equations 7.11–7.20.

Investment demand is given by equation 7.16:

$$I_N = [g_{0N} + g_{1N}(r_N + u) - g_{2N}(1 + x_N)\, i_W]\, K_N \qquad (7.16)$$

Equilibrium in the North is reached where investment-savings, fiscal and external accounts balance $[(I-S)_N + DEF_N = M_{SN} + M_{ON} - \theta M_{NS} - vm_{NO}Q_N - i_W(B_S - J_O - J_S)]$.

Using 7.6, 7.9, 7.10, 7.19 and 7.20, the macroeconomic balance in the North may be written as:

$$I_N = S_N(1 - t_N)\,[\tau(\omega_N/q_N + s_O\, vm_{NO})]\, Q_N + s_O\, vm_{NO}\, Q_N +$$
$$i_W DC_N - \Delta DC_N + (1 + x_S)\, i_W B_S - \Delta B_S - i_W J_S + \Delta J_S \qquad (7.16a)$$

Equation 7.16a states that *ex post* Northern private investment (I_N) is financed by savings from profit income, savings from oil exporters, savings from net interest income accruing to rentiers in the North, and acquisition of foreign assets by Southern profit earners (ΔJ_S), less government demand for domestic credits (ΔDC_N) and credit supplies to the South (ΔB_S). Equation 7.16a can also be expressed in growth terms, with the growth rate defined as $g_N = I_N/K_N$.

Further, the Northern profit rate is defined as:

$$r_N = [1 - (\omega_N/q_N + vm_{NO})]\, Q_N/K_N = \tau\,(1+\tau)^{-1} u$$

so that:

$$g_N = \frac{I_N}{K_N} = s_N(1-t_N) + s_0\,\varphi\,\tau^{-1}\,]\, r_N + (i_W - \widehat{dc}_N)\, dc_N$$
$$+ [i_W(1+x_S) - \hat{b}_S]\, b_S\,\kappa - (i_W - \hat{j}_S)\, j_S\,\kappa \qquad (7.16b)$$

where:

$$\hat{b}_S = \Delta B_S/B_S\,,\; b_S = B_S/K_S\,,\; \widehat{dc}_N = \Delta DC_N/DC_N\,,\; dc_N = DC_N/K_N,$$
$$\hat{j}_S = \Delta J_S/J_S,\;\; J_S = J_S/K_S \;\text{ and } \kappa = K_S/K_N$$
$$r_N = [1 - (\omega_N/q_N + vm_{NO})]\, Q_N/K_N = \tau\,(1+\tau)^{-1} u.$$

Equilibrium in the Northern commodity market is reached if investment demand equals the supply of finance, in other words:

$$g_{0N} + g_{1N}(r_N + u) - g_{2N}(1+x_N)\, i_W = [s_N(1-t_N) + s_O\,\varphi\,\tau^{-1}]\, r_N$$
$$+ (i_W - \widehat{dc}_N)\, dc_N + [\, i_W(1+x_S) - \hat{b}_S\,]\, b_S\kappa - (i_W - \hat{j}_S)\, j_S\kappa \qquad (7.16c)$$

Equation 7.16c indicates that both investment demand and savings are responsive to the Northern profit rate. A standard condition for Keynesian model stability is that the savings responsiveness is larger:

$$[s_N(1-t_N) + s_O\varphi\tau^{-1}\,]\, r_N \;>\; g_{1N}(r_N + u)$$

In the specifications of the present model, Northern market equilibrium and stability further depends on the interest rate sensitivity of investment and the growth of Northern and Southern public debt (see Appendix A7.1 for further details).

7.3.4 The global credit market

Credit rationing governs adjustment in the Southern segment of the market, but the market as a whole adjusts for the interest rate. Equation 7.27 specifies conditions for credit market equilibrium. After making substitution for Northern credit demand, using equations 7.24, 7.21, and

7.16 and market clearing implying that $ED_B = 0$, equation 7.27 in effect sets the world interest rate as:[11]

$$i_W = \frac{b_{1N}[g_{0N} + g_{1N}(r_N + u)]K_N + \Delta B_S + \Delta DC_N - \Delta J_N - \Delta J_0 - \Delta J_S}{b_{1N}[g_{2N}(1+x_N)]K_N} \tag{7.27a}$$

The interest rate will increase with a larger Northern investment demand, higher credit ceilings for Southern borrowers and higher bond-financing of the Northern fiscal deficit and will fall with higher deposit demand from all regions and the crowding-out effect of higher borrowing costs on Northern investment demand (g_{2N}).

7.3.5 How the economies interact

The way in which the Northern and Southern economies interact through commodity markets and the asset market can now be shown by deriving an expression relating the Southern growth rate to that of the North. This requires new expressions for the profit rates in both regions. The Southern profit rate equals:

$$r_S = \theta(1-\omega_S/q_S)Q_S/K_S$$

which – using equation 7.1b – can be rewritten as:

$$r_S = \frac{\alpha(1-t_N)[(1-\varphi)+(1-s_N)\tau^{-1}](1+\tau)^{-1}Q_N(1-\omega_S/q_S)Q_S/K_S}{Q_S-\omega_S(L_S+L_{Sg})-A}$$

Knowing that:

$$u = Q_N/K_N,\ \kappa = K_S/K_N \text{ and } r_N = \tau(1+\tau)^{-1}u$$

this can also be written as:

$$r_S = \alpha(1-t_N)\kappa^{-1}\left[\frac{(1-\omega_S/q_S)Q_S}{(1-\omega_S/q_S)Q_S-\omega_S L_{Sg}-A}\right]\left[\frac{(1-\varphi)+(1-s_N)\tau}{\tau}\right]r_N \tag{7.28}$$

The equilibrium profit rate in the North can be derived from 7.16c:

$$r_N = \frac{g_N-(i_W-\widehat{dc}_N)dc_N-[i_W(1+x_S)-\hat{b}_S]b_S\kappa+(i_W-\hat{j}_S)j_S\kappa}{s_N(1-t_N)+s_O\varphi\tau^{-1}} \tag{7.29}$$

The Southern growth rate can be derived from equation 7.2 as:

$$g_S = dQ_S / Q_S = \delta(I_S/K_S) + (1-\delta)k(I_{Sg}/K_S)$$

which can be rewritten after using equations 7.5 and 7.8, as:

$$g_S = \delta[s_S(1-t_S)r_S + \{\hat{b}_{Sp} - (1+x_S)\,i_W\}\,b_{Sp} - (\hat{j}_S - i_W)\,j_S]$$
$$+ (1-\delta)\,k\,[\Delta f^a_S + \{\hat{b}_{Sg} - (1+x_S)\,i_W\}\,b_{Sg} + t_S r_S - \theta\omega_S L_{Sg}/K_S]$$

and, after some reordering, as:

$$g_S = \delta[\{s_S(1-t_S) + \delta^{-1}(1-\delta)kt_S\}r_S + \{\hat{b}_{Sp} - (1+x_S)i_W\}b_{Sp} - (\hat{j}_S - i_W)j_S]$$
$$+ (1-\delta)\,k\,[\Delta f^a_S + \hat{b}_{Sg} - (1+x_S)i_W b_{Sg} - \theta\omega_S L_{Sg}/K_S] \qquad (7.2a)$$

where:

$$b_{Sp} = B_{Sp}/K_S,\ \hat{b}_{Sp} = (\Delta B_S - \Delta B_{Sg})/B_{Sp}$$
$$b_{Sg} = B_{Sg}/K_S,\ \hat{b}_{Sg} = \Delta B_{Sg}/B_{Sg} \text{ and } \Delta f^a_S = \Delta F^a_S/K_S.$$

Growth interactions between North and South can now be derived by relating the equilibrium growth conditions, i.e. by substituting 7.29 in 7.28 and the result in 7.2a:

$$g_S = \delta\,\{s_S(1-t_S) + \delta^{-1}(1-\delta)\,kt_S\}\,r_S\,\xi\,\alpha\,(1-t_N)\kappa^{-1}\,[(1-\varphi)\tau^{-1}$$
$$+ (1-s_N)\cdot\left[\frac{g_N - (i_W - \hat{dc}_N)dc_N - [i_W(1+x_S) - \hat{b}_S]b_S\kappa + (i_W - \hat{j}_S)j_S\kappa}{s_N(1-t_N) + s_0\varphi\tau^{-1}}\right]$$
$$+ \delta\,[\{\hat{b}_{Sp} - (1+x_S)\,i_W\}b_{Sp} - (\hat{j}_S - i_W)j_S\,]$$
$$+ (1-\delta)\,k\,[\Delta f^a_S + \{\hat{b}_{Sg} - (1+x_S)i_W\}b_{Sg} - \theta\,\omega_S\,L_{Sg}/K_S]$$

where:

$$\xi = \left[\frac{(1-\omega_S/q_S)Q_S}{(1-\omega_S/q_S)Q_S - \omega_S L_{Sg} - A}\right]$$

The coefficient ξ reflects the lower Engel elasticity in the North of the Southern commodity, in the case where $A > 0$. In this case ξ will be definitively greater than unity. This traditional structuralist assumption is, however, just one of the asymmetries in adjustment between North and South as analysed below. Reordering of the above result yields:

$$g_S = \delta\kappa^{-1}\nabla g_N + \nabla(\hat{dc}_N - i_W)dc_N\kappa^{-1}$$
$$+ (1-\delta)\,k\,(1+\nabla)\,[\hat{b}_{Sg} - (1+x_S)\,i_W]\,b_{Sg}$$

$$+ (1-\delta)k\Delta f_S^a - (1-\delta)\, k\, (\theta\, \omega_S\, L_{Sg}/K_S)$$
$$+ \delta(1+\nabla)\, [\hat{b}_{Sp} - (1+x_S)\, i_W]\, b_{Sp} - \delta\, (1+\nabla)\, (\hat{j}_S - i_W)\, j_S \qquad (7.30)$$

where:

$$\nabla = \frac{\{s_S(1-t_S)+\delta^{-1}\,(1-\delta)\,kt_s\}\,\xi\,\alpha(1-t_N)\,[\,(1-\varphi)\tau^{-1} + (1-s_N)]}{s_N(1-t_N) + s_0\,\varphi\,\tau^{-1}}$$

with:

$\nabla > 0$ for $0 < t_i < 1$, $0 < s_i < 1$, $0 < \delta < 1$, $k > 0$, $0 < \varphi < 1$ and $\xi > 0$.

The trade multiplier in North–South interactions is represented by ∇ in equation 7.30 and reflects the Keynesian and structuralist properties of the model, i.e. it falls with a higher Northern savings rate (s_N), higher OPEC savings (s_O) and higher raw material costs (φ) (leading to a lower Northern real wage and demand) and it will increase with a higher Southern savings rate (sS) and Northern propensity to consume the Southern good *(α)*. The trade multiplier determines how much Northern growth will be transferred into higher Southern welfare through trade expansion. Equation 7.30 shows further that Southern growth may expand with expansionary Northern fiscal policies ($\hat{dc}_N > i_W$), Southern net capital transfers [$\hat{b}_S > (1+x_S)\, i_W$ and $\Delta f_S^a > 0$], but fall with the accumulation of foreign assets ($\hat{j}_S > i_W$).

Equation 7.30 provides a basic model, the details of which will be discussed step by step in the next sections under three different conditions of financial interactions, i.e. without capital mobility; with foreign aid flows to the South, and with commercial bank credits; and foreign asset accumulation by Southern profit earners.

7.4 Asymmetric Adjustment with No Capital Mobility

This first case assumes no capital mobility between North and South, implying that $\Delta f_S^a = 0$, $b_{Sp} = 0$, $b_{Sg} = 0$ and $j_S = 0$. As a consequence, the Southern government budget has to balance, so that also: $\theta\omega_S L_{Sg} + I_{Sg} - t_S R_S = 0$. With these restrictions equation 7.30 reduces to:

$$g_S = \qquad (7.30a)$$

$$\delta\left[\frac{\{s_S(1-t_S)\}\xi\alpha(1-t_N)[(1-\varphi)\tau^{-1}+(1-s_N)}{s_N(1-t_N) + s_0\,\varphi\,\tau^{-1}}\right]\kappa^{-1}[g_N+(\hat{dc}_N-i_W)dc_N]$$

Equation 7.30a shows how the growth rates in North and South are related when there is equilibrium in commodity and asset markets. In this case of international capital immobility, the latter consists only of government securities, Northern bank deposits and 'domestic' credit supplies.

Equation 7.30a summarizes the view underlying the model assumptions that the North serves as the engine of growth for the South. It is debatable, of course, whether trade is the major or single source of growth for the South (see e.g. Riedel 1984), but as long as a major share of investment goods must be imported, the availability of foreign exchange will be a constraint to growth, as this model emphasizes. The focus is thus geared towards the nature of the trade interactions given the differing structural features of the Northern and Southern economies.

The multiplier in equation 7.30a is a slightly modified version of ∇ in 7.30. The asymmetrical adjustment process between both regions that results from the structuralist specifications of the model becomes immediately clear if equilibrium is disturbed by an exogenous shock. An oil price shock, for instance, will hit the South doubly hard in the short run as both the multiplier of equation 7.30a (through an increase in φ and, possibly, an increase in s_O) and g_N (from eq. 7.16c) will decrease. Additionally, lower demand in the North will put downward pressure on Southern commodity prices (through eq. 7.1b), i.e. the terms of trade (θ) will deteriorate, affecting Southern profits and export earnings, and therefore Southern growth.

Reflecting the Keynesian features of the model, an increase in the Northern savings rate will also have very unfavourable effects on the world economy. In the short run, Northern growth (and employment) decrease, which spreads to the South through a lower ∇, g_N and θ. If the shift in savings behaviour is permanent, the terms of trade of primary commodities will also deteriorate in the long run, reflecting that in the transition to a permanently slower rate of growth of the world economy, the South is more adversely affected than the North.

The essence of the trade interactions remains unchanged if the assumption of capital immobility is relaxed. The first round effects of capital transfers to the South may allow for a higher growth rate compensating the asymmetric trade adjustment. However, the nature and source of the capital movement as well as accumulated financial assets and liabilities appear critical in assessing the second round effects in the global adjustment process.

7.5 Global Adjustment and Aid Flows

Financial interactions between North and South in the form of official aid transfers from Northern to the Southern government, imply that $\Delta f_S^a > 0$, $b_S = 0$ and $j_S = 0$ and that equation 7.30 becomes:

$$g_S = \delta\kappa^{-1}\nabla g_N + \nabla\,(\widehat{dc}_N - i_W)\, dc_N\kappa^{-1} + (1-\delta)\, k\Delta f_S^a \\ - (1-\delta)\, k\, (\theta\omega_S L_{Sg}/K_S) \qquad (7.30b)$$

Aid flows are the principal source of external finance to a large number of (generally low-income) LDCs. The trade dependence and economic structure of most of these economies is perhaps closest to the characteristics of the South of the theoretical model presented here; that is, most official borrowers are largely agricultural economies, with primary exports generating most of the commodity-based foreign-exchange earnings.

All things being equal in the Southern economy, ΔF_S^a finances public sector investment less the resources needed to finance current expenditures which in turn are endogeous with the terms of trade $(\theta\omega_S L_{Sg}/K_S)$. A larger public sector wage bill will reduce available funds for public investment, assuming aid funds may be fungible.[12]

The model focuses on the global interactions. There will be a direct positive growth effect from aid-financed public investment. Indirect effects of aid flows from interdependence are not unambiguously positive, however; negative secondary effects may even offset the positive growth effects from productively allocated aid flows. The nature of these indirect effects depends to a large extent on the way in which the aid transfer is financed in the North. The model allows one to simulate alternative ways of financing an increase in aid budgets, i.e. through taxation or deficit financing. The mechanisms set in motion through both forms of financing affect demand in both regions and the world interest rate. The net outcome determines the effect of aid on the terms of trade and welfare in North and South and restates the classic transfer problem, as discussed in Chapters 3 and 6, in new terms. The impact on global adjustment can be analysed as follows.

Financing of increased aid transfers through bond financing $(\partial\widehat{dc}_N/\partial t > 0)$ may lead to a crowding out of private investment and output growth in the North (a lower g_N through 7.16c) as the interest rate will increase (through 7.27a). If the net effect is expansionary, demand for the Southern commodity is also expected to rise, while increased import capacity in the South stimulates Northern output growth, such that aid and trade would be mutually reinforcing along a Brandt Commission scheme (Brandt 1980). If Southern export supply effects are sluggish, the Southern terms of trade may improve and the 'secondary burden' will fall on the transferring economy. There are two reasons to question whether a mutual reinforcement process is sustainable under the model assumptions. Firstly, if – as assumed – aid is invested in infrastructure supporting primary production, supply effects $[(1-\delta)\, k\, \{ \Delta f_S^a - \theta\, \omega_S L_{Sg}/K_S\}]$ may dominate the demand effect $[(\alpha\, (1-t_N)\, \gamma\, g_N]$. Under the assumption that the Southern commodity is relatively income inelastic, the terms of trade will tend to deteriorate with sustained aid flows and the secondary burden falls on the recipient economy. Secondly, if aid transfers are substantial relative to Northern output, Northern domestic government debt will accumulate in the medium run, the fiscal deficit will increase through a the larger aid transfers and a higher interest burden. This will put further upward pressure on interest rates and enhance the crowding-out effect of Northern private investment with negative growth effects which will be transmitted to the South via falling demand for the Southern commodity.

'Global Keynesianism' might be more effective in raising the Southern growth rate, if the aid transfer could be financed through money creation. However, as indicated in the introductory section, in the present model specifications money and inflationary repercussions play no role.

Alternatively, the aid budget could be tax financed. A rise in t_N adequate to cover the aid budget avoids pressure on the global credit market. However, there is a more direct deflationary effect on the world economy through a downward effect on the North–South trade-income multiplier. The negative demand effect in the North together with a positive supply effect in the South will put downward pressure on the terms of trade (θ) (through 7.1b). This will be translated into lower Southern profits and savings (but also into a lower public sector wage bill). If these conditions hold, the North–South model thus provides a theoretical explanation *from a global perspective* of the often hypothesized negative relationship between foreign aid and domestic savings (see note 8).

In sum, aid may be beneficial to the South when financed through expansionary fiscal policies in the North. Major offsetting tendencies are nearby: crowding out of Southern private investment and falling terms of trade. The practical relevance of this conclusion is discussed at some length in the next chapter, but it will be clear that recent calls for doubling, or more, of aid flows to the poor countries (Fishlow 1987, Taylor 1990 and UNCTAD 1988) should be approached with caution as these proposals usually ignore the repercussions on global adjustment of the type analysed above.

7.6 Commercial Banking, 'Capital Flight' and Global Adjustment

Reintroducing a role for commercial banks implies a return to the result of equation 7.30:

$$\begin{aligned} g_S = {} & \delta\kappa^{-1}\nabla g_N + \nabla(\widehat{dc}_N - i_W)dc_N\kappa^{-1} + (1-\delta)\,k\,(1+\nabla)[\hat{b}_{Sg} \\ & -(1+x_S)i_W]b_{Sg} + (1-\delta)k\Delta f_S^a - (1-\delta)\,k\,(\theta\,\omega_S L_{Sg}/K_S) \\ & + \delta(1+\nabla)\,[\hat{b}_{Sp} - (1+x_S)i_W]b_{Sp} - \delta(1+\nabla)\,(\hat{j}_S - i_W)j_S \end{aligned} \tag{7.30}$$

As discussed in the previous chapters, in the 1970s about two dozen developing countries gained access to commercial bank lending. Most were middle-income countries, with relatively developed industrial sectors, oriented either towards export markets or protected domestic markets. The introduction of more diversified trade and production structures in the South would obviously enhance the degree of realism of the model and may yield qualitatively different results. However, attempts by others to insert such details in structuralist models of the kind presented here have shown that, on balance, trade asymmetries of the kind discussed in section 7.4 remain as long as the system continues to be demand-driven from the North and the South is foreign-exchange constrained (see Dominique 1985 and Marquez & Pauly 1987). None of these explicitly model North–South capital flows, however. To focus on the interactions between commodities markets and financial markets, and to keep the model simple at the same time, the South is assumed to be non-diversified and primary-exporting. As argued in Chapters 5 and 6, initial positions in trade (primary versus manufacturing) and industry (inwardly- versus outwardly-oriented) seem to provide some explanation of Southern economies being more or less prone to debt problems in the 1970s and 1980s. Under the present specifications such differences cannot be explained. The case specified here may provide, however, some deeper insights into interactions between trade and debt for the sub-group of private borrowers consisting of countries that were principally primary exporters in the 1970s and 1980s, for example Côte d'Ivoire, Peru, Ecuador, Chile, Argentina, Costa Rica and so on.

The effects of an oil price shock and a shift in Northern financial policies, the main economic events of the 1970s and 1980s, will be used to discuss the nature of the global interactions as captured in the model.

An oil price shock shifts income to oil exporters and surplus income from this region flows into the banking system (ΔJ_O). Northern output is affected from the demand side through a falling real wage (eq. 7.12). (With sticky Northern wages the oil price increase would act as a supply rather than as a demand shock.)[13]

Recessionary effects in the North are transmitted to the South via downward pressure in the terms of trade (eq. 7.1b). Global adjustment is mediated through the global capital market. Excess liquidity, resulting from higher credit creating capacity of the banks and initially falling Northern credit demand, put downward pressure on the interest rate. In the model, greater credit availability allows in principle for higher credit flows to the South (eq. 7.26), but this may be offset by the negative effect on creditworthiness of falling Southern exports and terms of trade. To induce the expansion of bank lending to the South after the first oil price increase, a shift in lending behaviour and creditworthiness assessment had to accompany the shift in the global savings-investment balance that took place in the early 1970s. Financial innovations reducing risks of sovereign lending to the South and reducing barriers of entry to the international loan market for smaller banks provided this institutional 'shock' which triggered oligopolistic bank competition over market shares and a revision of creditworthiness assessment. In the model such behavioural shifts are not endogenous, but would be reflected as downward adjustment imposed on the critical debt-export ratio in equation 7.26. Equation 7.30 shows that, in the short run, debt accumulation will foster faster Southern growth as long as the capital inflow exceeds the costs of accumulated debt: $[\hat{b}_{Sg} > (1 + x_S)\, i_W$ and $\hat{b}_{Sp} > (1 + x_S)\, i_W]$.

However, equation 7.30 suggests that the growth effect also depends, positively, on trade interactions (∇) and, negatively, on incentives to foreign asset accumulation by private investors in the South $[\delta(1+\nabla)(\hat{j}_S - i_W)\, j_S]$. Lower Northern demand and higher (foreign-financed, public) investment in the South will put downward pressure on the terms of trade and affect Southern profits. If Southern profit earners expect this trend to continue, there will be an incentive to private capital outflows (through eq. 7.23) to the detriment of domestic investment in export production and Southern growth.

A rise in the Northern fiscal deficit (ΔDC_N) will push up the world interest rate (through 7.27a), which will step up the Southern debt burden $[(1+x_S)\, i_W\, (b_{Sg}+b_{Sp})]$ and, for a given (or lower) availability of external finance, will reduce Southern investment (I_S and I_{Sg}) (eqs. 7.8 and 7.5).

Equation 7.30 summarizes a few other essential trade-offs in Northern and Southern adjustment implied by the model. Firstly, assume the fiscal expansion reflects increased development aid efforts benefiting the South. This has a direct positive impact on Southern welfare, depending on the productivity of public investment and the extent to which aid is not used for current public expenditures $[(1-\delta)K\,\{\Delta f_S^a-(\theta\,\omega_S\,L_{Sg}/K_S)\}]$. The secondary effects are upward pressure on the interest rate and lower Northern private investment. Subsequent effects are a higher debt burden for the South and larger incentives to profit earners to invest in foreign financial assets. The net outcome depends ultimately on the parameter values, but obviously, the higher the outstanding debt, the larger the negative impact resulting from higher interest rates. The same *systemic* conditions are likely to culminate in a debt crisis. With a high debt, higher interest rates affect Southern growth and export prospects and so reduce creditworthiness. Lower availability of external finance and a higher debt burden will bring the default option closer. In practice, different parts of the South may be affected through different channels. Official borrowers may benefit from higher aid transfers, but suffer from possible recessionary effects in the North. Private borrowers will be hit doubly through higher interest rates and slower Northern growth.

Secondly, the allocation of external finance to public or private sector borrowers in the South may be relevant for the Southern growth rate as there may exist productivity differentials between public and private investment. If that of private investment is larger $\delta>0.5$), then public sector external borrowing will lead to a higher average capital-output ratio and the growth impact of a unit increase in foreign finance will tend to become smaller. This seems to have happened in the case of many problem debtors, as suggested in Chapter 5.

The adjustment options for the South to resolve increasing internal and external transfer problems in face of an increasing debt burden are limited in the model structure. The Southern government could respond to emerging fiscal problems through tax reform, but while a tax increase may reduce the fiscal deficit, it will limit profits and investment resources available for primary production. An import cut to solve the external disequilibrium will slow down the Southern growth rate and induce a deterioration of the Northern trade balance and aggregate demand. Alternatively, the Southern government may try to cut back its expenditures by reducing public sector employment and lowering the institutional real wage. This will free resources for export production via higher profits and lower domestic demand for the Southern commodity. Higher export supplies can only be translated into higher foreign exchange earnings if there is adequate demand expansion in the North, or else the terms of trade will fall. If it is politically difficult to cut back on government expenditures and raise taxes and if the external debt burden has risen to a level where further access to fresh finance is cut off and the critical level of perceived debt repayment capacity is reached (eq. 7.25b), then debt repudiation will be seriously considered by the Southern government. The model takes this non-adjustment and the possibility of default as a base-line scenario. But fiscal adjustment (higher taxes, current expenditure cuts) also may fail to avert a debt crisis, since declining domestic demand would put downward pressure on the terms of trade and Southern profits and raise incentives towards the acquisition of foreign assets.

7.7 Concluding Remarks

The North–South model (STAC) developed in this chapter features a dual world economy with asymmetrical commodity market adjustment and with a segmented capital market in which the South has limited access due to donor stringency and credit rationing by multinational banks. The basic commodity market specifications were based on the model by Taylor (1981). Taylor's model, like many other theoretical and empirical world models (see Chapter 8), assumes a passive role for capital movements (i.e. accommodating regional trade deficits). STAC models these explicitly, assigning behavioural rules for public and private agents in both North and South and for international banking institutions. As in the Taylor model, the STAC model results show that trade and growth in the South are essentially determined by the Northern growth and savings rates. Because the model is demand driven from the North and due to fix-price versus flex-price adjustment difference between Northern and Southern commodity markets, exogenous recessionary demand effects on the Northern economy will hit the Southern economy even more adversely.

Foreign finance may reduce the South's foreign exchange constraint and enhance Southern welfare. Based on the empirical and theoretical investigations of Chapters 5 and 6, the world capital market has been specified with a segmented structure, with Southern access to official capital flows and bank credits dominated by supply conditions.

Assessing the global effects of enhanced aid transfers to the South, it was concluded that positive welfare effects from a higher Southern investment rate may easily be offset by lower terms of trade and recessionary effects in the North resulting from a bond or tax-financed aid budget. This restates in different terms the relevance of the classic transfer debate, where there is a strong underlying presumption that financial transfers from North to South are likely to create a secondary burden for the South. Such a conclusion is inconsistent with often asserted policy conclusions of the Brandt Commission type that productively invested massive aid transfers to the South will provide a major impetus to world economic growth and trade. Such policy studies usually fail to take account of financial trade-offs.

Under the model assumptions for the bank loan market, a debt crisis in the South is a likely systemic outcome. Structural asymmetries exist in bank lending behaviour and in the borrowing behaviour of Southern agents. The former is assumed to be in essence pro-cyclical with the export performance of the South being largely anti-cyclical. At low levels of outstanding debt, external borrowing is likely to contribute to Southern growth, but as debt accumulates this debt-led growth becomes unsustainable. Higher debt and slower growth will reduce creditworthiness and the availability of external finance while the increasing debt burden and tightened foreign exchange constraint will enhance the Southern demand for external finance. The system may gradually move to the limits of domestic Southern adjustment (zero public investment) which would lead the South to default on its debt obligations. Much of this story seems, though strongly stylized, very much in line with the analysis of the previous chapters.

An addendum to the numerous studies on aid flows, sovereign lending to developing countries and open-economy adjustment processes is that the model locates assumptions about banking lending behaviour and Southern economic adjustment options in a global framework and thus allows the taking into account of a number of general equilibrium considerations of the functioning of the world economy.

Models like the ones presented here obviously suffer from a number of limitations. The model results depend by definition on certain key assumptions. The aggregate nature of the model does inadequate justice to relevant features of and differences between countries within each region and economic sectors within each type of economy. Therefore, no claim for generalizable outcomes is made; the model results may vary should one of the basic specifications be changed (for instance, dropping the assumption of full specialization; allowance for manufactured exports from the South). The key point to be stressed is that the institutional setting of the world economy should be well captured in analyses of this kind. The STAC model is only a first step in this direction. As also emphasized in Chapter 6, the institutional behaviour and particularly the expectations and market perceptions of the main agents in the global credit market are modelled in a very rudimentary fashion and require further theoretical investigation.

The effort made in this chapter may further provide a useful outline for a more detailed, empirical model of the world economy. Having simpler analytical and fully tractable versions alongside, should strengthen the insights to be gained from such an ambitious project. In the next chapter, some policy simulations are made using a numerical version of the STAC model, and the results are compared with those of alternative theoretical and empirical world models.

8 The World Economy, External Shocks and Systemic Problems of North–South Interdependence

8.1 Introduction

The theoretical model developed in the previous chapter is an attempt to analyse in a rigorous manner structural asymmetries that exist in trade and financial interactions between industrialized and developing economies. Some of the key structural asymmetries brought out by that model related to the nature of financial interdependence. Following the empirical and theoretical analyses of Chapters 5 and 6, a restricted access of Southern economies to private international financial markets and to other (official) sources of external finance was hypothesized. The model results show that there remain few degrees of freedom to the South to determine its rate of growth. Even if world economic conditions seem favourable (demand expansion in the North, ample availability of finance), the South faces structural, offsetting factors which do not allow it to take full advantage of these. Such systemic problems suggest the absence of a 'hidden hand' which ensures that the decentralized decision-making of the principal actors (Northern governments and private agents, international banks and Southern governments) is compatible with optimal general welfare and an internationally efficient allocation of resources. This makes the case for pursuing structural change and more coordinated policy action.

The simulations with the STAC model presented below are mainly illustrative. Only tentative conclusions can be drawn from them, since the quantitative structure created for the model was not based on a complete econometric estimation of the main behavioural relations. Rather, a set of parameter values was imposed on the model, and an effort was made to obtain a plausible quantitative structure by basing the choice of parameters on plausible guesstimates derived from international statistics and empirical studies by others. Data problems (see Chapter 2) provided a constraint in deriving a consistent set of world accounts, making it impossible to produce a fully checked empirical version. The simulations include the effects of an oil price shock, tax- and deficit-financed increases in official aid flows and loan supply shocks.

The results are compared with those of other, empirical world models which focus on North–South macroeconomic interactions.

8.2 Model Adjustments and Solution

In order to perform simulations with the STAC model a solution algorithm was developed for the theoretical model set out in the previous chapter, after introducing a few modifications and additions. Firstly, non-negativity constraints were imposed on all non-financial endogenous variables. Secondly, the exogenous variables for government spending in the North (G_N) and foreign aid flows to the South (ΔF_S^a) were allowed to grow in fixed proportion with Northern output to avoid these falling out of line with the levels of the other endogenous variables in the system over several simulation periods, i.e.: $G_N = g_N Q_N$ and $\Delta F_S^a = tf_N Q_N$. In fact, although not following actual *ex ante* behaviour of all donors, in practice total aid flows to the South have indeed been a fairly stable proportion of Northern GNP (between 0.3 and 0.4 percent) over the past twenty years (see Chapter 5). Thirdly, a few responses of Southern governments and banks to a debt crisis were allowed for. As suggested in Chapter 7, Southern adjustment behaviour has to be specified if insufficient foreign finance is available to close the fiscal deficit. The following adjustment responses were identified: (i) if the debt burden surpasses the tolerable level as perceived by the Southern government (see the discussion of the Ω variable in Chapter 7), it will leap into payments arrears (which are capitalized in the Southern debt stock) and (ii) if no further funds can be mobilized by the government and the closing variable of the Southern fiscal balance, public investment (I_{Sg}), would tend to become negative, then I_{Sg} is set equal to zero and taxes are raised until the Southern fiscal account is balanced.[1] The banks are assumed to respond to payments arrears by the South by cuttin off further supplies of credits, even if the actual debt-export ratio is below the critical pre-fixed solvency level as perceived by the banks.

8.3 Parameter Values for Base Run

The numerical simulation exercises with the STAC model were executed for a set of chosen values for exogenous parameters and variables. To obtain a plausible quantitative structure of the model, key parameter values and base values of the exogenous variables were derived in part from the evidence in Chapter 5 (particularly the financial par-

Table 8.1 List of baseline values for exogenous parameters and variables

Exogenous parameters			Initial values of stock variables and constants		
b_{1N}	=	0.525	A	=	90
b_{1S}	=	0.425	B_N	=	7000
g_N	=	0.310	B_{Sg}	=	200
g_{0N}	=	0.110	B_{Sp}	=	150
g_{1N}	=	0.200	DC_N	=	3000
g_{2N}	=	2.800	J_N	=	10000
j_{0N}	=	0.050	J_O	=	600
j_{0S}	=	0.100	J_S	=	300
j_{1N}	=	1.000	K_N	=	60000
j_{1S}	=	0.700	K_S	=	5000
m_{NO}	=	0.035	K_{Sg}	=	2500
m_{ON}	=	0.350	L_{Sg}	=	150
q_N	=	10.000			
q_S	=	0.400			
s_N	=	0.400			
s_O (= $1-m_{ON}$)	=	0.650			
s_S	=	0.250			
t_N	=	0.300			
t_S	=	0.100			
tf_N	=	0.003			
x_N	=	0.100			
x_S	=	0.400			
α	=	0.036			
G_{Sp}	=	0.250			
G_{Sg}	=	0.160			
τ	=	0.400			
ω_S	=	0.080			
υ	=	1.000			
Ω	=	0.300			
$(B_S/\theta M_{NS})^{emax}$	=	2.000			

ameters for the South) and, to the extent available, from existing aggregate statistics and econometric evidence from other studies. Model sensitivity was tested for combinations of plausible ranges around the initially chosen empirical values (further observations about model sensitivity and stability are made below). The full list of base run values of exogenous variables and parameters appears in Table 8.1.

8.3.1 Parameters for the South

The productivity parameters for Southern private and public capital, σ_{Sp} and σ_{Sg} in equation 7.2, were fixed at 0.25 and 0.16 respectively. The estimates were based on recent econometric evidence on the relative contribution of public and private capital to growth in developing countries (Khan & Reinhart 1990 and Sarmad 1990), derived from cross-section analysis for a group of 24 countries. The evidence on the relative contribution to growth is mixed, suggesting a higher marginal productivity of private capital in the 1970s and of public capital in the 1980s. The base values for these parameters in the STAC model reflect a higher productivity for private capital as indicative for the two periods taken together.

Southern labour productivity (eq. 7.3), $q_S = 0.4$ (= US$ 400 at 1980 prices), is an average for the lower-income, primary exporting non-oil developing countries. Changing this parameter essentially affects employment in the South and for the given real wage the exportable surplus, which in turn is a determinant of the terms of trade (through eq. 7.1). The real wage in the South was set at $\omega_S = 0.08$, assuming a wage share in value added of 0.2 $[\omega_S = (\omega_S L_S/Q_S) \cdot q_S = 0.2 \times 0.4]$.[2]

The Southern tax rate (t_S) and the savings rate (s_S) were tested within plausible ranges of respectively 0.1–0.3 and 0.1–0.5 (cf. equations 7.5 and 7.7). Within these ranges model results remained in terms of tendency similar to the baseline run. The tax rate was set at the lower bound, $t_S = 0.1$. The average tax rate for non-oil developing countries in the mid-1980s was around 0.20, up from around 0.16 in the 1970s (see FitzGerald & Sarmad 1990; World Bank, 1990, 1985; and Chapter 5). The private savings rate (to non-wage income) was set at $s_S = 0.25$ for the baseline case. The Southern average private savings rate as a share of GNP has been estimated at between 0.15 and 0.20 for the late 1970s and 1980s (FitzGerald & Sarmad 1990 and Chapter 5), which, given the presumed wage share in GNP of 0.2, yields an approximate savings rate from profit incomes of between 0.19 and 0.25 $[S_{Sp} / \theta R_S = (S_{Sp} / \theta Q_S)$ /-

(1 – 0.2)].[3] Exogenous parameters for the financial variables in the Southern economy are identified further below.

8.3.2 Parameters for the North

Northern average labour productivity was set at $q_N = 10.0$ and was derived from World Bank data on GDP and employment in industrial countries. The relative labour productivity between North and South (q_N / q_S) is thus set at an initial level of 25.0, which seems to reflect productivity differentials between the North and the lower-income countries in the South. In the Northern wage-price function (eq. 7.12), the mark-up rate was set at $\tau = 0.4$, a value near econometric estimates obtained by Marquez & Pauly (1987) for the North in their application of the Taylor model. Their results for the Northern price function, using data for 1960-79, suggest a constant of 1.0 and 'mark-ups' of 0.33 on labour costs and 0.35 on non-oil raw material costs and 0.10 on oil input costs.

In the base run, the real price of oil ($v = P_O/P_N$) is set at 1.0 and the marginal input-output coefficient for oil was derived from the Northern long-run demand elasticity for oil as estimated by Marquez & Pauly, namely $\varepsilon_O = 1.34$, and the average oil import to output coefficient derived from trade and output statistics is 0.026 ($m_{NO} = 0.035$).

The Northern private savings rate, s_N, has been set at 0.4, derived as $s_N = 1 - c_N$, where c_N is the long-run propensity to consume in the North, estimated by Marquez & Pauly (1987) at 0.6. Northern tax and government spending rates (to GNP) average about 0.3. In the base run a modest tendency towards deficit spending is assumed by setting t_N and g_N (as indicated, for the simulations $G_N = g_N Q_N$ in equation 7.20) at respectively 0.30 and 0.31. Northern demand for Southern commodities (eq. 7.15a) has been assumed to be relatively income inelastic, as suggested earlier. In the model this is expressed by assigning a positive value to the constant A (see Chapter 7). From international trade statistics and Northern GDP data the average propensity of the North to import from the South was estimated to lie between 0.025 and 0.050. For the simulations α was set at 0.036.

Northern investment demand parameters were derived from econometric results obtained by Marquez & Pauly (1987) for a function similar to that hypothesized in the STAC model (eq. 7.16). The relevant coefficients for g_{0N}, g_{1N} and $-g_{2N}$ were set at respectively 0.11, 0.20 and -2.80 based on their estimates, all with expected signs, and after normalizing for K_N (instead of Q_N as in Marquez & Pauly).

Finally, as indicated, aid flows are endogenous to Northern output for the simulation exercises in order to maintain a level of flows which represent a more or less constant proportion of the size of the Northern economy. As shown in Chapter 5, the share of aid flows to Northern GNP has remained fairly constant at between 0.3 and 0.4 per cent since 1970. The start value for tf_N was thus set at 0.003.

8.3.3 Parameters for the oil-exporting region

The parameter for Northern demand for oil gas already been specified, leaving import demand of the oil economy, m_{ON}, as the remaining exogenous parameter. Trade and national accounts data indicate that the average import propensity of major oil exporters is in the order of magnitude of between 0.35 (1970s) and 0.5 (1980s).[4] The baseline case of the model takes the lower bound estimate.

8.3.4 Parameters for the credit market

Empirical evidence on the Northern deposit-demand function suggests that the stock-adjustment parameter j_{0N} might range between 0.05 and 0.50, while no firm estimates could be found for the rate-of-return response parameter j_{1N}.[5] For the numerical exercises the deposit demand parameters for the North were set at the lower bound (0.05) for j_{0N} and at a presumed 1.0 for j_{1N} which possibly overstates the significance of the rate-of-return responsiveness of Northern deposit demand. However, model results do not show great sensitivity to alternative values for j_{1N}.

Parameters for demand for external financial assets in the South were derived from the empirical evidence on 'capital flight' and other private capital outflows discussed in Chapter 5 (section 5.5.3 and note 27). The specification used in the STAC model was found significant in the case of the Philippines, yielding estimates for j_{0S} of 0.09 and for j_{1S} of between 0.4 and 0.8, depending on the functional specification (see Vos 1992). Other evidence for a sample of African countries suggested a j_{0S} of about 0.2 (Chapter 5, note 27), but j_{1S} was not significantly different from zero (Hermes & Lensink 1990). Pastor (1990) estimated j_{1S} at 0.32 for a sample of eight Latin American countries, but did not estimate j_{0S}. For the base run j_{0S} and j_{1S} were set at 0.1 and 0.7 respectively, where the first parameter may be a lower-bound and the latter an upper-bound estimate.

Interest-rate mark-ups on bank loans to North and South, x_N and x_S, were set at 0.1 and 0.4 respectively. At the average real interest rate (nominal LIBOR corrected for US inflation) of 3–4 per cent for the second half of the 1970s and 1980s implies a spread of 0.3–0.4 percentage points for the North and 1.2–1.6 percentage points for the South, which is in line with the evidence on spreads on publicly guaranteed loans given in Chapter 5 (Figures 5.2 and 5.6).

The analysis of Chapter 5 found a negative relationship between new bank lending and solvency indicators of the borrowing Southern economies (debt-GNP and debt-export ratios), although the corresponding parameter values shifted strongly between the different phases in bank lending to the South. These shifts were interpreted as changes in creditworthiness assessment and market confidence of the banks, which are captured in the model by the difference between a pre-set critical solvency parameter, $(B_S/\theta M_{NS})^{emax}$, and by the actual debt-export ratio and the confidence parameter b_{1S}. These parameters, determining the degree of credit rationing, were set at relatively low levels for the baseline case, reflecting 'prudent' borrowing and lending strategies, and were subsequently adjusted to simulate the impact of a 'loan supply shock' or change in borrowing behaviour of Southern governments. The critical solvency indicator as determined by the banks, $(B_S/\theta M_{NS})^{emax}$ (a maximum debt-export ratio), was set initially at a 'prudent' 2.0, and the confidence parameter b_{1S} at 0.425. Southern public sector demand for external borrowing was hypothesized to be constrained by a predetermined limit on debt-servicing capacity, Ω, as perceived by Southern government. This 'cap' on borrowing also defines the point at which the Southern goverment may consider default. No immediate quantitative evidence could be found for Ω, but as a policy variable it can reflect more or less prudent borrowing behaviour and hasten or delay the decision to default. For the base run it was set at 0.30 (i.e. a limit on interest payments on external debt of 30 per cent of total foreign exchange earnings).

8.3.5 Baseline run

The baseline run was calibrated using start values for the beginning of year stock variables which were set in proportion to the relative size of the three economies. Baseline values for 10 simulation periods are reported in Appendix Tables A8.1 and A8.2 for, respectively, a model version in which no bank lending takes place to the South and the full model version (see also below for the precise specification of these two versions).

The model converges in both versions for a global interest rate (i_W) of about 4 per cent, which shows a tendency to rise gradually. Base run estimates yield a practically stable endogenous Northern net investment rate of about 8 per cent of output. Base run estimates for output in the three regions (Q_N, Q_S, Q_O) roughly reflect actual shares in world output (7995, 1650 and 280, respectively in Table A8.2). In all regions output gradually increases over time, but the base run assumptions yield a widening income gap between North and South. Under parameter assumptions for the base run of the model version with bank lending to the South, government demand for external borrowing appears to widely exceed available bank lending ($\Delta B^d_{Sg} > \Delta B_S$), i.e. the public sector is rationed and there is no loan pushing to potential private borrowers in the South. Despite the rather strict credit rationing of Southern borrowers by banks the base run nevertheless tends towards a Southern debt crisis. A result discussed further below.

8.4 Stability and Dynamics

For the chosen parameter values and start values of stock variables, the stability conditions of the Jacobian of the reduced form of the model (see Appendix A7.1) hold for the base year.[6] The limits of the stability conditions of the model for each period were not formally analysed, but the stability of the numerical outcomes and model sensitivity were tested by performing a large number of simulations varying the key parameters one by one. It appears that model outcomes are most sensitive to the chosen parameters for Northern investment demand and the credit-rationing parameters for bank lending to the South. The reasons why the model is sensitive to these parameters and, for certain values fails to converge to equilibrium, are similar in each case. If the negative response parameter of investment demand to interest rate changes (g_{2N}) is large enough to make investment demand (I_N) zero even for very low real interest rates, then output levels in the North may fall to low levels. If the latter effect is such that the Southern terms of trade (θ) also approach zero, then Southern import capacity, profits and government income all approach zero. Because too many demand variables (e.g. I_N, I_{Sg}, M_{SN}) approach their non-negativity constraints (after which they are set equal to zero), the model fails to converge. This is a practical problem encountered when calibrating the model and testing a large number of simulations.

More important from a theoretical point of view are the stability conditions determined by the nature of the interactions between the markets. As indicated in Chapter 7, Keynesian stability conditions are essential to ensure equilibrium on the Northern commodity market and the world credit market, i.e. the savings response to Northern profitability should exceed that of the investment demand response less the responsiveness of Northern investment demand to the interest rate. Another potential source of instability relates to the interaction between the Northern and Southern commodity markets, i.e. the Northern income propensity to consume the Southern commodity should not exceed the savings responsiveness to output changes in the North. These stability conditions are not dissimilar to the ones found in other North-South models. See among others Taylor (1981) and van Wijnbergen (1985) on the first condition and Kanbur & Vines (1986) on the second. One example of violation of these stability conditions is the case in which Northern investment demand and output growth respond to the profit rate in the form of a diverging cobweb in a case of (near-)zero responsiveness of Northern investment to the interest rate combined with a high mark-up τ (near to unity). The world interest rate rises subsequently with increased credit demands, but the Southern terms of trade move upward faster and simultaneous equilibrium on all markets is not achieved. (See Appendix A7.1 for a further discussion of stability conditions.)

Another, more experimental test of the model properties was to look at the role of the credit-rationing rules of the banking system in model stability for the described set of parameters. This was tested by eliminating the credit rationing rules for Southern borrowers, i.e. by omitting the specific credit supply function for Southern borrowers (eq. 7.25) and by letting Southern demand for bank loans be directly part of the credit market clearing interest-rate function (7.27). The world credit market thus has become fully (price) interest-rate clearing in this adjusted model version. The results show that, due to the high elasticity of demand in the South for foreign exchange and the lifting of the supply-side constraint, the interest rate increases slowly in the first two simulation periods and then starts increasing exponentially. The debt-export ratio in the South is permitted to increase to staggering heights (above 8.0), while the high interest rate lowers the Northern investment level to zero and after about four simulation rounds the system fails to reach an equilibrium.[7] The robustness of this result has only been tested and confirmed for a small set of other parameter combinations (involving changes in the values of the parameters of the Northern investment function and the Southern credit demand function). Nevertheless it may be hypothesized that rationing in world credit markets has a logic and relevance for the stability of the world economic system as conceptualized through the STAC model. The credit-rationing rules applied by banks thus in effect appear to have a rationale beyond their own interests and risk-averse behaviour. However, as also follows from the analysis below, banks have only imperfect knowledge when they set credit limits and as bankers' expectations (exogenously imposed on the model) change due to changing credit market conditions they may set off a lending boom, endangering system stability. Such systemic tendencies seem obvious justifications for market regulation and third-party (e.g. IMF) interventions.

8.5 Model Simulations

Simulations in response to sustained permanent shocks have been performed for two model versions: (i) model I where the South has no access to the international banking system (i.e. b_{1S}, j_{ON}, j_{1N}, B_{Sg}, B_{Sp} and J_S are all set to zero); and (ii) the full model system (model II) with credit rationing rules for the South (baseline as described above). These two cases provide numerical simulations for the theoretical analysis of the previous chapter. Simulation results of the following permanent shocks and policy adjustments are reported:

(1) a doubling of the oil price ($v = 2$);

(2) an increase in official aid flows to the South up from baseline 0.3 per cent to the DAC target of 1 per cent of Northern output ($tf_N = 0.010$) for three alternative cases:
(2.1) bond financed;
(2.2) tax financed;
(2.3) budget cuts; and

(3) a bank loan supply shock produced by increasing creditworthiness of the South as perceived by the banks ($(B_S/\theta M_{NS})^{emax} = 3.0$).

Simulations 1, 2.1 and 2.2 are performed for both model versions and simulation 3 for model version (ii) only.

The above scenarios are inserted into the model with further unchanged behaviour and each agent pursuing its objectives as suggested by the model and specified in Chapter 7. In this sense one should interpret all simulations as examining the implications of non-cooperative policies on growth prospects in North and South. The results are shown as deviations from the baseline run for the equilibrium values of the world interest rate, the terms of trade, Northern and Southern output, Southern private capital outflows and world income distribution.

Figure 8.1a STAC model I: oil price shock and aid transfer (world interest rate, i_W)

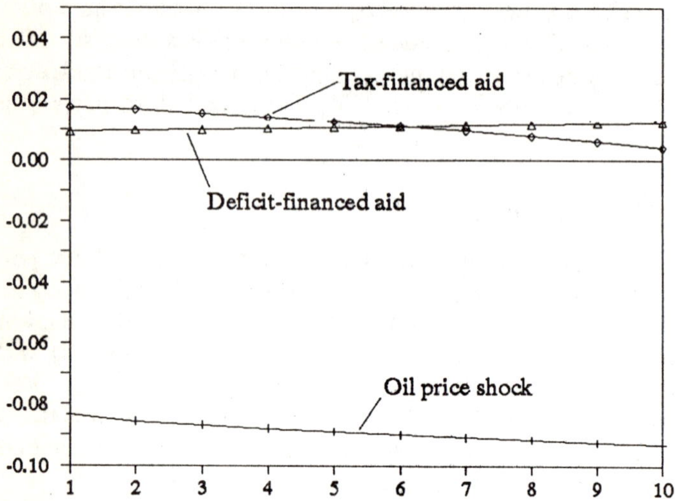

Figure 8.1b STAC model I: oil price shock and aid transfer (terms of trade, θ)

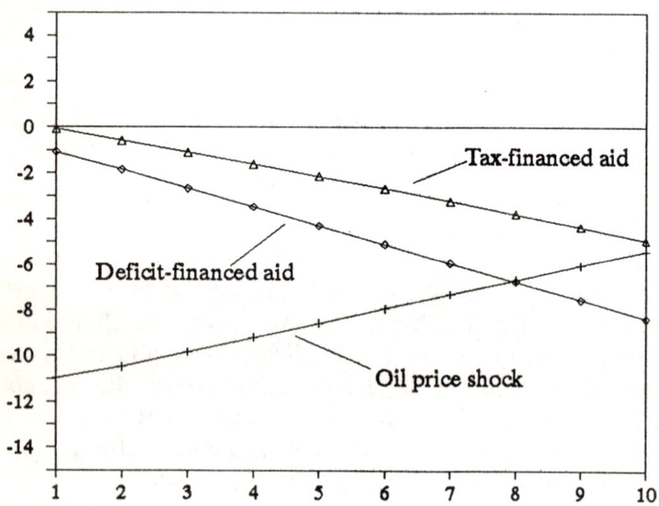

Figure 8.1c STAC model I: oil price shock and aid transfer (Northern output, Q_N)

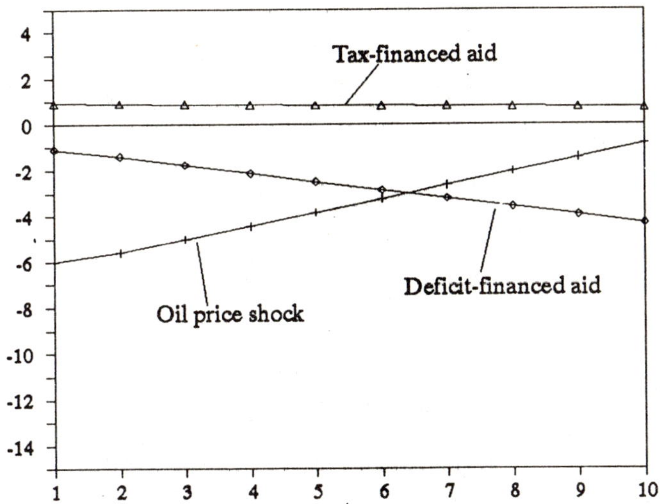

Figure 8.1d STAC model I: oil price shock and aid transfer (Southern output, Q_S)

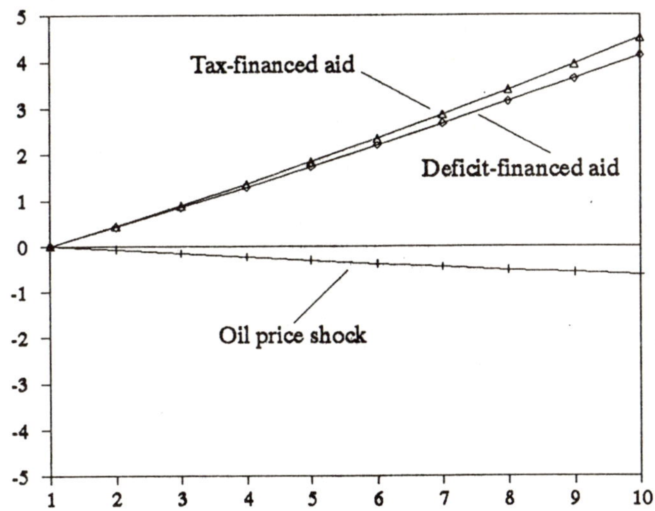

Figure 8.1e STAC model I: oil price shock and aid transfer (world income distribution, real)

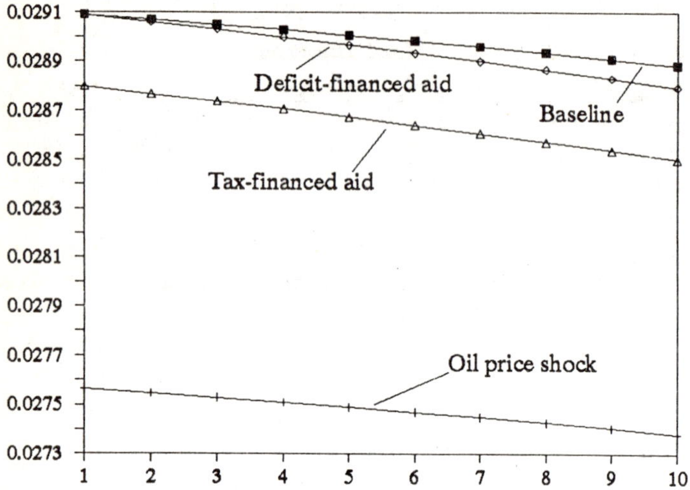

Figure 8.1f STAC model I: oil price shock and aid transfer (Southern savings, S_S)

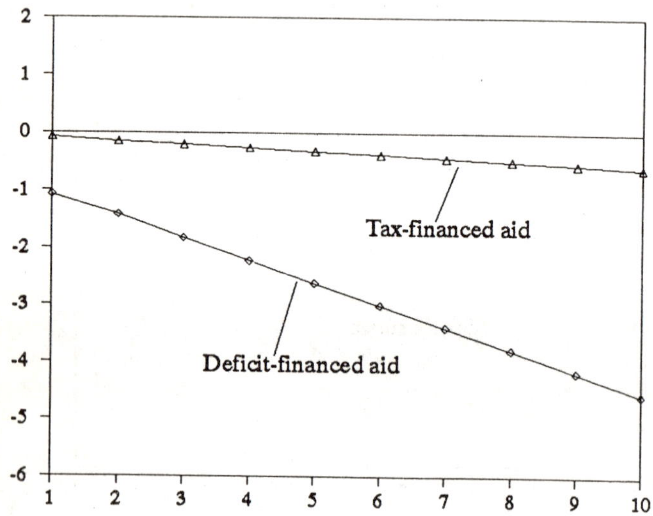

8.5.1 The effects of an oil price shock and increased aid flows in the case of no bank lending to the South (model I)

Figures 8.1a–e show the simulation results for (i) a doubling of the oil price and (ii) an increase in aid flows to the South from 0.3 to 1.0 per cent of Northern output financed by domestic borrowing or, alternatively, additional taxation of Northern incomes. The oil price shock has a downward effect on the world interest rate as a result of the fact that oil producers are high savers and deposit their savings surpluses in the Northern banking system (Figure 8.1a).

This model result is fully explained by the loanable funds effect of savings surpluses in the oil exporting region. The finding seems consistent with the events of the 1970s as discussed in Chapter 5. The outcome contrasts, however, with those of other empirical models which usually emphasize the supply side effects of a change in the price of oil. The models in Bruno & Sachs (1985) and McKibbin & Sachs (1991) are good examples; in these models a higher oil price creates recessionary effects in the Northern economies. Even though this depresses investment demand, the fall in world savings is even bigger in these models, so that the oil price increase leads to a higher, instead of a lower world interest rate. In the IMF's MULTIMOD model (Masson et al. 1988) an oil price increase (decrease) also depresses (stimulates) Northern output. Here the output effect is caused, however, by forward-looking behaviour: agents in the North anticipate the price increase (fall), thereby causing the long-term interest rate to increase (fall).

The terms of trade for the South suffer from falling demand in the North, but over time they tend to recover along with the Northern economy (Figure 8.1b). Under the model assumptions it is the Northern real wage that suffers most from the oil shock (eq. 7.12). Lower output demand also depresses the profit rate and thus Northern investment, but over time the lower interest rate allows for a gradual recovery (Figure 8.1c). In this case, Southern output growth tends to fall short of that in the base run case (Figure 8.1d). The South is hit through several channels. Lower growth rates in the North (particularly through the steeper fall in consumption growth) causes lower terms of trade and thus lower profits and investment. Since aid is a function of Northern output in the present model structure, foreign exchange availability is further eroded through declining aid flows. These results are as expected from the theoretical analysis of Chapter 7. Under these conditions North and South grow further apart as indicated by the world income distribution indicator ($\theta\, Q_S/Q_N$) in Figure 8.1e.

Recent pleas for substantial increases in aid flows from North to South (e.g. Fishlow 1987, Jepma 1990, Taylor 1990, Griffith-Jones 1989, UNCTAD 1988) might have been voiced with less vigour, if a number of potential trade-offs due to secondary global interdependence effects were considered explicitly as part of the proposal. Simulations of increased aid flows with the STAC model suggest two things: firstly, the beneficial growth effects of additional foreign exchange through official transfers may well be outweighed by reduced foreign exchange earnings in trade (through falling terms of trade); and, secondly, the way in which increased aid flows are financed also significantly influences net benefits for the South.

Figure 8.1a shows that the increase in aid flows leads to a higher world interest rate which has a negative impact on Northern investment and output growth.[8] This effect is higher in the first periods of adjustment if the official transfer is financed by additional Northern government borrowing. This causes excess demand for global credit and pushes up the world interest rate, which subsequently depresses Northern output growth, demand for the Southern commodity and the terms of trade for the South (Figures 8.1b and c). The latter effect is strengthened by the higher growth of Southern output, as the model assumes aid will lead to higher public investment which is complementary to primary production. Southern profits and tax income both gain from this volume effect, but these gains are more than outweighed by the lower terms of trade (*vis-à-vis* the baseline case). Lower profits and tax income imply lower private and public savings and thus confirm the hypothesis suggested in Chapter 7, that part of the presumed 'Griffin-effect' of savings substituting aid flows may well be caused by international transmission effects even where aid is assumed to be allocated for complementary productive investment (rather than government consumption). It also relates to the transfer debate and confirms the hypothesis of Chapter 7 that under the structuralist specifications of the world economy, the secondary burden (deteriorating terms of trade) of aid transfers falls on the recipient economy.

This strong and 'un-Keynesian' result tells us that there is no 'global free lunch'.[9] The model does not allow enhanced aid flows to be financed by monetary accommodation in the North. Under the present model assumptions, fiscal expansion leads to a higher world interest rate, leading to a fall in Northern investment demand and output. This recessionary effect seems to outweigh the positive demand effect from the larger import capacity in the South resulting from the aid transfer.

This also explains the intuitively less obvious result that the adverse global adjustment effects are significantly mitigated if the additional aid flow is financed from higher taxes on Northern incomes. The reported simulation presents the case of a rise in the Northern tax rate by 0.4 per cent of GNP. The initial effect on the interest rate (before it reaches it end-of-period equilibrium; see note 8) is significantly smaller than in the previous case, even though the new end-of-period equilibrium interest rate is not very different from that in the case of deficit financing. The new equilibrium interest rate is reached for a higher level of Northern output. This does not prevent the terms of trade from falling below the baseline values, however, due to the larger positive effect on Southern output from aid-financed public investment.

These issues are further investigated in the model version with endogenous commercial bank lending to the South.

8.5.2 Credit rationing, loan supply shocks and private capital outflows from the South (model II)

For the described set of parameter values and given the logic of the model concerning the asymmetric behaviour of Southern debtors and commercial creditors, there is an inherent tendency for debt crises to emerge in the South. The base run (Table A8.2) also yields such a result. Debt accumulation leads in the eighth period to a debt-export ratio which exceeds the critical solvency level as perceived by the banks (2.0) and banks stop new lending. Reduced foreign exchange availability in the next period brings thoughts of default to the minds of Southern borrowers as the critical interest payment to total foreign-exchange availability ratio is surpassed. Under the present model assumptions, the South will opt to default and will run interest payment arrears (*YARR*). New access to bank lending is virtually cut off, but since the model assumes the banks evaluate debt-export ratios and arrears positions from year to year, renewed access to the bank loan market is possible and in the base run this is the case in period 10. Running the model for subsequent periods produces another debt crisis within a few years. Runs for an alternative, and more realistic, case of a sustained 'revulsion' against bank lending to the South after a debt crisis and default generally reproduce, for the period after lending ceases, the tendencies discussed in the model without bank lending.

Debt crises thus appear as a systemic result of imperfect creditworthiness assessment and pro-cyclical lending behaviour of banks, rather than as products of particular exogenous shocks. The three simulations analysed below indicate that oil and loan-supply shocks may hasten the

Figure 8.2a STAC model II: oil price and loan shock (world interest rate, i_W)

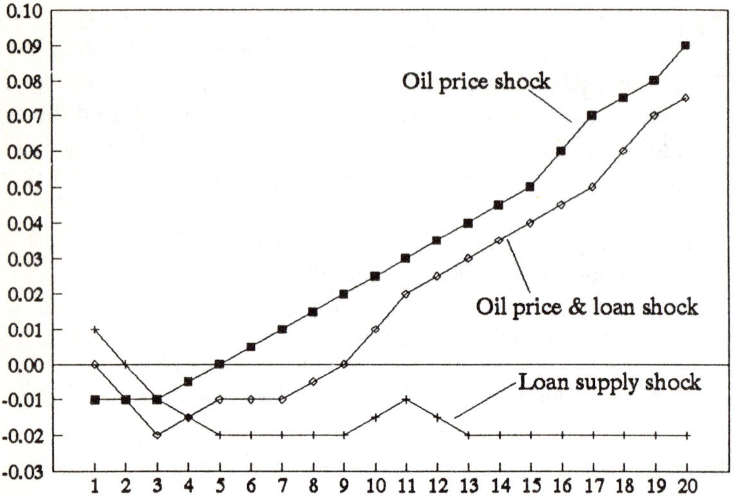

Figure 8.2b STAC model II: oil price and loan shock (terms of trade, θ)

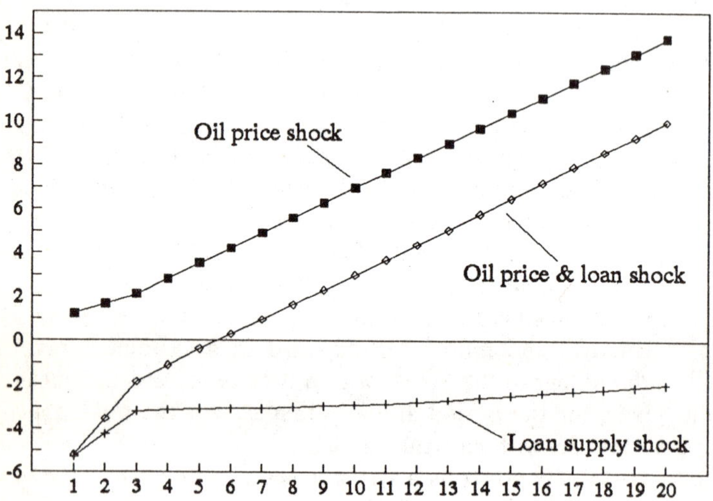

Figure 8.2c STAC model II: oil price and loan shock (Northern output, Q_N)

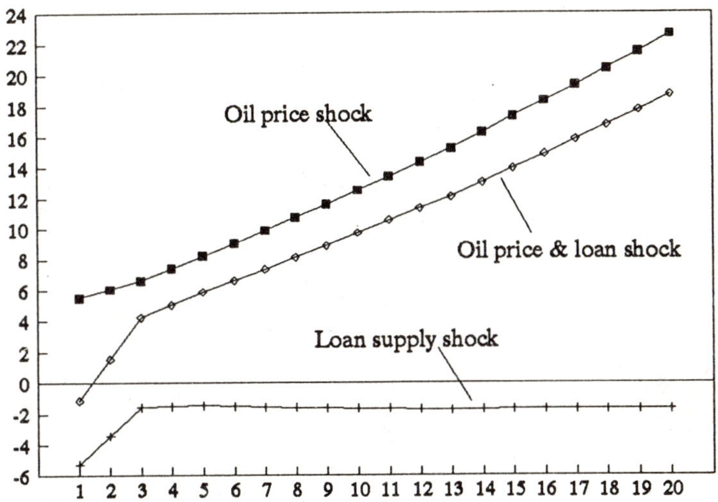

Figure 8.2d STAC model II: oil price and loan shock (Southern output, Q_S)

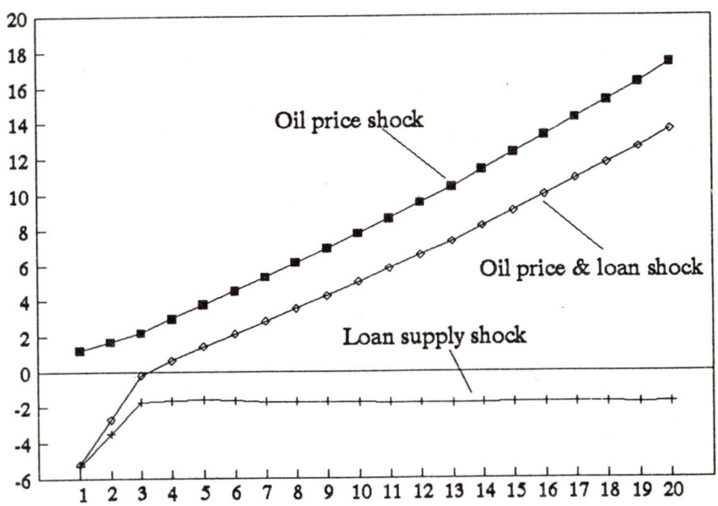

Figure 8.2e *STAC model II: oil price and loan shock (Southern savings, S_S)*

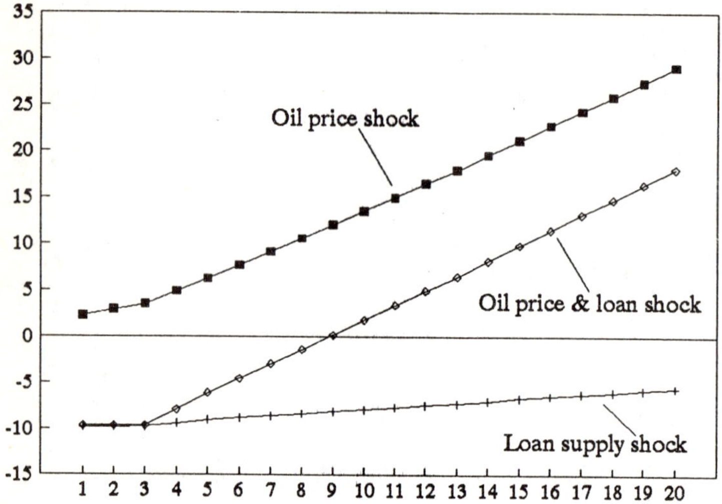

Figure 8.2f *STAC model II: oil price and loan shock (private foreign assets, J_S)*

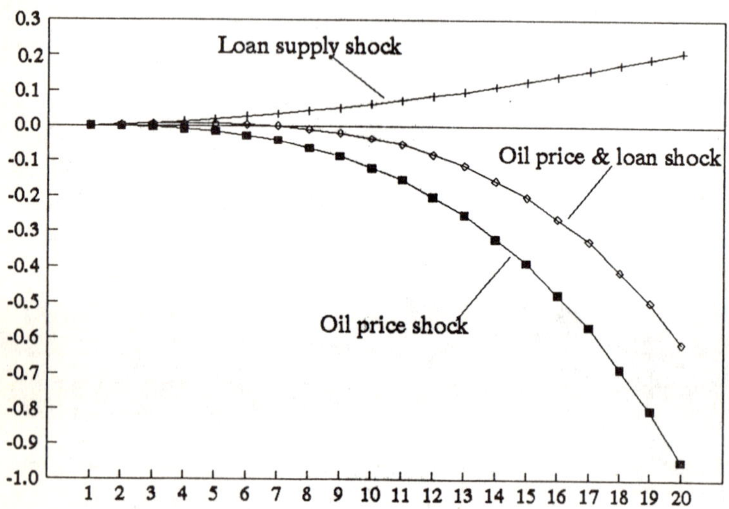

Figure 8.2g STAC model II: oil price and loan shock (payments arrears South)

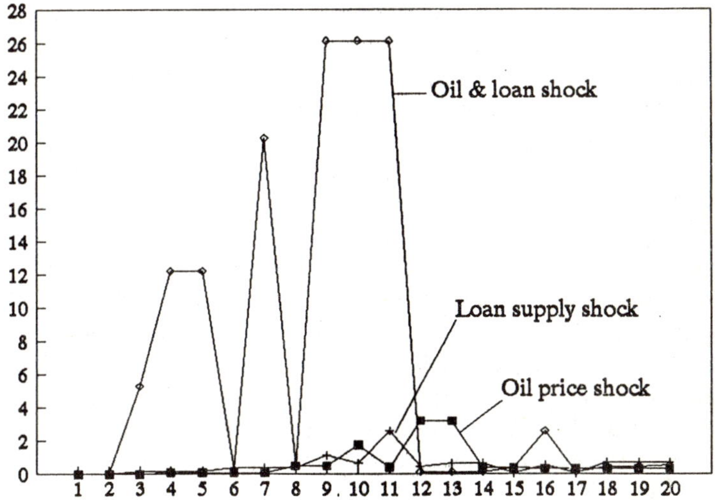

emergence of a debt crisis, while greater foreign exchange availability in the form of tax-financed official aid may delay the emergence of a crisis. The following simulations are reported:

(1) an oil price shock ($v = P_O / P_N = 2.0$);

(2) a loan-supply shock ($B_S/\theta M_{NS}^{emax} = 3.0$), in line with the events of the 1970s;

(3) a combination of (1) and (2);

(4) as (3), but in addition a bond-financed increase in aid flows (to $0.01Q_N$);

(5) as (3), but in addition a tax-financed increase in aid flows (to $0.01Q_N$); and

(6) as (3), but in addition an increase in aid flows (to $0.01Q_N$) financed through budget cuts in the North.

The results for the simulations 1–3 are reported for 20 simulation periods in Figures 8.2a–g. The oil price shock, as before, has an initial depressing effect on the world interest rate. However, this effect is short-

much more quickly than in the case with no bank lending to the South and results from enhanced demand for the Northern commodity from the South, allowed for by enhanced credit flows to the South.

A loan supply shock in turn puts upward pressure on the world interest rate. The model assumptions of a segmented global capital market imply that a softening of credit rationing rules increase global competition for loanable funds leading to the interest rate increase. This puts the world economy on a recessionary path. Northern output falls below the baseline no-shock case. Reduced Northern aggregate demand affects the Southern terms of trade (Figure 8.2b) and Southern output (Figure 8.2d). These factors also depress the world interest rate, however, without producing automatic recovery.

Simulation 3, which combines the oil price shock and the loan supply shock, provides no surprises. The results are between the opposite trends of the separate shocks. The global impact of an oil price shock of the simulated size, dominates the results. The global interest rate decreases (compared with the baseline) due to the increase in loanable funds caused by the shift in global income towards high-saving oil exporters. This effect is initially mitigated by the simultaneously imposed loan-supply shock. Economic recovery in the North after the oil price shock is not instantaneous (as in the single oil price shock simulation), but is nevertheless speedy (Figure 8.2c). These simulation results seem to be in line with the global macroeconomic events as described in Chapter 5. They confirm the importance of the loanable-funds effect of the oil price shock and its depressing impact on the world interest rate as pointed out above. The South benefits only gradually: Northern growth following the oil shock stimulates demand for Southern exports, while the loan supply shock stimulates Southern supply. The latter effect slows down terms of trade improvement for the South (Figure 8.2b) and thereby real income growth in this sector (Figure 8.2d).

Thus after a relatively short period of adjustment, the combined permanent oil and loan supply shock sets both North and South on an expansionary path. Nevertheless, this does not prevent the emergence of payments problems in the South. The critical debt-export ratio is reached after five periods and a negative net financial transfer leads the Southern government to opt for default in the sixth period (Figure 8.2g).

Enhanced public capital flows from North to South cannot resolve these systemic problems, but may mitigate some of the negative effects on the foreign exchange availability of the South and postpone the moment where the South will consider default.[10] Figures 8.3a–g report on simulations 4–6 showing the impact of increased aid transfers under dif-

Figure 8.3a STAC model II: increased aid transfers (world interest rate, i_W)

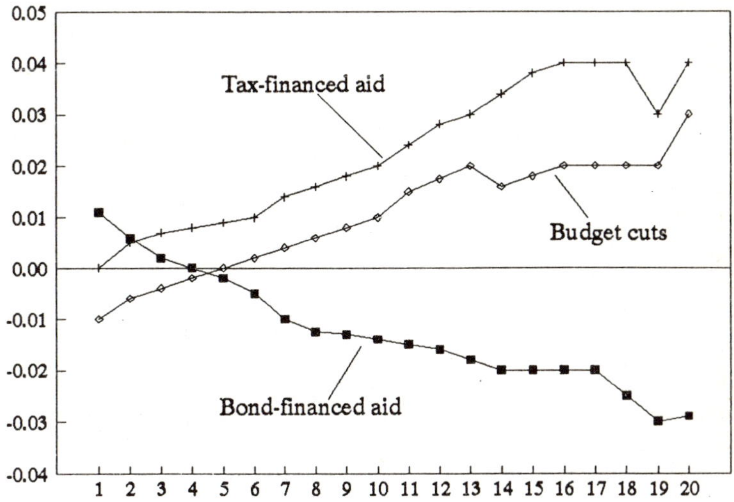

Figure 8.3b STAC model II: increased aid transfers (terms of trade, θ)

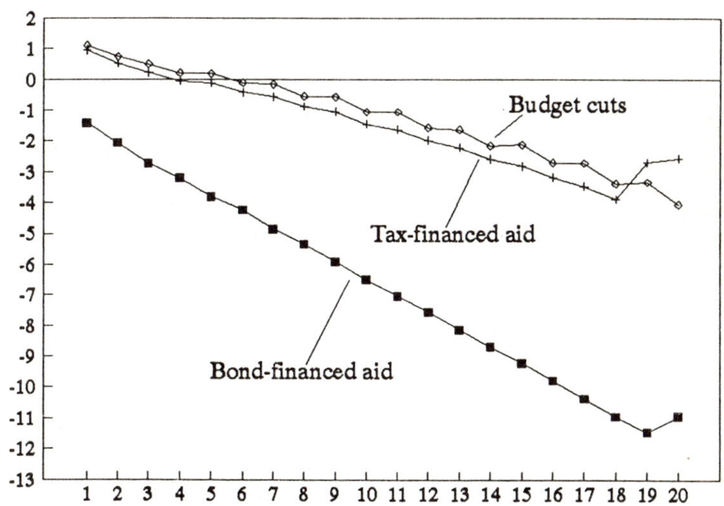

Figure 8.3c STAC model II: increased aid transfers (Northern output, Q_N)

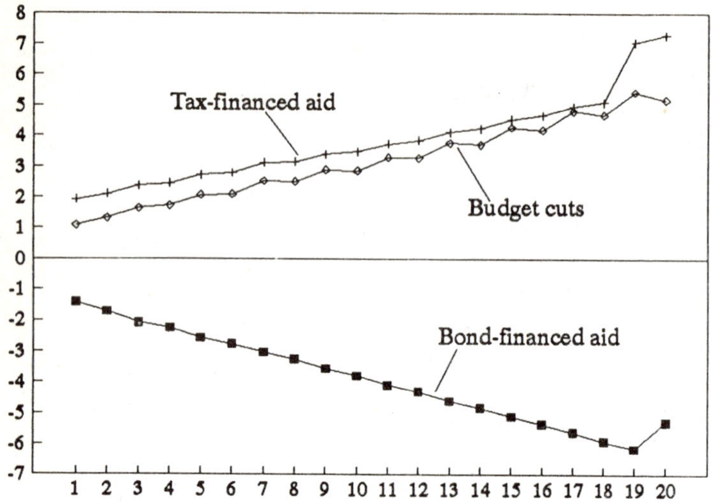

Figure 8.3d STAC model II: increased aid transfers (Southern output, θQ_S)

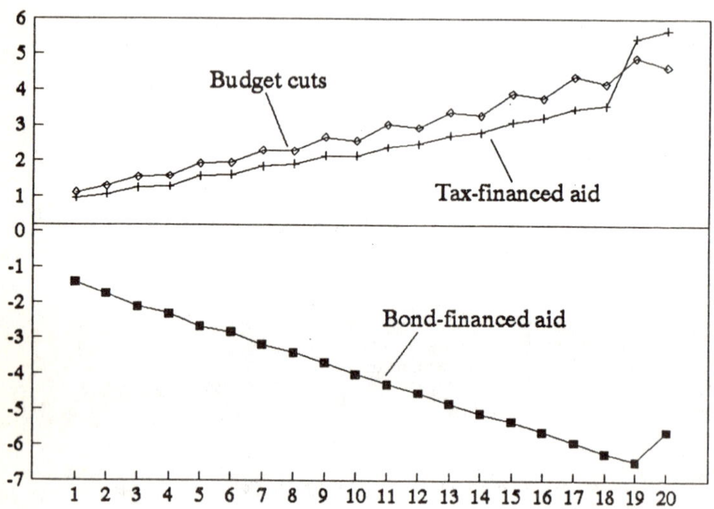

Figure 8.3e *STAC model II: increased aid transfers (private savings, South, θS_S)*

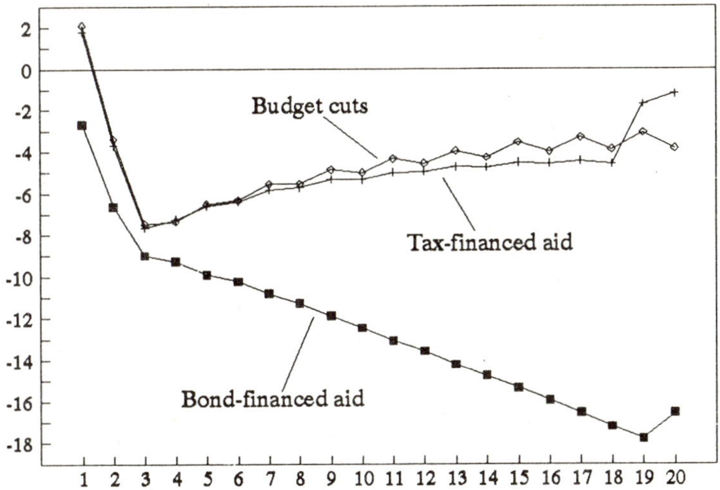

Figure 8.3f *STAC model II: increased aid transfers (private foreign assets, 'capital flight', J_S)*

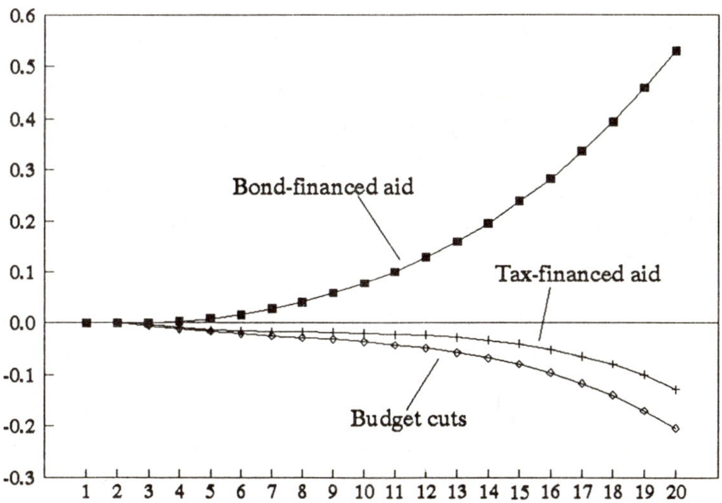

Figure 8.3g STAC model II: increased aid transfers (payments arrears South)

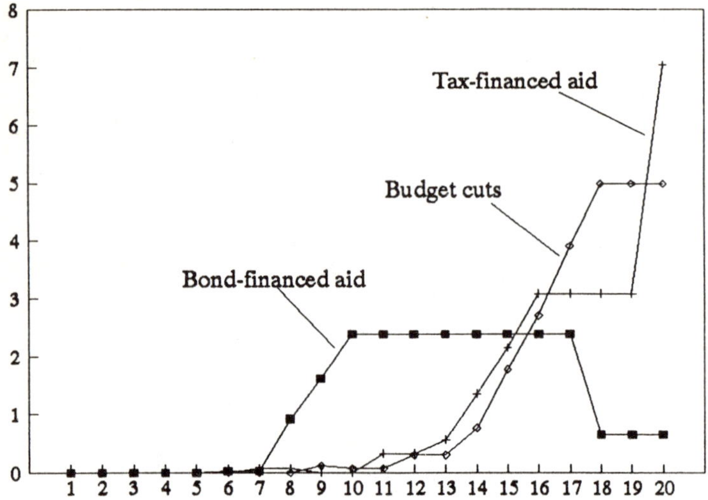

ferent financing assumptions. The graphs confirm the results obtained with the model version with no bank loans in the sense that an increase in aid flows financed by fiscal contraction in the North will be more beneficial to the South than a bond-financed increase. In the latter case as before, an initially higher equilibrium interest rate (Figure 8.3a) emerges at lower equilibrium output levels for Northern output. This means lower terms of trade, crowding-out of Southern profits and savings (Figure 8.3e) and larger incentives for 'capital flight' (Figure 8.3f). These reasons also underlie the earlier occurrence of a debt crisis (arrears significantly larger than zero) in the case of a bond-financed aid increase (i.e. in period 8 as against period 14 in the case of tax financing or budget cuts).

These simulations with the STAC model highlight some of the systemic risks attached to a redirection of financial resources from North to South. A Brandtian scheme of a 'virtuous circle' of trade and aid appears to be the less likely outcome. Besides the structural differences in the adjustment of the Northern and Southern economy assumed in the model, it could be said in addition that the monetary restraint implicitly imposed on the model is another factor determining the outcome. A more explicit and flexible role for money supply and demand functions is left for future versions of the STAC model. For the moment, it could be said that allowance for expansionary Northern monetary policy as a means to finance the increased aid transfer will not necessarily produce the free global lunch the Brandt report and other proposals would like to order. The effects of world inflation would then become crucial in determining the distribution of global adjustment costs. In any case, in the 1980s and early 1990s the priorities of policy makers in the major Northern economies have been to fight inflation and impose monetary restraints. In this sense the above simulations should be seen as an attempt to provide an analysis of the fundamentals of global adjustment in this period.

8.6 A Comparison with Other Applied North–South Models

Within the context of empirical global modelling experiments, relatively little explicit attention has been paid to macroeconomic interactions between North and South. Currie & Vines (1988) even suggest these interactions might form a crucial 'missing link' in current debates on international policy coordination. The experiments with the STAC model at best form a modest starting point to deal with this link and contribute to international policy debates. In its present state the simulations with the STAC model hold the middle ground between what has been labelled by Beenstock (1988) as the 'oracular' and the 'econometric' approaches to North–South modelling. The former refers to simulation exercises and the policy conclusions based on them, with arbitrarily set parameter values in a theoretical model,[11] while the latter approach searches for econometrically estimated parameters for behavioural relations.[12] The simulations with STAC were based on chosen parameter values which were imposed on the model, but the choices made were largely based on empirical evidence. Nevertheless, future work should include the construction of a better data base to elaborate an empirical version of the STAC model and preferably a more disaggregated structure of the world economy. Data constraints of the type discussed in Chapter 2 and elsewhere (Vos 1989) have thus far hampered the work in this direction.[13] In this respect the conclusions to be drawn from the analysis of the previous sections are limited and preliminary. Those that can be drawn can best be placed in a comparative perspective with the outcomes of experiments with other models that focus on North–South interactions.

8.6.1 STAC and large and small world models

The STAC model is distinguished from comparable models by (i) its explicit focus on the role of financial interactions between North and South, specifying (three) different types of capital movements (official aid transfers, commercial bank credits and acquisition of external bank assets by private agents in the South); (ii) the assumption of a strongly segmented world capital market with aid flows being supply-side determined by Northern government (donors) and credit rationing rules limiting bank loan supplies to the South; and (iii) inclusion of the consequences and possible responses to the dynamics of asset accumulation by the various agents and in particular to Southern external debt accumulation, i.e. the possibility of default by Southern borrowers and 'revulsion' of the banks against lending to the South in face of a debt crisis.

These elements are not entirely absent in all models, but if present they are based on different theoretical assumptions or fail to consider the full implications suggested in the STAC model.

Focusing on some of the more interesting empirical models, a distinction can be made between two types of world models. One is a group of *large* and disaggregated world models allowing the analysis of global interactions at the country level, or at least at a fairly large number of country groups. Another group of models can be labelled as *small* global models which distinguish only a small number of country blocs, North and South being the simplest disaggregation. Obviously, the STAC model falls in the second category. Tractability of the analytical structure and of simulation results is probably the main advantage of the 'small' approach. More detail and, possibly, more direct policy relevance, may be considered the advantage of the 'large' approach. The main interest here is, however, to compare the theoretical structure of the alternative models and the consequences that differences therein may have for conclusions derived from counterfactual analysis and policy simulations.

For reasons of comparability, attention will be concentrated on the small models. Concerning the larger model systems – like the World Bank's SIMLINK, the OECD's INTERLINK, the project LINK and SARUM – only a general comment is made here, namely that none of these explicitly model financial interactions between North and South.[14] Most tend to stress the structural asymmetry, also reflected in the STAC model, that growth in the Northern economies is demand determined and that growth in the Southern economies is limited by import capacity (i.e. export earnings determined in the North plus exogenous capital inflows). The Leontief model system is set up around fixed-price input-output accounting, while SIMLINK and INTERLINK leave out the intermediate demand disaggregation but add a role for commodity prices via the specification of price clearing excess demand functions for various commodities.[15] Capital flows between North and South are modelled either as exogenous flows or are residual (covering endogenous current account balances).

Turning to the small model systems, reference will be made to five comparable models which have received some attention in recent years.[16] These are the models by Marquez & Pauly (1987), Van Wijnbergen (1985, 1988), Beenstock (1988), and Currie & Vines et al. (1988) and the IMF's MULTIMOD (Masson et al. 1988). Table 8.2 gives a comparative overview of the most important model assumptions. The models show great similarity (with exception of the Beenstock model) with respect to the modelling of commodity market adjustment, assuming, as in STAC, a flex-price non-oil, primary commodity market and supply constrained production of primary output (and so determining Southern production conditions) and fixed-price and demand-constrained markets for manufactures (dominating Northern macro adjustment). More important differences exist in the modelling of financial interactions between North and South and the role of moving net financial asset positions on global adjustment. The differing features are detailed briefly below and the model outcomes are compared in each case to those of the STAC model.

8.6.2 A comparative perspective

The *Marquez-Pauly model* has a theoretical structure based, like the STAC model, on Taylor's North–South model, and several parameters used for the simulations with the STAC model were derived from the econometric specifications of this model. Marquez & Pauly consider exogenous aid flows, but do not specify behavioural rules for other capital flows which are thus simply residual to the endogenous current account balances of North and South. In general, their model results also show (as in Taylor 1981 and STAC, above) that not all regions benefit equally from world economic growth, with the South facing 'bleak prospects' (Marquez & Pauly 1987: 90). Their policy simulations, based on an optimal control approach, show further that only a framework of international policy coordination which would allow for a significantly larger weight for the policy targets of the South will help to direct its economy into a higher growth path. In the case of uncoordinated international policies, the model shows a different sensitivity to an oil price

Table 8.2 Comparison of the major characteristics of North-South models

Model	**Theoretical**	**Regions**	**Commodity markets by exporting region(s)**			**Capital markets**		
			Commodity type		*Type of market adjustment*	*Type of assets*	*Type of market adjustment*	*Dynamic stock adjustment of financial assets*
Marquez-Pauly	Kalecki-Lewis (Taylor 1981)	North (N) South (S) Oil exp. (O)	Primary, non-oil Manufactures Oil	S N, S S, O	Price-clearing Mark-up pricing Fix-price	Aid transfers Other	Exogenous Residual	no
van Wijnbergen	Keynesian-Lewis	North (N) South (S) Oil exp. (O)	Primary, non-oil Manufactures Oil	S N O	Price-clearing Fix-price Fix-price	Other (curr. account balance)	Interest-rate clearing	no
Beenstock	Monetarist	North (N) South (S)	Composite com.	N, S	Price-clearing	Money stock (N) Gov. debt (N) Southern debt Aid transfers	Interest-rate clearing (all fin. assets) Exogenous	yes

(Continued...)

(Table 8.2 Continued)

Model	Theoretical	Regions	Commodity markets by exporting region(s)			Capital markets		
			Commodity type		*Type of market adjustment*	*Type of assets*	*Type of market adjustment*	*Dynamic stock adjustment of financial assets*
Currie-Vines (MARK I)	Keynesian-Ration. exp. - Lewis	North (N) South (S)	Composite com. Primary, non-oil	N S	Fix-price (sh.t.) Price-clearing	Money stock(N) Southern debt	Interest-rate clearing money market (N) (Residual to CAD)[b]	no[a]
MULTIMOD (IMF)	Keynesian (Dyn. Mun-dell-Fleming) - Lewis	North (N,i=5) South (S,i=1) Oil exp. (O)	Primary, non-oil Manufactures Oil	S N, S all	Price-clearing Mark-up pricing Fix-price	Money stock(N), Gov. debt (N) Southern debt	Interest-rate clearing, each N market Credit rationing (liquidity crit.)	yes
STAC	Kalecki-Lewis - Oligop. Banking	North (N) South (S) Oil exp. (O)	Primary, non-oil Manufactures Oil	S N O	Price-clearing Mark-up pricing Fix-price	Aid transfers Southern Debt Private fin. assets (N, S, O) Gov. debt (N)	Exogenous Credit ratioining (solvency, market size) Portfolio choice and interest-rate clearing credit market	yes

Notes: a. Capital accumulation and stock adjustment included in second version (MARK II, see Muscatelli & Vines 1989).
b. Borrowing constraint imposed as policy variable to avoid model instability.

shock and increased aid flows than the STAC model due to differences in the specification. An oil price increase sets off a generalized and perpetuating recession in the world economy in the Marquez-Pauly model, mainly due to reduced exports to the South (and reduced import capacity of the South) exceeding the increase in exports to the oil-exporting economy. The STAC model, on the contrary, suggested a tendency towards recovery, as a consequence of the endogenous downward effect on the world interest rate of higher savings by oil exporters (in Marquez-Pauly the interest rate is exogenous). Marquez & Pauly also simulate the effects of a (permanent) increase in aid flows of US$ 24 billion per year (i.e. about 0.2 per cent of Northern GDP) and foresee, in the long run, accelerated growth in the South as a result. The STAC model also showed a positive response on Southern output, but this effect was mitigated and even off-set by falling terms of trade provoked by negative demand effects in the North resulting from the need to finance the additional aid flow. The problem with the Marquez-Pauly model is that it does not specify the source of finance of the increase in aid flows, nor does it account for the mentioned secondary effects. The beneficial effects of more aid thus seem to come like 'manna from heaven' in their case.

Van Wijnbergen (1985, 1988) develops a North–South model with more explicit financial interactions between North and South, applying a simple *flow* theory of loanable funds. Dynamics of debt stock accumulation, sovereign risk and other portfolio considerations are not taken into account. The main purpose of the model is to test whether the Ricardo-Barro Equivalence Theorem (see also Chapter 3) applies in financing the Northern fiscal deficit, or, if the 'debt-neutrality' hypothesis does not hold, what the implications are for global adjustment. Like most of the other models, van Wijnbergen assumes that Northern demand and current account balance are essentially demand determined, while the Southern economy is supply-constrained and its terms of trade depend on excess demand for its output (i.e. the market for the Southern commodity is price clearing). The empirical results show that no support can be found for the Ricardo-Barro equivalence theorem and that increases in the Northern fiscal deficit will be reflected in a higher *ex ante* world current account deficit. Bond-financing of the deficit will drive up the world interest rate and 'crowd out' finance available to the South. The STAC model also shows this, but along with it the dynamic consequences of debt accumulation in North and South. The higher interest rate and lower availability of new finance may trigger thoughts of default in the South at certain levels of debt accumulation and break up the 'normal' financial interactions between North and South.

Beenstock's econometric North–South model (Beenstock 1988) assumes neo-classical supply conditions in the North, while Northern aggregate demand is determined in monetarist fashion by the real money supply. Southern exports, assumed to consist mainly of non-oil primary commodities, are a function, not only of Northern GDP, but also of the South's own GDP, the real exchange rate and the terms of trade. The model emphasizes financial linkages, however. The model specifies *stocks* of financial assets and liabilities, but does not depart from a basic loanable-funds framework with the interest rate clearing the global credit market. Sovereign risk in lending to the South is assumed to be included in the interest rate. A crucial difference with the STAC model is that Beenstock explains capital movements to the South as being fully demand-determined: the South determines its desired level of indebtedness as a function of its level of development (following the 'debt-cycle' theory) and a target level of international reserves. Bank behaviour and supply constraints or credit rationing play no role. Debt increases with Southern growth and investment. Higher sovereign risk leads to a fall in desired borrowing. In a sense, credit market adjustment and the type of spill-over effects to the Northern economy are similar to the case of the STAC model version with a market-clearing bank loan market (see earlier in this chapter). Simulations with Beenstock's model which lead to increases in the Southern demand for external borrowing will tend to 'crowd out' Northern investment, since with unchanged Northern macroeconomic policies the world interest rate will move upwards. The STAC model without credit rationing also showed unambiguously that in this case debt-led growth would occur at the cost of Northern activity, but at the same time it was suggested that this cannot be sustained over a long period of time as the model enters into an unstable area.

While Marquez-Pauly, van Wijnbergen and Beenstock show model simulations based on econometrically estimated behavioural functions, *Currie & Vines* et al. (1988) report policy simulations using the 'oracular' approach.[17] A distinctive feature of the Currie-Vines model is the specification of Northern output as demand-determined in the short run, but supply-constrained in the long run. The Northern price adjusts according to an expectations-augmented Phillips curve. The South has features similar to those in most other models, i.e. producing a non-oil primary commodity of which output is supply-constrained and the price is market-clearing. Northern investors are allowed to hold speculative commodity stocks. The model does not specify capital accumulation in

North or South, so only short-run effects can be shown.[18] External debt is solely an accumulation of trade deficits. The interest rate is determined in the Northern money market and a policy rule constrains Southern demand for external borrowing by adjusting government spending (downwards) in the face of excessive debt accumulation. This policy rule appears necessary for model stability (Currie & Vines et al. 1988: 70) and thus provides a counterpart case to the STAC model in that either borrowing constraints, 'self-imposed' by the South, or credit-rationing, imposed by the banks, is required to ensure stability in models of this kind. Simulations with the Currie-Vines model suggest that demand expansion in the North may hurt the South via higher interest rates and hence a higher debt service burden. An additional feature of this model is that the higher rate of interest discourages speculative commodity stock holdings and so depresses commodity prices, despite the increase in Northern demand. Such a result is similar to the result following an increase in Northern government spending (e.g. through a higher aid budget) in the STAC model, but the underlying mechanism is different.

MULTIMOD (MULTI-region econometric MODel), constructed and maintained at the IMF, is in fact a medium-sized interregional macroeconomic model (Masson et al. 1988 and Masson, Symanski & Meredith 1990). It has more detail than the other models as it is built up around standard models for the major industrialized countries, a rudimentary model for high-income oil exporters while the group of other developing countries is treated as a whole. The fact that there is a standard model for industrialized countries which is structurally different from that for the developing countries makes the model comparable with the ones discussed above. The main linkages among the regions are modelled through endogenous determination of prices and volumes of traded goods and the endogenous determination through international economic linkages of exchange rates and interest rates. The signs of the international macroeconomic transmission effects and the magnitude of their domestic effects depend on a number of key parameters (determining, say, the slopes of the IS–LM curves), including the degree of wage and price stickiness, the elasticity of domestic absorption with respect to the interest rate, the degree of openness to trade and the size of trade elasticities. The Northern economies can be said to follow the basic outline of a dynamic version of the Mundell-Fleming model, but the model allows for rational expectations in determining portfolio behaviour in financial markets. Consumption demand in the North is determined by current income and net wealth and is affected by financial markets through the interest rate, rather than by allowing the interest rate to directly affect investment.

This IMF model follows the structuralist tradition of North–South modelling, by assuming economic performance in the South is constrained by external finance. In commodity trade, MULTIMOD assumes that primary commodities are only produced in the South at a flex-price. Oil is produced in all regions under fix-price conditions, while manufactures are also produced in all regions (but constitute imperfect substitutes) and relative prices of manufactures explain export and imports. There is no single price of manufactures, and export prices in each region move sluggishly as a function of domestic output prices (determined by a mark-up pricing rule over unit labour costs).

In MULTIMOD, international finance is also characterized by structural asymmetries. The Northern private sectors are assumed, as in STAC, to face an elastic supply of investment and current account financing, independent of their current account and net foreign asset (or liability) position. Contrariwise, credit supplies to the South are assumed to be rationed by (anonymous) Northern creditors and ceilings on credit flows are made dependent on expectations about the South ability to service debt, i.e. their creditworthiness as measured endogenously through the ratio of interest payment obligations to exports. Thus, Southern creditworthiness depends on a liquidity indicator in MULTIMOD, rather than a solvency indicator as in STAC. There is no specific demand function for external borrowing by Southern agents, but the South can influence its creditworthiness partly through policy variables that influence investment in the export sector. Unlike in the STAC model the possibility of a limit on debt servicing (default) is not considered. Further, neither the international banking system and the behaviour of banks nor their net asset positions with the South are apparent in the specifications of financial behaviour and balance of payments of the Northern economies. Credit rationing and debt accumulation thus only seem to work their way through in the system via their effect on new lending to the South (flow) and Southern import demand.

Despite these model differences, simulation results indicate a number of similar outcomes. One of the reported simulations (Masson et al. 1988 and Table A8.4) is that of an increase in US government spending of 1 percent, with no change in tax or monetary policy. The multiplier effect of government spending on GNP in the US is estimated endogenously in MULTIMOD at 1.2. However, this positive output effect disappears quickly, because of the 'crowding-out' effect of private demand due to higher interest rates and an appreciation of the dollar exchange rate. Other countries benefit from the initial demand expansion in the US and the depreciation of their currencies against the dollar. The rise in interest rates has unfavourable effects on the South because of higher debt service. The ratio of interest payments to exports rises, despite substantial export growth. Although primary commodity prices rise with respect to the baseline case as a consequence of the expansion of world demand, inflation in the Northern economies tends to be higher such that the Southern terms of trade are expected to fall. This result is quite similar to that obtained through the STAC model in case of a rise in Northern government spending (even where this takes the form of an increased aid budget for the South). Other simulations with MULTIMOD suggest, however, that the negative spillover effects for the South are mitigated if the spending injection takes place in the major surplus economies, particularly in Japan. There would still be upward on interest rates, but this might be partially compensated by a rise in real commodity prices.

Also in line with the results of the STAC model, increased aid flows to the South do not appear to be helpful on all scores. An aid injection of US$ 20 billion per year, financed by increased budget deficits in all industrial countries, permits initially higher import growth and a slightly higher economic growth rate, but these positive effects decay after a few years (see Masson et al. 1988 and Table A8.5). Larger foreign exchange availability leads to Southern output expansion, but over time leads to falling real commodity prices. Initially, the North benefits more than the South, in terms of export and output growth, from the financial transfer (which operates in like a fiscal impulse in the North). Output growth vanishes over time and the medium-term recessionary effects are larger than in the South, due to upward pressure on Northern interest rates which in turn also affect the debt-servicing burden of the South.

By and large STAC and MULTIMOD tend to generate a number of similar results concerning asymmetries in adjustment in North and South *vis-à-vis* a demand injection in the North and concerning the trade-offs attached to increased financial transfers to the South. Unlike STAC, however, MULTIMOD does not consider the effects of the operations of a complete international banking system, the possibility of default or capital flight from the South. A high debt servicing burden will hamper growth in the South, but the disruptive effects of a debt crisis and default are not included. STAC thus suggests that there are not only structural asymmetries in trade and financial interactions between North and South, but also that these may, without further policy action, put the presumed institutional arrangements, and thereby the world system, at risk.

8.7 Concluding Remarks

The simulations with the STAC model performed in this chapter largely confirm the presumed asymmetries in the global adjustment process elaborated in Chapter 7. Some additional results may be highlighted here. Firstly, under the presumed parameter values and structural North–South asymmetries, aid transfers do seem to present a transfer problem to the South as they impact negatively on the Southern terms of trade. The simulations also show that under the given assumptions, tax-financed aid transfers yield a smaller secondary burden for the South than do bond-financed aid transfers, assuming no other changes in Northern macroeconomic policies. Secondly, the presumed asymmetric behaviour of Northern commercial creditors (banks) and Southern debtors, combined with structuralist assumptions about North–South trade, appear to generate a systematic tendency towards a debt crisis. Such a conclusion hints at the need for more regulatory action in private financial markets and the need to redress trade interactions of the type presumed by the STAC model. The nature and impact of such structural changes cannot be directly addressed here, but require further analysis with alternative specifications of the STAC model. Thirdly, in addition to the stability requirements analysed in Chapter 7, simulations with alternative specifications of the model suggested that – though apparently inadequate to prevent debt crises – rationing of Southern borrowers with highly elastic demand for external finance contributes to system stability. Unconstrained access of Southern borrowers to the bank-loan market at a market-clearing interest rate showed unstable results as, for the given parameter values, the model would fail to converge to a new equilibrium after a number of adjustment periods.

The comparison with other, empirical North–South models suggests – since the commodity market specifications are largely similar – that these systemic problems depend largely on the way in which the institutional behaviour on financial markets is specified in the STAC model. It may therefore be concluded that – to the extent one accepts the way in which this behaviour is modelled in STAC has been adequately justified in the previous chapters – these systemic problems have been insufficiently recognized by existing model systems addressing the process of North–South interdependence and global adjustment.

9 Some Global Macroeconomic Policy Considerations

The model framework and simulation exercises discussed in Chapters 7 and 8 are far too aggregate to yield concrete policy conclusions. Moreover, the simulations in Chapter 8 have been as yet more 'oracular' than empirical. Nevertheless, it seems indispensable that international policy analyses are underpinned by general equilibrium frameworks that clearly bring out the structural features of the world economy. The STAC model tries to make a modest contribution in that direction.

Despite the recent surge of North–South models trying to take full account of trade and financial interactions, many influential international policy analyses are still based in partial-equilibrium approaches. Three examples may be mentioned.

Firstly, the World Bank and the International Monetary Fund still base most of their projections of growth and capital flows/requirements for developing countries on trends and accounting balances for individual countries and country groups, rather than focusing on a closed system taking account of global interactions.

Secondly, the influential policy model developed by Cline (1983, 1984, 1989) projects Southern indebtedness as a function of (exogenous) Northern variables (GNP, world interest rate, real dollar exchange rate). Since the outbreak of the debt crisis, Cline's conclusions have been unfailingly optimistic, e.g.: '... a critical threshold for industrial country growth in 1984–86 is 3 per cent annually. If this growth rate can be achieved, the debt problem of developing countries should be manageable and should show considerable improvement' (Cline 1983: 71). Cline's model has been particularly influential in circles of creditor governments, multilateral institutions and managers of multilateral banks. It underpinned predominant views, in the early stages of international debt management, that the debt problem is no more than a problem of 'illiquidity, not insolvency' (Cline 1983: 71), that commercial banks will be able to reduce their exposure to Southern debt and that the South will be able to 'grow out of its debt problems' provided it pursues 'appropriate adjustment policies'. The results of Cline's influential models critically depend on trade elasticity estimates (which comfortably meet Marshall-Lerner conditions in all cases), such that exchange-rate adjustment becomes effective to yield the required trade balance adjustments. Cline's 'elasticity optimism' is not shared by the models discussed in Chapter 8, which rather reflect a structuralist 'elasticity pessimism' in North-South trade adjustment. While this matter can be resolved through empirical research, a more fundamental shortcoming of Cline's modelling work as compared to the approach taken by the other models is its partial-equilibrium approach, in which repercussions of international trade on world market prices, global capital market adjustment and growth in each of the regions are not taken into account. When taken into account, as suggested by the STAC and several other North–South models, there is less reason for optimism about a positive-sum game in the global adjustment process.

Thirdly, the need for additional capital flows to developing countries to allow for better growth performance in the 1990s has been stressed in several recent policy reports and proposals from UNCTAD, the Group of 24 and WIDER, among others. Estimates of new capital requirements tend to be based in global aggregates of two- or three-gap model exercises for certain growth targets. Examples are in Fishlow (1987) and Taylor (1990). Taylor projects that, based on a large number of individual country estimates, a target annual growth rate of 4 per cent would require an annual net *positive* transfer from North to South of about US$ 40 billion, implying a major realignment of international capital movements and reversing the current (late 1980s) net *negative* financial transfer of about US$ 20 billion. As shown by the STAC model, a shift in foreign exchange resources of this magnitude (equalling about 0.6 per cent of Northern GNP) may have important global repercussions affecting Northern aggregate demand, the world interest rate and net international asset positions. Southern income gains from the net transfer may be offset by the impact on the terms of trade, borrowing costs and export prospects.

Despite these important shortcomings, such partial-equilibrium approaches retain their influence and remain the most practical type of framework for policy analysis. North-South modelling appears to be in an immature stage. The variety of models in Chapter 8 suggests there might be a consensus only about a very broad outline of an appropriate model framework, i.e. reflecting structural asymmetries between Northern and Southern economies with the latter being essentially supply and foreign-exchange constrained and with fewer degrees of freedom to determine its rate of growth. However, a wide variety of (conflicting) approaches exist with respect to modelling the precise trade and financial linkages between the two types of economies, while relatively little work has been done to develop more disaggregated model systems that can be used in concrete international policy debates. Academic achievement thus seems to lag well behind policy analysis requirements. A recent World Bank study formulates this pessimistically as: 'Even sophisticated computer models of the world economy are of limited use [for forecasting of world economic trends] because of the changes in the trading and financial interdependence of national economies.' (McCarthy & Fardoust 1990: 14).

But even if appropriate analytical tools were available, would these be able to support a better world economic management which could avoid the type of instabilities and asymmetric adjustment processes witnessed over the past decades? It is now widely believed this can be achieved by better international policy coordination (see e.g. Buiter & Marston 1985, Feldstein 1988, Sachs 1988a and Bryant et al. 1989). However, there is a seminal problem related to the lack of agreement on the objectives of international policy coordination among policy makers in different parts of the world.

Two types of academic responses to this problem are given in the literature on international policy coordination. Firstly, in one part of the literature the rationale for coordination is based on an *optimization process* by which national governments follow their own policy objections, but – through policy coordination – they internalize the effects of economic interdependence that no government can capture on its own. Applying this approach to their multi-region world model based on a mainstream macroeconomic framework, McKibbin & Sachs (1989) obtain a result which shows the developing countries as main beneficiaries of policy coordination among the Northern governments even if their objective functions merely take account of their collective self-interest. Applying a similar optimizing policy-coordination approach to Taylor's structuralist North–South model, Marquez & Pauly (1987) show in contrast that such a result can only be achieved if the framework for coordination allows for a significantly larger weight to the South's objective function (i.e. bargaining power) than in a case with equal weights for North and South. Comparing results from these two conflicting models points to an additional problem in assessing the potential benefits from international policy coordination: the relevant agents in the process may disagree about the underlying model justifying their action. As shown formally by Frankel (1988), optimization procedures in international policy coordination tend to yield highly unpredictable outcomes if agents use different models.

Secondly, another strand in the literature on international policy coordination argues for a process by which governments formulate and pursue collective, commonly agreed objectives to avoid instabilities in the adjustment process, to defend the international system against adverse economic and political shocks and/or to correct negative spill-over effects from uncoordinated action to certain parts of the system (e.g. the South due to structural asymmetries). Following Bryant (1987) and Griffith-Jones (1989), this may be labelled as a *public goods approach*, based on the argument that individual governments acting on their own and pursuing national objectives cannot achieve commonly shared objectives such as avoiding world economic instability or the reduction of world poverty. International policy reform documents such as those of the Brandt Commission (Brandt Commission 1980) hinged informally on this type of approach pleading for joint public action to foster development in the South, which – given the underlying global Keynesian framework (e.g. Jayawardena 1983) – may well turn out to be a positive-sum game for North and South.

Both approaches require for their implementation a proper institutional framework. Multilateral institutions like the IMF, the World Bank and the United Nations may provide such a framework for policy coordination, but in the 1970s and 1980s these have not been in the position to ensure international economic stability and equitable burden-sharing of the costs of global adjustment. The question of institutional reform and changing some of the rules of the game to take more account of the interests of the developing countries have been raised from various perspectives, but without producing fundamental changes (e.g. Stewart & Sengupta 1982, Dell 1987, UNCTAD 1987a and Versluysen 1989).

In practice, as a departure from previous experiences, the multilateral institutions, and particularly the IMF, did in fact become actively involved as third parties in negotiations between private creditors (the banks) and the debtor countries on debt-servicing problems in the 1980s. As discussed by Sachs (1988a), the role of the IMF in settling debt rescheduling agreements between the IMF and Mexico and the other major Latin American borrowers was backed by the US government, particularly because the lead banks with high exposure to developing country debt were the major US banks. The IMF also came into play as 'financial orchestrator' in the Paris Club reschedulings of official debt between creditor governments and debt countries, making such reschedulings contingent on an IMF agreement. The World Bank joined this game more actively after 1985, again pressured by the US government (Sachs 1988a: 249). This third-party intervention has led to more intensive bilateral and multilateral consultations between Northern creditors and Southern debtors and has given the lead banks the necessary 'time out' to reduce their exposure to developing country debt. It cannot be said, however, that it has brought the type of 'multilateral surveillance' which would be required for a better control of the intrinsic causes which underlie tendencies towards global financial instability, for a more stable access of developing countries to external finance and for a more equal burden-sharing of the costs of global instability. The efforts so far have focused too much on overcoming immediate debt-servicing problems and domestic adjustment in developing countries, but have underemphasized creditor-country responsibilities and the structural factors underlying the instability in private sources and conditions of lending.

Turning again to the analysis of Chapters 7 and 8 and taking note of the afore-mentioned policy considerations, a few tentative policy conclusions regarding financial interactions between North and South may be derived from the STAC model. These conclusions, which may be attached to the study as a whole, point in the direction of a framework for international policy coordination based on the *public goods approach* and one which would require changing some of the rules of the game:

1. Under the present conditions, most parts of the South will have to rely mainly on official capital transfers from the North to meet their capital and foreign exchange requirements in support of their development process. Private financial markets have proved to be an unstable source with a systemic risk of producing debt crises given the presumed (in the model), and empirically verified (Chapter 5), procyclical nature of commercial bank lending to the South. Factors leading to higher world interest rates produce recessionary effects in the North and spill over to the South in the form of reduced demand for (primary) exports and falling terms of trade, which in turn have a negative effect on the South's solvency and thus on its access to bank loans. Moreover, the banks, in the face of the debt crisis, seem to have changed their own rules by virtually stopping new lending to the South with no clear prospects to resume lending even if Southern economies restore their creditworthiness. If private lending is to play a role in the coming decades, it is likely that new incentives will be required, as well as institutional mechanisms providing better security against the risks involved for borrowers and lenders. As concluded in Chapter 4 and contrary to arguments

underlying some policy proposals made in the 1980s (Arndt & Drake 1985 and Lessard & Williamson 1985), historical experience suggests the private bond market is not necessarily a more stable and less risky source of future finance than commercial bank lending. This study provides an argument for stronger multilateral surveillance and regulation in the process of international financial intermediation between North and South. Tentatively, this could comprise new (public) guarantees to stimulate private international lending to developing countries, new bank and financial market regulatory measures to avoid potential new lending excesses and a strengthening of global macroeconomic policy coordination which simultaneously eyes commodity and financial market developments and gives more weight to creditor country responsibilities than presently is the case. This ambitious agenda raises, of course, many new questions, all well beyond the scope of this study.

2. The negative net financial resource transfer to the South (in the order of US$ 20 billion at the end of the 1980s) has been harmful to growth and development. Calls for substantial increases in official transfers to reverse this trend have to be approached with caution because of the potential general equilibrium effects of global economic interdependence. The 'global Keynesianism' approach of the Brandt Commission (1980) and recent pleas for substantial increases in net transfers from North to South are in part based on the presumption that increased aid flows to the South would lead to higher import demand and stimulate Northern growth. In contrast, simulations with the STAC model suggested that an increased transfer in orders of magnitude of, say, 0.3 to 0.7 per cent of Northern GNP (i.e. at the current level of Northern GNP about US$ 25 to 80 billion), can have a sufficiently large effect on the world interest rate to reduce aggregate demand in the North, thus affecting Southern income and foreign-exchange availability via higher debt-servicing obligations and the negative impact on terms of trade and export prospects. It should be repeated here that the STAC model does not permit inflationary financing of the additional flow of resources for the South, something which a global Keynesian approach would not exclude. Existing proposals are not very specific on the sources of finance, however. The simulations with the STAC model could be compared with a situation of enhanced aid flows in an international policy context of predominantly restrictive monetary policies in the North (as was the case in the 1980s).

The STAC model thus showed an apparently close link between official finance and the external debt overhang in the South. On the one hand, the additional aid flows have the effect of postponing immediate debt payment problems of Southern governments and thereby support (though not structurally) financial stability and bank profitability. On the other hand, the higher interest rate and lower aggregate demand in the North adversely affect the foreign exchange and solvency position of the South via an upward effect on debt servicing obligations and lower export prospects.

This story may vary, of course, for different parts of the South. In the low-income countries with little external commercial bank debt (official borrowers) the trade-off between aid and trade will predominate. The highly indebted countries in terms of bank debt (private borrowers) may feel most affected through the impact on financial markets. Thus, even if most of the additional aid would be meant for the poorer developing countries, other parts of the South may be affected through global interactions. More concretely, new programmes and financing schemes for Sub-Saharan Africa can have negative spill-over effects for the indebted Latin American countries, which makes it relevant, despite the enormous differences in external and development problems in both regions of the South, to make joint assessments of the global impact of aid programmes and joint proposals to deal with the debt crises in various parts of the Third World.

3. The way in which increased aid flows are financed has global implications. Under the assumptions of the STAC model, negative secondary spill-over effects from aid flows financed through tax increases or budget cuts seem smaller than operations financed by more government borrowing in the North. Moreover, more disaggregated world models (e.g. MULTIMOD), indicate that burden-sharing among Northern donors in order to effectuate such a transfer also may have global implications. If the main source of financing originates from the surplus countries (Japan in particular), simulations with MULTIMOD have suggested this will generate larger growth impulses for the South and mitigate, although not eliminate, adverse interest rate and terms of trade effects for the South. Such a conclusion could be seen, from the perspective of this chapter, as a mild support for proposals for a 'recycling' of the Japanese surplus, directing it into increased aid and debt reduction in the South (see Okita, Jayawardena & Sengupta 1987). The same conclusion is also

a critique of the proposal's insufficient attention to the secondary effects of such a redistribution of world savings on international financial and commodity markets.

These policy conclusions are, of course, of a rather general and tentative nature. The STAC model requires further elaboration, disaggregation and empirical foundations, if it is to serve as a tool in more practical international policy discussions. Given the issues at stake and given our relative ignorance about many of the involved global interactions, the development of competing North–South models will have to retain its high priority on the research agenda.

The STAC model assumes, based on the stylized facts analysed in Chapter 5, that the macroeconomic interactions between North and South are characterized by structural asymmetries and gives results showing potentially strong trade-offs between gains from trade, aid and private finance for the South. Coordinated policy action, that is, measures based on collectively defined objectives towards a better regulation of the world economy, greater stability of global financial markets and improvement of economic conditions in the South, seems a *sine qua non* to deal with such trade-offs.

The analysis has been at a high level of abstraction and aggregation which permits only rather general conclusions, as yet at some distance from concrete policy proposals. Nevertheless, analysis at this level is a necessary step toward a better understanding of the world economy. Considerably more work is required to provide policy makers with instruments that can design better-coordinated action towards a more stable and equitable world system.

Appendices

A1 Chapter 1

Country Classifications

The country classification underlying the empirical analysis of Chapter 5 distinguishes:

In the North
- Industrialized market economies (OECD)
- Industrialized (former) non-market economies (Eastern Europe)

In the South
- Major, high-income oil exporters
- Other developing countries, 'Official borrowers'
- Other developing countries, 'Private borrowers'
- Other developing countries, 'Diversified borrowers'
- Other developing countries, n.e.c.

As indicated in Chapter 1, most of the analysis concentrates on the North (OECD countries) and the South. Eastern Europe and 'other developing countries' are mostly absent in the analysis due to a lack of data, while 'Diversified borrowers' are brought in whenever the analysis requires. For the 'non-oil' developing countries, the principal classification criterion is the nature of external financial dependence as identified by the degree of access to distinct segments of the international capital market. 'Official borrowers' consist of countries which have over two thirds of long-term external debt from official sources. 'Private borrowers' are developing countries with more than two thirds of long-term external debt from private financial markets and other private suppliers. 'Diversified borrowers' have a more balanced structure of external debt (less than two thirds from official *and* less than two thirds from private sources).

The structure of outstanding external debt by source for each country was based on World Bank, *World Debt Tables*, covering the period 1975–87. Countries shifting within the period from one country group to another were classified according to the average structure of external debt for the period 1976-81.

Table A1.1 Country classification

NORTH

Market economies

*Australia, *Austria, *Belgium, *Canada, *Denmark, *Finland, *France, Greece, *Iceland, *Ireland, *Italy, *Japan, *Luxembourg, *Netherlands, *New Zealand, *Norway, Portugal, *Spain, *Sweden, *Switzerland, United Kingdom, *United States, *(former) W. Germany,

Former planned economies

Albania, Bulgaria, Czechland/Slovakia, German DR, Hungary, Poland, Romania, (former) USSR

SOUTH

Major high-income oil exporters

Bahrein, *Iran, *Iraq, *Kuwait, *Libya, Qatar, *Saudi Arabia, UAE

'Official borrowers'

Primary exporters

Belize, *Botswana, *Burkina Faso, *Burundi, Cape Verde, Central African Republic, Chad, Comoros, Djibouti, *Egypt†, *El Salvador, Eq. Guinea, *Ethiopia, *Fiji, Gambia, *Ghana, Grenada, *Guatemala, Guinea, Guinea-Bissau, Guyana, *Haiti, *Honduras, *Kenya, *Lesotho, *Liberia, *Madagascar, *Malawi, *Mali, *Mauretania, *Mauritius, *Myanmar, *Nicaragua, *Niger, *Rwanda, São Tomé, *Senegal, *Seychelles, *Sierra Leone, Solomon Islands, *Somalia, *Sri Lanka, St. Vincent, *Sudan, *Swaziland, *Syria†, *Tanzania, *Togo, Uganda, Vanuatu, W. Samoa, *Zaire, *Zambia

Exporters of manufactures

*Bangladesh, *India, *Jamaica, *Jordan, Lebanon, Malta, *Nepal, *Pakistan, *Tunisia, *Yemen AR

(Continued...)

(Table A1.1 Continued)

(South continued)

'Private borrowers'

Primary exporters

*Algeria†, *Argentina, Bahamas†, *Brazil, *Chile, Côte d'Ivoire, *Ecuador†, *Gabon †, *Malaysia, *Mexico†, *Nigeria†, *Panama, *Trinidad†, *Uruguay, *Venezuela†

Exporters of manufactures

*Korea Rep., *Philippines, *Singapore,

'Diversified borrowers'

Primary exporters

*Benin, *Bolivia, *Cameroon†, *Colombia, *Congo†, *Costa Rica, *Dominican Rep., *Indonesia†, *Morocco, *Papua NG, *Paraguay, *Peru, *Thailand, *Zimbabwe

Exporters of manufactures

Barbados, China, Cyprus, Israel, *Turkey

OTHER COUNTRIES, n.e.c.

Afghanistan, Am. Samoa, Angola, Anguilla, Antigua, Aruba, Bermuda, Bhutan, Brunei, Cambodia, Cayman Is., Cook Is., Christmas Is., Cuba, Dominica, Faeroe Is., Fr. Guiana, Fr. Polynesia, Gibraltar, Greenland, Guadaloupe, Guam, Hong Kong, Kiribati, Korea PDR, Lao PDR, Macao, Maldives, Malvinas, Martinique, Mayotte, Mongolia, Montserrat, Mozambique, Namibia, Nauru, Neth. Antil, N. Caledon, Oman, Réunion, S. Africa, St. Helena, St. Kitts, St. Pierre, Surinam, Tonga, Virgin Is., Yugoslavia, Taiwan, Tokelau Is., Turks Is., Vietnam, Îles Wallis, Wake Is.

Notes: * Included in the core sample of 102 countries used for the calculation of the global savings-investment balances and subsuquent analysis of Chapter 5.

† Net oil-exporting country.

Southern economies have been further subdivided in parts of the analysis according to commodity trade dependence. Countries of which more than 50 per cent of merchandise exports consist of primary commodities are classified as 'Primary exporters'. Those with 50 per cent or more of manufactures are classified as 'Exporters of manufactures'. Further, within the group of primary exporters, net oil exporters are distinguished if more than 50 per cent of total merchandise exports consist of crude oil.

Table A1.1 gives the full country classification. Developing countries marked with the † sign, are net oil exporters. Countries marked with an asterisk (*) belong to the core sample of 102 countries used for the calculation of the global savings-investment balances and subsequent analysis in Chapter 5.

A3 Chapter 3

A3.1 The Transfer Problem and Keynesian Income Multipliers

Section 3.3.1 discussed the classic transfer problem. The Keynesian income multiplier model has been used, next to the pure trade theory model, to clarify the problem. Here, the Keynesian income multiplier case is exemplified in a world consisting of two countries and two commodities, say North (N) and South (S), each producing their own commodity. Output is demand-driven in both economies and demand is determined by income as follows (adapting similar presentations by Johnson 1971 | 1958 and Dornbusch 1980):

$$Y_N = c_N Y_N + I_N + m_S Y_S - m_N Y_N \qquad (A3.1.1)$$

$$Y_S = c_S Y_S + I_S - m_S Y_S + m_N Y_N \qquad (A3.1.2)$$

$$T_S = m_S Y_S - m_N Y_N \qquad (A3.1.3)$$

with Y for output, I for investment and c and m for the propensities to consume and import respectively, while T_S is the *ex post* net transfer to the South equalling the Northern trade balance $(E_N - M_N)$. Differentiating totally and taking $d\,I_N$ as the increase in autonomous spending gives:

$$\begin{bmatrix} 0 & s_N + m_N & -m_S \\ 0 & -m_N & s_S + m_S \\ 1 & m_N & -m_S \end{bmatrix} \begin{bmatrix} d(E_N - M_N) \\ d\,Y_N \\ d\,Y_S \end{bmatrix} = \begin{bmatrix} d\,I_N \\ 0 \\ 0 \end{bmatrix} \qquad (A3.1.4)$$

where s represents the marginal savings rate [$s = (1 - c)$]. Solving for the changes in output and the Northern trade balance gives:

$$
\begin{aligned}
&dY_N/dI_N = (s_S + m_S)/\Delta \\
&dY_S/dI_N = m_N/\Delta \\
&d(E_N - M_N)/dI_N = -m_S s_S/\Delta
\end{aligned}
\qquad (A3.1.5)
$$

with:

$$\Delta = (s_N + m_N)(s_S + m_S) - m_N m_S > 0$$

In the case of a pure transfer financed by Northern taxpayers, spending in the North will depend on disposable income $Y_N - T_S$ and in the South it will depend on $Y_S + T_S$. Substituting for the new income definition in (A3.1.1–3) and defining domestic spending propensities as ($d = 1 - s - m$), one obtains:

$$
\begin{bmatrix} 0 & s_N + m_N & -m_S \\ 0 & -m_N & s_S + m_S \\ 1 & m_N & -m_S \end{bmatrix}
\begin{bmatrix} d(E_N - M_N) \\ dY_N \\ dY_S \end{bmatrix}
=
\begin{bmatrix} (m_S - d_N)\, dT_S \\ (d_S - m_N)\, dT_S \\ (m_S + m_N)\, dT_S \end{bmatrix}
\qquad (A3.1.6)
$$

Solving again for output and the Northern trade balance yields:

$$
\begin{aligned}
&dY_N/dT_S = (m_S s_N - d_N s_S)/\Delta \\
&dY_S/dT_S = (s_N d_S - s_S m_N)/\Delta \\
&d(E_N - M_N)/dT_S = (m_S s_N + m_N s_S)/\Delta
\end{aligned}
\qquad (A3.1.7)
$$

Note that T_S is the initial (exogenous) net transfer, which need not be equal to the *ex post* Northern trade balance after the income effects have taken place.

The effects of the transfer on total demand (and supply) in North and South depend on the spending propensities in North and South. Several cases may hold. Firstly, world spending and Southern output ($dY_S / dT_S > 0$) will increase if the Northern savings rate is higher and marginal domestic spending rates in the South are equal to Northern demand for the Southern commodity ($s_N > s_S$; $d_S = m_N$). Secondly, the redistribution of disposable income to the South due to a transfer will leave the level of world spending unchanged at equal savings rates and a higher domestic spending propensity in the South than the Northern propensity to spend on the Southern commodity ($s_N = s_S$; $d_S > m_N$), thus redistributing demand in favour of the South. Thirdly, the capital exporting North will benefit from a rise in world spending if $s_N > s_S$ and

$m_S = d_N$, or from a redistribution of demand in its favour if $s_N = s_S$ and $m_S > d_N$.

In each case, the net transfer on trade will be *undereffected* for the capital exporting country (see also Dornbusch 1980: Chapter 3). That is, net exports increase by less than the transfer because the disposable income of the transferring country falls and is not fully compensated by income multiplier effects in the receiving country, where part of the transfer becomes savings, so that net exports (the *ex post* trade surplus) of the transferring country increase by less than the transfer itself. Conversely, the receiving country will enjoy a positive effect on the trade balance (a smaller deficit).

Obviously these conclusions are limited by their key assumptions. Savings and spending propensities are given and remain unchanged. However, for instance, if the receiving country is foreign-exchange constrained, as many Southern economies are believed to be, then it is unlikely that the Southern import function will remain untouched by the transfer.

The possibility of changes in domestic spending and import propensities due to the transfer has been analysed by Johnson (1971 | 1958: 70-77) and yields a result which suggests, as argued by Ohlin, that the transfer may be either under- or overeffected, depending on the parameter values. This can be shown after assuming that the (given) propensities to save and import out of the (additional) transfer are not the same as the initial propensities, i.e.:

$$dY_N = (dT_S + s'_N T'_S)/s_N \qquad (A3.1.8)$$
$$dY_S = -(dT_S + s'_S T'_S)/s_S \qquad (A3.1.9)$$
$$dT_S = [m'_N + m'_S - (m_N s'_N/s_N) - (m_S s'_S/s_S) - 1](s_N s_S T'_S/\Delta) \qquad (A3.1.10)$$

where T'_S represents an exogenous increase in the transfer from North to South and m' and s' represent the changes in the demand for imports and in saving directly due to the financing of the transfer (in the North) or the spending of the transfer (in the South). From this modified income multiplier system it follows that the transfer will be over- or undereffected depending on the size of the change in the spending propensities due to the transfer, i.e. whether:

$$m'_N + m'_S \lesseqgtr m_N s'_N/s_N + m_S s'_S/s_S + 1$$

This condition also determines whether the terms of trade (or the exchange rate) will have to improve or deteriorate for the transferring country in order to reach a new global equilibrium. To establish this one would also have to include demand and supply responsiveness to the relative price.

A3.2 A North-South, Solow-Lewis Model: Capital Flows and Asymmetric Global Adjustment

A3.2.1 The basic model

The foundations of this model are ascribed to Findlay (1980, 1984). The North is a neo-classical economy. Full capacity use and full employment prevail and growth is determined by the natural rate. The South is a labour surplus and foreign exchange constrained economy. The presentation of the basic relations follow the exposition by Findlay (1984) and Ocampo (1986). First, the focus is on *trade* links between North and South along 'Solow-Lewis' lines, i.e. there is no capital mobility. Next, the impact of capital flows between both regions is assessed, assuming that these take place under perfect capital market conditions.

Consider a two-economy, two-commodity case. To keep the argument as simple as possible assume that North and South are both completely specialized in the production of one single composite good each. The North specializes in manufactures and the South in primary products. In the North, growth is at the natural rate, $g_N = g_N{}^*$, and the production function is assumed to satisfy neo-classical conditions so that we can write its intensive form (cf. Jones 1975) as:

$$q_N = q_N(k_N), \quad k_N = (K_N/L_N), \quad q_N = (Q_N/L_N) \qquad (A3.2.1)$$
$$q_N{}' > 0 \text{ and } q_N{}'' < 0, \text{ if } 0 < k < \infty$$

where q_N represents labour productivity in the North and k_N the capital-intensity ratio. The capital-labour ratio k_N changes over time according to:

$$\dot{k}_N = s_N q_N(k_N) - n k_N \qquad (A3.2.2)$$

where s_N is the constant proportion of income that is saved (and invested) and n a constant rate of growth in the Northern labour force. Northern demand for imports from the South, M_N, is a function of the Southern terms of trade, θ, and Northern consumer demand, $(1 - s_N)\, q_N L_N$:

$$\theta M_N = m_N L_N, \quad m_N = m_N[\theta, (1 - s_N)\, q_N] \qquad (A3.2.3)$$
$$\theta = P_S / P_N$$

Northern imports are valued in terms of the price of the Southern good (P_S). The propensity to import from the South in terms of the Northern commodity will be elastic to the terms of trade and Northern income. The propensity of Northern consumers to consume Northern goods is defined by $(1 - m_N)$. In this formulation both substitution and income effects are relevant. If, assumed here, both commodities are imperfect substitutes or complementary, then the income effect will dominate. A widely accepted assumption is that the primary commodity has the lower income elasticity (Prebisch-Singer), but here unitary income elasticities for both commodities are assumed to set a bench-mark case.

In the South, unlimited supplies of labour determine wages at the subsistence level and profits are the surplus over wages. The per worker surplus, z, is defined as:

$$z = q_S - w_S = k_S q_S'(k_S), \quad q_S = (Q_S/L_S), \quad k_S = (K_S/L_S) \qquad (A3.2.4)$$

where k_S is the capital-labour ratio at the given real wage and $q_S(k_S)$, the Southern production function. If one may assume that saving from wage income is negligible in the South – a realistic assumption if wages are at subsistence levels – Southern savings become a proportion of Southern profits ($S_S = s_S z L_S$). Total profits in terms of the Southern good are thus zL_S and since investment goods and thus also the Southern capital stock (K_S) is priced as a Northern good, the Southern profit rate becomes:

$$r_S = \theta z L_S / K_S = \theta z / k_S \qquad (A3.2.5)$$

If capital is internationally immobile, the Southern growth rate, $g_S = \dot{k}_S/K_S$, is constrained by domestic savings, i.e.:

$$g_S = s_S r_S \qquad (A3.2.6)$$

which expresses the Southern investment-savings balance in terms of its capital stock. Southern import demand is a function of investment demand and consumer demand:

$$M_S = (s_S \theta z + m_S) L_S, \qquad m_S = m_S[\theta^{-1}, (1 - s_S z) q_S] \qquad (A3.2.7)$$

where $(1 - s_S z)\, q_S$ is total consumption per worker in the South.

When there is no capital mobility and if labour markets clear in the North (in the South wages and profits are determined in labour surplus conditions), the short-term equilibrium of the model is determined through the commodity market balance. This can be expressed as the Southern trade balance, i.e. from equations A3.2.3 and A3.2.7:

$$s_S \theta z + m_S = \theta m_N \lambda^{-1}, \qquad \lambda = L_S / L_N \qquad (A3.2.8)$$

It can now be shown that Southern growth depends directly on its terms of trade, θ, in the short run. It is assumed that Southern goods are priced at the world market equilibrium price, so that if there is a relative scarcity of the Southern good, θ increases and Southern growth accelerates. In the steady state long-run, if both income elasticities of demand are unitary, both growth rates must be equal, i.e. $g_N = g_N^* = g_S$. The long-run, steady state terms of trade are thus, from equations A3.2.5 and A3.2.6 and given that the long-run rate of growth in the North implies that $g_N^* = s_N q_N (k_N) / k_N = n_N$:[1]

$$\theta^* = \frac{g_N^* k_S}{s_S z} = \frac{s_N q_N \kappa \lambda^{-1}}{s_S}, \qquad \kappa = K_S / K_N, \quad \lambda = L_S / L_N \qquad (A3.2.9)$$

In the steady state, the terms of trade will be stable, thus the trade balance equilibrium in equation A3.2.8 will determine long-run relative employment (λ^*):

$$\lambda^* = \frac{g_N^* k_S m_N^*}{s_S z (g_N k_S + m_S^*)} \qquad (A3.2.10)$$

where m_N^* and m_S^* are the per worker propensities to import consumer goods in North and South at the long-run terms of trade.

The behaviour of the world economy in the short and long run can now be discussed by means of equations A3.2.9 and A3.2.10. Trade (the capacity to import) is the 'engine of growth' for the South, but the speed at which the engine works is set by the growth rate of the North. If the demand for Southern goods in the North increases, i.e. the m_N function shifts up, the *short-run* effect would be that the Southern good becomes more scarce and the Southern terms of trade, θ, will increase and thus the Southern economy would grow.[2] The *long-run* rate of growth and relative prices would not be affected; thus the impact of a shift in the m_N schedule would go to relative employment in favour of the South. An increase in Northern productivity will have the same impact. An increase in the m_S function, however, would have an opposite effect.

The effect of a higher domestic savings rate in the South would increase Southern growth from equation A3.2.6, but from equation A3.2.9 it follows that θ would fall in the same proportion and leave the growth rate of the South unchanged in the long run. The decline in the long run terms of trade implies that the South would permanently 'export' higher savings and relative employment in the South would tend to fall. However, the total net effect of the changes depends further on the behaviour of per worker net import consumption in both regions, i.e. the change in m_N and m_S caused by the decline in θ and the increase in s_S.

The crux of the argument is that there is asymmetry in world economic adjustment, which is determined by an independent production function (and thus employment and profits) in the North and a trade dependent output growth in the South. There is a different impact on growth in both regions depending on whether growth, import demand or savings behaviour change in the North or in the South.

A3.2.2 Capital mobility and 'crowding out' of Southern capital

Capital mobility can be easily incorporated in the model. The simplest way to introduce capital mobility is to assume perfect capital markets. This assumption is usual in alternative specifications of North-South models with the above-outlined characteristics (cf. Burgstaller & Saavedra-Rivano 1984). Perfect capital mobility means that capital moves freely and is sensitive to differences in rates of return. It is reasonable to assume that capital will tend to flow from North to South implying $r_S > r_N$. Capital flows until rates of return are equalized $r^* = r_S = r_N$. Assume further that foreign capital is invested in primary production in the South under the same production conditions. The North will now invest in manufactures only up to a point where $q_M(k_M) = r^*$, where k_M is the capital-labour ratio in manufacturing at the point where international rates of return are equalized. The per worker foreign capital stock owned by the North can thus be defined as $f = k_N - k_M$. The Northern production function (equation A3.2.1) can now be rewritten as:

$$q_N = q_N(k_N - f) \qquad (A3.2.1a)$$

Per worker national income in North and South, y_N and y_S, become respectively:

$$y_N = q_N(k_N - f) + r^* f \qquad (A3.2.11a)$$
$$y_S = q_S(k_S + f\lambda^{-1}) - r^* f\lambda^{-1} \qquad (A3.2.11b)$$

Steady state conditions require that the long term terms of trade must continue to be equal to θ^*.[3] It can now be easily shown that asymmetric adjustment affects the Southern rate of accumulation. With a clearing capital market and applying Walras' law, stability follows if one of the commodity markets is in equilibrium. In primary commodity markets this means that the excess demand function for the Southern commodity is set equal to zero. In the case of no capital mobility, the demand for the Southern commodity is determined by Southern food demand, $(1 - m_S)(1 - s_S z)\, q_S$, and Southern exports, $\theta m_N (1 - s_N)\, q_N$. Total demand should equal total supply of primary commodities $[q_S(k_S)]$. Normalizing for Northern employment and spelling out the functions in equations A3.2.3 and A3.2.7, the excess demand function for the Southern commodity in case of capital immobility can be written as:

$$\theta^* m_N(\theta)\,(1 - s_N)\, q_N(k_N) + \\ [1 - m_S(\theta)]\,(1 - s_S z\,\theta^*)\, q_S(k_S)\,\lambda - q_S(k_S)\,\lambda = 0$$

which is the same as:

$$m_S(\theta)\,(1 - s_S z\,\theta^*)\, q_S(k_S)\,\lambda = \theta^* m_N(\theta)\,(1 - s_N)\, q_N(k_N) \qquad (A3.2.12a)$$

After allowing for capital mobility, import consumer demand functions for the North and the South become a function of per worker GNP (y), rather than per worker GDP (q), i.e. $m_N[\theta,\ (1 - s_N)\, y_N]$ and $m_S[\theta^{-1},\ (1 - s_S z\,\theta)\, y_S]$ *respectively. The excess demand function for the Southern good now becomes:*

$$m_S(\theta)\,(1 - s_S z\,\theta^*)\, q_S(k_S^0 + f)\,\lambda = \theta^* m_N(\theta)\,(1 - s_N)\, q_N(k_N - f) \\ + [\,\theta^*(1 - s_N)\, m_N(\theta) - (1 - s_S)\,(1 - m_S(\theta))\,]\, r^* f \qquad (A3.2.12b)$$

where k_S^0 is the new Southern capital stock owned by domestic proprietors. The second part of the right-hand side of equation A3.2.12b is Northern import demand from foreign investment income net of the propensity of Southern workers in the foreign owned industries to consume food (the Southern commodity). The latter is the result of the short term positive employment effect from foreign investments. From equations A3.2.12a and A3.2.12b it follows that $k_S > (k_S^0 + f)$, if $(1 - s_N)\, m_N > (1 - s_S)\,(1 - m_S)$. This condition holds if workers in the South have a high propensity to consume of the South's own commodity (food), relative to the food demand propensity from foreign investment income in the North. Such circumstances may not be far off the stylized facts of real life. The result is that Northern capital 'crowds out' Southern capital by entering primary production.[4] This conclusion is critical to the presumed mutual gains from trade and capital flows that are derived from Heckscher-Ohlin-Samuelson related models. The dual world economy model rather supports the propositions of the early imperialism theories of Hobson and Lenin. Notably, the conclusions are reached with neo-classical growth conditions in the North and no distortions in world capital markets.

The asymmetries in gains from trade and capital flows result from the basic assumptions of the model: the South is dependent on the North for its growth and, in the case with capital mobility, foreign assets are owned by the North. Capital mobility leads to a transfer of income back to the North, increasing Northern per worker income. The corresponding worsening of relative per worker income in the South is unlikely to be sufficiently compensated for by demand increase in the North, given savings and import propensities. In the short run asymmetries may be even larger. Foreign investment will tend to expand Southern supply, but given the insufficient demand adjustment from foreign investment income in the North, excess supply of primary commodities will cause the terms of trade to fall.

A3.3 The Mundell-Fleming Model

Figure 3.4 showed the IS-LM curves in a two-country Mundell-Fleming model with perfect capital mobility and fixed exchange rates. Here the slopes of the corresponding schedules are derived. For more extended multiplier analysis, including the case with flexible exchange rates, see e.g. Frenkel & Razin (1987).

The model system defined in equations 3.2 to 3.4 can be solved after total differentiation to obtain:

$$\begin{bmatrix} s_N+m_N & -m_S & 0 \\ -m_N & s_S+m_S & 0 \\ L_{yN} & L_{yN} & 1 \end{bmatrix} \begin{bmatrix} dY_N \\ dY_S \\ d(B_N+B_S) \end{bmatrix} = \begin{bmatrix} -D_{r\,N} \\ D_{r\,S} \\ L_{r\,N}+L_{r\,S} \end{bmatrix} dr \qquad (A3.3.1)$$

where D_r, L_r and L_y are partial derivatives with respect to the world interest rate (r) or the economy's income (y). The slopes for the IS- and LM-schedules for North and South can now be derived. For the IS-schedules one can obtain:

$$(dY_N/dr)\Big|_{IS_N} = \frac{-[m_S D_{rS} + (s_S+m_S)D_{rN}]}{\Delta} \qquad (A3.3.2)$$

$$(dY_S/dr)\Big|_{IS_S} = \frac{-[m_N D_{rN} + (s_N+m_N)D_{rS}]}{\Delta} \qquad (A3.3.3)$$

with as before (see Appendix A3.1), $\Delta = (s_N + m_N)(s_S + m_S) - m_N m_S > 0$.

The LM-schedules have the following slopes:

$$(dY_N/dr)\Big|_{LM_S} = \frac{L_{rN} + L_{rS} + L_{yS} D_{rS}/(s_S + m_S)}{L_{yN} + L_{yS} m_N/(s_S + m_S)} \qquad (A3.3.4)$$

$$(dY_S/dr)\Big|_{LM_S} = \frac{L_{rN} + L_{rS} + L_{yS} D_{rS}/(s_S + m_S)}{L_{yN} + L_{yS} m_N/(s_S + m_S)} \qquad (A3.3.5)$$

A4 Chapter 4

Statistical Appendix

Table A4.1 United States: foreign borrowing as a source of investment finance, 1869–1914

	Net foreign borrowing as a % of gross domestic investment
1869–78	5.1
1874–83	-2.7
1879–88	1.5
1884–93	5.8
1889–98	1.6
1894–1903	-5.3
1899–1908	-5.4
1904–1913	-1.1

Sources: Net foreign borrowing figures calculated from Mitchell's balance of payments data series (Mitchell 1982). Data on gross capital formation were taken from Kuznets (1961).

Table A4.2 *United States: foreign lending and investment by source, 1919-28 (milions of US$)*

	1919	1920	1921	1922	1923	1924	1925	1926	1927	1928
Government	2540	220	29	7	-54	-3	3	-10	-44	-30
Capital market (bonds)	2328	175	-30	-31	-91	-28	-27	-30	-46	-49
Bilateral capital transfers	212	45	59	38	37	25	30	20	2	19
Private	1001	1188	1038	1136	793	1333	1290	1218	1691	1887
Direct investment	94	154	111	153	148	182	268	351	351	558
Capital market (bonds, long-term and short-term capital)	75	400	477	669	317	812	649	506	985	983
Bilateral capital transfers	832	634	450	314	328	339	373	361	355	346
Total	3541	1408	1067	1143	739	1330	1293	1208	1647	1857
Memorandum item: Net lending according to Balance of Payments	3824	2844	1613	645	277	987	684	445	716	1012

Sources: US Department of Commerce, as reported in Eichengreen (1988); and Mitchell (1982).

Note: The large discrepancy between the memorandum item and the table's total indicates the difficulty in finding complete, comparable and consistent data on external debt and capital movements in the pre-war period.

Table A4.3 Urban/rural terms of trade in selected Latin American countries (indices 1929 = 100)

	Argentina	Brazil	Chile	Peru	Mexico
1925	n.a	91	n.a.	98	n.a.
1926	108	113	n.a.	94	n.a.
1927	107	108	n.a.	90	n.a.
1928	94	105	102	97	n.a.
1929	100	100	100	100	100
1930	119	95	108	100	108
1931	161	128	125	101	148
1932	179	125	125	106	168
1933	178	127	141	107	170
1934	163	128	138	106	155
1935	156	124	126	109	162
1936	129	136	114	107	160
1937	118	122	107	107	150
1938	131	128	109	104	155
1939	149	141	118	110	164

Source: Thorpe (1984: Statistical Appendix).

Notes: Argentina: wholesale prices, non-rural and rural;
Brazil and Mexico: implicit price deflators;
Chile and Peru: ratio of *general* wholesale price index and wholesale agricultural prices.

These data, it should be noted, are *not* accurate measures of the terms of trade.

Figure A4.1 UK: net transfers received from abroad,[a] 1863-1914 (percentage of GNP)

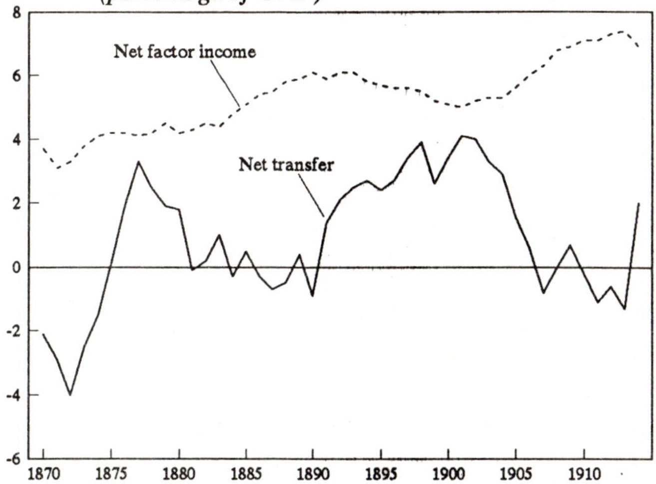

Source: Feinstein (1962)
Note: a. If negative, net transfer to abroad.

Figure A4.2 United States: net capital inflow, 1863-1914 (percentage of GNP)

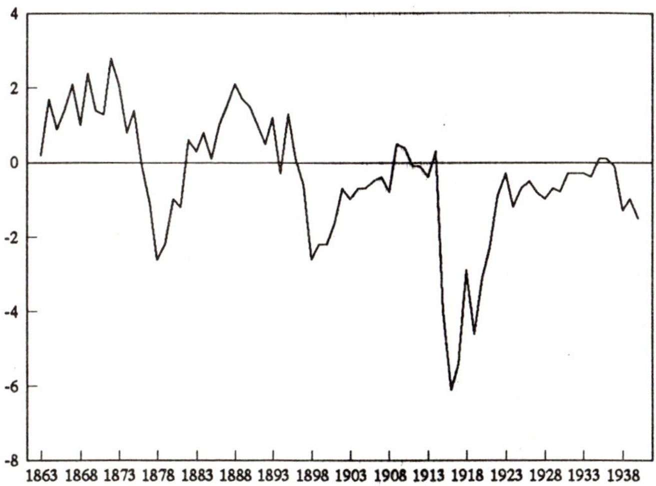

Source: Mitchell (1982)

Figure A4.3 *UK: net capital exports and domestic investment, 1918-39 (percentage of GNP)*

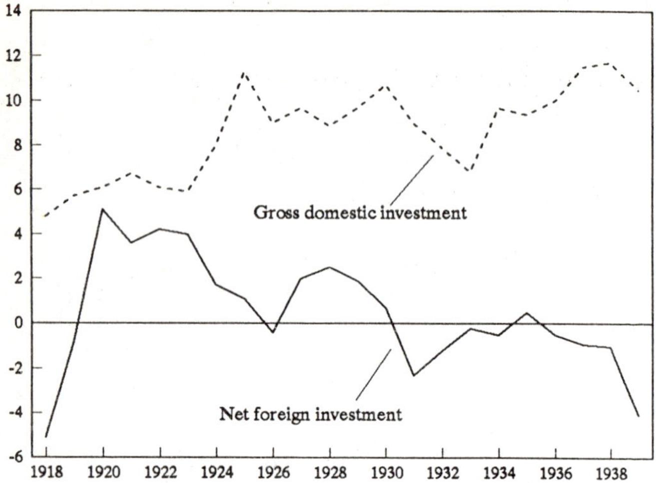

Source: Mitchell (1982)

Figure A4.4 *UK: net transfers received from abroad, 1918-39 (percentage of GNP)*

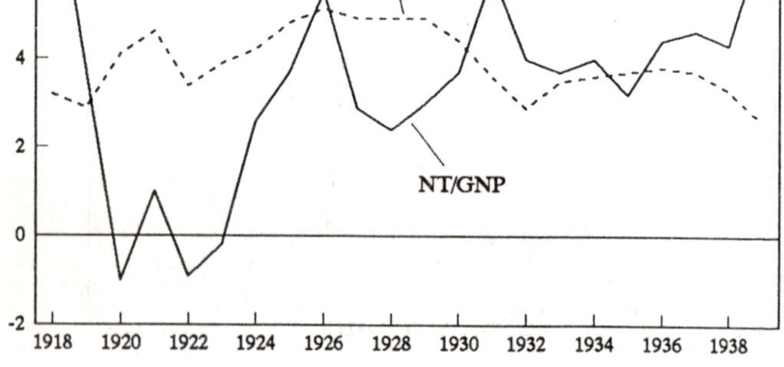

Source: Feinstein (1962)

Figure A4.5 Net ODA flows to LDCs, 1950-72 (millions of US$ at constant prices and exchange rates)

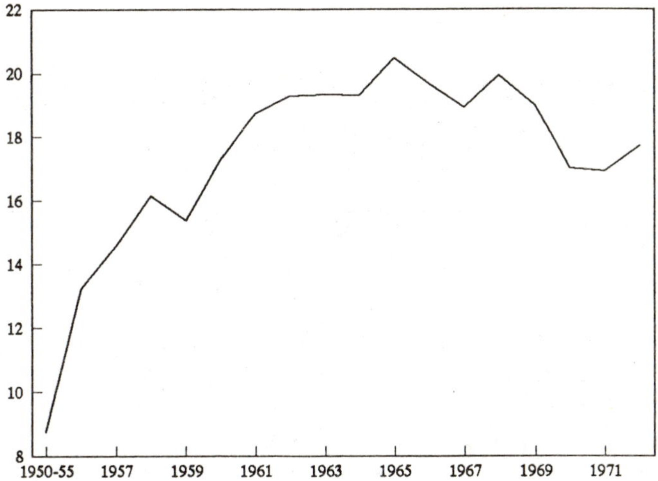

Source: OECD (1985)

Figure A4.6 Net ODA flows from DAC to LDCs, 1950-72 (percentage of GNP of donor countries)

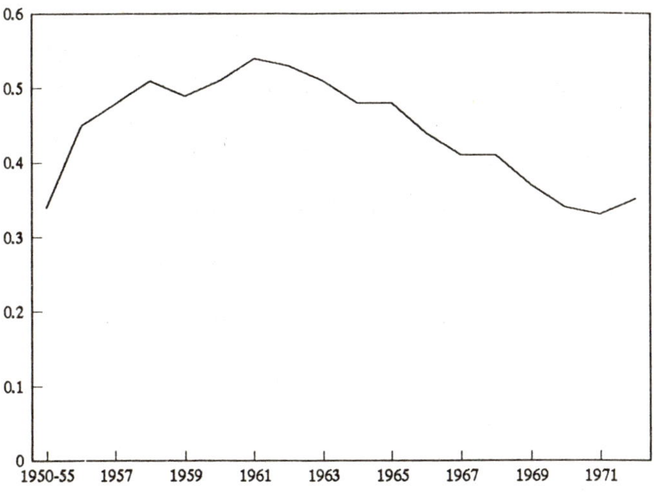

Source: OECD (1985)

A5 Chapter 5

Statistical Appendix

Table A5.1 Capital-importing LDCs: long-term debt by country group, type of borrowing institutions and sectoral allocation

	1970	1975	1980	1985	1988
LDC-OBs: Official Borrowers (n=36) (billions of US$)					
Total debt	18.7	40.7	101.3	178.3	238.7
Total long-term debt	18.7	40.7	89.5	158.9	213.3
Total Long-term Debt, by Institutional Borrower (percentage shares)					
Central Bank incl. IMF credit	3.8	12.1	11.9	15.6	12.5
Central Government	71.3	68.1	70.4	67.6	71.8
Rest of General Government	0.5	0.2	0.1	0.1	0.1
Non-financial public enterprises	14.6	11.8	12.5	12.4	11.1
Private sector, incl. non-guaranteed	9.8	7.8	5.2	4.3	4.4
By Economic Sector					
Traded goods sectors [a]	12.4	12.8	14.6	16.3	15.6
Non-traded goods sectors, of which:	59.3	58.9	54.1	46.7	45.0
Physical infrastructure	44.3	46.4	38.4	29.6	26.5
Energy	9.8	7.1	6.9	10.2	11.4
Public administration, defence	3.1	2.9	6.4	3.7	3.8
Other allocations, of which:	28.3	28.3	31.3	36.9	39.3
Debt reorganization	3.3	4.7	6.6	9.4	14.3
Balance of payment support	17.2	15.9	16.1	15.6	13.1
LDC-PBs: Private Borrowers (n=16) (billions of US$)					
Total debt	26.6	75.1	297.2	467.8	511.2
Total long-term debt	26.6	73.8	209.7	402.3	456.2
Total Long-term Debt by Institutional Borrower (percentage shares)					
Central Bank, incl. IMF credit	6.1	12.9	10.6	19.6	31.1
Central Government	19.9	18.5	21.1	34.7	42.4
Rest of General Government	1.0	1.4	1.7	2.5	1.1
Non-financial Public Enterprises	27.0	27.5	33.6	20.8	12.3
Private sector, incl. non-guaranteed	46.0	39.7	33.1	22.3	13.0

(Continued...)

(Table A5.1 Continued)

	1970	1975	1980	1985	1988
By Economic Sector					
Traded goods sectors	19.6	19.9	20.4	16.3	15.4
Non-traded goods sectors, of which:	67.8	68.7	71.6	59.0	52.6
Physical infrastructure	29.4	26.5	24.6	24.1	20.7
Energy	22.2	18.1	23.0	13.1	12.6
Public adminstration, defence	11.2	11.6	9.7	8.5	5.4
Other allocations, of which:	12.6	11.4	8.0	24.7	31.9
Debt reorganization	3.4	4.1	3.2	12.9	21.0
Balance of payment support	2.1	2.3	1.1	3.2	5.7
LDC-DBs: Diversified Borrowers (n=13) (billions of US$)					
Total debt	12.7	30.0	89.5	150.9	199.6
Total long-term debt	12.7	28.9	74.4	127.6	173.0
Total Long-term Debt by Institutional Borrower (percentage shares)					
Central Bank, incl. IMF credit	4.7	7.7	12.2	11.2	8.6
Central Government	53.9	49.0	53.9	58.1	64.0
Rest of General Government	1.6	1.2	0.7	1.0	1.1
Non-financial Public Enterprises	10.6	17.7	19.1	17.6	16.2
Private sector, incl. non-guaranteed	29.2	24.5	14.0	12.1	10.1
By Economic Sector					
Traded goods sectors	9.7	13.6	14.4	16.9	14.7
Non-traded goods sectors, of which:	41.0	48.8	53.4	55.0	62.4
Physical infrastructure	23.1	23.0	29.0	28.6	30.9
Energy	11.5	18.4	16.1	17.0	17.6
Public administration, defence	2.9	2.9	4.4	6.2	6.6
Other allocations, of which:	49.3	37.6	32.2	28.1	22.9
Debt reorganization	17.6	16.3	14.0	10.6	12.2
Balance of payment support	20.9	13.5	11.3	10.4	7.1

Source: World Bank, *Debtor Reporting System.*

Notes: Sample includes 65 LDCs, of which 36 are official borrowers, 16 are private borrowers and 13 are diversified borrowers.

a. Includes agriculture, forestry and fishing, mining and manufacturing industry.

Table A5.2 South: import structure by major commodity type, 1980-85 (percentage of total)

	LDC-OB	Sub-Saharan Africa	LDC-PB	LDC-DB
1980				
Food	15	13	12	10
Agr. materials	2	1	4	3
Fuels & ores	34	27	24	31
Manufactures	49	58	59	56
of which: machinery	(23)	(31)	(32)	(27)
Total	100	100	100	100
1985				
Food	17	14	11	9
Agr. materials	3	2	4	3
Fuels & ores	33	27	25	28
Manufactures	47	56	59	59
of which: machinery	(22)	(29)	(31)	(30)
Total	100	100	100	100

Source: UN International Trade Statistics.

Table A5.3 Official borrowers in Sub-Saharan Africa: internal and external balances, 1965-86 (percentage of GDP)

	1965-72	1973-77	1978-82	1983-86
Net transfer (T_S)	-0.4	5.6	7.0	3.3
Net External Financing ($\Delta F-\Delta J$)	1.7	7.1	7.9	3.0
Capital flight (ΔJ)	0.1	1.5	1.1	0.3
Public borrowing (ΔF)	1.8	8.6	9.0	3.3
External Balance, ($CA=E-M-R$)	-1.7	-7.1	-7.9	-3.0
Trade balance ($E-M$)	0.4	-5.6	-7.0	-3.3
Exports (E)	31.2	30.0	24.4	23.8
Imports (M)	30.8	35.6	31.4	27.1
Factor payments (R)	2.1	1.4	0.9	-0.3
Interest (iF)	0.6	0.8	1.0	1.5
Internal Balance ($S-I$)	-1.7	-7.1	-7.9	-3.0
Savings (S)	19.5	17.0	12.9	11.0
Investment (I)	21.2	24.1	20.7	14.0
Fiscal Balance ($T-G$)	-3.2	-6.4	-6.3	-4.0
Government expenditures (G)	21.1	23.8	21.6	21.3
Taxation (T)	17.9	17.4	15.3	17.3
Private savings surplus (S_p-I_p)	1.5	-0.7	-1.5	1.0

Sources and *Notes*: See Table 5.10a.

Table A5.4 ***Private borrowers – oil exporters: internal and external balances, 1965-86 (percentage of GDP)***

	1965-72	1973-77	1978-82	1983-86
Net External Financing ($\Delta F - \Delta J$)	2.5	0.0	-0.4	-3.6
Capital flight (ΔJ)	1.2	2.1	3.0	1.5
Public borrowing (ΔF)	3.7	2.1	2.6	-2.1
External Balance, ($CA=E-M-R$)	-2.5	0.0	0.4	3.6
Trade balance ($E-M$)	0.9	1.6	-0.4	6.9
Export (E)	14.1	17.8	18.6	20.8
Imports	13.3	16.2	19.0	13.9
Factor payments (R)	3.3	1.6	-0.8	3.3
Internal Balance ($S-I$)	-2.5	0.0	0.4	3.6
Savings (S)	18.9	26.0	24.1	21.6
Investment (I)	21.4	26.0	23.7	18.0
Fiscal Balance ($T-G$)	-1.2	-3.0	-4.9	-5.5
Government expenditures (G)	8.2	11.4	12.6	13.1
Taxation (T)	7.0	8.4	7.7	7.6
Private savings surplus (S_p-I_p)	-1.3	3.0	5.3	9.1

Sources and *Notes*: See Table 5.10a.

Table A5.5 Private borrowers – primary exporters: internal and external balances, 1965-86 (percentage of GDP)

	1965-72	1973-77	1978-82	1983-86
Net Transfer (T_S)	0.3	1.7	1.1	-5.0
Net External Financing ($\Delta F-\Delta J$)	0.9	3.0	3.5	-0.9
Capital flight (ΔJ)	2.2	2.0	3.1	2.9
Public borrowing (ΔF)	3.1	5.0	6.6	2.0
External Balance ($CA=E-M-R$)	-0.9	-3.0	-3.5	0.9
Trade balance ($E-M$)	0.3	-1.7	-1.1	5.0
Exports (E)	10.0	11.9	12.1	18.3
Imports (M)	9.7	13.7	13.1	13.3
Factor payments (R)	1.2	1.3	2.4	4.2
Internal Balance ($S-I$)	-0.9	-3.0	-3.5	0.9
Savings (S)	20.5	21.8	17.6	17.5
Investment (I)	21.4	24.9	21.1	16.6
Fiscal Balance ($T-G$)	-1.7	-1.7	-2.0	-2.7
Government expenditures (G)	13.0	14.5	15.7	16.0
Taxation (T)	11.3	12.8	13.7	13.3
Private savings surplus (S_p-I_p)	0.8	-1.3	-1.5	3.6

Sources and *Notes*: See Table 5.10a.

Table A5.6 Private borrowers – exporters of manufactures: internal and external balances, 1965-86 (percentage of GDP)

	1965-72	1973-77	1978-82	1983-86
Net Transfer (T_S)	4.9	4.3	5.4	0.7
Net External Financing ($\Delta F - \Delta J$)	7.0	6.1	7.2	2.9
Capital flight *(ΔJ)*	–	1.1	1.0	0.9
'Gross' borrowing *(ΔF)*	7.0	7.2	8.2	3.8
External Balance ($CA=E-M-R$)	-7.0	-6.1	-7.2	-2.9
Trade balance *($E-M$)*	-4.9	-4.3	-5.4	-0.7
Exports *(E)*	15.4	24.8	27.8	32.2
Imports *(M)*	20.3	29.1	33.2	32.8
Factor payments *(R)*	2.1	1.8	1.8	2.2
Internal Balance ($S-I$)	-7.0	-6.1	-7.2	-2.9
Savings *(S)*	15.6	22.4	22.9	23.5
Investment *(I)*	22.6	28.5	30.1	26.4
Fiscal Balance ($T-G$)	-0.9	-1.0	-1.9	-0.9
Government expenditure *(G)*	14.8	16.3	19.0	18.6
Taxation *(T)*	13.9	15.3	17.1	17.7
Private savings surplus ($S_p - I_p$)	-6.1	-5.1	-5.3	-2.0

Sources and *Notes*: See Table 5.10a.

A7 Chapter 7

Stability Conditions of the STAC Model

The solution and stability of the model depends on the properties of the excess demand functions for the three markets distinguished in the model. The Southern commodity market clears for the terms of trade θ, the Northern commodity market clears through output adjustment, Q_N, the global capital market for the world interest rate, i_W and the Northern government bond market. Market clearing functions may be expressed in their general form as:

Southern commodity market: $\dfrac{d\theta}{dt} = f[ED_S(Q_N, i_W, \theta)]$

Northern commodity market: $\dfrac{dQ_N}{dt} = f[ED_N(Q_N, i_W, \theta)]$

Global credit market: $\dfrac{di_W}{dt} = f[ED_B(Q_N, i_W, \theta)]$

Bond market: $DEF_N(Q_N, i_W, \theta) - \Delta DC_N = 0$

The excess demand function for the Southern commodity, ED_S, is determined by equations (7.1) and (7.15):

$$ED_S = \theta\omega_S(L_S + L_{Sg}) + \alpha(1 - t_N)\gamma Q_N + A\theta - \theta Q_S \qquad (A7.1)$$

which for the Northern commodity market, ED_N, can be written (from 7.13, and making substitutions using equations 7.14, 7.16, and 7.10 and knowing that Southern demand for the Northern commodity is composed of consumption demand by profit earners and investment goods: $M_{SN} = (1 - s_S)(1 - t_S)R_S + I_S + I_{Sg}$ as:

$$ED_N = (1-\alpha)(1-t_N)\gamma Q_N - A\theta + (1-s_S)(1-t_S)(1-\omega_S/q_S)\theta Q_S + (1-s_O)vm_{NO}Q_N + I_N + G_N + I_S + I_{Sg} - Q_N \qquad (A7.2)$$

which, after making the substitution for I_N using 7.16 becomes:

$$ED_N = -Q_N + (1-\alpha)(1-t_N)\gamma Q_N + (1-s_O)vm_{NO}Q_N + [g_{0N} + g_{1N}(r_N+u)]u^{-1}Q_N - A\theta + (1-s_S)(1-t_S)(1-\omega_S/q_S)\theta Q_S$$

$$-g_{2N}\,[\,i_W\,(1+x_N)]\,K_N + G_N + I_S + I_{Sg} \qquad (A7.2a)$$

The excess demand function for bank loans is given by equation 7.27:

$$ED_B = \Delta\, B_N^d + \Delta\, B_S - \Delta\, B^s \qquad (A7.3)$$

After making the substitutions using equations 7.21–24, 7.19, 7.16 and 7.11, and having defined $\varphi = vm_{NO}/(\omega_N/q_N + vm_{NO})$ and $r_N = \tau(1+\tau)^{-1}\,u$, this can also be written as:

$$\begin{aligned} ED_B = &-\theta\,[\,j_{1S}\,(i_W - r_S)_{-1} s_S\,(1-t_S)\,(1-\omega_S/q_S)\,Q_S] \\ &+ Q_N\,[(b_{1N}/u)\{g_{0N} + g_{1N}\,(r_N+u)\} - t_N\,(1-vm_{N0}) - s_0 vm_{N0} \\ &- j_{1N}\,(i_W - r_N)_{-1} s_N{}^{(1-t_N)}\, r_N/u] - i_W\,[\,b_{1N}\,\{\,g_{2N}(1+x_N)\,K_N\} \\ &+ DC_N - J_O - j_{1N}(i_W - r_N)_{-1}(DC_N + J_O + J_S) - j_{1S}(i_W - r_S)_{-1} \\ &\{J_S - (1+x_S)\,B_{Sp}\} + j_{1N}\,(i_W - r_N)_{-1}(1+x_S)\,(B_{Sg} + B_{Sp})] \\ &+ \Delta B_S + G_N + \Delta F_S^a - j_{0N} J_N - j_{0S} J_S \end{aligned} \qquad (A7.3a)$$

The Jacobian matrix, *J*, for this system is:

$$J = \begin{bmatrix} \omega_S\,(L_S + L_{Sg}) + A - Q_S, & \alpha(1-t_N)\gamma & 0 \\ \begin{array}{l}(1-s_S)(1-t_S)\\ (1-\omega_S/q_S)Q_S - A\end{array} & \begin{array}{l}-1 + (1-\alpha)(1-t_N)\gamma \\ + (1-s_O)vm_{NO} \\ + u^{-1}[g_{0N} + g_{1N}(r_N + u)]\end{array} & -g_{2N}(1+x_N)K_N \\ \begin{array}{l}-j_{1S}(i_W - r_S)_{-1}s_S(1-t_S)\\ (1-\omega_S/q_S)Q_S\end{array} & \begin{array}{l}u^{-1}b_{1N}\{\,g_{ON} + g_{1N}\,(r_N+u)\}\\ -t_N(1-vm_{NO}) - s_O vm_{NO}\\ -j_{1N}(i_W - r_N)_{-1}s_N\\ (1-t_N)r_N u^{-1}\end{array} & \begin{array}{l}-b_{1N}\,\{\,g_{2N}\,(1+x_N)\,K_N\,\}\\ -DC_N + J_O\\ +j_{1N}(i_W - r_N)_{-1}\,\{DC_N\\ +J_O + J_S - 1 + x_S)(B_{Sg} + B_{Sp})\}\\ +j_{1S}(i_W - r_S)_{-1}\{J_S -\\ (1+x_S)B_{Sp}\}\end{array} \end{bmatrix}$$

in:

$$\begin{bmatrix} ED_S \\ ED_N \\ ED_B \end{bmatrix} = \begin{bmatrix} J \end{bmatrix} \begin{bmatrix} d\theta/dt \\ dQ_N/dt \\ di_W/dt \end{bmatrix} \qquad (A7.4)$$

For the system to be stable, the trace of the Jacobian should be negative and the determinant of the matrix should be positive. Given that most parameter and variable values are positive, the likelihood of stability may be assessed even with these complex terms. The trace is the algebraic sum of the elements of the main diagonal: $a_{11} + a_{22} + a_{33}$.

The expected values are:

$a_{11}<0$,

assuming Southern output is larger than domestic demand and the existence of South-North trade.

$a_{22}<0$,

if the 'Keynesian stability' condition of a quicker savings response to output changes than the response of investment holds. Note that total Northern output, Q_N, less the terms relating to Northern and oil-exporters' consumption demand $[(1-\alpha)(1-t_N)\gamma+(1-s_O)vm_{NO}]Q_N$ refers to the savings supply in the North that is directly dependent on Northern output.

$a_{33} < 0$,

for a large enough Northern physical capital stock (K_N) and government debt (DC_N) *vis-à-vis* deposit holdings of oil exporters and deposit demand response in North and South resulting from positive net asset positions.

As long as all elements of the trace are negative or $\left|a_{11}+a_{22}\right| > a_{33}$, then the sum of the trace elements may be expected to be negative.

The determinant of the 3 × 3 Jacobian is given by:

$$\Delta = a_{11}a_{22}a_{33}-a_{12}a_{21}a_{33} + a_{12}a_{23}a_{31}-a_{13}a_{22}a_{31} + a_{13}a_{21}a_{33}-a_{11}a_{23}a_{32}$$

The expected signs can be traced by looking at the individual components:

$a_{11}a_{22}a_{33}<0$,

if all individual components are negative (but may be positive if $a_{33} > 0$ due to the asset-liability structures of the different agents as indicated above).

$-a_{12}a_{21}a_{33}<0$,

as $a_{12}>0$ with positive parameters and $0<(t_N, \alpha)<1$; $a_{21}>0$ for the same reason and $0<(s_S, t_S)<1$; and if $a_{33}<0$ (see above).

$a_{12}a_{23}a_{31}<0$,

as $a_{12}>0$; a_{23} is clearly negative; and $a_{31}>0$ for positive parameter values.

$a_{13}a_{22}a_{31}=0$

and $a_{13}\,a_{21}\,a_{33}=0$, as $a_{13}=0$

$-a_{11}a_{23}a_{32}>0$,

as $a_{11}<0$ and $a_{23}<0$, while $a_{32}<0$ if Northern private credit demand response to higher profitability is smaller than Northern tax rate plus oil exporters savings rate plus Northern private deposit demand response parameters to savings and profitability.

Stability thus need not be preserved, but under the above conditions the determinant will be positive if:

$$\left|a_{11}a_{22}a_{33}\right| + \left|a_{12}a_{23}a_{31}\right| < \left|a_{12}a_{21}a_{33}\right| + \left|a_{11}a_{23}a_{32}\right|$$

Looking at the terms in pairs, these conditions may hold if:

$\left|a_{11}a_{22}a_{33}\right| < \left|a_{12}a_{21}a_{33}\right|$,

which holds if the Northern propensity to import the Southern commodity times consumption demand of Southern profit earners ($a_{12}a_{21}$) is larger than the Southern export volume times the difference between the Northern savings-investment response to output ($a_{11}a_{22}$).

$\left|a_{12}a_{23}a_{31}\right| < \left|a_{11}a_{23}a_{32}\right|$,

which holds if $\left|a_{12}a_{31}\right| < \left|a_{11}a_{32}\right|$, i.e. if the Southern export volume (a_{11}) times the Northern private credit demand response to higher profitability less oil-exporters' and Northern private agents' deposit demand parameters (a_{32}) is larger than the Northern propensity to import the Southern commodity (a_{12}) times the Southern foreign asset demand response to rate-of-return differentials (a_{31}).

Stability is thus not unambiguously ensured by the model assumptions. If Keynesian stability does not apply to the North, or if, for instance, Southern profit earners have a stronger incentive to accumulate foreign assets to the detriment of export production, there is no certainty of model stability. Stability further appears to depend strongly on asset and liability positions of Northern and Southern public and private agents. A large deposit demand response resulting from large accumulated net financial private asset positions in North, South and the region of oil exporters may be another source of system instability. This latter possibility may imply, since the model allows for stock adjustment from one period to another, that initial stability may be disturbed over time with shifting asset and liability positions.

A8 Chapter 8

Statistical Appendix

Table A8.1 *STAC model: baseline case, model version with official aid flows only, no bank lending to South*

	1	2	3	4	5	6	7	8	9	10
Endogenous variables										
ΔB_S	0	0	0	0	0	0	0	0	0	0
ΔB_{S_g}	0	0	0	0	0	0	0	0	0	0
ΔDC_N	276.11	297.50	319.86	343.84	369.56	397.13	426.69	458.39	492.39	528.86
I_N	500.76	530.07	559.16	589.77	621.90	655.63	691.04	728.18	767.13	807.98
I_S	33.51	35.45	37.36	39.38	41.50	43.71	46.03	48.47	51.02	53.69
I_{S_g}	32.73	34.65	36.55	38.56	40.66	42.87	45.19	47.62	50.17	52.85
i_W	0.0419	0.0422	0.0425	0.0428	0.0431	0.0435	0.0438	0.0441	0.0445	0.0449
ΔJ_N	556.06	587.91	619.83	653.47	688.85	726.08	765.23	806.41	849.71	895.23
ΔJ_S	0	0	0	0	0	0	0	0	0	0
ΔJ_O	170.73	186.65	203.27	221.16	240.42	261.12	283.39	307.34	333.10	360.81
L_S	4125.00	4159.04	4195.05	4233.02	4273.06	4315.26	4359.72	4406.57	4455.91	4507.86
M_{NS}	1308.00	1318.89	1330.42	1342.57	1355.38	1368.88	1383.11	1398.10	1413.89	1430.52
M_{ON}	78.39	82.98	87.53	92.33	97.36	102.64	108.18	113.99	120.09	126.49
M_{SN}	166.77	176.43	186.01	196.08	206.64	217.71	229.32	241.49	254.24	267.59
Q_N	6399.36	6773.95	7145.71	7536.87	7947.54	8378.60	8831.04	9305.67	9803.49	10325.49
Q_S	1650.00	1663.61	1678.02	1693.21	1709.22	1726.10	1743.89	1762.63	1782.36	1803.15
Q_O	223.98	237.09	250.10	263.79	278.16	293.25	309.09	325.70	343.12	361.39

(Continued...)

(*Table A8.1 Continued*)

	1	2	3	4	5	6	7	8	9	10
R_S	148.93	157.54	166.07	175.03	184.42	194.27	204.60	215.41	226.74	238.60
r_N	0.0305	0.0320	0.0335	0.0350	0.0365	0.0381	0.0398	0.0414	0.0432	0.0449
S_N	606.14	640.92	675.75	712.44	751.04	791.64	834.33	879.22	926.42	976.03
S_S	33.51	35.45	37.36	39.38	41.50	43.71	46.03	48.47	51.02	53.69
	0.1128	0.1184	0.1237	0.1292	0.1349	0.1407	0.1467	0.1528	0.1590	0.1654
YARR	0	0	0	0	0	0	0	0	0	0
Updated stock variables										
K_N	60000.00	60500.76	61030.82	61589.98	62179.75	62801.65	63457.28	64148.32	64876.49	65643.62
K_S	5000.00	5033.51	5068.95	5106.32	5145.70	5187.20	5230.91	5276.94	5325.41	5376.42
K_{S_g}	2500.00	2532.73	2567.38	2603.93	2642.49	2683.15	2726.02	2771.21	2818.82	2869.00
B_N	7000.00	7450.68	7927.74	8430.98	8961.77	9521.49	10111.56	10733.49	11388.85	12079.26
B_{S_g}	0	0	0	0	0	0	0	0	0	0
B_{S_p}	0	0	0	0	0	0	0	0	0	0
B_S	0	0	0	0	0	0	0	0	0	0
$B_S/\theta M_{NS}^{emax}$	0	0	0	0	0	0	0	0	0	0
DC_N	3000.00	3276.11	3573.61	3893.46	4237.31	4606.86	5003.99	5430.68	5889.07	6381.46
J_N	10000.00	10556.06	11143.97	11763.80	12417.27	13106.12	13832.20	14597.43	15403.84	16253.54
J_S	0	0	0	0	0	0	0	0	0	0
J_O	700.00	770.73	957.38	1160.64	1381.81	1622.22	1883.34	2166.74	2474.08	2807.18

Table A8.2 *STAC model: baseline case for complete model version with endogenous aid flows and commercial bank lending to the South*

	1	2	3	4	5	6	7	8	9	10	11	12
Endogenous variables												
ΔB^s	466.94	489.97	516.91	544.03	573.66	603.26	635.93	668.19	704.30	778.68	860.78	902.85
ΔB^d_N	464.26	463.32	510.54	508.63	569.16	560.86	635.05	616.62	709.26	775.31	862.53	902.85
ΔB_S	2.68	26.65	6.37	35.40	4.49	42.40	0.89	51.57	-4.95	3.37	-1.75	0.00
ΔB_{Sg}	2.68	26.65	6.37	35.40	4.49	42.40	0.89	51.57	0.00	3.37	0.00	0.00
ΔB^d_{Sg}	114.00	113.48	144.38	149.52	193.40	196.82	251.15	249.53	317.76	394.11	477.39	504.50
C_N	4787.75	4961.37	5294.20	5494.54	5882.60	6084.01	6532.35	6726.68	7250.72	7991.86	8849.57	9282.98
ΔDC_N	313.62	334.94	363.52	388.67	422.24	450.71	490.01	522.08	568.26	656.73	760.45	817.12
I_N	640.36	639.06	704.19	701.56	785.05	773.59	875.93	850.51	978.28	1069.39	1189.70	1245.31
I_S	30.61	32.16	35.00	36.74	40.07	41.86	45.74	47.52	47.11	59.02	65.00	70.89
I_{Sg}	19.53	44.29	24.34	54.07	23.46	61.85	20.22	71.85	34.07	25.29	42.70	43.59
i_W	0.0433	0.0437	0.0440	0.0443	0.0447	0.0451	0.0454	0.0458	0.0462	0.0469	0.0477	0.0481
ΔJ_N	557.33	585.17	617.15	649.73	685.05	720.85	759.99	799.33	842.77	933.57	1034.38	1086.77
ΔJ_S	15.32	15.97	16.75	17.52	18.38	19.20	20.13	21.01	22.02	24.02	26.20	27.26
ΔJ_O	207.91	223.77	246.52	265.45	292.48	313.91	345.82	369.93	407.78	477.82	560.65	605.94
L_S	4125.00	4151.94	4189.76	4221.37	4265.96	4300.38	4351.29	4387.96	4446.40	4548.74	4665.30	4723.00
M_{NS}	1308.00	1316.62	1328.72	1338.84	1353.11	1364.12	1380.41	1392.15	1410.85	1443.60	1480.90	1499.36
M_{ON}	97.95	101.50	108.31	112.41	120.35	124.47	133.64	137.62	148.34	163.50	181.05	189.92
M_{SN}	176.22	207.04	198.53	235.18	217.70	263.36	237.22	295.60	256.85	291.53	316.71	334.59

(Continued...)

(Table A8.2 Continued)

	1	2	3	4	5	6	7	8	9	10	11	12
Q_N	7995.92	8285.87	8841.71	9176.30	9824.3	10160.7	10909.53	11234.07	12109.26	13347.02	14779.46	15503.29
Q_S	1650.00	1660.78	1675.90	1688.55	1706.38	1720.15	1740.52	1755.19	1778.56	1819.50	1866.12	1889.20
Q_O	279.86	290.01	309.46	321.17	343.85	355.63	381.83	393.19	423.82	467.15	517.28	542.62
r_N	0.0374	0.0383	0.0405	0.0415	0.0440	0.0449	0.0476	0.0484	0.0515	0.0551	0.0592	0.0611
r_S	0.0374	0.0385	0.0407	0.0420	0.0446	0.0457	0.0486	0.0496	0.0530	0.0572	0.0618	0.0640
S_N	733.43	760.91	810.74	842.62	900.61	933.55	1000.85	1033.19	1097.67	1226.03	1339.75	1407.43
S_S	45.93	48.13	51.75	54.26	58.45	61.07	65.86	68.53	74.08	83.05	92.95	98.15
	0.1415	0.1456	0.1539	0.1584	0.1677	0.1719	0.1822	0.1860	0.1976	0.2125	0.2291	0.2371
YARR	0.00	0.00	0.05	0.05	0.32	0.03	0.03	0.03	14.13	1.62	21.79	21.79
Updated Stock Variables												
K_N	60000.0	60640.3	61279.4	61983.6	62685.1	63470.2	64243.82	65119.74	65970.25	67910.56	70031.96	71221.66
K_S	5000.00	5030.61	5062.77	5097.7	5134.5	5174.5	5216.44	5262.17	5309.69	5411.35	5531.86	5596.85
K_{S_g}	2500.00	2519.53	2563.82	2588.1	2642.24	2665.6	2727.54	2747.76	2819.61	2916.62	3019.72	3062.42
B_N	7000.00	7464.26	7927.58	8438.1	8946.75	9515.9	10076.77	10711.81	11328.43	12735.16	14273.17	15135.70
B_{S_g}	200.00	202.68	229.34	235.7	271.21	276.02	318.45	319.36	370.96	427.82	489.35	511.15
B_{S_p}	150.00	150.00	150.00	150.0	150.00	150.00	150.00	150.00	150.00	145.05	145.05	143.30
B_S	350.00	352.68	379.34	385.7	421.21	426.02	468.45	469.36	520.96	572.87	634.40	654.45
$B_S/\theta M_{NS-1}$	1.99	1.91	1.98	1.89	1.99	1.88	2.00	1.87	2.01	1.99	2.00	1.93
DC_N	3000.00	3313.62	3648.56	4012.08	4400.75	4822.99	5273.70	5763.71	6285.79	7460.20	8818.00	9578.45
J_N	10000.0	10557.3	11142.5	11759.6	12409.3	13094.4	13815.29	14575.28	15374.61	17103.20	19018.38	20052.76
J_S	300.00	315.32	331.29	348.04	365.57	383.94	403.14	423.27	444.28	489.24	538.31	564.51
J_O	600.00	807.91	1031.68	1278.20	1543.65	1836.13	2150.04	2495.86	2865.79	3710.29	4700.09	5260.74

Table A8.3 *STAC model: baseline case, model version with no credit rationing and interest-rate clearing world credit market*

	1	2	3	4	5	6	7	8	9	10
Endogenous variables										
ΔB^s	470.85	494.53	521.52	549.98	580.37	610.98	569.28	0	0	0
ΔB^d_N	451.36	460.77	456.76	415.53	288.03	0	0	0	0	0
ΔB_S	19.49	33.77	64.76	134.45	292.34	652.85	2121.44	0	0	0
ΔB_{Sg}	19.49	33.77	64.76	134.45	292.34	652.85	2121.44	0	0	0
ΔB^d_{Sg}	19.49	33.77	64.76	134.45	292.34	652.85	2121.44	0	0	0
C_N	4749.52	4949.21	5127.72	5194.18	4989.75	4556.52	15043.22	0	0	0
ΔDC_N	308.21	330.08	352.47	371.92	382.41	389.6	975.21	0	0	0
I_N	622.57	635.54	630.02	573.14	397.28	0	0	0	0	0
I_S	30.27	32.04	33.54	34.05	32.15	28.33	124.75	0	0	0
I_{Sg}	32.13	46.18	75.92	141.8	290.04	628.59	2043.48	0	0	0
i_W	0.0433	0.0436	0.044	0.0444	0.0447	0.0461	0.08	0	0	0
ΔJ_N	557.28	585.4	617.11	650.65	686.58	725.95	788.62	0	0	0
ΔJ_S	15.32	15.98	16.75	17.57	18.45	19.44	21.39	0	0	0
ΔJ_O	206.46	223.24	240.13	253.68	257.75	255.2	734.49	0	0	0
L_S	4125	4156.77	4195.27	4246.6	4324.6	4460.71	4729.85	0	0	0
M_{NS}	1308	1318.17	1330.49	1346.91	1371.87	1415.43	1501.55	0	0	0
M_{ON}	97.17	101.25	104.91	106.26	102.08	93.22	307.76	0	0	0
M_{SN}	187.49	208.47	244.3	312.31	453.09	776.16	2560.19	0	0	0

(Continued...)

(Table A8.3 Continued)

	1	2	3	4	5	6	7	8	9	10
Q_N	7932.07	8265.56	8563.69	8674.68	8333.27	7609.74	25123.33	0	0	0
Q_S	1650.00	1662.71	1678.11	1698.64	1729.84	1784.28	1891.94	0	0	0
Q_O	277.62	289.29	299.73	303.61	291.66	266.34	879.32	0	0	0
r_N	0.0371	0.0383	0.0392	0.0393	0.0374	0.034	0.1121	0	0	0
r_S	0.0371	0.0384	0.0395	0.0397	0.0378	0.0342	0.1119	0	0	0
S_N	728.49	760.16	790.35	808.27	795.82	767.8	2340.78	0	0	0
S_S	45.59	48.01	50.29	51.61	50.6	47.77	146.14	0	0	0
	0.1404	0.1451	0.1488	0.1488	0.1401	0.1238	0.3837	0	0	0
YARR	0	0	0	0	0	0	0	0	0	0
Updated Stock Variables										
K_N	60000	60622.57	61258.11	61888.13	62461.27	62858.55	62858.55	62858.55	0	0
K_S	5000	5030.27	5062.31	5095.85	5129.89	5162.04	5190.38	5315.12	0	0
K_{S_g}	2500	2532.13	2578.31	2654.23	2796.03	3086.08	3714.66	5758.14	0	0
B_N	7000	7451.36	7912.13	8368.89	8784.42	9072.45	9072.45	9072.45	0	0
B_{S_g}	200	219.49	253.26	318.02	452.47	744.81	1397.66	3519.1	0	0
B_{S_p}	150	150	150	150	150	150	150	150	0	0
B_S	350	369.49	403.26	468.02	602.47	894.81	1547.66	3669.1	0	0
$B_S/\theta M_{NS\text{-}1}$	1.99	2.01	2.11	2.36	3.01	4.65	8.83	6.37	0	0
DC_N	3000	3308.21	3638.29	3990.76	4362.68	4745.09	5134.69	6109.9	0	0
J_N	10000	10557.28	11142.68	11759.79	12410.44	13097.02	13822.97	14611.59	0	0
J_S	300	315.32	331.3	348.05	365.61	384.06	403.5	424.88	0	0
J_O	600	806.46	1029.7	1269.83	1523.51	1781.26	2036.46	2770.95	0	0

Table A8.4 MULTIMOD: increase of US government spending by 1 per cent of GNP (percentage deviation from baseline, unless otherwise noted)

	1988	1989	1990	1991	1993	1995
Major industrial countries						
United States						
Real GNP	1.1	1.2	1.2	1.0	0.6	0.1
Real domestic demand	1.4	1.7	1.7	1.6	1.4	1.3
GNP deflator	0.3	1.0	2.1	3.5	6.9	10.5
Long-term interest rate (in %)	0.5	0.5	0.5	0.5	0.5	0.4
Short-term interest rate (in %)	0.1	0.3	0.4	0.5	0.9	1.2
Nominal effective exchange rate[1]	2.3	2.2	2.1	2.1	1.8	1.3
Current account balance[2]	-0.2	-0.3	-0.3	-0.4	-0.5	-0.7
Fiscal balance[2]	-0.8	-0.8	-0.9	-1.0	-1.2	-1.4
Gross private investment[2]	0.1	0.3	0.3	0.2	0.0	-0.1
Japan						
Real GNP	0.3	0.4	0.5	0.5	0.3	0.3
GNP deflator	0.4	1.0	1.9	2.9	4.7	5.8
Short-term interest rate (in %)	0.1	0.2	0.3	0.4	0.7	0.8
Exchange rate ($/Yen)	-2.1	-2.0	-1.9	-1.9	-1.6	-1.1
Current account balance[2]	0.1	0.1	0.2	0.2	0.2	0.3
Germany[3]						
Real GNP		0.3	0.4	0.5	0.5	0.4
GNP deflator	0.3	0.9	1.8	2.7	4.7	5.9
Short-term interest rate (in %)	0.1	0.2	0.3	0.4	0.7	0.8
Exchange rate ($/DM)	-2.5	-2.4	-2.4	-2.3	-2.0	-1.5
Current account balance[2]	0.1	0.1	0.2	0.2	0.3	0.4
Other major industrial countries						
Real GNP	0.1	0.1	0.2	0.2	0.2	0.2
GNP deflator	0.4	1.2	2.1	3.1	5.0	6.1
Short-term interest rate (in %)	0.1	0.2	0.3	0.4	0.7	0.8
Nominal effective exchange rate[1]	-0.3	-0.3	-0.2	-0.2	-0.1	0.0
Current account balance[2]	0.1	0.1	0.1	0.1	0.1	0.1

(Continued...)

(*Table A8.4 Continued*)

	1988	1989	1990	1991	1993	1995
Other industrial countries						
Real GNP	0.2	0.5	0.5	0.4	0.4	0.4
GNP deflator	0.4	1.1	2.0	3.0	4.6	5.5
Current account balance[2]	0.1	0.2	0.2	0.2	0.3	0.3
High-income oil-exporting countries						
Real GDP	0.3	0.3	0.2	0.0	-0.5	-1.0
Other developing countries						
Real GDP	0.2	0.3	0.4	0.4	0.5	0.6
GNP deflator	0.5	1.2	2.1	3.1	5.1	6.5
Real imports	0.6	0.4	0.3	0.1	-0.3	-0.6
Interest payments/exports[4]	0.1	0.3	0.5	0.7	0.8	1.0
Current account balance[2]	0.0	0.0	0.0	0.0	0.0	0.0
World prices						
Price of oil (in dollars)	-1.1	-0.4	0.6	1.8	4.3	6.6
Price index of commodities	-0.1	0.5	1.2	2.1	3.9	5.8

Source: Masson et al. (1988: Table 11).

Notes:
1. A positive value indicates an appreciation.
2. In per cent of baseline GNP/GDP.
3. Effects as simulated for conditions before German Unification. On the impact of the unification, see Masson & Meredith (1990) and Vos (1993).
4. Change in level.

Table A8.5 MULTIMOD: increase in financing flows to the South of US$ 20 billion per year (percentage deviation from baseline case, unless otherwise noted)

	1988	1989	1990	1991	1993	1995
Major industrial countries						
United States						
Real GNP	0.3	0.3	0.3	0.2	-0.2	-0.4
GNP deflator	0.1	0.3	0.5	0.8	1.3	1.3
Long-term interest rate (in %)	0.0	0.1	0.1	0.1	0.0	0.0
Short-term interest rate (in %)	0.1	0.1	0.1	0.1	0.1	0.1
Nominal effective exchange rate[1]	-0.2	-0.2	-0.1	0.1	0.3	0.3
Current account balance[2]	-0.1	-0.1	-0.1	-0.1	-0.1	-0.1
Japan						
Real GNP	0.4	0.5	0.4	0.3	-0.2	-0.2
GNP deflator	0.2	0.6	1.0	1.2	1.2	0.6
Short-term interest rate (in %)	0.1	0.1	0.2	0.2	0.1	0.0
Long-term interest rate (in %)	0.0	0.0	0.0	0.0	0.0	0.0
Exchange rate ($/Yen)	0.2	0.1	0.0	-0.1	-0.3	-0.3
Current account balance[2]	0.2	0.1	0.1	0.1	0.0	0.0
Germany[3]						
Real GNP	0.4	0.5	0.4	0.3	-0.3	-0.3
GNP deflator	0.2	0.6	1.0	1.3	1.4	0.8
Short-term interest rate (in %)	0.1	0.1	0.2	0.2	0.1	0.1
Long-term interest rate (in %)	0.1	0.1	0.0	0.0	0.0	0.0
Exchange rate ($/DM)	0.2	0.2	0.1	0.0	-0.2	-0.3
Current account balance[2]	0.2	0.1	0.1	0.1	0.0	0.1
Other major industrial countries						
Real GNP	0.4	0.5	0.4	0.2	-0.3	-0.2
GNP deflator	0.3	0.7	1.1	1.4	1.2	0.5
Short-term interest rate (in %)	0.1	0.2	0.2	0.2	0.1	0.0
Long-term interest rate (in %)	0.1	0.1	0.1	0.1	0.0	0.0
Nominal effective exchange rate[1]	0.1	0.1	0.0	0.0	0.0	0.0
Current account balance[2]	0.2	0.2	0.1	0.1	0.0	0.0

(Continued...)

(Table A8.5 Continued)

	1988	1989	1990	1991	1993	1995
Other industrial countries						
Real GNP	0.5	0.6	0.5	0.3	-0.2	-0.3
GNP deflator	0.3	0.7	1.1	1.4	1.3	0.6
Current account balance[2]	0.2	0.2	0.2	0.2	0.0	0.0
High-income oil-exporting countries						
Real GDP	0.5	0.4	0.3	0.1	-0.5	-0.5
Other developing countries						
Real GDP	0.0	0.1	0.1	0.0	0.0	0.0
GNP deflator	0.2	0.6	0.9	1.2	1.1	0.6
Real imports	3.7	3.3	2.9	2.5	-0.5	-0.3
Interest payments/exports[4]	-0.1	-0.1	0.0	0.0	0.2	0.2
Current account balance[2]	0.0	0.0	0.0	0.0	0.0	0.0
World prices						
Price of oil (in dollars)	0.3	0.6	0.9	1.1	1.1	0.7
Price index of commodities	1.5	1.5	1.2	0.9	-0.4	-0.3

Source: Masson et al. (1988: Table 18).

Notes:
1. A positive value indicates an appreciation.
2. In per cent of baseline GNP/GDP.
3. See note 3 to Table A8.4.
4. Change in level.

Notes

Chapter 1

1. McKinnon (1977) concluded that 'lack of government restrictions created a model of efficiency in international banking', while Dufey & Giddy (1978: 193) argued at the time that 'in the international context the Euromarkets facilitate market-induced credit allocation at the expense of government-induced allocation . . . Indeed, probably no other single force has made such a great contribution to the efficient international allocation of credit as have the Eurocurrency markets.'

2. Such optimism can be read for instance in the 1983 *World Economic Outlook* (IMF 1983: 9):

    > [t]he aggregate current account deficit of the non-oil developing countries could be expected to settle in the neighborhood of 14 per cent of their (LDCs, R.V.) exports of goods and services. This is a considerably lower ratio than in 1981-82 and similar to the average for the latter part of the 1970s. A deficit of this size should not pose serious financing problems or unmanageable debt burdens in the aggregate.

    This was the major result of the Fund's 'central' scenario at the time and it was suggested that the commercial banks need not worry too much about LDC creditworthiness. Cline's influential simulation model (Cline 1983) yielded similar conclusions. The banks nevertheless did not appear to share the same optimism and withdrew from new voluntary lending to LDCs.

3. Bryant (1988) gives a similar presentation of the conventional view on the role of external finance.

4. Cross & Hempel (1973: 207 and 280; cited in Devlin 1987) state that 'no well-run bank can take a passive attitude towards lending'; 'successful banks . . . are those that have found the means to make more loans than their neighbours and to make some loans that their neighbours would not make at all' and, further, 'in a competitive world, it is not enough to be a good fellow; *one must aggressively seek business*' (italics are mine).

5. One may picture this country ranking as follows. Potential borrowers are ranked according to broadly defined, easily identifiable groups on the basis of a country risk analysis, e.g. A, B, C, D and E where A are mostly OECD countries, B more industrialized, middle-income LDCs and further down are the poorer LDCs and possibly the politically highly unstable countries.

This risk evaluation is translated into quantitatively fixed credit ceilings per country or into rationing points. At the bottom of the list (say, D and E countries) credit ceilings will be low or zero and the countries concerned are thus effectively rationed out of the market.

6. Such an outcome is consistent with various theoretical assumptions. One approach is the Fleming-Mundell IS-LM model applied to two or more economies (see e.g. Frenkel & Razin 1987; but see further Chapters 3, 5 and 6).

Chapter 2

1. The lack of a global accounting framework to collect information on the world economy obliges researchers to study debt and adjustment using inconsistent data sources for key variables, despite ongoing efforts towards more standardized definitions (see e.g. Tims & Waelbroeck 1982 and World Bank/BIS/IMF/OECD 1988). At present, no single consistent data system exists which allows simultaneous analysis of international linkages in trade and finance. At best such world accounts could be built from separate data systems like the aggregate national SNA accounts, standardized UN trade statistics, World Bank debt statistics and IMF balance-of-payments data. However, apart from the fact that these data sets show differences in concepts and coverage (see World Bank/BIS/IMF/OECD 1988), they also do not systematically specify *all* international linkages on a source-user basis (except the UN trade statistics and partially in the World Bank Debtor Reporting System). On-going research at the Institute of Social Studies in The Hague aims to (re)organize existing data into a world accounting (WAM) framework (Vos 1989; Luttik 1992; de Jong, Vos, Jellema & Zebregs 1993). Perhaps a bit less ambitious are recent efforts being made at the World Bank (McCarthy et al. 1989) in this direction. Gray & Gray (1989) define a basic international flow-of-funds system, but without fully integrating it with the real internal and external balances across economies.

Chapter 3

1. The presentation follows the exposition by Grubel (1982: 6-7); and a similar one can be found in Ruffin (1984: 255-6) and in many textbooks on international trade.

2. In a survey of the literature on the ways in which banks evaluate risk, Devlin (1987: 38-39) finds that loan pricing does not play a role in risk aversion. Empirical evidence reported by Blask (1977) also confirms that country risk evaluation by banks does not appear to be a determinant of interest rates, spreads or fees.

3. For instance, Isenman (1976) combines a number of potential determinants (income and population of recipient country, balance of payments variables and political variables) of bias in aid supplies in a single regression equation which is subsequently estimated with aid flows from different sources as dependent variable. Since the regression equation is not derived as a 'reduced-form' equation, potential interdependence between the independent variables is only tested for statistical correlation, not for analytical causality.

4. The evidence presented by Frey (1984) is based on earlier estimates supplied by Dudley (1979). The following regression results were obtained using cross-section data for 17 industrialized countries over the period 1972-74:

A_i/N =	δ_0	$+\delta_1 y_i$	$+\delta_2(A_0/N_i)$	$+\delta_3(1/N_i)$	
Bilateral:	-3.86	0.003	0.02	-14.10	$\bar{R}^2$=.55
		(3.60)	(2.29)	(-1.70)	
Multilateral:	-3.09	0.002	0.04	5.22	$\bar{R}^2$=.43
		(2.42)	(2.21)	(0.82)	

where:

A_i = Aid supplied by donor country *i*;
N_i = Population of donor country *i*;
y_i = GNP per capita of donor country *i*;
A_o/N_i = Aid supplied by other donors in the donor reference group (standardized by the population of the donor *i*).

A two-stage least squares simultaneous estimation procedure was applied, because A_i depends on A_o and A_o on A_i, provided $\delta_2 \neq 0$. The hypothesized 'bandwagon' effect in aid-giving would be confirmed by a positive and significant value for δ_2, which appears to be the case in this specification. The values in parentheses are t-statistics.

5. Other surveys of the debate are in Johnson (1958), Reisen & von Trotsenburg (1988: Appendix) and Eaton (1989).

6. See also Eaton (1989) and Buiter (1989) for similar presentations.

7. Chichilnisky's model (Chichilnilsky 1980) was heavily criticized for mathematical errors in deriving the results (see e.g. Gunning 1983a, Srinivasan & Bhagwati 1983, Ranney 1984 and Saavedra-Rivano 1984). Lysy (1985) restates Chichilnisky's model omitting the mathematical errors and, as discussed in the text, shows that the results of the initial model can still be obtained but under other critical assumptions than those of Chichilnisky.

8. A distortion is defined in the sense of Bhagwati (1971) as failure to reach the Paretian condition of equality between domestic and foreign rates of transformation, e.g. due to the failure to exercise a monopoly power in trade.

9. In another paper (Bhagwati, Brecher & Hatta 1985) show that immiserizing transfers may also result in a two-country context, again in a general framework of trade and distortions.

10. The negative welfare effects of capital inflows in a tariff-protected economy and capital flows leading to foreign-ownership and profit remittances can be analysed as summarized by Cardoso & Dornbusch (1989a:1408-9). Assume a small economy producing two commodities, exportable x and importable m. Domestic consumption is determined by a utility function $U(C_{Sx}, C_{Sm})$. The domestic and international relative price of the importable are defined as θ and θ^* and consumption and output are labelled C_S and Q_S. The marginal welfare effect of a capital inflow can be determined after utility maximization and using a budget constraint at world prices as:

    $$dU/U_x = [(dQ_{Sx} + \theta^* dQ_{Sm} - r^* dK^*) + (\theta - \theta^*)dC_{Sm}]$$

    Protection will imply that $(\theta - \theta^*) > 0$, i.e. importables are overvalued, while dC_{Sm} will depend on the income effect, i.e. have the same sign of dU. Thus, the first term on the right-hand side of the equation will determine the direction of the welfare effect. The term expresses output increase at international prices less profit remittances. Since profit maximization implies that rents are equal to the domestic price output increase, i.e. $dQ_{Sx} + \theta^* dQ_{Sm} = r^* dK^*$, it follows that:

    $$dU/U_x = (\theta - \theta^*)\theta^* [dC_{Sm} - dQ_{Sm}]$$

    If dQ_{Sm} is positive, which follows if importables are capital intensive, then welfare must decline *vis-à-vis* the situation without capital inflows.

11. Note that Lewis' own North-South model (Lewis 1969) retains a dual structure in both economies, while the models discussed in this section assume complete specialization in a dual world economy.

12. The presentation of the basic two-country IS-LM model is quite standard. The simple model presentation here adapts presentations in Hamada (1985) and Dornbusch (1980: Chapter 10). Hickman (1988) gives a similar simple model structure, but adds equations for the determination of aggregate supply.

13. The papers by Chenery and associates provide the seminal references for country level analyses (see Chenery 1979 for a collection and consolidation). More recent exercises have been applied at the country and global level, estimating total financial requirements for the South. See Fishlow (1987) for an exercise for the Group of 24 using a modified two-gap specification and Taylor (1990) using a three-gap (private savings, fiscal and external gaps) approach. See also Bacha (1990) on the three-gap model.

14. Other disequilibrium or fix-price specifications of the two-gap model are in Gunning (1983b), Waelbroeck (1984) and Standaert (1985). The dependent-economy model is also referred to as the Meade-Salter-Swan model for

adjustment in the small, open economy (see e.g. Dornbusch 1980 for a basic exposition). A basic text on disequilibrium macroeconomics is Malinvaud (1977).

15. This presumed link between the domestic relative price and the real exchange rate arises from a simple argument. Suppose that the *nominal* price of NT-goods (P_{NT}) were given. Then adjustments in the equilibrium relative price would have to come through changes in the nominal price of T-goods (P_T). Given world prices, this means that the exchange rate would have to adjust. A net transfer from abroad would call for an appreciation so as to raise the relative price of NT-goods (P_{NT}/P_T) or the *real* exchange rate. With nominal prices given, changes in the exchange rate will bring about a change in relative prices. (See also Dornbusch 1980.)

16. See van Wijnbergen (1984b) for the formal exposition of the conditions under which wage indexing yields this result.

Chapter 4

1. See among others Davis (1976), Seiber (1982) and Das (1986) for accounts of early history.

2. Some authors see Paris as the strongest financial centre in the world before 1914. Kindleberger (1978: 191-2) concludes that the whole question emphasizes the rivalry between France and Britain, as well as the sensitive political nature of international finance. However, both the empirical evidence on international capital movements and the sterling domination of the Gold Standard point at London as having been the major financial centre. The Paris market trailed by a considerable margin.

3. Hughes (1979) indicates that net capital inflows averaged 50 per cent of domestic investment in Australia in the 1880s and rose to nearly 70 per cent in some years in the 1860s and 1880s. Dunning (1970) provides data according to which inflows to Canada averaged 7.5 per cent of GNP and 30 to 40 per cent of investment between 1870 and 1910. As documented by Ford (1962), capital inflows to Argentina were also enormous. There was a major boom in foreign lending to Argentina in the 1880s and another one between 1905 and 1914 (Ford 1962), with annual flows ranging from 12 to 15 per cent of GNP and financing about 40 per cent of total investment.

4. Regression results for the link between UK net capital exports and the domestic investment rate point at a significant inverse correlation. For the period 1870-1914 the following result was obtained:

$$\ln(\Delta F/Y)_N = \underset{(-6.06)}{-4.99} \quad \underset{(-2.24)}{-0.684} \ln(I/Y)_N \qquad R^2 = 0.11 \quad DW = 1.61$$

T-statistics are between parentheses. Data are taken from Feinstein (1962).

5. Dunning (1970: 164 ff.) finds UK investment in the US highly responsive to changes in the relative profitability of US and UK investment. However, he relates the *stock* of UK investment in the US to an index of share prices in US versus that in the UK. Re-estimation of the relation between the index of new (flow) foreign investment by the UK in the US relative to domestic investment in the UK and the relative profitability index (i.e. relating the two curves of Figure 3.3), using Dunning's data, yields a lower responsiveness, at a lower, though still significant, level of confidence:

$$\ln(\Delta F_{UK/US}/I_{UK}) = \underset{(0.235)}{1.11 + 0.492} \ln(r_{US}/r_{UK}) \quad R^2 = 0.10 \quad DW = 2.26$$

with the standard error for the regression coefficient between parentheses. Data are for 1871-1913. The regression coefficient is significant at the 5 per cent-level of confidence. Using a lag-specification for the relative profitability (the lagged variable being a proxy for expected yield differentials) improves the regression result somewhat:

$$\ln(\Delta F_{UK/US}/I_{UK}) = \underset{(0.222)}{0.63 + 0.726} \ln(r_{US}/r_{UK}) \quad R^2 = 0.21 \quad DW = 2.08$$

6. Feis (1930: 106) cites an 1875 report of the Select Committee on Foreign Loans of English Parliament on recent defaults in Central America, which put the blame on intermediaries in the foreign bond market, as these showed: 'reckless disregard for the borrower, misuse of loan proceeds, commissions so usurious that no honest borrower would submit to them, collusion between government representatives and issuers, and falsification of the market to dispose of the bonds.'

7. For a more extensive discussion, see Ford (1956) and Fishlow (1989).

8. See Fishlow (1989) for a discussion of the debt crisis of the 1890s in Argentina and Brazil.

9. Just before and in the first year of the Argentine debt crisis of the early 1890s, there was a steep increase in the fiscal deficit, largely due to increased government spending. Fiscal surpluses of the mid-1880s turned into major deficits, starting in 1889 with a deficit of 24 per cent of total government revenue, rising to almost 200 per cent in 1891 (calculated from data supplied in Mitchell 1982). The budget deficit was reduced in subsequent years, partly due to conditionality of foreign creditors. By 1899 Argentina was back on an almost balanced budget. In Brazil problems emerged later in the 1890s, showing major but fluctuating deficits as from 1892 onwards up to 41 per cent of government revenue in 1894 and over 100 per cent in 1898. The deficit was adjusted in one year to a small surplus in 1899. (Data are as before from Mitchell 1982.)

10. It is quite possible that the Argentinian and Brazilian debt crises were exacerbated by early forms of private capital flight. Argentine and Brazilian

private investors already had a tradition of buying up Argentine and Brazilian foreign bonds issued in London and Paris (Platt 1984, Kindleberger 1987). These politically influential groups favoured creditor intervention: the debt crisis caused bonds to fall well below their par value, while externally imposed conditionality gave new risk insurance and ensured larger repayment.

11. Great Britain had to give up 15 per cent of its foreign assets, France about half and Germany nearly all (Dunning 1970).

12. Brazil, for instance, borrowed in the 1920s to finance a growing stockpile of unsold commodities. In the mid-1920s there was an increase of 75 per cent in coffee stocks financed indirectly by long-term foreign capital, which served the purpose of preventing a fall in coffee prices (Maddison 1985, Fishlow 1985).

13. Under the Pax Brittanica, international capital flows averaged US$ 1 billion per year at 1913 prices between 1870 and 1914, while US foreign lending averaged about US$ 0.7 billion per year at constant prices between 1919 and 1929 (US$ 1.2 billion at current prices). The absolute size of international capital movements in the 1920s is small compared to those reached in the 1970s (see also Chapter 5). For the more recent period I estimated these would average by the end of the decade (1978-82) between US$ 30 and 40 billion per year at 1913 prices. In relative terms, measured against world GDP or GDP of the major creditor countries, however, the size of the flows in the 1970s is comparable to that of the 1890s and 1920s.

    It should be noted that these comparative historical data are rough estimates and that data problems hamper the construction of a consistent historical series. The estimates were derived as follows. For the period 1865-1914 stock data were applied. In section 4.2.1 it was indicated that total outstanding external liabilities were estimated at US$ 4 billion in 1865 and US$ 44 billion in 1914, which, correcting for the general price increases in the US, leads to an average flow of about US$ 1 billion at 1913 prices. Data for the 1920s were derived from Tables 4.4, 4.5 and A4.2 and the sources mentioned there. Roughly, US external claims increase by about US$ 8 billion (current prices) between 1919 and 1929, or US$ 0.8 billion per year. Since US foreign lending accounted for about two thirds of estimates of total new foreign lending and investment for the world as a whole (see also Dunning 1970: 19), the overall total is estimated at US$ 1.2 billion per annum. Adjusted for dollar price inflation this is about US$ 0.7 billion at 1913 prices. The estimates for 1978-82 refer to (i) net new *cross-the-border* bank lending and internationally traded bonds as recorded in IMF/BIS data on international financial markets and which flows are estimated in 'gross terms' at US$ 210 million per year in current prices (gross) in this period and at US$ 120 billion when corrected for redepositing of bank loans, redemptions and purchases of international bonds and double counting for bonds taken up by banks for the underpinning of their international lending activity (Table 5.3,

Chapter 5 and Watson et al. 1986, 1988); (ii) direct foreign investments (outgoing) for all countries as derived from IMF, Balance of Payments Statistics (US$ 45 billion per year); and (iii) total lending from official sources (outgoing and to LDCs only) which averaged about US$ 75 billion per year between 1978 and 1982. The current dollar price total for this period is thus US$ 330 billion including double counting in financial market activity and US$ 240 billion if corrected for this. Estimated at 1913 prices the latter would amount to an annual flow of about US$ 30 billion.

14. Data calculated from Mitchell (1983).

15. The predominant form the banks used to raise funds in the bond market was the investment trust, which pooled subscriptions of investors, placed management in hands of specialists and issued long-term securities entitling holders to a share in the trust's earnings. Following the British model and practice, these new financial institutions invested heavily in foreign bonds (Eichengreen 1988).

16. A US government report summarizes the international lending practices of the 1920s this way:

> Under the high-pressure salesmanship methods by which foreign issues were solicited and sold, our loans proved to be their undoing. The flotation of one loan frequently came to be regarded as adequate justification for further issues to the same borrower or the same country without regard to the growing burden of indebtedness. (H. Lary, *The United States in the World Economy*, Washington: US Department of Commerce, 1943; quoted in Davis 1976: 21)

Lewis (1938: 377) writes:

> Whereas in the middle decades of the nineteenth century American promotors had scoured Europe in search of foreign lenders, in 1925-29 they were searching the world over for foreign borrowers. At one time, according to the testimony before the Senate Committee on Finance investigating the sale of foreign securities in the United States, there were 29 representatives of American financial houses in Colombia alone trying to negotiate loans for the national government, for the departments and for other possible borrowers.

17. Regression analysis for the correlation between US net capital exports and domestic investment rates gives the following result for 1920-1935:

$$\ln(\Delta F/Y)_N = \underset{(-8.51)}{-4.28} + \underset{(1.86)}{0.388}\ln(I/Y)_N \quad R^2 = 0.22 \quad DW = 2.34$$

T-statistics are between parentheses; the regression coefficient is significant at the 5 per cent-level of confidence and its sign is positive as expected. Data are derived from Mitchell (1982).

18. Both internal and external causes contributed to the 'Great Crash'. On the internal causes, historical analyses have pointed at a number of domestic structural problems facing the US economy (Galbraith 1955, Thorp 1984): (i) the unequal income distribution led to a tendency towards excess supply and excess savings, as productivity had increased sharply in the 1920s but mass purchasing power had not; (ii) an unhealthy corporate structure; and (iii) an unhealthy banking structure with a large number of small banks with unsound liability-to-capital ratios. As the stock market boomed in the US on a wave of speculation related to the savings surplus of the rich, US interest rates peaked in 1928, after which US capital exports began to fall sharply, increasing the transfer problem for the debtor countries. Turning to the external causes, the economic weaknesses of the major economy interacted with the prevailing world economic conditions. Jointly with the internal causes, the large accumulated foreign debt in several countries combined with an excess supply of primary commodities would have provoked the crash. The transfer problem of the borrowing nations forced them to run export surpluses (mainly of primary commodities) while domestic demand in the major creditor country contracted. This provoked a collapse of commodity markets, debt-servicing problems in the debtor countries, a deepening of the recession in the major creditor countries and, consequently, risk-adverse behaviour (if not panic) on the stock exchange and in financial markets.

    Other, less convincing, explanations, particularly those prevailing in the monetarist-Keynesian debate, focus on much more aggregate questions such as whether the crash was caused by monetary policy (Friedman & Schwartz 1963) or by an autonomous fall in aggregate demand (Temin 1976). Brunner (1981) provides an overview of the monetarist-Keynesian debate on cause and effect in the Great Depression.

19. Abreu (1984) documents this in more detail.

20. No conclusive evidence exists on the mechanisms of the recovery. A mainstream interpretation is that domestic industrial growth was promoted by state-led demand expansion and shifts in relative prices induced by the import-substituting industrialization policies (ECLA 1950, Thorp & Londoño 1984). An additional explanation is that this output growth would not have been possible without the income distribution shifts and the investments in domestic production capacity that had already taken place in the 1920s (FitzGerald 1984). At least in the larger Latin American countries, some infrastructural and industrial capacity had already been built up during the boom in international lending. The collapse of export prices shifted income distribution in favour of non-agricultural profit incomes, because the internal terms of trade moved against food production (see Appendix Table A4.3) which allowed workers to maintain their real wages (in terms of food production), while wage costs for industrial producers (in terms of industrial prices) could be kept low. The latter was especially strong where major export crops were at the same time major food items (Peru, Argentina and

Mexico). Also in the case of major coffee exporters (Colombia, Brazil) domestic food prices followed the coffee price (Thorp & Londoño 1984, Malan et al. 1977). This, in combination with the available production capacity and effective import substitution, allowed for high accumulation rates in industrial sectors despite the foreign-exchange constraint. A number of smaller Latin American countries, e.g. Bolivia, Ecuador, and those in Central America, were not able to pursue a similar adjustment strategy. They lacked even the beginning of an industrial base, leaving them with little option but to wait for export recovery.

21. Proposals to set up a plan along these lines for Latin America were rejected by both the Truman and Eisenhower administrations. According to Griffith-Jones (1984), the main reasons were political; Latin America was considered to play a very secondary role in the Cold War.

22. The US expanded aid to India and Pakistan as well as to Latin America. The latter expansion was motivated by the 'Alliance for Progress', the political response to US fear of a repetition of the Cuban revolution elsewhere on the continent.

23. At a more aggregate level, cross-section analysis on the basis of data for the late 1960s has suggested a negative correlation between aid and national savings (Griffin 1970, Weisskopf 1972). Thus, not all aid went into productive investment. Obviously, an important part of the aid was probably never intended for that purpose, but rather took the form of food aid, social services projects, and so on. However, institutional and sectoral adjustments are likely to be at the background of the observed negative correlation, factors far more complex than what such simple correlations can tell us.

24. Where these occurred in the 1950s and 1960s (e.g. in Argentina, Brazil, Chile, Ghana, Indonesia, Peru and Turkey) the accumulation of short-term debt (trade and other) to finance budget deficits and long-term projects, created debt servicing problems when terms of trade deteriorated and export earnings fell (World Bank 1985: 16).

Chapter 5

1. International banking and financial statistics are largely incompatible with balance of payments statistics. For a discussion see IMF (1987a), World Bank/IMF/BIS/OECD (1988) and Vos (1988a). The concept of a World Accounting Matrix (WAM) has been designed as a tool which among other things can reconcile different data sources (Vos 1989). However, at time of writing no time series of WAMs were available, so that while appropriate time series for individual data sources are used for the analysis in this chapter, they ignore possible discrepancies between comparable statistics in different tables. In this respect the figures used in Table 5.4 and those in Fig-

ure 5.1 show some discrepancies, but due to differences in coverage these are not directly traceable.

2. The table defines private international *financial* markets as *cross-border* bank transactions and international bond issues only. The flow of international bank lending is net of redepositing among banks and new international bonds are net of redemptions and repurchases, and of double counting; that is, bonds taken up by commercial banks to underpin their international lending activity are excluded. The focus is thus on international financial transactions between non-banks.

3. Vos (1986: Table A.7) reports on available evidence from BIS and IMF data. Balance of payments data on the current account surplus of the major oil exporters and available data on their foreign investments from financial market data show a reasonable match until 1980, after which the different sources show large statistical discrepancies. Between 1974 and 1981 the stylized pattern of the use of the financial surplus of oil exporters is that about 50 per cent flows into bank deposits (largely in Eurobank deposits), 25 per cent is channeled directly to non-oil developing countries in the form of official transfers and concessional loans and the remaining share is invested in Northern government securities (particularly in the US), other direct and portfolio investment and financial support to multilateral agencies. Between 1980 and 1983 investment in US government securities increase, while there is a withdrawal of bank deposits.

4. It seems reasonable to assume that the first oil shock should not be regarded as completely 'exogenous', determined by OPEC price-setting policies, but that it resulted partly from surging demand for oil generated by rapid growth in the major industrial countries and, in the later 1970s, in major developing countries as well; see, for example, Haberler (1986: 85) and Pereira, Ulph & Tims (1987).

5. See among others Sachs (1981), Feldstein (1983), Dooley, Frankel & Mathieson (1987).

6. The Eurocurrency market is the term for foreign currency deposits in banks located outside the country that issues the currency in which the deposit is denominated. About 70 per cent of all Eurocurrency deposits are denominated in dollars and the first banks to accept such deposits were located in Europe – two reasons for the custom to speak of the *Euro*dollar market. European financial centres still dominate the Eurocurrency market (particularly London), but financial *offshore* centres, located in Hong Kong, Singapore, Panama and a number of Caribbean islands, have gained importance.

   In the early years, influenced by growing world trade and with the dollar as the international reserve currency, the Eurocurrency market constituted an attractive portfolio because of the convenience of holding short-term dollar deposits in a bank on the same continent as one's business, and because of the market's freedom from bank regulations and from capital controls by the United States authorities. From 1964 to 1973 the market expanded further as bank lending by US banks to abroad was restricted in an attempt to cure the economy's tendency towards balance of payments deficits. This tended to raise interest rates abroad, including in the Eurocurrency markets, relative to those in the United States. Since international corporations (in particular) were not prohibited from switching dollar accounts from US banks to Eurobanks, they could take advantage of the higher interest rates. This process was abetted by the US Interest Equalization Tax Law of 1964-73 which increased the after-tax interest rate differential between US and foreign interest rates on dollar holdings and by the still prevailing Glass-Steagall Act of 1933 separating commercial and investment banking in the United States and thereby barring banks from underwriting bonds.

7. Folkerts-Landau (1985) summarizes the legal aspects. If the foreign creditor is a large and nationally influential private entity in a developing country, then its domestic assets have also proven to be immune from seizure by a foreign creditor. In theory, the Sovereign Immunities Act of 1976 removed the doctrine of absolute 'sovereign immunity' from US courts as the act proclaims that immunity will not be recognized if the relevant borrower is a *commercial* agent of a foreign state or its agencies. In practice, however, it remains difficult for creditors to lay hands on the foreign assets of debtors, even if held in a bank that forms part of the loan syndicate, because it will be difficult to match the identities of of particular private borrowers and private depositors as the former tend to be limited liability firms and the latter individuals. This problem of 'sovereign risk' holds particularly in the case of developing countries. Moreover, domestic courts in developing countries do not tend to give foreign creditors equal standing with the resident borrowers.

8. This insurance changed the domestic financial system of the industrialized countries, but also indirectly covered risks on domestic and foreign loans. In most industrial countries this process of institutional change was completed by the early 1970s, either through direct state control and ownership as in Italy or via automatic discounting facilities as in France, Germany and the United Kingdom. In the United States the Federal Deposit Insurance Corporation (FDIC), founded in 1934, was transformed from an agency that could merge bankrupt banks and supply some refunding to individual depositors in failing banks, into a financial stabilization agency that guarantees the total deposit and debt liabilities of the major banks. These domestic financial changes were arranged internationally through the Bank of International Settlements (BIS), the meeting point of the presidents of the central banks of the major countries. Insurance against default risk and the understandings of international commercial banks about the lender-of-last-resort obligations of the national central banks encouraged bank lending to developing countries.

9. For full descriptions of the mechanics of loan syndication, see Bee (1975), McDonald (1982) and Lewis & Davis (1987).

10. Data derived from World Bank, *World Debt Tables*, computer tapes (1987/88).

11. For detailed accounts of the collection and exchange of information and the establishment of criteria for country risk indicators, see Devlin (1986: 195 ff), Gwynne (1983: 22-26) and Bogdanowicz-Bindert & Sacks (1984). The latter suggests that new entrants often relied heavily on the 'placement memoranda' prepared by the lead banks, which were little more than sophisticated tourist guides, prepared as sales documents rather than serious analytical statements on the country (Ibid.: 71).

12. The spreads refer to public and publicly guaranteed debt and may thus be expected to reflect sovereign risk.

13. *Euromoney*'s 'country-risk league tables' of creditworthiness rankings of sovereign borrowers just before (1982) and after (1983) the debt crisis show that following behind the industrialized countries (with only somewhat lower rankings for Italy, Spain and Greece), is a large group of middle-income LDCs and Eastern European sovereign borrowers. Low-income countries are at the bottom-end, with high-ranked China and India as exceptions. A comparison of the 1982 and 1983 tables shows a steep fall towards the bottom of the listing for debt-ridden countries like Brazil and Poland, while other hard hit countries like Mexico and Argentina began to show recoveries in creditworthiness scores as early as 1983. By 1988, most of the Latin American debtor countries shared the ranks of low-income countries, but the overall ordering showed similar patterns as in 1982-83. (See *Euromoney*, October 1983 and September 1988.) Comparisons over time of these rankings are difficult, however, because of various changes in coverage and methodology. Noteworthy are the major changes in presentation, country coverage and method of creditworthiness measurement in the years prior to February 1982 and after the debt crisis (as of September 1982). Multinational banks tend to have their own ranking systems, but *Euromoney*'s list is considered to be influential.

14. This 'follow-the-herd' credo is lucidly discussed in Guttentag & Herring (1985). Sachs (1984b) interprets this type of behaviour as *rational* lending strategies as he contends that in making their decisions, bankers must anticipate actions of other banks: ' Since no bank alone can extend all the credit that Mexico or Brazil needs to stay afloat, it is prudent for each bank to lend new money only if other banks are making new loans as well. Because of this interdependence of the banks' decisions, aggregate bank lending may stop not because the country's position has changed, but because each individual bank believes that all of the other banks have decided to stop lending . . .'.

15. As indicated, banks showed a strong increase in risk-aversion against lending to the South in the 1980s. This conclusion can also be drawn on the basis of the recent empirical literature on creditworthiness of developing countries. Some of the applied models are discussed below. A more simple test executed in the context of this study confirms the hypothesis of a shifting market perception. Simple regression analysis confirms this, using the flow of new lending (ΔF) as dependent variable and as independent variables debt-to-GNP (F/Y) and debt-service ratios [$(a+i)F/E$], both lagged one year, which are taken as solvency and liquidity indicators of borrowers (expected creditworthiness). Pooled time-series and cross-section data for a sample of 16 major private borrowers from the World Debt Tables yield for 1974-81 and 1982-88 (t-statistics are in parentheses):

1974-81:

$$\ln(\Delta F) = \underset{(-19.7)}{-6.9} \quad \underset{(-3.1)}{-0.63} \ln(F/Y)_{-1} \quad \underset{(6.6)}{+1.03} \ln[(a+i)F/E]_{-1}$$

$\bar{R}^2 = 0.23$ $F = 21.8$ $DW = 1.73$ $n = 148$

1982-88:

$$\ln(\Delta F) = \underset{(5.4)}{5.9} \quad \underset{(-4.3)}{-2.99} \ln(F/Y)_{-1} \quad \underset{(2.8)}{+2.64} \ln[(a+i)(F/E)]_{-1}$$

$\bar{R}^2 = 0.15$ $F = 10.5$ $DW = 1.57$ $n = 119.$

All coefficients are significant at the 1 per cent level of confidence. The substantial increase in the coefficient for solvency (F/Y) reflects the 'loan revulsion' in the 1980s, while the positive sign of the parameter of borrowers' liquidity, and the increase therein in the 1980s, probably means that much of the new borrowing was needed to service debt. The same result is obtained (though with higher parameter values) if the debt–export ratio (F/E) is used as solvency indicator.

The independent variables have been found to be significant in several other econometric studies analysing credit rationing and creditworthiness assessment in bank lending behaviour to the South. These exercises provide insight into the extent of the shifts in behavioural patterns. McDonald (1982) gives a useful review of several models. The most common independent variables found to be significant are GNP per capita, the debt/GNP or debt/export ratio and the debt service ratio (and related variables, such as GNP growth, export growth and terms of trade). GNP per capita performs well on a large sample of developing countries, including low-income countries, and confirms our earlier hypothesis of the existence of different risk classes between Southern borrowers. Classics in this literature are the papers by Frank & Cline (1971), applying a discriminant analysis, Feder & Just (1977) who suggest the use of binary logit models, and Eaton & Gersovitz (1981), who include a 'regime-switching' econometric technique to allow for the possibility of disequilibrium credit markets. Hajivassiliou (1989) extends the model of Eaton-Gersovitz and uses panel data. The excercise confirms the structural breaks in behaviour also observed in the text, but Hajivassiliou warns that one cannot extrapolate the model results without incorporating recent data, which amounts to saying that the model has little predictive value. Even if the above-mentioned factors are the relevant explanatory variables, they do not indicate the point of borrower solvency at which banks will be willing to resume lending in the 1990s. Perceived creditworthiness instead seems highly dependent on institutional factors and subjective determinants of the market confidence of private creditors.

16. As indicated these results confirm those of earlier studies, see for example Edelman & Chenery (1977), Dowling & Hiemenz (1985). The regression analysis underlying Figure 5.5 uses OECD data on bilateral aid and World Bank data for population size and GNP per capita. Bilateral aid flows were averaged for the period 1983-86 and divided by the 1986 population size for 76 developing countries. Regression results were as follows:

1983-86:

$$\ln(AID/P) = \underset{(-1.67)}{-3.16} \; \underset{(-6.42)}{-0.58} \ln(P) \; \underset{(2.78)}{+3.69} \ln(Y/P) \; \underset{(-3.08)}{-0.70} \ln(Y/P)^2$$

$\bar{R}^2(adj.) = 0.398 \quad F = 17.5 \quad DW = 2.35 \quad n = 76$

where:

AID = Bilateral aid flow from DAC countries to LDCs.
P = Population size.
Y = GNP (US$).

T-statistics are between parentheses; the regression coefficients are significant at the 1 per cent level, the constant at 10 per cent level.

The above regression model yielded the best results using alternative specifications of the same variables. The results are similar for comparative estimates in earlier periods:

1969–72:

$$\ln(AID/P) = \underset{(-1.20)}{-4.58} \; \underset{(-7.77)}{-0.57} \ln(P) \; \underset{(2.08)}{+2.75} \ln(Y/P) \; \underset{(-2.36)}{-0.27} \ln(Y/P)^2$$

$\bar{R}^2(adj.) = 0.410 \quad F = 22.5 \quad DW = 2.35 \quad n = 76$

It is worth noting that this non-linear functional relationship holds for bilateral aid flows only. Total aid flows (bilateral and multilateral) show a better fit for a more linear relationship between aid per capita and population size and GNP per capita:

1983–86:

$$\ln(AIDtot/P) = \underset{(-10.40)}{2.98} \; \underset{(-9.81)}{-0.64} \ln(P) \; \underset{(-3.85)}{-0.36} \ln(Y/P)$$

$\bar{R}^2(adj.) = 0.410 \quad F = 22.5 \quad DW = 2.35 \quad n = 76$

Regressions with 'aid to GNP' as dependent variables gave outcomes similar to those presented here.

17. See (among others) Nicoletti (1988), Masson & Knight (1986) and Van Wijnbergen (1988).

18. Data were derived from IMF, *Balance of Payments Statistics Yearbook, 1989.*

19. Singer (1989) supplies evidence, on the basis of cross-country calculations for Latin American debtors, that higher debt pressure (measured by the debt service ratio) is positively related with the expansion of export volumes, but negatively correlated with export unit values and the terms of trade. Singer calls the shift 'desperation export sales'. Information from commodity market trends confirms the 'fallacy of composition' of export promotion in many countries. The quantity of Latin American copper exports, for instance, rose by 12 per cent and the copper price fell by 35 per cent between 1980 and 1985, so that the value of exports fell by 28 per cent. For ten 'core' commodities mainly exported by Southern economies, the volume of exports rose by 8 per cent while the average export unit value fell by 26 per cent and the export value by 21 per cent. The implied elasticity of demand (around 0.3 in each case) agrees with other empirical findings (Singer 1989) and underpins the hypothesis that simultaneous supply expansion by a large enough number of producers leads to perverse export-earning effects in primary commodity markets.

20. Following a liquidity crisis in servicing short-term external debt, the Philippine Central Bank has, since the early 1970s, maintained a relatively developed system of external debt management. External borrowing was constrained by putting a cap of 20 per cent on total debt service payments to total foreign exchange earnings. In practice the cap did not act, however, as a real limit on external borrowing. The critical ratio only referred to debt service on long-term external debt, while net inflows (long-term and short-term) were part of the denominator. The limit on borrowing would be based on the actual debt service-to-total foreign exchange availability ratio of the previous year. Clearly, with high capital inflows in one year, permitted borrowing in the next year could increase further. See for a further analysis on the nature of this debt management system, introduced under Republic Act 6142 of November 1970, Dohner & Intal (1989) and Lamberte, Lim, Vos & Yap (1992).

21. Rewriting equation 4.5, the usual formulation of the debt-dynamics accounting rule is:

    $$\Delta f_S = [i-(p_S - p_N)-g_{S_e}] f_S + t_S$$

    where Δf_S is taken to be the adjusting variable.

22. In value terms, import adjustment in the 1980s has tended to be proportional over all import categories, since import structures by major commodity groups have not been subject to major shifts (see Appendix Table A5.2). For the South as a whole the share of capital goods imports (machinery) is typically about 30 per cent of total merchandise imports plus domestic investment and this share was more or less sustained between 1980 and 1990. The pattern is similar for the different country groups. However, given the decline of real commodity prices relative to manufactured goods prices in this period, this constancy in the *value* structure of imports of LDCs tends to reflect falling shares for manufactures, and particularly machinery, in the *volume* structure of imports. The contraction in import demand thus contributed to falling investment ratios and growth rates.

23. Public sector data for developing countries are weak and often not easily comparable across countries (World Bank 1988). The IMF *Government Finance Statistics* probably form the most complete data set, though comparable data are restricted to central government budgets only. Tables 5.10a-d use this source of information to give an approximation of the fiscal balance.

24. Various definitions of the real exchange rate exist. The relative price of home goods to foreign goods (or non-traded/traded goods) is one of them. See Dornbusch (1988) for a useful overview.

25. A shift towards more capital-intensive investment projects with long gestation lags will push up capital-output ratios and may create adjustment problems and falling output if external and internal financing resources are restrained. A crude indicator of the productivity of investment can be obtained by using gross fixed investment and GDP growth data to compute marginal capital-output ratios. Table 5.12 shows average ICORs for three subperiods since 1973. The change in these ICORs over time suggests an overall tendency towards increasing capital-output ratios. Official and diversified borrowers show no such trend, but private borrowers and particularly oil-exporters and non-oil primary exporters with recent major debt problems show a substantial increase in their ICORs. Under the present method of estimation, ICORs shift upwards and tend to fluctuate strongly in trough years of the business cycle; some were even cancelled out by negative GDP growth in several LDCs during the 1980s. ICORs will be lower and more stable during peak years (Lluch 1986). The estimates for 1983-86 reflect trough years for most official and private borrowers and thus may be less indicative; however, the upward shift in the preceding periods could perhaps be seen as an indication of a move towards lower investment productivity during the period of heavy external borrowing.

    Nevertheless, this evidence is at best indicative; it does not provide definitive conclusions regarding the efficiency of externally financed investment in the 1970s.

26. Available evidence indicates that during the major boom period of commercial bank lending to the Third World, 1978-82, all major private borrowers reported in the Morgan Guarantee, *World Financial Markets* showed a significant real appreciation of their exchange rate. Most Latin American borrowers have attempted to use the exchange rate as part of import-substitution policies and as an anti-inflationary device by not devaluing to compensate for domestic price increases. The ensuing overvaluation of the currency curtailed export profits and promoted imports and it is likely that they reflect the sectoral shift in spending towards non-traded goods. It is therefore noteworthy that countries like Argentina, Brazil and Chile also show real appreciation despite the substantial import liberalization and relatively flexible exchange-rate policies they pursued in the 1970s. Large-scale external borrowing may be part of the explanation of such trends. After the debt crisis in mid-1982, net transfers from external sources declined steeply and most LDC-PB implemented large devaluations.

    Real appreciation of exchange rates has also been observed in many 'official borrowers'. ODA flows may lead to excess demand for non-traded goods (via a larger fiscal deficit) *ex ante* and, with traded goods prices fixed in the world market, this will lead to real appreciation of the exchange rate (assuming a correspondence between the relative price of traded and non-traded goods and the real exchange rate). Econometric evidence to support this hypothesis (van Wijnbergen 1986b: Table 1) shows a positive elasticity of the real exchange rate with respect to the real volume of aid flows for a number of official borrowers in Sub-Saharan Africa over the period 1969-83. Van Wijnbergen finds that the size of the elasticities (summed over two years) ranges from a low 0.20 in Tanzania to a high 0.87 in Ghana, with Kenya, Egypt and Malawi between the two. Parameter estimates, based on time series data for 1969-83, are significant in all countries except Tanzania. The evidence is suggestive, but the country sample is small and more analysis is required to disentangle the precise mechanisms of the observed link. Bearing these reservations in mind, the evidence shows that aid flows may create macroeconomic side-effects by exerting upward pressure on the real exchange rate. Real exchange rate appreciation may provide a disincentive to export production and incentives for resource shifts towards non-traded goods sectors and, possibly, for the growth of parallel markets.

27. Pastor (1990), Hermes & Lensink (1990) and Vos (1992) apply comparable econometric specifications to similar definitions of private foreign asset acquisition. Pastor (1990) measures resident capital outflow for eight Latin American private borrowers (Argentina, Brazil, Chile, Colombia, Mexico, Peru, Uruguay, and Venezuela) from balance of payments data by taking change in external debt and foreign direct investment inflows and substracting the current account deficit and change in reserves. It thus includes foreign asset acquisition by the domestic banking sector. This last element is excluded from the estimates of ΔJ_S in Tables 5.10a-d and Table 5.15. Hermes & Lensink (1990) use the same definition as Pastor, but also exclude

the banking sector. Vos (1992) also uses this non-bank concept, but in addition gives estimates for trade misinvoicing and unrecording of workers' remittances from abroad. The main econometric results are:

Pastor for Latin America (pooled regression, 1973-86)

(i) Total sample (n = 82)

$$\Delta J_S/\theta E_S = \underset{(-1.21)}{0.08p} \; \underset{(3.57)}{+0.32\,FINC} \; \underset{(2.11)}{+0.003\,RER} \; \underset{(2.40)}{+2.62} \; (\Delta F_S/Y_S) \; \underset{(-2.77)}{-1.33\,g_S}$$

$R^2 = 0.49$

(ii) Countries without capital controls (n = 35)

$$\Delta J_S/\theta E_S = \underset{(-1.68)}{0.19p} \; \underset{(1.77)}{+0.25\,FINC} \; \underset{(1.55)}{+0.004\,RER} \; \underset{(2.34)}{+4.88} \; (\Delta F_S/Y_S) \; \underset{(-1.67)}{-1.76\,g_S}$$

$R^2 = 0.53$

(iii) Countries with capital controls (n = 47)

$$\Delta J_S/\theta E_S = \underset{(-1.68)}{0.02p} \; \underset{(1.68)}{+0.23\,FINC} \; \underset{(0.45)}{+0.001\,RER} \; \underset{(0.53)}{+0.63} \; (\Delta F_S/Y_S) \; \underset{(-1.36)}{-0.65\,g_S}$$

$R^2 = 0.02$

Hermes & Lensink (1990) for six Sub-Saharan African countries
(pooled regression 1976-87, n = 59)

$$\Delta J_S/Y_S = \underset{(-2.17)}{-0.02} \; \underset{(0.07)}{+\,0.002\,FINC} \; \underset{(9.62)}{+0.75} \; (\Delta F_S/Y_S)$$

$R^2 = 0.63$ $\quad F = 47.5$

$$\Delta J_S/Y_S = \underset{(-2.52)}{-0.04} \; \underset{(1.32)}{+\,0.037\text{p}} \; \underset{(1.25)}{+\,0.0008\,\text{RER}} \; \underset{(9.54)}{+\,0.76} \; (\Delta F_S/Y_S)$$

$R^2 = 0.65$ $\quad F = 34.2$

Vos (1992) for the Philippines (time series 1972-88)

$$\Delta J_S/Y_S = \underset{(-3.03)}{0.21} \; \underset{(1.86)}{+0.365FINC} \; \underset{(-3.20)}{-0.216RER} \; \underset{(2.10)}{+0.54} \; (\Delta Fs/Ys) \; \underset{(2.91)}{+0.09} \; (Js/Ys)_{-1}$$

$R^2 = 0.58$ $\quad DW = 2.10$ $\quad F = 6.42$

where:

Js = stock of private foreign asset holdings;
Ys = GDP or GNP;
θEs = total exports;
p = domestic inflation rate;
$FINC$ = exchange rate adjusted rate-of-return differential (regression for Philippines refers to real interest differentials, LIBOR and Phil-

ippine T-Bills, lagged one year); RER is expected real exchange rate depreciation (appreciation, in Philippine case);

g_S = GDP growth rate.

28. Using the data from Hermes & Lensink (1990: Table 1 and 2) and GNP figures from the World Tables (1989/90), the following regression results were obtained:

$$\text{(i)}\ \Delta J_S/Y_S = \underset{(0.19)}{0.01} + \underset{(6.38)}{0.24}\ (J_S/Y_S)_{-1}$$

$R^2 = 0.36$ $F = 98.4$ n = 65

$$\text{(ii)}\ \Delta J_S/Y_S = \underset{(-0.81)}{-0.03} + \underset{(3.64)}{0.18}\ (J_S/Y_S)_{-1}$$

$R^2 = 0.27$ $F = 107.7$ n = 35

where equation (i) uses the residual balance of payments measure for private foreign asset accumulation (see note 29) and equation (ii) uses estimates derived from IMF banking statistics (*International Financial Statistics*, line 7xrd) for external non-resident deposit holdings.

29. A not uncommon feature of lifestyles of rich households is to have children studying abroad and spending at least part of the year in the North. One child studying in the US and one foreign trip might require US$ 30,000 per year. Assume for argument's sake that because of foreign exchange restrictions this is not financed from current domestic income, but from yields on foreign assets. If the average rate of return on dollar-denominated assets is 6 per cent (1989), a foreign asset position of at least half a million dollars would be required. Applying these assumptions for the Philippines, possibly 0.1 per cent of Philippine households (i.e. about 1000 households) may be in such a position. This would imply a target level of foreign asset holdings of US$ 5 billion, or US$ 2.5 billion if half of consumptive spending abroad would be financed out of domestic income. In the latter case one quarter of total estimated private foreign asset holdings would still be explained by this type of asset demand.

30. See Sachs (1988a) for an extensive analysis of creditor-country government intervention. The US government in particular intervened right from the start, in pressing for the settlement of Mexico's liquidity problems in 1982 by calling for a rescheduling operation supported with IMF credits. This was to become the model for 'rescue' operations in the rest of the LDC-PBs with debt servicing problems.

31. New net long-term official lending to LDC-OBs was US$ 74 billion (accumulated) between 1983 and 1988. Total arrears amounted to US$ 65 billion in the same period. (Estimates based on IMF, *Balance of Payments Statistics*, various issues.)

Chapter 6

1. Spreads are thus viewed as a 'mark-up' over the base rate. Spreads and interest rates moved broadly in the same direction in the 1970s and 1980s, although the mark-up fell with enhanced competition in the 1970s and increased in the 1980s. The latter tendency has been explained in Chapter 5 (but see also Folkerts-Landau 1985) as a result of the inclusion of the cost of debt rescheduling in the spread, rather than as a mechanism of risk aversion.

2. Guttentag & Herring (1985, 1986) seek determinants in the cognitive psychology of decision-makers inside banks and loan syndicates. Perceptions of default probability related to bank lending in the 1970s could not be based on rational expectations based on past experience. The assessment of country risk has to be based on a meagre statistical record. Furthermore, since the last major period of lending to LDCs, the 1920s, the world economy has changed structurally. None of the new generation of bankers had direct experience with the episode of defaults of the 1930s. Subjective perceptions thus will have dominated lending decisions. 'Ignorant' of the experience of the 1930s, bankers tended to perceive default risk as low in the 1970s. By the late 1970s many, particularly US, banks must have seen the risk of high shares of developing country debt in their portfolios and high debt-export ratios of many of their debtors. That banks continued, and even increased lending was a sign of 'disaster myopia'. This would explain why many LDC borrowers experienced an increase in international bank loans shortly before actually entering into debt service problems (Brau & Williams 1983, Eaton & Taylor 1986, Chapter 5). As loans built up and perceived risk grew in the late 1970s and early 1980s, banks felt pressures to retreat from lending to the South. Instead, perhaps hoping to avoid a payments crisis or incapable of admitting having funded apparently bad loans, they increased lending (particularly in short maturities) just before the crisis set in. Guttentag and Herring see this as an example of cognitive dissonance, 'a psychological mechanism designed to protect the decision-maker's self-esteem when information arises that casts doubt on the wisdom of past decisions' (Guttentag & Herring 1985: 133).

3. In many cases banks enhanced the attractiveness of commercial borrowing by providing untied loans at free disposition. Devlin (1986: Tables 40-41) gives evidence for Peru and Bolivia (both diversified borrowers, LDC–DBs), with substantial debts to commercial banks. In both cases free-disposition loans formed a substantial proportion of bank lending: 49 per cent of commercial bank lending to Peru in the 1970s was used for refinancing of outstanding debt and debt-servicing and another 28 per cent consisted of free-disposition loans. In Bolivia, between 1970 and 1979, an average of 18 per cent of total borrowing from banks went to refinancing and 43 per cent consisted of free-disposition loans.

4. Even under very adverse circumstances, defensive lending may be in the interest of creditors by avoiding an almost certain debt repudiation by a borrower and increasing the expected present value of the existing debt. Krugman (1989) clarifies the point as follows. Let B be a country's outstanding debt and d be the subjective discount that creditors place on that debt (e.g. inferred from the secondary market price for the debt, if that market is sufficiently well developed). The argument for defensive lending now rests on the assumption that by relending part of the interest obligations to the debtor, and thus averting an immediate liquidity crisis, creditors can reduce the discount to d'. The cost of defensive lending will be the expected loss of possible (partial) non-servicing on the new lending ($d'L$, with L being the value of new lending), while the benefit will be an increase in the value of existing claims: $(d-d')B$. Defensive lending will be beneficial to the creditor as long as:

   $$d'L < (d - d')B$$

   The difficulty is of course to predict the effect of L on d, and to explain why the commercial banks did not opt for a defensive lending strategy in the 1980s. Another difficulty inherent to defensive lending may be that of a 'free-rider problem'. Collectively, it may be clear that new lending by creditors will raise the expected value of the *collective* claims of all creditors, but for each *individual* creditor it may be preferable not to participate and even to withdraw its own credits to leave the debt burden to the other banks. (Sachs 1984a gives a formal theoretical analysis of the 'free rider problem'.) This incentive will be larger for the smaller banks in the syndicate. The concentration of debt in the hands of the large leading banks leads one to expect that the withdrawal of the smaller banks will only have a minor effect on net bank lending, as indeed seems to have been the case in practice (Krugman 1989). However, the simplest explanation for the low new bank lending to problem debtors in the 1980s is given in the text: they did not have to because they felt their bargaining position was strong enough and support was given by 'third parties' to protect their claims.

5. Notice that $CA_N=(I_N-S_N)_p+DEF_N$ and further that the Northern fiscal deficit includes aid supplies (ΔA) on the expenditure side and the financing of the Northern deficit equals the change in government debt and the change in money holdings (borrowing with the Central Bank): $DEF_N = \Delta DC_N - \Delta H_N$.

Chapter 7

1. A convenient, complementary assumption is that with the imported capital goods, modern technical production conditions tend to be introduced, so that growth in the South does not absorb the labour surplus.

2. Findlay (1980, 1984) assumes neo-classical, steady-state growth conditions for the Northern economy. See also Chapter 3.

3. Dominique (1985) supplies a version of the Taylor-model including a Southern region exporting manufactures, but sustains the overall model conclusions drawn in the two-region specification. Marquez & Pauly (1987) supply an empirical version of the Taylor model, but include in the Southern economy exports of oil, non-oil primary commodities and manufactures. In accordance with the theoretical model, the econometric model predicts bleak prospects for the South as with its current bargaining position in the world economy the region is not able to benefit on equal terms with the North from a worldwide economic recovery.

4. See Sawyer (1985) for suggestions of how to model wage bargaining in a Kaleckian macroeconomic framework.

5. Recent empirical investigations into the relative contribution of public and private investment on output growth can be found in Khan & Reinhart (1990) and Sarmad (1990). Conclusions vary. The former study concludes, for a cross-section of 21 developing countries, that during the 1970s the contribution of public investment was not significantly different from zero. Sarmad's study confirms these results for the 1970s, but suggests that during the 1980s the marginal productivity of public capital was positive and significantly different from zero and even higher than that of private capital investment.

6. Alternatively, the mark-up could be made a function of factors determining the degree of monopoly (such as the level of concentration, the degree of collusion and the elasticity of demand; see e.g. Cowling 1981). In the model the assumption of excess capacity in the North is maintained throughout. An adjustable mark-up, t, may be allowed for if the possibility of full capacity is left open. Assume potential output (the capacity constraint) of the manufactured commodity is determined through a simple production function. Actual output is determined by demand. If capacity limits are reached, e.g. due to a faster growth of consumption than investment, it is assumed that the market power of firms is enhanced and further demand pressure will drive up the mark-up (τ) to correct the excess demand situation (a higher τ will drive down $_N$ and so consumption demand, and will increase the rate of profit and stimulate investment in production capacity). The following relations may be formalized:

$Q_N^{max} = \sigma_N K_N$ potential output

where σ_N is a given output-capital ratio. Output adjustment conditions may be formulated as:

$dQ_N/dt = g(Q_N, Q_N^{max})$ if $u < u^{max}$

$d\tau/dt = f(Q_N, Q_N^{max})$ if $u = u^{max}$

where:

$u^{max} = Q_N^{max}/K_N$ and $u = Q_N/K_N$

The mark-up adjustment in response to demand pressures when capacity limits are reached is in full agreement with the Kaleckian interpretation of an oligopolistic market structure.

7. The Northern labour market is not spelled out in the present model version, but – as suggested by Sawyer (1982, 1985) – this wage determination from oligopolistic firm behaviour may be combined with the real wage bargaining of organized labour. Since this is not at the heart of the present analysis, the Northern wage rate is set, in effect exogenously, by equation 7.12a.
8. Zero savings out of wage income is an extreme version of the differential savings proposition usually applied in the structuralist literature and in post-Keynesian and Kaleckian economics. In the present model, the distribution of wages and profits is determined by the degree of monopoly. The level of output and the level of real wages (in terms of the Northern commodity) are heavily influenced by the interaction of wage demands and profit demands. In this view, the impact of differential savings propensities is further reduced and at the limit those propensities merely serve to translate wages and profits into levels of consumption and savings (see also Sawyer 1985).
9. The credit supply function for the Southern market segment adapts the function given in Chapter 6 (equation 6.5). As no separate risk classes within the South are distinguished by the STAC model, the variables which were seen to determine *a priori* access to the market, i.e. income per capita and economic size were omitted from 7.25.
10. I am indebted to David Vines and Lance Taylor for comments and suggestions on this point.
11. In Appendix A7.1 a more complete substitution of the endogenous variables in equation 7.27 is made. This has not been pursued in the text, where a more tractable presentation is given.
12. Simple cross-section regression analyses of the impact of foreign aid on savings and investment in developing countries have yielded some academic controversies and have led to a wide range of estimates for the share of aid presumably allocated to consumption. Based on the econometric evidence a reasonable range of the value of this share would be between 0.2 and 0.8.

    Griffin (1970) estimates for 32 LDCs a coefficient of 0.73 (data 1962-64). In an more recent study, he reaches an estimate of 0.48, for a smaller sample of 12 LDCs, using pooled cross-section data for three points in time (Griffin 1986). Weisskopf (1972) reports that approximately 23 per cent of net foreign capital inflows substitute for domestic savings. Own estimates (Vos 1988b) suggest a negative link between domestic savings and foreign capital inflows, with a parameter value of 0.39 for private borrowers in the group of LDCs for 1966-72. The estimate falls to 0.31 for 1973-79, but increases to 0.88 for 1980-86. Official borrowers also show fluctuating values over time. For the same periods the coefficient for LDC-OBs was 0.76, 0.36 and 0.55, respectively.

13. See for instance Bruno & Sachs (1985) for the interpretation of the oil price increase as a supply shock. See also Chapter 8, where simulations with an oil price shock are discussed, on alternative assumptions yielding different outcomes of oil price increases.

Chapter 8

1. In practice zero public investment levels need not be the bottom line. As analysed in Chapter 5, public investment rates in many LDCs rose strongly as a consequence of the foreign lending boom of the 1970s and were heavily cut during the years of debt crisis and reduced access to external borrowing, but on average remained above pre-lending boom levels. The simulation exercises thus assume stronger adjustment than actually may have taken place.
2. Rough estimate based on available wage rate data and employment data for wage-earners and self-employed for low- and lower middle-income primary exporting countries (World Bank, *World Tables*; ILO, *International Labour Statistics*).
3. A recent IMF study gives an estimate of a total marginal savings rate for the South of 0.29 (Aghevli et al. 1990).
4. The long-run import demand elasticity of major oil exporters is very close to unity, according to econometric results obtained by Marquez & Pauly (1987).
5. A pooled regression estimating real demand for time and savings deposits (ΔJ_N) for the five major industrialized countries (US, Japan, Germany, France and UK) for the period 1970-88 gave the following result:

$$\Delta J_N/GNP_N)_i = \underset{(-1.66)}{-0.023} + \underset{(6.25)}{0.135\,(J_N/GNP_N)_{i-1}} \underset{(-0.79)}{-0.001\,(i_W - r_N)_{i-1}}$$

$$R^2_{adj} = 0.68 \qquad DW = 1.60 \qquad F = 61.5$$

where i_{W_i} is the real deposit rate on time and savings deposits in each country and r_{N_i} is a proxy of the real rate of return on other domestic investments (in most cases the real return on government bonds). Looking at time-series results, the coefficient for the rate-of-return differential (j_{1N}) was found significant for Japan (positive) and Germany (negative) but showing opposite signs. No significant relationship could be found for the other three countries. This ambiguous result may well be caused by specification problems. The effect of interest rates on deposit demand is usually analysed as part of broader money demand functions. The stock-adjustment parameter (j_{0N}) varies from 0.05 for France, 0.24 for the US and Japan and 0.47 for Germany.

6. For the given values the trace of the Jacobian in Appendix A7.1 is negative and the determinant positive.
7. The results for the base run are reported in the Appendix in Table A8.3.
8. The substantial rise in aid and Northern demand for government bonds appears to have had only a small effect on the interest rate (Figure 8.1a). The additional official transfer of 0.7 per cent of Northern GNP seems to have upped the interest rate less than 0.02 percentage points. However, the figure shows the new end-of-period interest rate, which accounts for the simultaneous adjustment of Northern investment demand to initial upward pressures on the interest rate due to the 'aid shock'. The intermediate iteration results before reaching the end-of-period equilibrium suggest that a rise in aid flows of this magnitude initially pushes up the interest rate by around one percentage point, after which it gradually falls to its new equilibrium.
9. I should thank David Vines who suggested putting it in these terms.
10. A further way in which not only banks, but also the Northern government (donor community), respond to an arrears position of the South is not considered in the present set of simulations. The model should also allow official capital to be debt creating and interest bearing (now ΔF_S^a is to be interpreted as unrequited transfers or grants), since donors (and multilateral agents) in the first instance are more likely to respond to arrears on their accounts than to those on payment obligations of the South to the commercial banks.
11. Examples along this line can be found in e.g. Oudiz & Sachs (1984) and Currie & Vines et al. (1988).
12. Examples include a model elaborated by Beenstock himself (Beenstock 1988) and small, empirical North-South models by Marquez & Pauly (1987), van Wijnbergen (1985, 1988) and Masson, et al. (1988). The Marquez-Pauly model is an empirical version of Taylor's North-South model (Taylor 1981), while Masson, et al. describe the IMF's MULTIMOD model currently used in the IMF's assessment of global projections and policy coordination scenarios. These models are all discussed further in the text below.
13. A more elaborate data base is currently being developed at the Institute of Social Studies using the world accounting matrix (WAM) framework referred to in Chapter 2. See Vos (1989), Luttik (1992) and de Jong, Vos, Jellema & Zebregs (1993).

14. See Leontief et al. (1977) on the Leontief regional world model; Hicks et al. (1976) and Tims & Waelbroeck (1982) on SIMLINK; OECD (1982) and Richardson (1987) on INTERLINK; Filator, Hickman & Klein (1983) on the country models and global linkage system coordinated through the LINK project; and Jepma (1988) on the SARUM model.

    Further, mention could be made of work at IIASA and associated research groups which have generated a system of linked national agricultural policy models (IIASA/FAP) to study the world food problem (see Parikh & Tims 1987). As in the LINK project the linkages between the models in IIASA/FAP are essentially through commodity trade; financial interactions are not explicitly modelled.

15. That is, other than including net capital flows either as passive, accommodating financial transfers to cover endogenous current account balances or as fully exogenous, aggregate net flows.

16. Muscatelli & Vines (1989) give another review of the state of art of recent North-South modelling efforts.

17. See also Muscatelli & Vines (1989) for a further elaboration of the Currie-Vines model. Work is in progress for a more disaggregated and empirical version along the lines of the theoretical Currie-Vines model.

18. A later version of this model does include capital accumulation (see Muscatelli & Vines 1989), however.

Appendix A3

1. For the full elaboration of neo-classical growth conditions in the long-run steady state, see e.g. Jones (1975), pp. 69ff.

2. Note, however, that this result is achieved for unitary income elasticities for both commodities and no output adjustment in the North. In the Kalecki-Lewis model treated in Chapter 7, the Northern economy is characterized by excess capacity, allowing for demand-driven output adjustment.

3. For a steady state, Southern capital must grow at the same rate n, i.e. the growth rate of the Northern labour force, which continues to be the sole determinant of the expansion of the system as a whole. Thus, the terms of trade continue to be set according to the conditions of equation A3.2.9:

   $$\theta^* = g_N^* k_S / s_S z = n k_S / s_S z$$

4. This conclusion has also been reached by Findlay (1984), Burgstaller & Saavedra-Rivano (1984) and Quibria (1986). The latter two also discuss the stability conditions of this type of North-South model system.

Bibliography

Abreu, M. de Paivo (1984) 'Argentina and Brazil during the 1930s: The impact of British and American international economic policies', in: R. Thorp (ed.) pp. 144-62.

Adler, J. (ed.) (1967) *Capital Movements and Economic Development*. London: Macmillan.

Aghevli, B. et al. (1990) *The Role of National Saving in the World Economy*. IMF Occasional Paper No. 67, Washington DC: International Monetary Fund.

Almansi, A. (1988) 'Patterns of External Adjustment in LDCs: Do we understand them?', University of Michigan, Ann Arbor (mimeo).

Anthony, M. & A. Hughes Hallet (1992) 'How Successfully Do We Measure Capital Flight? The empirical evidence from five developing countries', *Journal of Development Studies*, 28(3): 538-56.

Arndt, H.W. & P.J. Drake (1985) 'Bank Loans or Bonds: Some lessons from historical experience', *Banca Nazionale del Lavoro Quarterly Review*, 38: 373-92.

Avramovic, D. et al. (1964) *Economic Growth and External Debt*. Baltimore: Johns Hopkins University Press.

Bacha, E. (1984) 'Growth with Limited Supplies of Foreign Exchange: A re-appraisal of the two-gap model', in: M. Syrquin, L. Taylor & L. Westphal (eds), pp. 263-80.

Bacha, E. (1990) 'A Three-gap Model of Foreign Transfers and the GDP Growth Rate in Developing Countries', *Journal of Development Economics*, 32: 279-96.

Bain, J.S. (1956) *Barriers to New Competition*. Cambridge, MA: Harvard University Press.

Balassa, B., G. Bueno, P. Kuczynski & M. Simonsen (1986) *Toward Renewed Economic Growth in Latin America*. Washington DC: Institute for International Economics.

Bardhan, P. (1967) 'Optimal Foreign Borrowing', in: K. Shell (ed.) *Essays on the Theory of Optimal Growth*. Cambridge, MA: MIT Press, pp. 117-28.

Barro, R. (1974) 'Are Government Bonds Net Wealth?' *Journal of Political Economy*, 82(6): 1095-117.

Bee, R. (1975) 'Syndication', in: J. Mathis (ed.) *Offshore Lending by U.S. Commercial Banks*. Philadelphia: Robert Morriss Associates, pp. 151-65.

Beenstock, M. (1980) 'Political Econometry of Official Development Assistance', *World Development*, 8(2): 137-44.

Beenstock, M. (1988) 'An Econometric Investigation of North-South Interdependence', in: D. Currie & D. Vines (eds), pp. 32-62.

Berg, A. & Sachs, J. (1988) 'The Debt Crisis: Structural explanations of country performance', *Journal of Development Economics*, 29(3): 271-306.

Bergsten, F., W. Cline & J. Williamson (1985) *Bank Lending to Developing Countries: The Policy Alternatives*. Washington DC: Institute for International Economics.

Bevan, D., P. Collier & J.W. Gunning (1987) 'Consequences of a Commodity Boom in a Controlled Economy: Accumulation and redistribution in Kenya 1975-83', *The World Bank Economic Review*, 1(3): 489-513.

Bhagwati, J. (1958) 'Immiserizing Growth: A geometrical note', *Review of Economic Studies*, 25(June): 201-205.

Bhagwati, J. (1971) 'The Generalized Theory of Distortions and Welfare', in: J. Bhagwati et al. (eds) *Trade, Balance of Payments and Growth*. Amsterdam: North-Holland, pp. 69-90.

Bhagwati, J., R. Brecher & T. Hatta (1983) 'The Generalized Theory of Transfers and Welfare: Bilateral transfers in a multilateral world', *American Economic Review*, 73(4): 606-18.

Bhagwati, J., R. Brecher & T. Hatta (1984) 'The Paradoxes of Immiserizing Growth and Donor-enriching 'Recipient-immiserizing' Transfers: A tale of two literatures', *Weltwirtschaftliches Archiv*, 120(2): 228-43.

Bhagwati, J., R. Brecher & T. Hatta (1985) 'The Generalized Theory of Transfers and Welfare: Exogenous (policy-imposed) and endogenous (transfer-induced) distortions', *Quarterly Journal of Economics*, 100(3): 697-714.

BIS/OECD (various years and issues) *Statistics on External Indebtedness*. Paris and Basel: Bank for International Settlements and Organization for Economic Cooperation and Development.

Black, J. & J. Dunning (eds) *International Capital Movements*. London: Macmillan.

Blask, J. (1977) 'A Survey of Country Evaluation Systems in Use', in: S. Goodman (ed.) *Financing and Risk in Developing Countries*. Washington DC: US EXIM Bank, pp. 77-82.

Bogdanowicz-Bindert, C. & P. Sacks (1984) 'The Role of Information: Closing the barn door', in: R. Feinberg & V. Kailab (eds) *Uncertain Future. Commercial Banks and the Third World*. London: Transaction Books, pp. 69-78.

Brandt Commission Report (1980) *North-South: A Programme for Survival*. New York: Pan.

Brau, E. & R. Williams et al. (1983) *Recent Multilateral Debt Reschedulings with Official and Bank Creditors*. IMF Occasional Paper No. 25, Washington DC: IMF.

Brecher, R. & J. Bhagwati (1981) 'Foreign Trade and the Theory of Trade and Welfare', *Journal of Political Economy*, 89(3): 497-511.

Brecher, R. & C. Diaz-Alejandro (1977) 'Tariffs, Foreign Capital and Immizerizing Growth', *Journal of International Economics*, 7: 317-22.

Brown, B. (1987) *The Flight of International Capital. A Contemporary History*. London: Croom Helm.

Brown, R.P.C. (1992) *Public Debt and Private Wealth. Debt, Capital Flight and the IMF in Sudan*. London/Basingstoke: Macmillan.

Brunner, K. (ed.) (1981) *The Great Depression Revisited*. Boston: Kluwer-Nijhoff.

Bruno, M. (1984) 'Petrodollars and the Different Growth Performance of Industrial and Middle-income Countries in the 1970s', in: M. Syrquin, L. Taylor & L. Westphal (eds), pp. 363-90.

Bruno, M. & J. Sachs (1985) *Economics of World-Wide Stagflation*. Oxford: Basil Blackwell.

Bryant, R. (1987) *International Financial Intermediation*. Washington DC: The Brookings Institution.

Bryant, R. (1988) 'Discussion of Commodities, Debt and North-South Cooperation', in: D. Currie & D. Vines (eds), pp. 141-46.

Bryant, R. & R. Portes (eds) (1987) *Global Macroeconomics. Policy Conflict and Cooperation*. London: Macmillan (for CEPR and IEA).

Bryant, R. et al. (eds) (1988) *Empirical Macroeconomics for Interdependent Economies*. Washington DC: The Brookings Institution.

Bryant, R., D. Currie, J. Frenkel, P. Masson & R. Portes (eds) (1989) *Macroeconomic Policies in an Interdependent World*. Washington DC: IMF (with The Brookings Institution and CEPR).

Buiter, W. (1989) *Budgetary Policy, International and Intertemporal Trade in the Global Economy*. Amsterdam: North-Holland.

Buiter, W. & R. Marston (eds) (1985) *International Economic Policy Coordination*. Cambridge: Cambridge University Press.

Buiter, W. & J. Tobin (1979) 'Debt Neutrality: A brief review of doctrine and evidence', in: G. von Furstenberg (ed.) *Social Security Versus Private Saving*. Cambridge, MA: Ballinger.

Burgstaller, A. (1985) 'North-South Trade and Capital Flows in a Ricardian Model of Accumulation', *Journal of International Economics*, 18(3/4): 241-60.

Burgstaller, A. & N. Saavedra-Rivano (1984) 'Capital Mobility and Growth in a North-South Model', *Journal of Development Economics*, 15: 213-37.

Burneaux, J., F. Delorme, I. Lienert, J. Martin & D. van der Mensbrugghe (1989) 'Economy-wide Effects of Agricultural Policies in OECD Countries: A GE approach using the WALRAS model', Paper presented at the OECD/World Bank Symposium on 'Agricultural Liberalization: Implications for developing countries', Paris, 5-6 October.

Cairncross, A. (1953) *Home and Foreign Investment, 1870-1913*. London: Cambridge University Press.

Calvo, G., R. Findlay, P. Kouri & J. de Macedo (eds) (1989) *Debt, Stabilization and Development*. Oxford: Basil Blackwell.

Cardoso (1987) *Inflation, Growth and the Real Exchange Rate*. New York: Garland.

Cardoso, E. & R. Dornbusch (1989a) 'Foreign Private Capital Flows', in: H.B. Chenery & T.N. Srinivasan (eds), pp. 1388-439.

Cardoso, E. & R. Dornbusch (1989b) 'Brazilian Debt Crises: Past and present', in: B. Eichengreen & P. Lindert (eds) *The International Debt Crisis in Historical Perspective*. Cambridge, MA: MIT Press, pp. 106-39.

Cassen, R. et al. (1987) *Does Aid Work?*. Oxford: Oxford University Press.

Casson, M. (1982) 'The Theory of Foreign Direct Investment', in: J. Black & J. Dunning (eds), pp. 22-57.

Chapman, S. (1984) *The Rise of Merchant Banking*. London: Allen & Unwin.

Chenery, H.B. (1979) *Structural Change and Development Policy*. New York, London: Oxford University Press.

Chenery, H.B. & M. Bruno (1962) 'Development Alternatives in an Open Economy: The case of Israel', *Economic Journal*, 72(285): 79-103 (March).

Chenery, H.B. & T.N. Srinivisan (eds) (1988) *Handbook of Development Economics. Vol. I*. Amsterdam: North-Holland.

Chenery, H.B. & T.N. Srinivisan (eds) (1989) *Handbook of Development Economics. Vol. II*. Amsterdam: North-Holland.

Chichilnisky, G. (1980) 'Basic Goods and the Effects of Commodity Transfers and the International Economic Order', *Journal of Development Economics*, 7(4): 505-19.

Chichilnisky, G. (1983) 'The Transfer Problem with Three Agents Once Again', *Journal of Development Economics*, 13(2): 237-48.

Clarke, R. (1985) *Industrial Economics*. Oxford: Basil Blackwell.

Cline, W. (1983) *International Debt and the Stability of the World Economy*. Policy Analyses in International Economics No. 4, Washington DC: Institute for International Economics.

Cline, W. (1984) *International Debt. Systemic Risk and Policy Response*. Washington DC: Institute for International Economics.

Cline, W. (1989) *United States External Adjustment and the World Economy*. Washington DC: Institute for International Economics.

Cooper, R. & J. Sachs (1985) 'Borrowing Abroad: The debtor's perspective', in: G. Smith & J. Cuddington (eds), pp. 21-60.

Corbo, V., M. Goldstein & M. Khan (eds) (1987) *Growth-oriented Adjustment Programs*. Washington DC: IMF and World Bank.

Corden, M. (1984) 'Booming Sector and Dutch Disease Economics: survey and consolidation', *Oxford Economic Papers*, 36: 359-80.

Cowling, K. (1981) 'Oligopoly, Distribution and the Rate of Profit', *European Economic Review*, 15(2): 195-224.

Crook, C. (1992) 'World Economy: Fear of finance', *Economist*, September 19-25, London.

Cross, H. & G. Hempel (1973) *Management Policies for Commercial Banks*. Englewood Cliffs, NJ: Prentice Hall (2nd Edn).

Crosswell, M. (1981) 'Growth, Poverty Alleviation and Foreign Assistance', in: D. Leipziger (ed.) *Basic Needs and Development*. Cambridge, MA: Oelgeschlager, Gunn & Hain, pp. 181-218.

Cuddington, J. (1986) *Capital Flight: Estimates, Issues and Explanations*. Princeton Studies in International Finance No. 58, Princeton, NJ: Princeton University Press.

Cuddington, J. (1987) 'Macroeconomic Determinants of Capital Flight: An econometric investigation', in: D. Lessard & J. Williamson (eds), pp. 85-96.

Cumby, R. & R. Levich (1987) 'On the Definition and Magnitude of Recent Capital Flight', in: D. Lessard & J. Williamson (eds), pp. 27-84.

Currie, D., D. Vines et al. (1988) 'North-South Interactions: A general equilibrium framework for the study of strategic issues', in: D. Currie & D. Vines (eds), pp. 65-100.

Currie, D. & D. Vines (eds) (1988) *Macroeconomic Interactions Between North and South*. Cambridge: Cambridge University Press (for CEPR and IEA).

Darity, W. (1987) 'Debt, Finance, Production and Trade in a North-South Model: The surplus approach', *Cambridge Journal of Economics*, 11: 211-27.

Darity, W. & B. Horn (1988) *The Loan Pushers. The Role of Commercial Banks in the International Debt Crisis*. Cambridge, MA: Ballinger.

Das, D. (1986) *Migration of Financial Resources to Developing Countries*. London: Macmillan.

Davis, S. (1976) *The Euro-bank: Its Origins, Management and Outlook*. London: Macmillan.

De Melo, J. (1987) 'The Macroeconomic Effects of Foreign Aid: Issues and evidence', Paper presented at the Conference on North-South Cooperation in Retrospect and Prospect, University of Groningen, Groningen.

Dean, A., M. Durand, J. Fallon & P. Hoeller (1990) 'Savings Trends and Behaviour in OECD Countries', *OECD Economic Studies*, 14 (Spring): 7-58.

Dell, S. (ed.) (1987) *The International Monetary System and its Reform. Papers Prepared for the Group of Twenty-Four*. Amsterdam: North-Holland.

Deppler, M. & M. Williamson (1987) 'Capital Flight: Concepts, measurement and issues', in: IMF, *Staff Studies for the World Economic Outlook*. Washington DC: IMF, pp. 39-58.

Devlin, R. (1986) 'Debt and Crisis in Latin America: The supply-side of the story', unpublished PhD thesis, The American University, Washington DC.

Devlin, R. (1987) 'The Structure and Performance of International Banking During the 1970s and its Impact on the Crisis in Latin America', The Helen Kellogg Institute for International Studies Working Paper No. 90, Notre Dame: University of Notre Dame.

Devlin, R. (1989) *Debt and Crisis in Latin America. The Supply-side of the Story*. Princeton: Princeton University Press.

Dixit, A. & V. Norman (1980) *The Theory of International Trade*. Cambridge: Cambridge University Press.

Dohner, R. & P. Intal (1989) 'The Marcos Legacy: Economic policy and foreign debt in the Philippines', in: J. Sachs & S. Collins (eds) *Developing Country Debt and Economic Performance. Volume 3: Country Studies – Indonesia,*

Korea, Philippines, Turkey. Chicago: University of Chicago Press (for NBER).

Domar, E. (1950) 'The Effect of Foreign Investment on the Balance of Payments', *American Economic Review*, 40(5): 805-26.

Dominique, C. (1985) 'Trade Links and Dependency Theory: An addendum to Taylor's assessment', *Trade and Development* (UNCTAD), 6: 241-54.

Dooley, M. (1986) 'Country-specific Risk Premiums, Capital Flight and Net Investment Income Payments in Selected Developing Countries', DM 86/17, Washington DC: International Monetary Fund.

Dooley, M., J. Frankel & D. Mathieson (1987) 'International Capital Mobility: What do saving-investment correlations tell us?', *IMF Staff Papers*, 34(3): 503-30.

Dornbusch, R. (1976) 'Expectations and Exchange Rate Dynamics', *Journal of Political Economy*, 84(6): 1161-76.

Dornbusch, R. (1980) *Open Economy Macroeconomics*. New York: Basic Books.

Dornbusch, R. (1985) 'External Debt, Budget Deficits and Disequilibrium Exchange Rates', in: G. Smith & J. Cuddington (eds), pp. 213-35.

Dornbusch, R. (1987) 'Comment', in: D. Lessard & J. Williamson (eds), pp. 145-51.

Dornbusch, R. (1988) 'Overvaluation and the Trade Balance', in: R. Dornbusch & F.L. Helmers (eds), pp. 80-107.

Dornbusch, R. & F.L. Helmers (eds) (1988) *The Open Economy. Tools for Policy-makers in Developing Countries*. Oxford: Oxford University Press (for EDI).

Dornbusch, R. & S. Fischer (1987) 'International Capital Flows and the World Debt Problem', in: A. Razin & E. Sadka (eds), pp. 211-54.

Dowling, J. & U. Hiemenz (1985) 'Biases in the Allocation of Foreign Aid: Some new evidence', *World Development*, 13(4): 535-41.

Dudley, L. (1979) 'Foreign Aid and the Theory of Alliances', *Review of Economics and Statistics*, 61: 564-71.

Dudley, L. & C. Montmarquette (1976) 'A Model of the Supply of Bilateral Foreign Aid', *American Economic Review*, 66(1): 132-42.

Dufey, G. & I. Giddy (1978) *The International Money Market*. Englewoods Cliffs, NJ: Prentice Hall.

Dunning, J. (1970) *Studies in International Investment*. London: Allen & Unwin.

Dunning, J. (1981) 'Explaining the International Direct Investment Position of Countries: Towards a dynamic or developmental approach', *Weltwirtschaftliches Archiv*, 117: 30-64.

Dunning, J. & J. Cantwell (1987) *Directory of Statistics of International Investment and Production*. London: Macmillan.

Dutt, A.K. (1988) 'Trade, Debt and Uneven Development in a North-South Model', Department of Economics, Florida International University, Miami (mimeo).

Eaton, J. (1987) 'Public Debt Guarantees and Private Capital Flight', *The World Bank Economic Review*, 1(3): 377-95.

Eaton, J. (1989) 'Foreign Public Capital Flows', in: H.B. Chenery & T.N. Srinivasan (eds), pp. 1305-86.

Eaton, J. & M. Gersovitz (1980) 'LDC Participation in International Financial Markets. Debt and Reserves', *Journal of Development Economics*, 7(1): 3-21.

Eaton, J. & M. Gersovitz (1981) 'Debt with Potential Repudiation: Theoretical and empirical analysis', *Review of Economic Studies*, 48: 286-309.

Eaton, J. & M. Gersovitz (1989) 'Country Risk Analysis and the Organization of International Capital Transfer', in: G. Calvo, R. Findlay, P. Kouri & J. de Macedo (eds), pp. 109-29.

Eaton, J., M. Gersovitz & J. Stiglitz (1986) 'The Pure Theory of Country Risk', *European Economic Review*, 30: 481-513.

Eaton, J. & L. Taylor (1986) 'Developing Country Finance and Debt', *Journal of Development Economics*, 22: 209-65.

ECLA (1950) *Economic Survey of Latin America, 1949*. New York: United Nations.

ECLA (1965) *External Financing in Latin America*. New York: United Nations.

ECLAC (1990) *Latin America and the Caribbean: Options to Reduce the Debt Burden*. Santiago: United Nations Economic Commission for Latin America and the Caribbean.

Edelman, J. & H.B. Chenery (1977) 'Aid and Income Distribution', in: J. Bhagwati (ed.) *New International Economic Order: The North-South Debate*. Cambridge, MA: MIT Press, pp. 27-49.

Edwards, S. (1984) 'Coffee, Money and Inflation in Colombia', *World Development*, 12(11/12): 1107-17.

Edwards, S. & S. van Wijnbergen (1989) 'Disequilibrium and Structural Adjustment', in: H.B. Chenery & T.N. Srinivasan (eds), pp. 1481-533.

Eichengreen, B. (1988) 'Till Debt Do Us Part: The US capital market and foreign lending', CEPR Discussion Paper Series No. 212, London: Centre for Economic Policy Research.

Eichengreen, B. & R. Portes (1986) 'Debt and Default in the 1930s. Causes and consequences', *European Economic Review*, 30(3): 599-640.

Eichengreen, B. & R. Portes (1987) 'The Anatomy of Financial Crisis', in R. Portes & A. Swoboda (eds) *Threats to International Financial Stability*. Cambridge: Cambridge University Press, pp. 10-58.

Eichengreen, B. & R. Portes (1989) 'Dealing with Debt: The 1930s and 1980s', in: I. Diwan & I. Husain (eds) *Dealing with the Debt Crisis*. Washington DC: World Bank, pp. 69-85.

Ensign, M. (1988) *Images and Behavior of Private Bank Lending to Developing Countries*. New York: Gordon and Breach Science Publishers.

Feder, G. & R. Just (1977) 'A Study of Debt-servicing Capacity Applying Logit Analysis', *Journal of Development Economics*, 4: 25-38.

Feder, G. & L. Uy (1985) 'The Determinants of International Creditworthiness and their Policy Implications', *Journal of Policy Modeling*, 7(1): 133-56.

Feinstein, C. (1962) *National Income, Expenditure and Output of the United Kingdom, 1855-1965*. Cambridge: Cambridge University Press.

Feis, H. (1930) *Europe, the World's Banker. 1870-1914*. New Haven, CN: Yale University Press.

Feldstein, M. (1983) 'Domestic Saving and International Capital Movements in the Long Run and in the Short Run', *European Economic Review*, 21: 129-51.

Feldstein, M. (ed.) (1988) *International Economic Cooperation*. Chicago: Chicago University Press (for NBER).

Feldstein, M. & C. Horioka (1980) 'Domestic Saving and International Capital Flows', *Economic Journal*, 90: 314-29 (June).

Filator, V., B. Hickman & L. Klein (1983) 'Long-term Simulations with the Project LINK System 1978-85', in: B. Hickman (ed.), pp. 29-52.

Findlay, R. (1973) *International Trade and Development Economics*. New York: Columbia University Press.

Findlay, R. (1980) 'The Terms of Trade and Equilibrium Growth in the World Economy', *American Economic Review*, 70(2): 291-99.

Findlay, R. (1984) 'Growth and Development in Trade Models', in: R.W. Jones & P. Kenen (eds) *Handbook of International Economics*. Vol. I, Amsterdam: North-Holland, pp. 185-236.

Fishlow, A. (1985) 'Lessons from the Past: Capital markets during the nineteenth century and the inter-war period', *International Organization*, 39(3): 383-439.

Fishlow, A. (1987) 'Capital Requirements in Developing Countries in the Next Decade', *Journal of Development Planning*, 17: 245-91.

Fishlow, A. (1989) 'Lessons of the 1890s for the 1980s', in: G. Calvo, R. Findlay, P. Kouri & J. de Macedo (eds), pp. 19-47.

FitzGerald, E.V.K. (1984) 'Appendix: A Note on Income Distribution, Accumulation and Recovery in the Depression: An alternative view', in: R. Thorp (ed.), pp. 266-78.

FitzGerald, E.V.K. & K. Sarmad (1990) 'Public and Private Sector Capital Account Behaviour in Less Developed Countries, 1970-88', ISS Money, Finance and Development Working Paper Series, No. 36, The Hague.

FitzGerald, E.V.K. & R. Vos (1989) *Financing Economic Development. A Structural Approach to Monetary Policy*. Aldershot: Gower.

Fleming, J.M. (1962) 'Domestic Financial Policies Under Fixed and Floating Exchange Rates', *IMF Staff Papers*, 9(3): 369-79.

Folkerts-Landau, D. (1985) 'The Changing Role of International Bank Lending in Development Finance', *IMF Staff Papers*, 32(2): 317-63.

Ford, A. (1956) 'Argentina and the Baring Crisis of 1890', *Oxford Economic Papers*, 8: 302-20.

Ford, A. (1962) *The Gold Standard 1880-1914. Britain and Argentina*. London: Clarendon Press.

Frank, C. & W. Cline (1971) 'Measurement of Debt-servicing Capacity', *Journal of International Economics*, 1: 327-44.

Frankel, J.A. (1988) 'The Implications of Conflicting Models for Coordination Between Monetary and Fiscal Policy-makers', in: R. Bryant et al. (eds), pp. 238-54.

Frankel, J.A. (1991) 'International Capital Mobility: A review', *American Economic Review*, 81(1): 78-99 (March).

Frenkel, J. & A. Razin (1987) 'The Mundell-Fleming Model a Quarter of a Century Later: A unified exposition', *IMF Staff Papers*, 34(4): 567-620.

Frenkel, J. & H.G. Johnson (eds) (1976) *The Monetary Approach to the Balance of Payments*. Chicago: Chicago University Press.

Frey, B. (1984) *International Political Economics*. Oxford: Basil Blackwell.

Friedman, B. (1983) *The World Debt Dilemma: Managing Country Risk*. Philadelphia: Robert Morriss Associates.

Friedman, M. & A. Schwartz (1963) *A Monetary History of the United States*. Princeton, NJ: Princeton University Press.

Galbis, V. (1987) 'La liberalización del sector financiero bajo condiciones oligopólicas y las estructuras de los "holdings" bancarios', in: S. Roca (ed.) *Estabilización y ajuste estructural en América Latina*. Lima: IDE/ESAN.

Galbraith, J.K. (1955) *The Great Crash 1929*. London: Hamish Hamilton.

GATT (various years) *International Trade*. Geneva: GATT.

Gersovitz, M., C. Diaz-Alejandro, G. Ranis & M. Rosenzweig (eds) (1982) *The Theory and Experience of Economic Development. Essays in Honour of Sir W. Arthur Lewis*. London: Allen & Unwin.

Gilbert, C. (1990) 'Expectation Formation in Equilibrium and Disequilibrium Commodity Market Models', Paper presented at CEPR Conference on Commodity Prices, London (March).

Goldsbrough, D. & I. Zaidi (1986) 'Transmission of Economic Influences from Industrial to Developing Countries', in: IMF (1986), *Staff Studies for the World Economic Outlook*. Washington DC: IMF, pp. 150-95.

Gray, P. (1982) 'Towards a Unified Theory of International Trade, International Production and Foreign Direct Investment', in: J. Black & J. Dunning (eds), pp. 58-83.

Gray, P. & J. Gray (1989) 'International Payments in a Flow-of-funds Format', *Journal of Post-Keynesian Economics*, 11(2): 241-60.

Griffin, K. (1970) 'Foreign Capital, Domestic Savings and Economic Development', *Bulletin of the Oxford Institute of Economics and Statistics*, 32: 99-112.

Griffin, K. (1978) *International Inequality and National Poverty*. London: Macmillan.

Griffin, K. (1986) 'Doubts About Aid', *IDS Bulletin*, 17(2): 36-45.

Griffith-Jones, S. (1984) *International Finance and Latin America*. London: Croom Helm.

Griffith-Jones, S. (ed.) (1988) *Managing World Debt*. Hemel Hempstead: Harvester-Wheatsheaf.

Griffith-Jones, S. (1989) 'International Economic Management, International Liquidity and Resource Transfers in the 1990s', Brighton Institute of Development Studies (mimeo).

Grilli, E. & M.C. Yang (1988) 'Primary Commodity Prices, Manufactured Goods Prices and the Terms of Trade of Developing Countries: What the long run shows', *The World Bank Economic Review*, 2(1): 1-47.

Grubel, H. (1977) 'A Theory of Multinational Banking', *Banca Nazionale del Lavoro Quarterly Review*, September: 349-63.

Grubel, H. (1982) 'The Theory of International Capital Movements', in: J. Black & J. Dunning (eds), pp. 1-21.

Gulati, S. (1987) 'A Note on Trade Misinvoicing', in: D. Lessard & J. Williamson (eds) pp. 68-78.

Gunning, J.W. (1983a) 'The Transfer Problem, a Rejoinder', *Journal of Development Economics*, 13: 249-50.

Gunning, J.W. (1983b) 'Rationing in an Open Economy: Fix-price equilibrium and two-gap models', *European Economic Review*, 23: 71-98.

Gupta, S., A. Schwartz & R. Padula (1979) 'The World Bank Model for global Interdependence: A quantitative framework for the World Development Report', *Journal of Policy Modeling*, 1(2): 179-200.

Guttentag, J. & R. Herring (1985) 'Commercial Bank Lending to Developing Countries: From overlending to structural reform', in: G. Smith & J. Cuddington (eds), pp. 129-50.

Guttentag, J. & R. Herring (1986) *Disaster Myopia in International Banking*. Essays in International Finance No. 164, International Finance Section, Princeton University, Princeton: Princeton University Press.

Gwynne, S. (1983) 'Adventures in the Loan Trade', *Harper's*, September: 22-26.

Haberler, G. (1986) 'The Slowdown of the World Economy and the Problem of Stagflation', in: D. Lal & M. Wolf (eds), pp. 48-90.

Hajivassilou, V. (1989) 'Do the Secondary Markets Believe in Life After Debt?' in: I. Diwan & I. Husain (eds) *Dealing with the Debt Crisis*. Washington DC: The World Bank, pp. 276-91.

Hamada, K. (1985) *The Political Economy of International Monetary Interdependence*. Cambridge, MA: MIT Press.

Harberger, A. (1980) 'Vignettes on the World Capital Market', *American Economic Review*, 70 (May, Papers and Proceedings): 331-37.

Harberger, A. (1985) 'Lessons for Debtor-country Managers and Policy-makers', in: G. Smith & J. Cuddington (eds), pp. 236-57.

Harris, J. (1986) 'Macroeconomic Adjustment in Sudan: 1972-85', Paper presented at WIDER Conference on Stabilization and Adjustment Policies, Helsinki, August (mimeo).

Helleiner, G. (1987) 'Balance of Payments Experience and Growth Prospects of Developing Countries. A synthesis', in: UNCTAD (1987b), pp. 125-206.

Helleiner, G. (1988) 'Primary Commodity Markets: Recent trends and research requirements', in: K.A. Elliott & J. Williamson (eds) *World Economic Problems*. Washington DC: Institute for International Economics, pp. 197-215.

Helleiner, G. (1989) 'Transnational Corporations and Direct Foreign Investment', in: H.B. Chenery & T.N. Srinivasan (eds), pp. 1441-80.

Heller, P. (1988) 'Ageing, Savings and Pensions in the G-7 Countries: 1980-2025', IMF Working Paper (mimeo).

Hermes, N. & R. Lensink (1990) 'Capital Flight from Six Sub-Saharan African Countries', Research Memorandum No. 381, University of Groningen, Groningen.

Hickman, B. (ed.) (1983) *Global International Economic Models*. Amsterdam: North-Holland.

Hickman, B. (1988) 'The US Economy and the International Transmission Mechanism', in: R. Bryant et al. (eds), pp. 92-130.

Hicks, N., with P. Pollak, F. Pinto, J. Gunning, R. Williams, H. Elkington, E. Brook & J. de Vries (1976) 'A Model of Trade and Growth for the Developing World: The SIMLINK model', *European Economic Review*, 7(3): 239-55.

Hufbauer, G. (1975) ' The Multinational Corporation and Direct Investment', in: P. Kenen (ed.) (1975) *International Trade and Finance*. Cambridge: Cambridge University Press, pp. 253-319.

Hughes, H. (1979) 'Debt and Development: The role of foreign capital in economic growth', *World Development*, 7(2): 95-112.

Hughes Hallet, A. (1988) 'Commodities, Debt and North-South Cooperation: A cautionary tale from the structuralist camp', in: D. Currie & D. Vines (eds), pp. 106-40.

Hume, D. (1752| 1971) 'Of the Balance of Trade', reprinted in: R. Cooper (ed.) *International Finance*. Harmondworth: Penguin, pp. 25-37.

Hymer, S. (1976) *The International Operations of National Firms*. Cambridge, MA: MIT Press.

IMF (1977) *The Monetary Approach to The Balance of Payments*. Washington DC: IMF.

IMF (1983) *World Economic Outlook 1983*. Washington DC: IMF.

IMF (1985) *Foreign Private Investment in Developing Countries*. IMF Occasional Paper No. 33, Washington DC: IMF.

IMF (1987a) *Report on the World Current Account Discrepancy*. Washington DC: IMF.

IMF (1987b) *World Economic Outlook 1987*. IMF, Washington DC

IMF (1987c) *Theoretical Aspects of the Design of Fund-supported Adjustment Programs*. Washington DC: IMF.

IMF (1988) *World Economic Outlook 1988*. Washington DC: IMF.

IMF (1989) *World Economic Outlook 1989*. Washington DC: IMF.

IMF (1990) *World Economic Outlook 1990*. Washington DC: IMF.

IMF (1991) *Determinants and Systemic Consequences of International Capital Flows*. IMF Occasional Paper No. 77, Washington DC: IMF.

IMF (1992) *Report on the Measurement of International Capital Flows*. Washington DC: IMF.

IMF (various years) *International Financial Statistics*. Computer tapes, Washington DC: IMF.

IMF (various years) *Balance of Payments Statistics*. Computer tapes, Washington DC: IMF.

IMF (various years) *Direction of Trade Statistics Yearbook*. Washington DC: IMF.

IMF (various years) *Primary Commodities, Market Developments and Outlook*. Washington DC: IMF.

Inter-American Development Bank (1983) *External Debt and Economic Development in Latin America*. Washington DC: IDB.

Isenman, P. (1976) 'Biases in Aid Allocations Against Poorer and Larger Countries, *World Development*, 4(8): 631-41.

Ize, A. and G. Ortiz (1986) 'Fiscal Rigidities, Public Debt and Capital Flight', *IMF Staff Papers*, 34(2): 311-32.

Jayawardena, L. (1983) 'International Keynesianism – A solution to the world crisis?', in: K. Jansen (ed.) *Monetarism and the Third World*. London: Frank Cass, pp. 149-74.

Jepma, C.J. (1988) 'Some Broad Development Policy Scenarios', in: C.J. Jepma (ed.) *North-South Co-operation in Retrospect and Prospect*. London: Routledge, pp. 207-25.

Jepma, C.J. (1990) 'LDC Financial Requirements Through the 1990s', Paper presented at Development Economics Seminar, January, Institute of Social Studies, The Hague.

Johnson, H.G. (1958) 'The Transfer Problem and Exchange Stability', in: *International Trade and Economic Growth*. London: Allen & Unwin, pp. 169-90 (reprinted in: R. Cooper (ed.) *International Finance*. Harmondsworth: Penguin, pp. 62-86).

Johnson, H.G. (1967) 'The Possibility of Income Losses from Increased Efficiency or Factor Accumulation in the Presence of Tariffs', *Economic Journal*, 77: 151-54.

Jones, H. (1975) *An Introduction to Modern Theories of Economic Growth*. London: Nelson.

Jones, R. (1967) 'International Capital movements and the Theory of Tariffs and Trade', *Quarterly Journal of Economics*, 81: 1-38.

Jones, R. (1979) *Essays in Trade Theory*. Amsterdam: North-Holland.

Jones, R. & P. Kenen (eds) (1984) *Handbook of International Economics*. Vol. I, Amsterdam: North-Holland.

Jones, R. & P. Neary (1984) 'The Positive Theory of International Trade', in: R. Jones & P. Kenen (eds), pp. 2-62.

Jong, N. de, R. Vos, T. Jellema & H. Zebregs (1993) 'Trade and Financial Flows in a World Accounting Framework: Balanced WAMs for 1989-90', ISS Working Paper Series on Money, Finance and Development No. 52, The Hague: Institute of Social Studies.

Kalecki, M. (1971) *Selected Essays on the Dynamics of the Capitalist Economy*. Cambridge: Cambridge University Press.

Kanbur, R. and D. Vines (1986) 'North-South Interaction and Commod Control, *Journal of Development Economics*, 23(2): 371-87.

Kemp, M. (1966) 'The Gain from International Trade and Investment: A neo-Heckscher-Ohlin approach', *American Economic Review*, 56: 788-809.

Kenwood, A. & A. Lougheed (1971) *The Growth of the International Economy, 1820-1960*. London: Allen & Unwin.

Keynes, J.M. (1923) *A Tract on Monetary Reform*. London: Macmillan. Reprinted in: D. Moggridge (ed.) *The Collected Writings of John Maynard Keynes*. Vol. IV.

Keynes, J.M. (1929a) 'The German Transfer Problem', *Economic Journal* (March): 1-7. Reprinted in: D. Moggridge (ed.) *The Collected Writings of John Maynard Keynes*. Vol. XI, pp. 451-59.

Keynes, J.M. (1929b) 'The reparations problem', *Economic Journal* (June). Reprinted in: D. Moggridge (ed.) *The Collected Writings of John Maynard Keynes*. Vol. XI, pp. 468-72.

Keynes, J.M. (1929c) 'Mr. Keynes' Views on the Transfer Problem. A reply by Mr. Keynes', *Economic Journal* (September). Reprinted in: D. Moggridge (ed.) *The Collected Writings of John Maynard Keynes*. Vol. XI, pp. 475-80.

Keynes, J.M. (1931) 'The Consequences to the Banks of the Collapse of Money Values', in: J.M. Keynes, *Essays in Persuasion*. New York: Norton (1963 edn).

Khan, M. & Reinhart, C. (1990) 'Private Investment and Economic Growth in Developing Countries', *World Development*, 18(1): 19-27.

Khan, M. & N. Ul Haque (1985) ' Foreign Borrowing and Capital Flight', *IMF Staff Papers*, 32(4): 606-28.

Kharas, H. & J. Levinsohn (1988) 'LDC Savings Rates and Debt Crisis', *World Development*, 16(7): 779-86.

Kindleberger, C. (1973) *The World in Depression, 1929-39*. Berkeley: University of California.

Kindleberger, C. (1978) *Manias, Panics and Crashes: A History of Financial Crises*. New York: Basic Books.

Kindleberger, C. (1982) 'The Cyclical Pattern of Long-term Lending', in: M. Gersovitz et al. (eds) pp. 300-12.

Kletzer, K. (1984) 'Asymmetries of Information and LDC Borrowing with Sovereign Risk', *Economic Journal*, 94: 287-308 (June).

Kletzer, K. & P. Bardhan (1987), 'Credit Markets and Patterns of International Trade', *Journal of Development Economics*, 27: 57-70.

Kouri, P. & M. Porter (1974) 'International Capital Flows and Portfolio Equilibrium', *Journal of Political Economy*, 82(3): 443-68.

Krueger, A. (1987) 'Aspects of Capital Flows Between Developing and Developed Countries', in: A. Razin & E. Sadka (eds), pp. 255-82.

Krugman, P. (1979a) 'A Model of Innovation, Technology Transfer and the World Distribution of Income', *Journal of Political Economy*, 87: 253-66.

Krugman, P. (1979b) 'Increasing Returns, Monopolistic Competition and International Trade', *Journal of International Economics*, 9: 469-79.

Krugman, P. (1985) 'International Debt Strategies in an Uncertain World', in: G. Smith & J. Cuddington (eds), pp. 79-100.

Krugman, P. (1989) 'Private Capital Flows to Problem Debtors', in: J. Sachs (ed.) pp. 299-330.

Krugman, P. & R. Baldwin (1987) 'The Persistence of the US Trade Deficit', *Brookings Papers on Economic Activity*, 1:1-43.

Kuznets, S. (1961) *Capital in the American Economy: Its Formation and its Financing*. Princeton, NJ: Princeton University Press.

Lal, D. & S. van Wijnbergen (1985) 'Government Deficits, the Real Interest Rate and LDC Debt. On global crowding out', *European Economic Review*, 29(1): 157-91.

Lamberte, M., J. Lim, R. Vos & J. Yap (1992) *External Finance and Structural Adjustment in the Philippines, 1970-1990*. Manila: PIDS-ISS.

Lary, H. (1943) *The United States in the World Economy*. Washington DC: US Department of Commerce.

Leontief, W. (1936) 'Note on the Pure Theory of Capital Transfer', in: *Explorations in Economics: Notes and Essays Contributed in Honor of F.W. Taussig*. New York: McGraw Hill, pp. 84-91.

Leontief, W. et al. (1977) *The Future of the World Economy*. New York: Oxford University Press.

Lessard, D. & J. Williamson (1985) *Financial Intermediation beyond the Debt Crisis*. Institute of International Economics Policy Analyses No. 12, Washington DC: Institute for International Economics.

Lessard, D. & J. Williamson (eds) (1987) *Capital Flight and Third World Debt*. Washington DC: Institute for International Economics.

Lewis, C. (1938) *America's Stake in International Investment*. Washington DC: The Brookings Institution.

Lewis, M. & K. Davis (1987) *Domestic and International Banking*. Oxford: Philip Allen Publishers.

Lewis, W.A. (1954) 'Economic Development with Unlimited Supplies of Labour', *The Manchester School*, 22: 139-91 (May).

Lewis, W.A. (1969) *Aspects of Tropical Trade, 1883-1965*. Stockholm: Almquist and Wiksell.

Lewis, W.A. (1977) *The Evolution of the International Economic Order*. Princeton, NJ: Princeton University Press.

Lewis, W.A. (1978) *Growth and Fluctuations 1870-1914*. London: Allen & Unwin.

Lindert, P. & P. Morton (1989) 'How Sovereign Debt Has Worked', in: J. Sachs (ed.) pp. 39-106.

Llewellyn, D. (1980) *International Financial Integration. The Limits of Sovereignty*. London: Macmillan.

Lluch, C. (1986) 'ICORs, Savings Rates and Determinants of Public Expenditure in Developing Countries', in: D. Lal & M. Wolf (eds) *Stagflation, Savings and the State. Perspectives on the Global Economy*. Oxford: Oxford University Press, pp. 361-94.

Lowe, A. (1970) *On Economic Knowledge. Toward a Science of Political Economics*. New York: Harper and Row.

Luttik, J. (1990) 'The World Accounting Matrix: A first approximation', Paper presented at the IDS-ISS seminar on 'Structural adjustment and Macroeconomic Problems in Developing Countries', 1-2 November, Institute of Social Studies, The Hague

Luttik, J. (1992) *Trade and Finance in a World Accounting Matrix*. PhD dissertation, University of Amsterdam, Institute of Social Studies, Amsterdam/The Hague.

Lynn, R. & F.D. McCarthy (1989) 'Recent Economic Performance of Developing Countries', World Bank Policy, Planning and Research Working Papers, WPS 229, Washington DC: World Bank.

Lysy, F. (1985) 'Graciela Chichilnisky's Model of North-South Trade', *Journal of Development Economics*, 18(2/3): 429-61.

McCarthy, F.D. & S. Fardoust (1990) 'Economic Issues for the 1990s', in: F.D. McCarthy (ed.) *Problems of Developing Countries in the 1990s*. World Bank Discussion Papers 97, Washington DC: World Bank.

McCarthy, F.D., B. Laury, M. Riordan, & J.P. Zhou (1989) 'Global Accounting Framework (GAF): The basic system', Economic Analysis and Projections Division, International Economics Department, World Bank (mimeo).

MacDougall, G. (1960) 'The Benefits and Costs of Private Investment from Abroad: A theoretical approach', *Economic Record*, 36: 13-35.

McDonald, D. (1982) 'Debt Capacity and Developing Country Borrowing', *IMF Staff Papers*, 29(4): 603-40.

Machlup, F. (1943) *International Trade and the National Income Multiplier*. Philadelphia: The Blakestone Company.

McKibbin, W. & J. Sachs (1989) 'Implications of Policy Rules for the World Economy', in: R. Bryant et al. (eds), pp. 151-94.

McKibbin, W. & J. Sachs (1991) *Global Linkages, Macroeconomic Interdependence and Cooperation in the World Economy*. Washington DC: The Brookings Institution.

McKinley, R. & I. Little (1978a) 'The German Aid Relationship: A test of the recipient need and the donor interest models of the distribution of German bilateral aid, 1961-70', *European Journal of Political Research*, 6: 235-57.

McKinley, R. & I. Little (1978b) 'A Foreign Policy Model of the Distribution of UK Bilateral Aid 1960-70', British *Journal of Political Science*, 8: 313-32.

McKinley, R. & I. Little (1979) 'The US Aid Relationship: A test of the recipient need and donor interest models', *Political Studies*, 27: 236-50.

McKinnon, R. (1977) *The Euro-currency Market*. Essays on International Finance No. 125, Princeton, NJ: Princeton University Press.

McKinnon, R. (1984) 'The International Capital Market and economic Liberalization in LDCs', *The Developing Economies*, 22(3): 476-81.

Maddison, A. (1985) *Two Crises: Latin America and Asia, 1929-38 and 1973-83*. Paris: OECD (Development Centre Studies).

Makin, J. (1984) *The Global Debt Crisis. America's Growing Involvement*. New York: Basic Books.

Malan, P. et al. (1977) *Política económica externa e industrializaçao no Brasil, 1939/52*. Rio de Janeiro: Universidad Católica.

Malinvaud, E. (1977) *The Theory of Unemployment Reconsidered*. Oxford: Basil Blackwell (2nd edn: 1985).

Marquez, J. & P. Pauly (1987) 'International Policy Coordination and Growth Prospects of Developing Countries', *Journal of Development Economics* 25(1): 89-104.

Marris, S. (1985) *Deficits and the Dollar: The World Economy at Risk*. Washington DC: Institute for International Economics.

Masson, P. & M. Knight (1986) 'International Transmission of Fiscal Policies in Major Industrial Countries', *IMF Staff Papers*, 33(3): 387-438.

Masson, P. & G. Meredith (1990) 'Domestic and International Consequences of German Unification', in: L. Lipschitz & D. McDonald (eds) *German Unification. Economic Issues*. IMF Occasional Paper No. 75, Washington DC: International Monetary Fund, pp. 93-114.

Masson, P., S. Symanski, R. Haas & M. Dooley (1988) 'MULTIMOD – A multi-region Econometric Model', in: IMF, *Staff Studies for the World Economic Outlook*. Washington DC: IMF, pp. 50-104.

Masson, P., S. Symanski and G. Meredith (1990) *MULTIMOD Mark II: A Revised and Extended Model*. IMF Occasional Paper No. 71, Washington DC: International Monetary Fund.

Meade, J. (1951) *The Theory of International Economic Policy. Volume 1: The Balance of Payments*. London: Oxford University Press.

Metzler, L. (1942) 'The Transfer Problem Reconsidered', *Journal of Political Economy*, 50: 397-414.

Mikesell, R.F. (1968) *The Economics of Foreign Aid*. London: Wiedenfeld & Nicolson.

Minsky, H. (1982) *Can 'It' Happen Again? Essays on Instability and Finance*. Armonk: M.E. Sharpe.

Mintz, I. (1951) *Deterioration of the Quality of Foreign Bonds Issued in the United States, 1920-30*. New York: National Bureau of Economic Research.

Mitchell, B. (1978) *European Historical Statistics, 1750-1970*. London: Macmillan.

Mitchell, B. (1982) *International Historical Statistics. Africa and Asia*. London: Macmillan.

Mitchell, B. (1983) *International Historical Statistics. The Americas and Australasia*. London: Macmillan.

Modigliani, F. (1958) 'New Developments on the Oligopoly Front', *Journal of Political Economy*, 66: 215-32.

Molana, H. & D. Vines (1988) 'North-South Growth and Terms of Trade: A model on Kaldorian lines', CEPR Discussion Paper Series No. 248, London: Centre for Economic Policy Research.

Morgan, E. & W. Thomas (1962) *The Stock Exchange: Its History and Functions*. London: Elek.

Mosley, P. (1981) 'Models of the Aid Allocation Process', *Political Studies*, 29: 245-53.

Mosley, P. (1985) 'The Political Economy of Foreign Aid: A model of the market for a public good', *Economic Development and Cultural Change*, 33(1): 373-93.

Mosley, P. (1987) *Overseas Aid: Its Defence and Reform*. Brighton: Wheatsheaf Books.

Mundell, R. (1960) 'The Monetary Dynamics of International Adjustment Under Fixed and Flexible Rates', *Quarterly Journal of Economics*, 74: 227-57 (May).

Mundell, R. (1963) 'Capital Mobility and Stabilization Policy Under Fixed and Flexible Exchange Rates', *Canadian Journal of Economic and Political Science*, 29: 475-85 (November).

Mundell, R. (1968) *International Economics*. New York, London: Macmillan.

Muscatelli, A. & D. Vines (1989) 'Macroeconomic Interactions Between the North and South', in: R. Bryant et al. (eds), pp. 381-412.

Muscatelli, A. and D. Vines (1991) 'Third World Debt and Macroeconomic Interactions Between North and South', *Journal of Development Studies*, 27(3): 146-66.

Naylor, R.T. (1987) *Hot Money and the Politics of Debt*. London: Unwin.

Nicoletti, G. (1988) 'A Cross-country Analysis of Private Consumption, Inflation and the Debt Neutrality Hypothesis', *OECD Economic Studies*, 11: 43-87 (Autumn).

Nurkse, R. (1954) 'International Investment Today in the Light of Nineteenth-century Experience', *Economic Journal*, 64: 744-58.

Nurkse, R. (1959) *Patterns of Trade and Development*. Stockholm: Almquist and Wiksell.

Obstfeld, M. (1986) 'Capital Mobility in the World Economy: Theory and measurement', in: K. Brunner & A. Meltzer (eds) *The National Bureau Method, International Capital Mobility and Other Essays, Carnegie-Rochester Series on Public Policy*, 24: 55-103 (Spring).

Ocampo, J.A. (1986) 'New Developments in Trade Theory and LDCs', *Journal of Development Economics*, 22: 129-70.

OECD (1972) *Development Cooperation. Report 1972*. Paris: OECD.

OECD (1981) *International Investment and Multinational Enterprises. Recent International Direct Investment Trends*. Paris: OECD.

OECD (1982) 'The OECD INTERLINK System', Economics and Statistics Department, OECD, Paris (mimeo).

OECD (1985) *Twenty-five Years of Development Cooperation. A Review. 1985 Report*. OECD, Paris.

OECD (1987) *Financing and External Debt of Developing Countries. 1986 Survey*. Paris: OECD.

OECD (1988) *Development Cooperation. Chairman's Report 1988*. Paris: OECD.

OECD (various years) *International Financial Market Trends*. Paris: OECD.

Ohlin, B. (1929) 'Transfer Difficulties: Real and imagined', *Economic Journal*, June: 172-78.

Ohlin, B. (1935) *Interregional and International Trade*. Cambridge, MA: Harvard University Press.

Okita, S., L. Jayawardena & A. Sengupta (1987) *Mobilizing International Surpluses for World Development: A WIDER Plan for a Japanese Initiative*. WIDER Study Group Series No. 2, Helsinki: UNU/WIDER.

Page, D. & W. Rogers (1982) 'Trends in Eurocurrency Credit Participation, 1972-80', in: Group of Thirty, *Risks in International Lending*. New York: Group of Thirty, pp. 57-70.

Parikh, K. & W. Tims (1987) 'Hunger Amidst Abundance – Causes and Cures. Executive summary', International Institute for Applied Systems Analysis (IIASA), Laxenburg, Austria (mimeo).

Park, Y. (1985) 'Korea's Experience with External Debt Management', in: G. Smith & J. Cuddington (eds), pp. 289-328.

Pastor, M. (1990) 'Capital Flight from Latin America', *World Development* 18(1): 1-18.

Pereira, A., A. Ulph & W. Tims (1987) *Socio-economic and Policy Implications of Energy Price Increases*. Aldershot: Gower.

Pfefferman, G. & A. Madarassy (1989) 'Trends in Private Investment of Thirty Developing Countries', World Bank/IFC Discussion Paper No. 6, Washington DC: World Bank.

Pincus, J. (1965) *Economic Aid and International Cost-Sharing*. Baltimore: Johns Hopkins University Press.

Platt, D. (1984) *Foreign Finance in Continental Europe and the USA, 1815-1870. Quantities, Origins, Function and Distribution*. London: Allen & Unwin.

Polak, J.J. (1957) 'Monetary Analysis of Income Formation and Payments Problems', *IMF Staff Papers*, 6(1): 1-50.

Portes, R. & A. Swoboda (eds) (1987) *Threats to the International Financial System*. Cambridge: Cambridge University Press (CEPR and NBER).

Prebisch, R. (1950) *The Economic Development of Latin America and its Principal Problems*. New York: United Nations.

Prebisch, R. (1959) 'Commercial Policy in the Underdeveloped Countries', *American Economic Review*, 49: 251-73.

Purvis, D. (1978) 'Dynamic Models of Portfolio Behaviour: More on pitfalls in financial model building', *American Economic Review*, 68(2): 403-9.

Quibria, M. (1986) 'A Note on Foreign Investment, the Savings Function and Immizerization of National Welfare', *Journal of Development Economics*, 21: 361-72.

Ranney, S. (1984) 'Terms of Trade and Domestic Distribution: A comment', *Journal of Development Economics*, 15(1-3): 89-96.

Razin, A. & E. Sadka (eds) (1987) *Economic Policy in Theory and Practice*. London: Macmillan.

Reisen, H. & A. von Trotsenburg (1988) *The Budgetary and Transfer Problem of Major Debtor Countries*. Paris: OECD Development Centre.

Richardson, P. (1987) 'A Review of the Simulation Properties of OECD's INTERLINK Model', OECD Department of Statistics Working Papers No. 47, Paris: OECD.

Rendell, R. (1980) *International Financial Law*. London: Euromoney Publications.

Riedel, J. (1984) *Myths and Reality of External Constraints on Development*. Aldershot: Gower.

Rodriguez, M. (1987) 'Consequences of Capital Flight for Latin American Debtor Dountries', in: D. Lessard & J. Williamson (eds), pp. 129-44.

Rose, M. & P. Snowden (1988) 'Bond Issues as a Replacement for Bank Lending to LDCs: A reconsideration of the lessons of the 19th century for the present day', *World Development* 16(7): 771-78.

Ruffin, R. (1984) 'International Factor Movements', in: R. Jones & P. Kenen (eds), pp. 237-88.

Rybcynznski, T. (1955) 'Factor Endowment and Relative Commodity Prices', *Economica*, 22: 336-41.

Saavedra-Rivano, N. (1984) 'Terms of Trade and Domestic Distribution: A comment', *Journal of Development Economics*, 15(1-3): 111-15.

Sachs, J. (1981) 'The Current Account and Macroeconomic Adjustment in the 1970s', *Brookings Papers on Economic Activity*, No. 1: 201-68.

Sachs, J. (1984a) *Theoretical Issues in International Borrowing*. Princeton Studies in International Finance No. 54, Princeton, NJ: Princeton University Press.

Sachs, J. (1984b) 'Comment', *Brookings Papers on Economic Activity*, No. 2.

Sachs, J. (1988a) 'International Policy Coordination: The case of the developing country debt problem', in: M. Feldstein (ed.), pp. 233-78.

Sachs, J. (1988b) 'New Approaches to the Latin American Debt Crisis', Harvard University, Cambridge, MA (mimeo).

Sachs, J. (1989), 'Introduction', in: J. Sachs (ed.), pp. 1-35.

Sachs, J. (ed.) (1989) *Developing Country Debt and Economic Performance. Volume 1: The International Financial System*. Chicago: University of Chicago Press (for NBER).

Sachs, J. & D. Cohen (1982) 'LDC Borrowing with Default Risk', NBER Working Paper Series No. 925, Cambridge, MA: National Bureau of Economic Research.

Sampson, A. (1981) *The Money Lenders: Bankers in a Dangerous World*. London: Hodder and Stoughton.

Samuelson, P. (1947) *Foundations of Economic Analysis*. Cambridge, MA: Harvard University Press.

Samuelson, P. (1948) 'International Trade and the Equalization of Factor Prices', Economic Journal, 58: 163-84.

Samuelson, P. (1952) 'The Transfer Problem and Transport Costs: The terms of trade when impediments are absent', *Economic Journal*, 62: 278-304.

Samuelson, P. (1954) 'The Transfer Problem and Transport Costs, II: Analysis of effects of trade impediments', *Economic Journal*, 64: 264-89.

Sarmad, K. (1990) 'Public and Private Investment and Economic Growth', ISS Money, Finance and Development Working Paper Series, No. 34, The Hague.

Saunders, A. (1987) 'The Inter-bank Market, Contagion Effects and International Financial Crisis', in: R. Portes & A. Swoboda (eds), pp. 196-230.

Saunders, P. & A. Dean (1986) 'The International Debt Situation and Linkages Between Developing Countries and the OECD', *OECD Economic Outlook*, Autumn: 155-203.

Sawyer, M. (1982) *Macroeconomics in Question*. Brighton: Wheatsheaf.

Sawyer, M. (1985) 'Towards a Post-Kaleckian Macroeconomics', in: P. Arestis & T. Skouras (eds) *Post-Keynesian Economic Theory. A Challenge to Neo-Classical Economics*. Brighton: Wheatsheaf, pp. 146-79.

Seiber, M. (1982) *International Borrowing by Developing Countries*. New York: Pergamon Press.

Simon, M. (1967) 'The Pattern of New British Portfolio Foreign Investment', in: J. Adler (ed.), pp. 33-70.

Simonsen, H. (1985) 'The Developing-country Debt Problem', in: G. Smith & J. Cuddington (eds), pp. 101-26.

Singer, H. (1950) 'The Distribution of Gains Between Investing and Borrowing Countries', *American Economic Review*, 40: 473-85.

Singer, H. (1989) 'The Relationship Between Debt Pressures, Adjustment Policies and Deterioration of the Terms of Trade for Developing Countries', Public Lecture, Institute of Social Studies, The Hague, May (mimeo).

Sjaastad, L. (1983) 'International Debt Quagmire: To whom do we owe it?', *The World Economy*, 6: 305-24 (September).

Smith, G. & J. Cuddington (eds) (1985) *International Debt and the Developing Countries*. World Bank Symposium, Washington DC: World Bank.

Solís, L. & E. Zedillo (1985) 'The Foreign Debt of Mexico', in: G. Smith & J. Cuddington (eds), pp. 258-88.

Srinivasan, T.N. & J. Bhagwati (1983) 'On Transfer Paradoxes and Immiserizing Growth: Part I', *Journal of Development Economics*, 13: 251-52.

Standaert, S. (1985) 'The Foreign Exchange Constraint, Suppression of the Trade Deficit and the Shadow Price of Foreign Exchange in a Fix-price Economy', *Journal of Development Economics*, 18: 37-50.

Stewart, F. (1984) 'Recent Theories of International Trade: Some implications for the South', in: H. Kierzkowski (ed.) *Monopolistic Competition and International Trade*. Oxford: Oxford University Press.

Stewart, F. & A. Sengupta (1982) *International Financial Cooperation. A Framework for Change*. London: Frances Pinter.

Stiglitz, J. & A. Weiss (1981) 'Credit Rationing in Markets with Imperfect Information', *American Economic Review*, 71(2): 393-410.

Sylos-Labini, P. (1962) *Oligopoly and Technical Progress*. Cambridge, MA: Harvard University Press.

Syrquin, M., L. Taylor & L. Westphal (eds) (1984) *Economic Structure and Performance. Essays in Honor of Hollis B. Chenery*. New York: Academic Press.

Taussig, F.W. (1928) *International Trade*. London: Macmillan.

Taylor, L. (1981) 'North-South Trade and Southern Growth: Bleak prospects from the structuralist point of view', *Journal of International Economics*, 11: 589-602.

Taylor, L. (1983) *Structuralist Macroeconomics*. New York: Basic Books.

Taylor, L. (1985) 'Debt Crises, North-South, North-North and in Between', Cambridge, MA, MIT (mimeo).

Taylor, L. (1990) 'Foreign Resource Flows and Developing Country Growth: A three-gap model', in: F.D. McCarthy (ed.) *Problems of Developing Countries in the 1990s*. World Bank Discussion Papers 97, Washington DC: World Bank, pp. 49-90.

Temin, P. (1976) *Did Monetary Forces Cause the Great Depression?* New York: Norton.

Thirlwall, A.P. (1972) *Growth and Development*. London: Macmillan.

Thirlwall, A. & J. Bergevin (1985) 'Trends, Cycles and Asymmetries in the Terms of Trade of Primary Commodities from Developed and Less Developed Countries', *World Development*, 13(7): 805-17.

Thomas, B. (1967) 'The Historical Record of International Capital Movements to 1913', in: J. Adler (ed.), pp. 3-32.

Thorp, R. (1984) 'Introduction', in R. Thorp (ed.), pp. 1-16.

Thorp, R. (ed.) (1984) *Latin America in the 1930s. The Role of the Periphery in World Crisis*. London: Macmillan.

Thorp, R. & C. Londoño (1984) ' The Effect of the Great Depression on the Economies of Peru and Colombia', in: R. Thorp (ed.), pp. 81-116.

Tims, W. & J. Waelbroeck (1982) *Global Modeling in the World Bank, 1973-76*. World Bank Staff Working Paper No. 544, Washington DC: World Bank.

Tobin, J. (1969) 'A General Equilibrium Approach to Monetary Theory', *Journal of Money, Credit and Banking*, 1: 15-29 (February).

Tobin, J. (1980) *Asset Accumulation and Economic Activity*. Oxford: Basil Blackwell.

Triffin, R. (1947) 'National Central Banking and the International Economy', *International Monetary Studies*, Postwar Economic Studies No. 7, Board of Governors of the Federal Reserve System, Washington DC.

Triffin, R. (1960) *Gold and the Dollar Crisis*. New Haven, CN: Yale University Press.

Triffin, R. (1964) *The Evolution of the International Monetary System: Historical Reappraisal and Future Perspectives*, Princeton Studies in International Finance No. 12, Princeton, NJ: Princeton University Press.

UNCTAD (1987a) *Trade and Development Report 1987*. Geneva: UNCTAD.

UNCTAD (1987b) *International Monetary and Financial Issues for Developing Countries*. Geneva: UNCTAD.

UNCTAD (1988) *Trade and Development Report 1988*. Geneva: UNCTAD.
UNCTAD (various years) *Handbook of International Trade and Payments Statistics*. New York: United Nations.
United Nations (1948) *Public Debt, 1914-46*. Department of Economic Affairs, Lake Success, New York: United Nations.
United Nations (1949) *International Capital Movements During the Inter-War Period*. Department of Economic Affairs, Lake Success, New York: United Nations.
United Nations (1954) *The International Flow of Private Capital*. Department of Economic Affairs, Lake Success, New York: United Nations.
United Nations (1968) *A System of National Accounts*, Studies in Methods Series F No. 2 Rev. 3, New York: United Nations.
United Nations (various years) *International Trade Statistics*. New York: United Nations.
Van Arkadie, B. (ed.) (1986) 'External Finance and Policy Adjustment in Africa. A special issue', *Development and Change*, 17(3): 371-581.
VerLoren van Themaat, J. (1982) 'Waarom geven landen hulp?' *Economisch Statistische Berichten*, 67(3339): 64-65 (20 January).
Versluysen, E. (1989) 'A Review of Recent Proposals to Solve the Debt Overhang', Paper presented at the World Bank Conference 'Dealing with the Debt Crisis', Washington DC, January.
Vines, D. (1984) 'A North-South Growth Model Along Kaldorian Lines', CEPR Discussion Paper No. 26, London: Centre for Economic Policy Research.
Vos, R. (1986) 'World Accounts of trade, Finance and Accumulation', Working Paper Sub-Series on Money, Finance and Development No. 16, The Hague: Institute of Social Studies.
Vos, R. (1988a) 'Accounting for the World Economy', Working Paper Sub-Series on Money, Finance and Development No. 26, The Hague: Institute of Social Studies.
Vos, R. (1988b) 'Savings, Investment and Foreign Capital Flows: Have capital markets become more integrated?', *Journal of Development Studies*, 24(3): 310-34.
Vos, R. (1989) 'Accounting for the World Economy', *Review of Income and Wealth*, 35(4): 389-408.
Vos, R. (1992) 'Private Asset Accumulation, Not Just Capital Flight: Evidence from the Philippines', *Journal of Development Studies*, 28(3): 500-37.
Vos, R. (1993) 'Prospects of Capital Flows to Developing Countries in the 1990s. The global macroeconomic trade-offs', UNCTAD, *International Monetary Issues for the 1990s*. New York: United Nations, pp. 1-50.
Waelbroeck, J. (1984) 'Capital, Foreign Exchange and Growth: The two-gap and labor-income-flow views', in: M. Syrquin, L. Taylor & L. Westphal (eds), pp. 281-94.
Watson, M. et al. (1984) *International Capital Markets. Developments and Prospects 1984*. IMF Occasional Paper No. 31, Washington DC: IMF.

Watson, M. et al. (1986) *International Capital Markets. Developments and Prospects 1986*. IMF Occasional Paper No. 43, Washington DC: IMF.

Watson, M. et al. (1988) *International Capital Markets. Developments and Prospects, 1988*. Washington DC: IMF.

Weisskopf, T. (1972) 'The Impact of foreign Capital Inflows on Domestic Savings in Underdeveloped Countries', *Journal of International Economics*, 2: 25-38.

Weston, R. (1980) *Domestic and Multinational Banking*. New York: Columbia University Press.

Wijnbergen, S. van (1983) 'Credit Policy, Inflation and Growth in a Financially Repressed Economy', *Journal of Development Economics*, 13(3): 45-65.

Wijnbergen, S. van (1984a) 'The Dutch Disease: A disease after all?', *Economic Journal*, 94: 41-55.

Wijnbergen, S. van (1984b) 'Inflation, Employment and the Dutch Disease in Oil-exporting Countries: A short-term disequilibrium analysis', *Quarterly Journal of Economics*, 99: 233-50 (May).

Wijnbergen, S. van (1985) 'Interdependence Revisited: A developing countries perspective on macroeconomic management and trade policy in the industrialized world', *Economic Policy*, 1(1): 81-114.

Wijnbergen, S. van (1986a) 'Macroeconomic Effects of the Effectiveness of Foreign Aid: On the two-gap model, home goods and real exchange rate misalignment', *Journal of International Economics*, 21: 82-116.

Wijnbergen, S. van (1986b) 'Aid, Export Promotion and the Real Exchange Rate: An African dilemma', Development Research Department Discussion Paper No. DRD199, World Bank, Washington DC.

Wijnbergen, S. van (1988) 'Fiscal Policy, Trade Intervention and World Interest Rates: An empirical analysis', in: J. Frenkel (ed.) *International Aspects of Fiscal Policy*. Chicago: University of Chicago Press (for NBER), pp. 273-300.

Wilber, C. & R. Harrison (1978) 'The Methodological Basis of Institutional Economics: Pattern model, story-telling and holism', *Journal of Economic Issues*, 12: 61-89 (March).

Williams, J. (1920) *Argentine International Trade Under Inconvertible Paper Money. 1880-1900*. Cambridge, MA: Harvard University Press.

Williamson, J. (1983) *The Open Economy and the World Economy*. New York: Basic Books.

Williamson, M. (1987) 'Acquisition of Foreign Assets by Developing Countries', International Monetary Fund, Washington DC (mimeo).

Woodruff, W. (1967) *Impact of Western Man. A Study of Europe's Role in the World Economy 1750-1960*. Washington DC: Press of the University of America.

World Bank (1985) *World Development Report 1985*. New York: Oxford University Press.

World Bank (1987) *World Development Report 1987*. New York: Oxford University Press.

World Bank (1988) *World Development Report 1988*. New York: Oxford University Press.

World Bank (1990) *World Development Report 1990*. New York: Oxford University Press.

World Bank (various years) *World Debt Tables*. Washington DC: World Bank.

World Bank (various years) *World Tables*. Washington DC: World Bank.

World Bank/IMF/BIS/OECD (1988), *External Debt. Definition, Statistical Coverage and Methodology*. Paris: OECD.

Index